Understanding
the
Cold War

Works by Adam B. Ulam

Understanding the Cold War: A Historian's Personal Reflections (2002)

The Bolsheviks (1998; 1965)

Prophets and Conspirators in Pre-Revolutionary Russia (1998; 1977)

The Communists: The Story of Power and Lost Illusions, 1948-1991 (1992)

Stalin: The Man and His Era (1989; 1973)

The Kirov Affair (1988)

Dangerous Relations: The Soviet Union in World Politics,
1970-1982 (1983)

Russia's Failed Revolutions (1981)

The Unfinished Revolution (1979; 1960)

The Rivals: America and Russia Since World War II (1978)

In The Name of the People (1977; 1972)

Ideologies and Illusions: Revolutionary Thought from Herzen to Solzhenitsyn (1976)

A History of Soviet Russia (1976)

Expansion and Coexistence: Soviet Foreign Policy, 1917-73 (1976; 1974)

Patterns of Government: The Major Political Systems
of Europe (Samuel H. Beer, Adam B. Ulam) (1973)

The Fall of the American University (1972)

The New Face of Soviet Totalitarianism (1963)

The Russian Political System (1955)

Titoism and the Cominform (1952)

The Philosophical Foundations of English Socialism (1951)

Second, expanded edition

Adam B. Ulam

A Historian's Personal Reflections

Understanding
the
Cold War

with a new introduction by **Paul Hollander**

 **Transaction Publishers**
New Brunswick (U.S.A.) and London (U.K.)

Library of Congress Catalog Number: 2001052297
ISBN: 0-7658-0885-4
Printed in the United States of America

Library of Congress Cataloging-in-Publication Data

Ulam, Adam Bruno, 1922-
    Understanding the Cold War : a historian's personal reflections / Adam B. Ulam.—2nd, expanded ed. / with a new introduction by Paul Hollander.
        p. cm.
    Includes index.
    ISBN 0-7658-0885-4 (pbk. : alk. paper)
        1. Cold War. 2. World politics—1945- 3. Soviet Union—Foreign relations—1945-1991. 4. United States—Foreign relations—1945-1989. 5. Ulam, Adam Bruno, 1922- I. Title.

D847 .U43 2001
909.82'5—dc21   2001052297

In Memory of Stanislaw Ulam

Contents

Preface

Adam Ulam was, in the words of one of his colleagues John Kenneth Galbraith, "the central spokesman on Soviet and Russian matters at Harvard...for close on half a century." He died on March 28, 2000, in his seventy-eighth year, shortly after finishing this, his nineteenth book.

Knowing that it would be his final book, and hoping to see it in print before he died, Adam decided with my help to publish it under the auspices of his own publishing company, which he founded from his hospital bed. He named it "Leopolis Press," after the medieval Latin name of Lwów, Poland (now Lviv, Ukraine), where he was born and which had the lion as its emblem.

The book was not intended as a formal work of scholarship. Adam's account of his education in Lwów, and of his life in America as a student and professor, continually gave way to his historian's passion for understanding the meaning of great events. Though he reminisced about the vanished way of life he experienced growing up in Lwów during the 1920s and 30s, he directed most of his energy to a commentary on trends in America and the world, and a reflection on the extraordinary events of the 1980s and 1990s in Eastern Europe and Russia, all told with the exceptional style and wit that puts his writing into a unique category. Adam entitled his book *Understanding the Cold War: A Historian's Personal Reflections.* What he meant by this title is subject to interpretation. Rather than a rigorous scholarly analysis of how best to understand the Cold War, I believe he meant "understanding" to refer to how he himself came to understand the Cold War, and this evolution of understanding is as autobiographical as any of the "personal reflections."

The emergence of new biographical material illuminating his life in Poland and the early years in the United States demands its inclusion in this second edition, published by Transaction Publishers. To suggest the contours of what Adam did not set down, or of what he himself did not know, about events that shaped his past, I have as-

ix

sembled in these pages passages by those who spoke about Adam, or about matters of which he himself was unable to speak. One of these was the Holocaust, which, although he seldom mentioned it, was very much with him for the rest of his life. It must be emphasized, however, that he never saw himself as a "victim." He was raised as an assimilated Polish Jew; and after he came to this country, he assimilated himself into American culture.

The biographical passages of this book describe Adam Ulam's personal and scholarly voyage. Adam's accounts of his story were characterized by what Stephen Kotkin (in his review of the first edition, entitled "Kremlinologist as Hero"), calls "...The zestful storyteller who favors the wink and nod...the telling anecdote." They were that. But considering his life now, it seems to me that Adam's existence despite his highly successful professional career was both poignant and tragic. His story begins with his early years in the beautiful, highly civilized, intellectually vibrant, cultivated city of Lwów with its fine balance of ethnic and religious groups, and follows with his abrupt, life-saving departure from Poland at age sixteen. The sudden, dreadful destruction of that way of life brought with it haunting, if repressed, nightmares of what happened to those left behind. It continues with his and his brother Stanislaw's unexpected impoverished state after reaching these shores, with Adam's legal status in this country in jeopardy until 1944, his education dependent on his older brother's meager resources. To realize, in the light of this background, that he devoted the rest of his life to seeking an understanding of how the 20th century could unleash such terrible forces is to demonstrate that Adam Ulam was indeed "Kremlinologist as Hero."

Mary H. B. Ulam

Introduction

Adam Ulam: Understanding the Cold War: A Historian's Reflections

It was an unexpected honor and welcome obligation to provide an introduction for Adam Ulam's last book although it is never easy to offer commentary on or new insight into the work of great minds. The task was not made easier by having known him for over three and a half decades and by the admiration for his work and ideas. Both the man and his ideas were complex, stimulating and highly original. That he passed away less than two years ago makes the task seem still more difficult—there is the temptation to eulogize the recently departed rather than focus on his ideas and scholarship which this last book also testifies to.

Adam Ulam was one of a remarkable group of scholars and writers of Polish origin whose contribution to the Western understanding of Soviet communism and its ideological underpinnings was unique and enormous. They include Zbigniew Brzezisnki, Jerzy Gliksman, Leszek Kolakowski, Leo Labedz, Czeslav Milosz, Richard Pipes, and Andrzej Walicki.

As a professor of government throughout his life at Harvard University and twice director of its Russian Research Center Adam Ulam was well positioned to enlarge and influence whatever was known about Soviet-Communist affairs in this country and elsewhere. He accomplished this through both teaching and research, exchanging information with a "steady stream" of visitors from communist countries and by advising members of our government and Congress, as well as the president. His personality too, I believe, magnified the influence of his ideas.

I first met him in 1963 when I was a young assistant professor at Harvard in what was then called the Department of Social Relations.

I was also a research fellow at the Russian Research Center where I had an office and spent most of my time; my office was actually next to his and there was plenty of opportunity for informal communications encouraged by his approachability and total lack of stuffiness. Adam Ulam's self-esteem did not rest on impressing those around him by how busy he was.

In the years and decades that followed my departure from Harvard (in 1968) I visited him when I was in Cambridge, perhaps two or three times a year. During an additional year and a half between 1974 and 1976 that I spent at the Center (while on leave from my school) once more I resumed almost daily contact with him—not that we invariably discussed weighty scholarly or intellectual concerns although (unlike many in the Center) I was unable to converse with him about the Red Socks as I was devoid of interest in baseball.

I believe that I saw him last sometime in 1997 in his Center office when he was already in poor health and spirit. On that final occasion much of the conversation was more intimate than usual revolving around age, ill health and bodily decline.

After my arrival at Harvard back in 1963 it did not take long to discover (with great pleasure) that Adam Ulam's views of the world, politics, Soviet affairs, Soviet-American relations, American academia and society were quite similar to mine. These shared dispositions became apparent in our conversations and deepened as I became familiar with his work; they have been further confirmed and enlarged by the autobiographical recollections here introduced. I was especially struck by the similarities in the ways of life of his family in Lwow and mine in Budapest back in the first half of the past century.

We both came from assimilated Jewish families—his Polish, mine Hungarian; we both had (different) accents; we both came to this country at an early age: Adam much earlier at sixteen, myself at twenty-seven (I left Hungary at twenty-four). We both spent much of our professional lives thinking and writing about Soviet/communist affairs, Western/Soviet relations, questions of Marxist-Leninist theory and Soviet (and other) communist practice. I fully subscribed to the pithy summation of the essential characteristic of Soviet communism he provides in this volume: "However unnatural and repugnant it may seem to the Western mind, the fact remains that the destiny of the Soviet state was for most of its existence determined not by its people, not by impersonal social and economic forces, but by the decisions, first of a despot, then by that of a small oligarchy..." (250). Ulam was one of very few people who had the nerve and insight to make such an assertion and hold on to it throughout his professional career.

We both believed that through much of its existence it was appropriate to characterize the Soviet Union as "totalitarian" and the concept was not merely a creation of cold war propaganda or personal animosity toward the USSR and other communist systems. Having grown up in a communist country I also found much truth in his observation that "life under Communism has a curious make-believe characteristic: its ultimate element, lack of individual freedom, tends to make other problems appear distant and relatively unimportant." He added, wisely, "it would take some time after the fall of the Soviet Union to make the former subjects of Communism realize that freedom brings its own uncertainties and dilemmas" (358).

I quoted him long ago in my writing when he compared, in a refreshingly iconoclastic manner, the power struggle within the Soviet leadership following Stalin's death to the way Mafiosi settled their disputes—an observation reproduced in this volume: "...in order to understand the current political game in the USSR, it was less instructive to study Marx and Lenin than to reread the accounts of Al Capone's struggles with rival gangs in prohibition-era Chicago..." (185).

Adam Ulam also succeeded in putting his finger on the mainspring of the attraction Western intellectuals felt toward communist systems and Marxist ideas (a topic to which I devoted more than one book):

> One suspects that most of these scientists, artists, writers and the like who adopted the Communist creed did so not out of misguided idealism, but precisely because Communism did demand unquestioning obedience and faith in the Party and the leader. The most telling evidence that it was a kind of intellectual masochism rather than idealism...appears in the decreasing popularity of Communism in the West after Stalin's death. A "normal" police state ruled by a committee of elderly bureaucrats didn't have the same appeal as a phantasmagoric terror-driven society headed by an infallible leader. (338)

One might say that we both had a morbid fascination with these matters, notwithstanding our shared abhorrence. Adam was interested in the nature of the Soviet system, its historical origin, antecedents in Russian history, the ideas that provided its original inspiration and the major figures who created it and its relationship with the West and especially the United States. (He knew far more about

all these matters than I.) I was most interested in how a highly repressive and depriving political system such as the Soviet could stay
in power over long periods of time and how appealing ideals came
to provide motivation and justification for its repressive policies and
practices.

For all these reasons, not surprisingly, he came close to being a
"role model" though I suspect he would not care for the term and its
trendy associations. I had great admiration for his work, his impressive productivity and understanding of the Soviet system and its
origins. I also found him personally appealing—his wit, sense of
gentle humor, the inclination to understatement, the reticence and
modesty unusual in a person of his academic status and renown. I
admired his scholarly intellectual style, too: he was the proverbial
"lone scholar," not the "team player," not the academic operator,
grantsman, "networker," wheeler-dealer. Unlike many of his colleagues in the upper reaches of the academic world he rarely attended conferences, he did not seem anxious to rub shoulders with
the rich, famous and powerful, he was unconcerned with his "vis-
ibility," and did not chase after publicity. It is difficult to imagine
him having "power lunches" in order to advance his career or image, or to invite to his house those who would be useful profession-
ally. Astonishingly enough he seemed to be a man who attained his
eminence and position for no other reason than intellectual-schol-
arly merit, brilliance and hard work—although clearly his work was
his pleasure, the center of his life and he seemed to produce his
books effortlessly in regular succession.

A key element of his personality and personal appeal was the
total lack of pomposity, posturing, and interest in conveying a bloated
self-importance, all too characteristic of successful academics, indeed among the successful in any walk of life. As one of his friends
Samuel Beer wrote, "Adam was not a person to exert the slightest
effort to make a good first impression. He would not lift a little finger in that sort of self-advancement" (148). His reflectiveness, detachment, gentleness, tolerance and attraction to English culture and
customs (a self-confessed Anglophile) are *somewhat* reminiscent of
Saul Bellow's literary character, Mr. Sammler—another emigré from
Poland (an aspiring scholar), an honorable man and witness to the
horrors of this century, at once appreciative of and somewhat bewil-
dered by his new homeland, another upholder of the best traditions
and ideas Europe has produced.

Adam Ulam was well liked even by those who did not share his worldview and politics; many of his colleagues were willing to overlook his "political incorrectness" perhaps because of his personal charm and because his rejection of the conventional political wisdom of his times was good humored as reflected, for example, in his *The Fall of the American University* (1972). The latter, I learned in the pages that follow, was refused by his "regular publishers, who said it was not consistent with the 'political correctness' of the time" (248).

Although Adam Ulam disliked many of the politically correct trends that flourished and proliferated since the late 1960s he managed to convey his distaste for them without rancor or bitterness and he was not particularly vocal criticizing them, as he self-critically admits on these pages ("Having criticized my colleagues for their attitude in the face of assaults on the university, I confess with some regret that I myself was far from being an active defender of it" [235]). But he persisted in refusing to idealize or romanticize the 1960s. As he writes in this volume: "I still grow impatient when I hear people express nostalgia for the 'idealism'...and 'activism' of the 1960s. It is a huge oversimplification to hold that young rebels are always prompted by idealism....Youthful passion and combativeness are just not synonymous with idealism" (232-233). Unlike some of his contemporaries among American academic intellectuals he was well aware of the profound differences between the protest movements of the late 1960s in the West and those in the Communist countries in the same period: "...those occurrences in the Communist world had completely different roots and just happened to coincide with the crisis in the West" (227).

He had little patience with the "cold war revisionists" and told a congressional committee that "revisionism was based on bad history, and on the inappropriate assumption that there must be two sides to every political argument" (315). Nor did he believe that the Soviet system "could evolve peacefully into 'socialism with a human face'" (319). He realized that the vitality of Soviet communism was closely connected to Soviet expansionism and that the system's "legitimacy...[was] based on the myth of Communism inheriting the world" (317). He came to the conclusion (as did I) that a crucial determinant of the Collapse was the loss of self-confidence of the rulers (335). He, too, believed that the great unraveling had mostly internal causes, among them the unintended consequences of Gorbachev's policies and his personality. Memorably he observed:

"...there were two Gorbachevs: one an unsparing critic of the system, seeing its history as rooted in crime, falsehood, and brutal abuse of power by its rulers; and the other, a defender of Communism eager to preserve it as a higher and more progressive form of society....for the remainder of his ill-fated reign the two Gorbachevs would continuously and incongruously struggle with each other" (451).

The volume here introduced has the great virtue of acquainting the reader both with important details of its author's personal and professional life and the highlights of his academic interests, findings and points of view while also providing a highly informed commentary on major world events in the second half of the past century. Although much of the book does indeed focus on the Cold War there are substantial autobiographical sections interspersed with accounts and recollections of those who knew him: members of his family, colleagues and friends. The thoughtful and revealing analysis of major world events is enlivened by entertaining anecdotes of major turning points of his life (e.g. taking the last boat out of Poland in 1939 a week before the Nazi invasion) and recollections of people of a variety of accomplishments and claims to fame he met and knew. They included Yuri Arbatov, Yuri Afanasyev, Yelena Bonner, McGeorge Bundy, Milovan Djilas, John Kenneth Galbraith, Petro Grigorenko, George Kennan, Henry Kissinger (he was a student of Ulam), Herbert Marcuse, Roy Medvedev, John von Neuman, Andreas Papandreou and Pierre Trudeau (both fellow students at Harvard who went on to become prime ministers in their respective countries), Joseph Schumpeter (his teacher at Harvard), and Teresa Toranska among many others. There was also a "steady stream" of Soviet and East European visitors to his office over the decades even when he was reviled in the Soviet press.

Much of the book consists of retrospective reflections and reassessments of his earlier work and ruminations on where he was right and wrong regarding the nature of the Soviet systems and its relationship to the West. Ulam has no hesitation to admit errors or misjudgments (he often quotes them) and especially his failure to anticipate the collapse of the Soviet Union. In these respects, too, he differed from most scholars and academic stars of similar stature who seem compelled to insist that they were always right.

This volume also faithfully echoes his overall orientation and approach to history and politics. Adam Ulam was a real humanist in more than one way; he placed specific human beings, their ideas and beliefs at the center of historical events and developments. He was interested in particular individuals, in their psychology as well as actions and policies they pursued (as also importantly reflected in the biographies he wrote), in personal decisions and their impact on historical events. But he was also well aware of the part played by the contingent, accidental and unexpected aspects of history and politics. His work had a problem-solving dimension: he raised specific questions, he sought to solve historical riddles (e.g., why and by whom was Kirov murdered? Or, "...were those millions of people destroyed [under Stalin] who were innocent of any real or potential opposition to the regime, because of the dictator's genuine conviction that treason was widespread or was it the result of his cynical conclusion that the safety of his power required periodic sacrificial offerings of multitudes of innocent people in addition to those he really mistrusted?" [265]).

Ulam's recreational hobby, detective-mystery novels might have served him well in his professional "historian-detective work;" as he notes in this volume, "the search for the solution of all interesting problems of history does partake of detective work" (200).

Although he lived in a period when the social sciences aspired to greater respectability by becoming more "scientific" and "theoretical"—often by embracing a new, ponderous and esoteric vocabulary—he vigorously resisted these trends and fads. He wrote in clear, jargon-free language; in his work as in his personal life he avoided posturing. He was also modest enough to realize that the social sciences cannot provide the kind and wealth of information the natural sciences do: "in the social sciences there can be no experts. A scholar may have amassed extensive knowledge of Russian history, economics, etc., yet it doesn't follow that his advice on American policies about the USSR would be necessarily more perspicacious or valuable than that of a layman guided by common sense" (190).

Modestly entitled, *Understanding the Cold War: A Historian's Reflections* is a well-rounded portrait of the man and his ideas, social background and times; it is also a worthy conclusion to the work and life of a man who personified both a simple decency and a profound understanding of the major and complex problems and conflicts of our times.

Paul Hollander
Northampton, Massachusetts
August 2001

Acknowledgments

It is hard to imagine how the manuscript for the first edition of this book could have gone forward without the generous support and astute editing of the professional material by Professor Ulam's close friend and former student, Abbott Gleason, the Barnaby Conrad and Mary Critchfield Keeney Professor of History, at Brown University.

I am indebted to Allen Lynch, Associate Professor of Russian History, at University of Virginia, for taking the time to go over the manuscript and for his invaluable suggestions.

In preparing the second edition, I want to thank the editorial staff of Leopolis Press, Robert C. Johnston and John Tytus for their fine editorial work and computer skills.

Thanks also to Liubko Hajda, director of the Ukrainian Institute, Harvard University and to Patricia Blake, Research Associate, Davis Center, Harvard University and to Angela Stent, Professor of History, Georgetown University, for their editorial suggestions. George Suboczewski, reviewer for the Polish Library's Newsletter, Washington DC. was kind enough to comment on the book and point out several important errors

Finally, I could not have undertaken this project were it not for the unflagging and wonderful support of Alexander and Joseph Ulam during a time that continues to be sad for all of us.

Mary H. B. Ulam

List of People Quoted in the Text

SB: Samuel H. Beer, Eaton Professor of the Science of Government, Emeritus, Harvard University

LB: Louis Begley, writer and lawyer

MK: Mark Kramer, Director, Cold War Studies Project, Harvard University

HR: Henry Rosovsky, Lewis P. and Linda L. Geyser University Professor Emeritus, former Dean of the Faculty of Arts and Sciences, Harvard University

AS: Angela Stent, Professor of Government, Georgetown University

GS: Gwendolyn Stewart, Adam Ulam's last student; author of *Russia Redux*

NT: Nina Tumarkin, Professor of History, Wellesley College

GV: George Volsky, retired journalist, formerly with *The New York Times*

JU: Joseph Ulam, son of Adam Ulam

Part One

Farewell to Poland

1

The Ulams' Lwów

About Lwów...Manners and the café culture...elementary and secondary education...learning about America

Lwów, Lvov, Lviv have been different versions of the name of my hometown (to be sure after the partition of Poland in the 18th century, it became for its Austrian masters Lemberg, and as such it stayed on the world's maps, but none of the natives used this form). For the Poles it has been and remains Lwów, from the Middle Ages to the partition of Poland, one of the main urban centers of the old Polish Lithuanian Commonwealth, third largest city in the reborn Polish State after 1918. With the Hitler-Stalin deal in 1939, eastern Poland, and with it the city, became part of the Soviets' loot, and after the horrifying interval of the German occupation (1941-1944) it stayed on the map of the USSR in its Russian form, Lvov. Indisputably Polish in its ethnic character and culture as the city was, southeastern Poland in which it is situated is nationally and linguistically predominantly Ukrainian.

At the Yalta conference, President Roosevelt pleaded with Stalin that Lwów be returned to liberated Poland, but Stalin would not allow it. And so when the Soviet empire crumbled in 1991, and Ukraine became independent, the city of my childhood again changed a consonant in its name, becoming officially Ukrainian Lviv. How much history can be evoked by altering a single letter!

The awareness that I was living on the political fault line of eastern Europe came to me very early. I had heard my elders talk about dangerous developments all over the world: the depression, the war in the Far East and other portents of the horrors to come.

My first distinct memory of a political event is of the most ominous one: a Polish news broadcast from Berlin on the occasion of

3

Adolf Hitler being appointed chancellor of Germany. The correspondent's voice was strained: the news came as a surprise to him as to most political analysts. True, the Nazis' popular support had grown with the severity of the depression gripping the country. But that support had crested, the party losing votes in the last election; one could hope democratic forces would reassert themselves. And then unexpectedly the old President Hindenburg appointed Hitler to head the government. The reporter was wiser than the majority of political pundits: once in power the Nazis would never surrender it, no matter what future elections and other constitutional paraphernalia. Hitler's deputy, Goering, in a radio address celebrating the occasion recounted how a prominent Socialist sought him out and begged that he be allowed by the new regime to keep his job as a notary public. So much for your German democratic forces! Jubilant gangs of storm troopers were roaming the streets of Berlin and provincial cities.

At the time I found the event more intriguing than alarming. The young are seldom afraid of things and situations with which they are not familiar. War was something I had not experienced. Lwów had suffered Russian occupation in World War I, and at its end was the scene of armed struggle between the Poles and the Ukrainians. War to my mind was something which took place between armies of soldiers, hardly affecting the civilians. My father and brother had already instructed me about what Hitler represented. But I had also learned (one absorbed as if by osmosis in the Poland of the time), that Germany was a traditional enemy, and that any German government would, if it could, reclaim Polish territories Germany had to surrender after World War I. In a way, Hitler and his thugs, sure to outrage public opinion, would be less dangerous to Poland than their respectable countrymen playing on Western sympathies for poor Germany so horribly treated by the Versailles Treaty.

Austrian Poles' privileged status contributed to a certain if good-natured feeling of superiority over their fellow nationals from elsewhere, a feeling which lingered after the reunification. Russia's former subjects were believed to have imbibed some of the harshness and lack of ceremoniousness allegedly characteristic of their erstwhile masters. Those who had been under the Hohenzollerns had not been fully emancipated from the haughtiness and overseriousness typical of a German milieu. In contrast to such flaws the natives of Galicia believed themselves to be light hearted, tolerant, and appreciative of the finer things in life.

A sociologist might be skeptical of such generalizations, and whatever the regional differences they were being quickly homogenized in independent Poland. But it is indisputable that some of the flavor of Vienna had rubbed off on the culture of my part of the country. Architecture of the modern part of the city was reminiscent of certain quarters of the Austrian capital. Personal manners were elaborately ritualized. I would later discover how easy it was in America to make friends. In Poland, the process just as the entire social etiquette was much more complex and formal.

Take such seemingly simple courtesies as kissing the hand of your women acquaintances Upon meeting them or saying goodbye, the practice was quite widespread all over the Continent in those distant days before the explosion of feminism. But in formerly Austrian Poland it was elaborated into an intricate ceremonial which continued to be practiced after 1918, and remained the subject of dispute as to its details. The most fundamental one touched on the question of who was entitled to this form of salutation. Of course one kissed the hand of married ladies. But how about the unmarried ones? One would not do so with a young girl, not without arousing suspicion that the gesture meant more than a social amenity. But what was the proper procedure with regard to an older spinster? This was the subject of considerable contention.

Then there was the question of the mechanics. The most accepted form was for the man to bow while planting his lips on the palm of the right hand (left handers were an oppressed minority being usually forced to switch in their childhood). But how, if at all, should one incline one's head while performing the rite and should it be nuanced according to the woman's social status and/or the degree of her closeness to the man? There was yet another technique, one frowned upon by the traditionalists as suggestive of possible romantic intent: the hand was snatched impulsively and the kiss deposited on the fingers rather than on the palm. There was no Polish Emily Post to lay down the law to the contending factions.

The equally elaborate rules regulated social intercourse between men. That endearing American custom of people even of the most recent acquaintance calling each other by their first names was unthinkable. People could be friends for years and yet would address each other by Mr. with the verb in third person singular (e.g., does Mr. X desire some vodka?). Closer intimacy was signaled by inserting a companion's first name after Mr. but retaining the third person singular. Only very very old friends and relatives would reach the level of complete familiarity (X, dost thou want vodka?). I shall spare the reader other convolutions of the procedure, such as when it was proper to use the diminutive form of one's first name, etc. In the People's Poland, such bourgeois feudal practices were officially frowned upon. Instead of "Pan," and its feminine equivalent, "Pani," you were supposed to use "citizen" and "citizeness," and employ the second-person plural, which before the war was regularly used in talking to a person of lower social standing, e.g., by a city dweller to a peasant. Like many Communist innovations, this one never really took hold and finally expired with the demise of the "People's Poland." Except for forms of address implying social inferiority, those folk customs had really been innocuous, and the abandonment of "citizen," all the more obnoxious because it aped the Soviet "comrade," was a logical result of post -1989 Poland throwing off the yoke of Communism.

To be sure, social distinctions in prewar Poland instead of being obscured or concealed were only too discernible in everyday manners. There was none of your "Hi!" or wave of the hand in passing a casual acquaintance in the street. If one encountered a social superior, the proper greeting was a broad sweeping gesture with one's hat. For men of lesser status one lifted the hat only slightly, or just touched it with the hand. Even when very young I felt the custom not only demeaning but ridiculous. Fortunately, new Poland has emancipated itself not only from Communism but also from that social backwardness and crudeness which hung so heavily over the country between the two world wars.

But to return to Vienna's contribution to my hometown's life. It would be excessive to ascribe the café culture which permeated Lwów to the lingering Austrian influence. Coffeehouses, bistros, and similar establishments have promoted sociability for centuries and all over the Continent; and they have been gathering places for artists, professionals, and politicians. In some ways, their function has been similar to that of the British or American club, but there are significant differences. In the first place the coffeehouse is egalitarian; it serves anyone who can afford a cup of coffee or a glass of beer and not just a select clientele. In the second place one frequents a club, i.e., drops in there after work for a drink, meal, game of squash etc. The real business of life is done at home and the place of work. The café goer reverses this routine. He spends his day in the coffeehouses with but occasional visits to his office and home. It is not surprising that being incompatible with the Anglo Saxon work ethic the institution never caught on in Britain or America, what passes for cafés there being in fact closer to bars or restaurants, rather than to their Paris or Vienna namesakes.

Lwów's café culture followed the Austrian rather than the French model insofar as the customers were almost exclusively recruited from the middle class, rather that from a wide social spectrum, and the staple of consumption was in fact coffee rather than liquor. Of course one did occasionally order a drink or a meal, but for serious drinking you would go to a bar and for a festive dinner or lunch to a restaurant. Custom prescribed that no matter what or how much one consumed one could stay indefinitely. Most cafés were also reading rooms. No sooner would a habitué be seated at his usual table than the waiter would bring him newspapers, Polish or foreign, of his usual choice. The café goer would attend to his correspondence, write a lecture, confer with his business associates, or simply sit drinking coffee, smoking and reflecting. The surrounding atmosphere depended on the time of day. In the morning conversations were as a rule subdued; people attended to their business and did not seek to socialize. In the afternoons, the place became more animated; friends felt free to join you at your table. But it was in the evening that the café would become really crowded and noisy. Husbands, having discharged their domestic duties by dining at home, would abandon wives and children and repair to their favorite spot, there to argue and gossip for hours usually with the same men they would see night after night.

It would not be atypical, say, for a university professor after a morning lecture to attend a café, then to have breakfast and read newspapers. Then after lunch and a brief visit to his office he would turn to another place of refreshment where he might chat about his subject with some students and colleagues. And after supper yet another café, this time with his senior associates and personal friends. My brother Stan, when a young student of mathematics, would often spend a social hour with a couple of his professors in the Café Roma. After lunch they usually moved across the street to the Scottish Café there to be joined by other mathematicians. Some would play chess, others would kibitz and chat. But on occasions, the gathering turned into a veritable seminar with the problems and theorems discussed written down in a large notebook. As my brother was to reminisce, " I recall a session with Mazur and Banach at the Scottish Café which lasted seventeen hours without interruptions except for meals" [S. M. Ulam, *Adventures of a Mathematician*, New York p.33]. The book of problems kept in the custody of the café's staff grew with the years, new theorems and problems being added by the participants in the café symposia right up to the German occupation of 1941. It was then hidden and miraculously survived the war. The *Scottish Book* was translated into English by my brother and became widely known to the international mathematical community as a memento not only of scientific achievement but of a way of life long gone. Communism was not tolerant of leisurely and unhurried sociability represented by the café culture. One could not lightheartedly engage in free animated chatter; the man at the next table might have well have been an informer. Nor is the budding capitalism in Eastern Europe likely to revive the old institution, so contrary to the American notion of how people ought to spend their time. Today's café is in tune with the brave new world of the global market and the entrepreneurial spirit. One visits it occasionally and briefly.

My knowledge of that bygone tradition was derived not only from observing my elders. Beginning when I was twelve or thirteen my father would occasionally let me join him at his Sunday morning sessions in the coffee houses. It was a special treat; children were not as a rule seen in the establishments. Very early, after having been fortified by tea, we would set forth on a stroll through the still deserted streets to our destination. It was usually the Café Roma, which had nothing Italian about it but was favored because of its large collection of newspapers both Polish and foreign. We breakfasted in the still largely empty emporium. It must have been barely eight or nine in the morning. Then followed what had been the main purpose of the expedition: the reading of the newspapers. My father followed the longstanding habit, acquired before the war, of, after skimming one or two Polish journals, becoming engrossed in Vienna's *Neue Freie Presse*. To my mind this was rather hard to understand: Vienna was now the capital of a small insignificant country. But in Austrian Poland, the liberal Viennese paper had been quite popular and my father, deeply conservative, remained faithful to the habits of his youth. What was happening in Austria was for him of interest second only to the interest he took in Polish politics, and the inroads made there by the growing impact of the Nazis, a source of deep concern.

Despite Poland's semi-authoritarian regime, opposition parties were tolerated, and I favored the latter for my reading. Not that I had as yet any definite political outlook or any hankering after a specific ideology. But it was intriguing to follow political arguments and views clashing with those that official propaganda tried to drive into our heads in the schools, and to take note of veiled hints of scandal and corruption in high places (For if too overt, an article would be banned and its space in the newspaper would be left blank).The natural re-belliousness of youth combined with an aversion, which persists to this day, against the unctuous and pompous ways in which those in authority, and not only in nondemocratic countries, tend to present their actions and motivations. One must be fair: apart from its treat-ment of domestic politics, it was the Warsaw regime's main organ *Gazeta Polska* (Polish Gazette) which represented the best in jour-nalism. It had excellent correspondents in the major European capi-tals, and the analyses of the politics of the respective countries, es-pecially of Britain, France, and the USSR, were most instructive, in some ways superior to what I could read in the leading Western journals. For a daily paper, an inordinate amount of space was de-voted to articles about cultural and historical subjects, usually by leading authorities in the given field. I could now read English and French. *Le Matin* kept me informed and troubled by the turbulent politics of France in the 1930s. *The Times* and *The Daily Telegraph* conveyed on the contrary the impression of the solidity of British politics, but also, alas, of the irresolution and to me the inexplicable restraint of London's policies toward the dictators. Like most Poles of my background I was brought up in the belief in the enormous power and masterful diplomacy of Great Britain. Pax Britannia was for me a vital element of the world order even as Hitler, Stalin, and Mussolini threatened the world itself. Britannia still ruled the waves, even if the American Navy was at least its equal. Why then did the British put up with Hitler's impudence and Mussolini's provocations? Questioning my elders did not produce satisfactory answers, since they also adhered to that 19th century image of Britain; and for Po-land, the 19th century did not really end until 1939. In politics we were all Anglophiles, just as when it came to the arts and culture in general most educated Poles were enamored of France. Paris was the most potent magnet for those traveling abroad.

My interest in world affairs was thus spawned in a Lwów coffee house. It was not as yet informed by first hand experience, for until my journey to the United States at the age of sixteen, I had never really traveled abroad. The only experience of a non Polish environment came in early childhood. My family used to summer on the Baltic in the resort town of Sopot, then part of the territory of the free city of Danzig; today, near Polish Gdansk. The city, long under the sovereignty of the old Polish commonwealth, came, after the Partitions, to be under Prussian rule. The peacemakers after World War I had to manage reconciling the heavily German population of the area with the promise in one of President Wilson's Fourteen Points that independent Poland should have a port on the Baltic. The ill-fated compromise turned Danzig into a free city under the League of Nations; i.e., an entity having complete political self government but with special rights reserved to Poland, a perfect recipe for an additional strain on the already tense relations between the new state and Germany. Predictably, Polish vacationers were not popular in Sopot, but they provided employment; and for them it was the country's only seaside resort.

I have one vivid recollection from my summers on the Baltic. Most of my time was spent on the beach playing with other children. But on one occasion (I was eight or nine) my governess felt the need of a cultural diversion and most ill-advisedly took me along with her for a concert. The program consisted of several choral pieces by Wagner. I don't know whether this is a rule whenever Wagner is performed in Germany, but on this occasion the audience behaved as if it were in church: no chatter between numbers, no clapping or anything else which might profane the sublime message of the music. Needless to say my own mood was one of boredom rather than veneration. But one number aroused my amusement, not so much on account of the music, but of the appearance of the performers: several corpulent gentlemen in formal morning attire were emitting, to me, raucous sounds in an unintelligible language. They finally concluded and made their bows. There ensued another interlude of decorous silence conducive to meditation, but not for long: because it was so quiet, the whole room became startled by an outburst of loud childish laughter. The charm was broken. Heads turned toward the culprit; there were shouts of indignation. A lady in a neighboring seat raised her umbrella as if to strike my poor governess, who hurriedly dragged me out of the concert hall. Whenever I hear Wagner I still recall my uncultured behavior on my first acquaintance with him.

Not long after this incident the free city of Danzig stopped being free except in name. Its good citizens entrusted their government to the followers of Hitler, and the city turned into a miniature Third Reich. We stopped spending summers in Sopot. My only trip to the Baltic after 1933 came on the occasion of my departure to the United States six years later.

During those years the family became dispersed. My mother's illness required periodic trips to Vienna then famed throughout Europe for its medical facilities, and she died there in early 1938. My sister [Stefania] got married. Brother Stan finally moved to the United States, returning to Poland just for the summers. Much younger than the two of them, I was now left very much to my own devices, father's professional obligations taking most of his time.

The economic circumstances of my family turned quite modest in those years. Father was a very successful lawyer but even so his practice was not very remunerative during the years of economic crisis. He continued working for his clients, mostly professional people and landowners, even when they remained delinquent with their fees. One simply did not abandon one's client-friends but waited patiently, sometimes indefinitely, until they were able to pay. One such debtor whose financial distress did not evidently make him abandon expensive habits was the cause of my father's relapse into an unfortunate addiction. During their consultations he kept offering him choice Cuban cigars and my father finally succumbed, with foreseeable consequences.

There was one bizarre fringe benefit enjoyed by the legal profession. Very occasionally my father took criminal cases. It was generally understood that lawyers so employed enjoyed immunity from the activities of their prospective clients, i.e., professional thieves. This surely sounds incredible, but I remember one occasion when my father's stolen fur coat reappeared with an anonymous note of apology for such an unprofessional act, the writer protesting that he had not known whose coat he had stolen. There was certainly some honor among the thieves of Lwów.

Despite such intriguing sidelines of the profession, I had no inclination to be a lawyer. In contrast to the beginning of the century when my father joined the bar, the field was overcrowded. (Curiously enough, at the time when most American law schools did not admit women, in backward pre-939 Poland they were on absolutely equal terms when it came to admission to law courses at the university and proceeding into the profession.) After graduating in Law one had to spend seven years clerking with an established lawyer before being allowed to practice on one's own, i.e., one would be about thirty before reaching professional independence. Under existing political conditions, a law degree in itself was not, unlike how it was in the West, a key which might open many doors. To work in state administration, e.g., not that I had the slightest inclination in that direction, required both the right political orientation and "pull."

A similarly melancholy situation prevailed in the teaching profession. Like most of the Continental institutions of higher learning, Polish universities were non-residential and as a rule had very large classes. Thus, though there were relatively few higher schools for a population of about 33 million, they spawned graduates in numbers quite disproportionate to employment opportunities in the depression years. With few university chairs in a given discipline, an average Ph.D. was lucky to secure the position of a high school teacher where the teaching load virtually precluded scholarly research and writing. My brother's early achievements in mathematics notwithstanding, he would have had difficulties in obtaining the position of even a docent (equivalent to an assistant professor in the U.S., but usually unpaid). It was a very discouraging situation for a youngster like myself who very early decided that his vocation was one of historian and student of international affairs.

My formal education did little to advance those goals. At twelve I began to attend the local gymnasium, or public high school. Until shortly before, it had been patterned after the general continental model of the secondary school: eight years of general education culminating in an examination, a stressful experience for most students; for if one failed in even one subject, one was barred from entering the university and had to repeat the test next year. But, in 1931, the government, which ran all the schools, altered the educational structure. The term of the elementary school, which taught little beyond the "Three R's," was lengthened by two years, and that of the gymnasium correspondingly shortened. Before, the prospective student had the choice between several types of high school, e.g., one centered on classical studies, another which stressed modern languages, etc. Now the curriculum was strictly homogenized. A Polish minister of education might well have emulated that legendary French counterpart of his, who, when asked by a foreign visitor about methods of instruction, pulled out his watch and announced that at this hour in every history class in every French lycée, Hannibal was crossing the Alps.

Much as I enjoyed some subjects, I found the gymnasium in general a cheerless institution. During my first years in America I thought that all public schools were greatly superior to those in the Poland of my youth. They had a relaxed atmosphere in contrast to the stultifying discipline of the gymnasium. Students had a wide choice of subjects, rather than a uniform curriculum. You did not learn by rote as was the case in my school. And there were sports and games and not just exercises in calisthenics.

But then in the seventies and eighties, observing what was going on in American high schools, I had, alas, to modify my previous judgments. Few would seriously maintain that what was happening at the pre-college level of education does credit to the American way of life. Quite aside from drugs and violence, the average public or private high school fails to instill in its students that intellectual discipline so essential to the absorption of knowledge, future professional training, and civilized living in general.

Now in retrospect some of the pedagogical techniques to which I was subjected no longer appear to me so useless or repugnant. Take memorizing long passages from Latin and Polish poets, rules of grammar of foreign languages, and other practices which today would spark off a rebellion in an American classroom. They provide useful mental discipline and are of help, I am convinced, even in unrelated intellectual endeavor. Nor should one dismiss a grading system and a strict code of conduct as necessary aids to the process of learning. By trying to make education easy and painless we are in fact punishing the young by depriving them of the skills and knowledge which at their age they could absorb quickly and firmly, and which might later in life require an incommensurate amount of effort and time.

Having said that, I am still far from extolling my own high school, the Tadeusz Kósciuszko gymnasium in the city of Lwów. Its physical appearance was unprepossessing: a nondescript large four story building. Unlike other schools of this kind mine did not have a playing field, not even a courtyard, the students spilling out into the street during free periods. But even had it had the physical facilities, it is unlikely we would have had a sports team of any kind. The notion of athletic competition between schools was as unthinkable as a university funding a soccer team. Education and sports simply did not mix, although sports from soccer to tennis were becoming increasingly popular. There was thus little to relieve the intense and at times oppressive atmosphere of my school years. Of course youngsters' spirits would still bubble over in the usual deviltry: drawing teachers' caricatures on the blackboards, roughhousing during recess, and other forms of rebellion against the adult world, as well as imitating its bad habits, like smoking secretly in the lavatories. Penalties if caught in the act were severe. The culprit would be sent home with a letter to his parents. For something as minor as talking in class an offender might be required to leave his seat and stand against the wall. For habitual offenders there was the dreaded grade of unsatisfactory for conduct, which meant one had to repeat the class. The teachers were poorly paid and grossly overworked. Not a few vented their resentment against the system by being rude or even brutal in their treatment of the students. Those who found it difficult to keep up with their studies could expect little help or attention to their special needs, instead an unfeeling teacher would make them the butt of ridicule or insulting language. I compared notes with my brother, who attended the same school in the twenties, and found that in his time punishments were much less frequent, and that teacher student relations were much more civilized. Another unfortunate innovation was that we were required to wear military-style uniforms both in and outside the school, which we saw as an unwelcome intrusion of authority into our private lives. I no sooner got home that I would discard the despised costume and resume my civilian identity. It made me feel freer.

Yet the majority of teachers were both competent and civil in their deportment. And, despite the pressures the system placed upon them a handful managed to show obvious delight in their subject as well as the ability to communicate it to their pupils. I remember with special gratitude my teachers of Polish literature, one an elderly gentleman who had begun his pedagogical career before World War I, the other a fairly recent graduate of the university. The older one adhered to the traditional approach: treatment of the greats and near greats of Polish poetry and fiction from the purely esthetic point of view and yet in terms transcending the platitudes of the textbook. For most people, the taste for poetry does not come naturally, nor does the ability to distinguish real poets from hacks. Also if we are honest we must also admit that we find our first attempts at reading the masterpieces of world literature heavy going, and to be completely honest, boring. And in fact after the school years, and this was true even before the age of TV, most people give up trying, and if they read novels at all, they are of the usual crime and sex genre. (I do not include the genuine mystery story of which I have been a lifelong devotee). It is only when one is young that one can be immunized against such philistinism. And it usually takes a parent, friend, but most often an exceptional teacher to do the trick. The teacher I remember had the ability to present the most reader resistant literary classic in a seductive light. Through his lectures it appeared endowed with intriguing and hitherto unsuspected subtleties of construction, style, and personal characterizations a book to be reread rather than put aside after one had passed the examination.

If his approach to what were considered masterpieces of Polish literature was too reverential, then that of his younger colleague offered a needed corrective. He stressed the historical and social background of literature. This would seem to be commonplace, yet for some, it was new in the school setting. To question the artistic stature or to probe into the personal life of one corner of a literary luminary was considered impermissible, bordering on unpatriotic. A young mind was not to be troubled by unnecessary insights into a great man's weaknesses, whether artistic or personal. Critics and biographers might dispute the historical veracity of the novels by X, discuss at length whether his sexual impotence affected the poetry of Y, but such indecorous subjects did not belong in the classroom.

Our young teacher disregarded the taboos, not, I am sure, for the sake of keeping popularity, but simply as part of what he considered to be an adult and realistic treatment of literature. His critical approach did not even spare one recognized as the greatest national idol among the prose writers, Henryk Sienkiewicz. Known abroad and crowned with the Nobel Prize, mainly for his *Quo Vadis*, Sienkiewicz captured the imagination of the reader at home with his immensely readable novels on themes from Polish history. His trilogy recounting the wars that beset the Polish Lithuanian Commonwealth from the highest point in its fortunes in 1648 through the next forty years attained the status of a national monument and as such were sacrosanct in the eyes of his artistically minded countrymen. By the same token the modern critic, finds a lot to criticize: Sienkiewicz's view of history is frequently colored by his strong nationalism often bordering on jingoism, and his characters are cast from the same mould: The Poles (unless they happen to be traitors to the commonwealth) are virtuous, often endowed with superhuman courage; their foreign enemies as a rule villainous and low-minded. Equally uncomplicated are the portraits of the heroines: incredibly and unfashionably chaste, they manage to preserve their purity against all odds through the most harrowing ordeals; and it is still as virgins that they become spouses of appropriate heroes. And one suspects what has irked many critics is the fact that this author for all his unfashionable ways has remained the most popular writer in the Polish language. Even during the Communist rule in Poland, Sienkiewicz, despite the fervently Catholic spirit of his novels, was being republished and read.

A balanced judgment such as our teacher was trying to impart, set the writer in the context of his times and milieu. The historical novels were published when the chances of recovering Poland's independence seemed at their lowest point in the 19th century. He wrote expressly to bolster his countrymen's spirit and to remind them of the past occasions when Poland faced and overcame almost equally desperate situations. Against his flaws as a writer must be set his superb mastery as a narrator, the vividness of his style, superb descriptions of nature. His non-historical fiction, especially his novellas written on contemporary 19th century themes show his versatility in employing the realistic genre.

I also have fond memories of my Latin teacher, a stately figure, reminiscent of the typical Polish provincial nobleman of old, uniquely cordial and even comradely in his dealings with the students. At the same time, he maintained his dignity and knew how to arouse interest not only in the language but in Roman life and the relevance of antiquity to modern life. We covered a wide swath of Latin literature, from Caesar to Tacitus; in poetry, from Ovid to Horace. I am not convinced that we don't lose something in our own education by eliminating the ancient languages from the curriculum. Well, there is always Hollywood to regale us with its version of ancient history. Some years ago I was idly turning the television dial, and came to what to me remains the high point of Hollywood's Cleopatra: The Egyptian queen (Elizabeth Taylor) is being introduced to Caesar (Rex Harrison) and her first words to the Roman conqueror are: "Caesar, I've been reading your *Commentaries*." Just like at a New York literary cocktail party! It is true that I did very well in Latin, and Polish literature, and in fact was graded A in practically all my subjects every year. A conspicuous exception was mathematics where my marks alternated between "satisfactory" (C) and "good" (B). Any amateur psychologist would undoubtedly ascribe my mediocre performance in mathematics to the fact that my brother was already recognized as a brilliant mathematician. I would plead that my less than brilliant achievements and subsequent aversion to the subject were largely caused by the trauma induced by the treatment received at the hands of my mathematics teacher whom I viewed as a sadist. Perhaps those not particularly talented in mathematics, tend to view their experience with that rigorous discipline as the low point of their school years. Still the man's dealings with his pupils was undoubtedly harsh, and unlikely to promote their self esteem or facilitate the mastering the techniques of the queen of the sciences. There were practically no lectures, students were supposed to learn the assignments from the textbook, and then in the classroom, they would be summoned to the blackboard to write out an exercise under dictation, and then without a single word of explanation or encouragement, expected to solve it. The teacher seated behind his desk would scan his student list to choose the victims of the day. As he turned the pages of the notebook, those whose names began with a letter low in the alphabet would breathe more easily, those in its upper reaches grew increasingly alarmed. Finally a name was called out and the designated student advanced to the site of his ordeal. The slightest slip in calculation and the unfortunate youngster would be curtly sent back to his seat. A few such mishaps (there were no written examinations) and one was failed and had to repeat the school year. The crushing effect of that terror on my psyche can be judged by the fact that once when another teacher taught mathematics for the first semester I was graded A at its end, but then the torturer took over again and I barely emerged with a C for the year.

Well, perhaps the school years would not prepare you for life if they were invariably and monotonously enjoyable. Even under ideal conditions and with the most devoted corps of teachers, the continental gymnasium was in a way somewhat reminiscent of pre-World War II colonies. Like the natives, students could not be expected to know what was good for them, but had to be told by the administrator-teacher. Their naturally anarchic dispositions had to be curbed by strict discipline if law and order were to prevail in the colony school. Freedom would come only after the emancipation, and in the case of the high school students, it really would come after a set period, seven or eight years. The transition from gymnasium to university was in fact a tremendous leap to freedom. Young men and women were completely freed from the constraints of their previous existence. Unlike students in the residential American and English colleges, or even their nonresident affiliates, the European university student was completely exempt from any rules to do with his personal life. Nor did he have to attend lectures if he did not feel like it. For an eighteen-year-old it was an abrupt, often bewildering jump from the realm of dependence to that of independence. No more uniform. He or she was as free as any other citizen, freer as a matter of fact, for society looked indulgently at minor transgressions. The privileged status of university youth was symbolized by the fact that even in a semi authoritarian Poland, and even in the old Tsarist Russia, the police could enter the university premises only if summoned by its authorities.

For all the accelerating political crisis I had little sense of its dimensions. The press was more strictly censored than before, and though an avid newspaper reader, I realized only much later that in 1937 the country was shaken by widespread peasant riots and that on several occasions the police had fired their weapons in dispersing demonstrations. The same year, I believe, there was a mass workers' protest meeting in Lwów. The police again fired into the crowd and at least one person was killed. One would think that in a city of some 350,000 people one could not have remained ignorant of the tragedy, but I lived in a different district and was not apprised of the events till several days later. All of which helped me to understand later on how in a really totalitarian society, in the Soviet Union in 1932-1933, an inhabitant of Moscow could remain unaware that millions of peasants were starving in the south in Ukraine.

What one could not miss was the rising tide of anti-Semitism. The government's position on the issue was ambiguous. In general its attitude during the immediate prewar years was one of what the authorities undoubtedly considered a "respectable" variety of intolerance: lamenting both anti-Jewish excesses and the fact that there were so many Jews in Poland, severe limitations on Jewish access to government-controlled positions (which included university professorships) and reluctance to curb anti-Semitic propaganda, which was the staple commodity of the radical right.

Extremism often appeals to the young, but in such cases it is usually their elders who plant the seeds of intolerance in their minds. I could observe this process in my school. In a class of about fifty students, there had been until 1937-1938 no tension between Catholics and Jews. But then one began to hear anti-Semitic remarks. Most often they were uttered rather shamefacedly and not targeted at Jewish colleagues, obviously something the speaker picked up from a newspaper or an older relative. More serious and saddening were the developments at the universities. The radical right succeeded in capturing a sizable proportion of the student body. The young zealots, if that be the proper term, sought to submit Jewish students to all sorts of chicanery; at the Lwów university, they pressed the authorities to require Jews attending lectures to be confined exclusively to the left row of seats. Demonstrations against liberal-minded professors, scuffles in the hallways, and student strikes, became almost daily features of university life. The shock was all the greater because Lwów had always been proud of its ethnic and religious pluralism (probably the only city in the world outside of Jerusalem which was the seat of three Catholic archbishops of the Roman, Greek, and Armenian rites) and of their long-standing harmony between the different national communities. Anti-Semitism in Poland never reached anything like the level of savagery it displayed even in pre-war Nazi Germany. Nor did it ever succeed in capturing, as in France at the time of the Dreyfus affair, a large part of the intellectual community. Few of the university professors displayed any sympathy with the newfangled form of barbarism. But the aggressive intolerance was a blemish on the tradition of the nation that had fought for so long for the right of independent existence under the slogan "for our own and universal freedom."

My immediate family was well-to-do but hardly rich. Many years later after my brother's death one of his professorial colleagues wrote an obituary in which he presented the Ulams of Lwów as local Rothschilds. He must have been carried away by the emotion of the moment in his desire to embellish his dead friend's origins. In fact my cousin owned a small bank, and we had some very rich relatives, but our own material circumstances were quite middle class. But for whatever reasons, I cannot recall anyone in the family discussing the idea of emigration. My brother for professional reasons had to seek an academic career abroad, but he returned home every summer. What was happening in the universities, however, was a strong factor in persuading my parents and myself that unlike my much older brother and sister, I should pursue higher studies abroad. Already at fourteen and being a fervent Anglophile I hoped to go to college in England. But then not having been abroad and with my brother in the States, it appeared logical that I should seek my higher education there.

America for a Polish boy of my generation and background was still an exotic land. Our earliest initiation into what we thought was America came through the adventure stories of Karl May, a fantastically popular and prolific writer. The mainstay of his huge corpus of works were the stories of his alleged exploits among the Indians of the Wild West where he became a blood brother of an Apache chief, and helped his tribe against the treacherous Comanches (though soon disenchanted with May, I long remained pro-Apache and anti-Comanche). We all adored the author-hero (who in fact never set foot outside his native Germany), appropriately known as Old Shatterhand, who had two unique skills: the ability to crawl unnoticed close to a fire around which Comanche chiefs or other malefactors took counsel and thus learn their evil plans, and a punch which without inflicting permanent damage made its recipient unconscious for exactly thirty minutes. But May's appeal was not likely to last long after age 12. There followed more solid fare. James Fenimore Cooper, Mark Twain, and on the adventure side, Zane Grey. But as I got older, my view of American contemporary life was influenced by reading Sinclair Lewis, Upton Sinclair, and Theodore Dreiser, none of them likely to induce a very favorable view of American life at that time. In addition, my Anglophilia was also fed by mystery stories, and here England 's advantage over the U.S. appeared insuperable: where were the American counterparts of Dorothy Sayers, Agatha Christie, and Conan Doyle?

I was not much of a moviegoer; so that American films could not counteract my passion for things British. In fact Hollywood in the thirties was in some ways an outpost of the British empire, movies on the imperial themes, e.g., *Lives of a Bengal Lancer, Gunga Din* among its most notable productions, British actors and actresses, some of its outstanding stars.

Two years before my actual departure I began a systematic study of American history and culture. My brother took out subscriptions for me to American newspapers and periodicals. I was amazed to receive my first packet of the Sunday *New York Times*: what tremendous bulk! How many different parts and features! American politics were a new and exciting discovery. In Britain the political scene was entirely dominated by the Conservatives. In France it was one of chaos. One need not recall what was going on in Germany and Italy, or in Spain during the Spanish Civil War. But in America, President Roosevelt for all his overwhelming victory in the elections and democratic majorities in both houses of Congress, saw much of his legislation blocked by the Supreme Court, by the "nine old men" (actually six of them). At first it was incomprehensible to me how a handful of justices could thwart what for, the most part, was a clear mandate of the majority of the electorate. I sympathized with Roosevelt's "court-packing" scheme. It is only later that I began to understand the complex constitutional nexus tying American politics and the judiciary. Today I still wonder whether judicial review in its present form is a desirable feature in a democracy and at times entertain a blasphemous thought that in today's world perhaps a parliamentary system like Britain's would for the United States be preferable to the presidential one.

As for many progressively minded Europeans, Roosevelt even then was the outstanding democratic leader of the West. England's Baldwin and Chamberlain (even before Munich) were politicians with a pre-1914 mentality incapable of understanding the challenge of the times. One admired Winston Churchill for his spirited campaign to awaken his countrymen to the danger of Nazi Germany. But he was out of power, and his chivalrous but fatuous defense of Edward VIII in the abdication crisis of 1936 made his chances of achieving it seem quite remote. FDR presided over a social revolution, and it was clear it if that had depended solely on him, he would have disabused American society of the delusion of isolationism.

I have a capricious memory; poor when it comes to remembering faces and names, quite good for historical facts and trivia. A few years ago, I found myself in the company of several specialists in American politics. One of them announced that a colleague of his has just been made Bertrand Snell Professor of political science and challenged his fellow experts to identify the man after whom the chair was named. They all failed and it fell to me, an outsider, to provide the answer. I remember unfolding the *New York Times* forty or so years before and coming across a photograph of Snell, then the Republican minority leader in the House of Representatives. Through books, journals, and my habit of leafing in idle moments through the *World Almanac* I acquired an extensive knowledge of data about U.S. history and politics before I set foot on American soil. In the future this preparation would enable to amaze my friends with my instant recall of obscure facts (e.g., the vice presidential candidate in 1928, Ted Williams's batting average in one of his less successful years) and usually collect on bets when challenged.

My expertise in trivia also extended to British and French history, not to speak of Poland's. In fact my interest in America was as yet unconnected with any clear idea that it should become home for the rest of my life. For the time being, 1937-1939, all that was clear to me was my future college career there. Beyond that I do not recall any decision about my eventual profession. My uncertainty I can recognize now was due partly to my immaturity and consequent indolence: in due time things somehow will arrange themselves, why worry about them now. Consciously it did not occur to me that I would be embarking on a completely new life in a strange country, that I might never see my father again, nor, for decades, (never, as it turned out [ed.]) the city and country of my birth.

Yet at the same time, I also recognize, I had a dim and uneasy feeling of irretrievable change both in my world and in the world at large. Whatever the elements of stability, the firm point and direction was in flux not only because of normal adolescent developments but also because of what was happening around me. My mother was in the final phase of her cruel illness, and much as my parents wanted to spare me the knowledge of the hopelessness of her condition, I had a presentiment I would not see her again after her departure to Vienna for yet another operation. My brother was away; my sister left home upon her marriage. The unraveling of my childhood world was compounded by what was happening in Polish society and the world beyond it. The Warsaw regime, split between the traditional and those who favored an outright authoritarian if not frankly fascist route, seemed less and less capable of coping with the economic crisis and political disturbances. Had the war not come, it is conceivable the country would have experienced a right-wing coup and a violent clash between the regime and forces on the left represented by the more radical elements of the Socialist and Peasant parties. Anti-Semitism was increasing. There was still a world of difference between living in Poland, even if one was a Jew or an opponent of the regime, and living in Germany. But there was a definite change in the political atmosphere, and one could almost feel it physically like a man suddenly transported to a much higher altitude and having to gasp for air as if unable to acclimatize to a new environment. The government's foreign policy was a case in question. The foundation of Poland's security and territorial integrity was the alliance with France. (Of course no one, including Hitler's generals, suspected how frail that foundation would turn out to be in 1939-1940.) But, and not without some reason, the Warsaw regime felt that it was being patronized by the French rather than treated as a real ally, and that Paris insisted on special treatment for the French capitalists in Poland, and there were other grievances not unusual for the weaker partner in any alliance. Beyond it the France of the Popular Front was ideologically not pleasing to the increasingly authoritarian Warsaw rulers. Confident that if the worst came they should still have the invincible French army to help them, Poland's leaders embarked on a political flirtation with Germany and Italy. Warsaw understood the 1934 nonaggression treaty with German as reflecting Hitler's recognition that Poland was a great power and could not be provoked or attacked with impunity. The nationalistic megalomania was not confined to the government circles. I remember my high school history teacher, a very intelligent and prescient woman, commented on the pact with satisfaction because it showed, according to her, that Poland could no longer be treated as a mere client of France.

The Czech crisis of the summer of 1938 completed my disillusionment with the Polish political system and its future prospects. Before it I had not been able to emancipate myself completely from a feeling of loyalty to that system, much as I knew its defects. It is difficult when one is young to resist or question what is being drummed into one's head in school and the majority of the media. I did resent the fascist-like features of the political situation, the Warsaw rulers' flirtation with Hitler, their equanimity in the face of rising anti-Semitism. But before the summer of 1938 I still believed, as did many others, that the more liberal elements within the ruling groups would prevail. Paradoxically, one could even draw some comfort from the worsening international situation: surely those responsible for the country's security had to see that it depended ultimately on the Western democracies, and that they would not be eager to help if the regime continued to gravitate toward fascism. It was one thing to entertain visiting Nazi and Fascist dignitaries and another to lend indirect assistance to one of Hitler's nefarious schemes.

That hope of the alleged "healthy" elements within the regime restraining themselves had to be seriously undermined by Warsaw's complicity in the first place, of partitioning Czechoslovakia (and how inglorious for a country that itself had been the victim of partitions!). Perhaps even more than the immorality of carving out a piece of the prostrated land, it was the stupidity of this policy which made one lose respect for the rulers. Anything which strengthened Hitler, any new conquest, served only to whet his appetite. And there was a considerable probability that Poland would be next on his menu.

It is impossible for me to recall precisely my view of the world on the eve of my departure from Poland. I was thoroughly permeated by Polish culture—yet as the above testifies, increasingly alienated from the political situation in my country. My Jewishness was also of an ambivalent nature. I reacted with strong indignation to manifestations of anti-Semitism, yet neither knew nor was drawn to specifically Jewish culture or customs. While very religious when very young, by sixteen I had turned agnostic. It seemed to me then and I continue to believe so now that true religious experience cannot be based merely on the acceptance of the moral code and precepts of a given creed but must be accompanied by faith in its supernatural part. For better or worse, probably the worse, science has made it impossible to believe in the way our ancestors did. I respect and envy the people who believe in the totality of a given creed but I am baffled by the question of how such belief can be combined with true tolerance. Nor do I understand strict atheism, which to me appears based on the presumption that we know all there is to know about the universe and human destiny. Perhaps any discussion of such a fundamental problem must raise more questions than they answer. A seventeenth-century English philosopher formulated one solution of the problem which, though humorous, is, I suspect, widely and covertly practiced: "wise men have only one religion," and about which one it is, "wise men don't tell."

Here I digress. If my attitude about religious, but also political, matters, may appear rather passionless, unbecoming to the rebellious spirit of youth, then at least a partial explanation could be derived from what happened in my childhood. No, I do not refer to some dramatic trauma but to but to the personality of my governess, perhaps a pretentious term for a peasant-born girl who took care of me and whose influence on the child's mind was all the greater in view of my mother's illness and frequent trips abroad. Zosie (Sophie) was a very good person but much addicted to reading trashy sentimental novels, and playing on the piano and singing the dreadful hits of the period. The words of the most risqué are still firmly imprinted in my memory, something which would undoubtedly please Dr. Freud since at that early age my mind was obviously innocent of the mysteries of sex. Here is one example: "And from this moment we shall live the joyous life of bees and butterflies: Ecstatic all night, longing all day long. Oh, marvel of my caresses, wonder of my dreams, what do we care about the world and other people?" Sounds more rhapsodic if no less idiotic in Polish (e.g., "Shouldn't daytime bring welcome rest rather than the craving for more?")

Needless to say those pursuits of my governess were greatly restricted by her duties in taking care of a seven or eight year old. What was most time consuming on this count was the need to satisfy my constant pestering her for explanations: Why do I have to dream in a certain way, why do the grownups smoke, why about everything under the sun. And to economize on our conversations so that she had more time to devote to reading and singing, she developed an infallible technique: all my "whys" were answered with an imperturbable "such is the custom." After some initial resistance, I acquiesced in her explanations and accepted them as satisfactory answers to most problems touching my conduct and my *Weltanschauung*.

Perhaps this early indoctrination has not entirely worn off to this very day and may be blamed for my generally conservative attitude on many issues. But as time went on the influence of my governess's philosophy waned. Certainly what was happening in Polish politics, not to mention the world at large, could not be explained in terms of tradition. On the contrary, the traditions of humanity and toleration were on the defensive all over Europe. And then some "customs" I discovered were quite bad; persistence in traditional attitudes and practices when the times called for change, often led to disastrous results. I was never drawn to a radical philosophy, but in the last prewar years the one political movement which attracted my sympathy was the Polish Socialist Party Before 1914 the party had played the leading role in the struggle for independence. In independent Poland it stoutly fought for democracy and after Pilsudski's death it was the main force opposing the fatuous foreign and domestic politics of the government. Its ideology at least insofar as the leadership was concerned was but little influenced by dogmatic Marxism, and it was firmly opposed to Communism. The latter's strength among the working classes was not considerable, mainly because of its identification with the Soviet Union, which for a Pole was much clearer and more compromising than to a French or Italian worker and intellectual. But for all of its proud tradition and considerable following, the Socialist Party assented to the fatal policies of the government.

2

The Last Summer

Doubt, denial and indifference about war...a trip to the mountains...preparing to leave for America...

In the fall of 1938, I applied through my brother for admission to Brown University in Providence. He taught there while a Senior Fellow at Harvard and advised me probably wisely, and coming fresh from abroad, that a small college would be better for my initiation into American life than a big school in a big city like Columbia or Harvard. Brown at that time had an entering class of four hundred. I was accepted as a freshman with the class of '43, and beginning with the fall of '38 I intensified my preparation for a new country and a new life. I felt neither exultation nor regret at my forthcoming departure. It did not occur to me that I would not see my father or sister again, that all of my friends and classmates would disappear from my life, a great majority of them victims of the coming war. My separation from my homeland was thought to be provisional for four years, and I would be coming back, just as my brother had, every summer.

Not that like Mr. Neville Chamberlain I believed in peace in our time. But everything that fall seemed to indicate that the European crisis would fester for a few years without actually coming to war. Hitler had scored dazzling successes, and within the last two years had swallowed Austria and the German part of Czechoslovakia. Why should he now stretch his luck? The natural thing for him to do, I believed with many others in Europe that autumn, was to sit quietly for some time, thus strengthening the hand of Chamberlain and other appeasers in the West.

Ah, but had he been capable of such rationality, Hitler would not have been Hitler. Following Munich he immediately began preparing to grab which remained of Czechoslovakia and intoxicated by his previous victories began simultaneously to press Poland. What he demanded probably seemed to the tyrant to be the height of magnanimity on his part: just Danzig and a German-owned easement through the "Polish Corridor" linking East Prussia with the rest of Germany. Danzig, for all practical purposes. was already part of the Reich; the extraterritorial road was not a big deal. But obtuse though the Polish government had been, it would have taken complete idiocy not to realize that those demands represented for Germany just an appetizer and to grant them would be the first and decisive step in making the country a dependency of Hitler's as it would be soon: March, 1939, demonstrated this when German nabbed what remained of Czechoslovakia.

Conscious that the revelation of the German blackmail meant absolute bankruptcy of his policy, Polish Foreign Minister Beck withheld Hitler's demands from the public as well as from the West. Had it been done before March, 1939 he would have been hounded out of office. I remember my father, who was far from a militant nationalist, becoming indignant at seeing a photo of Beck visiting Hitler in Berchtesgaden when Germany's demands were still secret. There he was, holding his hat in his hand looking for all the world like a supplicant, while Hitler, looking stern, kept his hat on his head. Beck retained his job only because Hitler's demands became known at the same time as the British declaration that His Majesty's government would come to Poland's help in the case of aggression. With Germany's swallowing of what was left of Czechoslovakia, Chamberlain finally realized the fatuity of his trust in Hitler's reasonableness. And so for a few months longer Beck could pose as a master statesman who secured Britain's and France's guarantees that this time Hitler's blackmail would not work.

Remembering Munich one could still take British and French assurances with a grain of salt (as evidently did Hitler). Didn't Paris and London practically to the last moment keep supporting the Czechs, only to press them in the end to surrender? Reading French papers like Le Matin I was aware that that a segment of French public opinion would have been content to leave Poland to her own, or rather to Hitler's, devices. "Should we die for Danzig?" was the title of one of the defeatist articles in the press. But like most of my contemporaries, in fact most Poles, I knew that the country would never capitulate; there could be no repetition of Munich.

As of the spring of '39 many still believed that there would be no war in near future and hardly anybody could foresee that the nation was on the eve of the greatest catastrophe in its history. It was generally held that Hitler's previous successes had been achieved largely through bluff. This time it would not work. The Germans had to know that Poland would fight, even if she had to fight alone, and that to invade her would take months if not more and much German blood. The nature of modern warfare was little understood, and not only in Poland. But if anything, ignorance on that subject was probably more widespread there than elsewhere. When General Maurice Gamelin, the commander-in-chief of the French army, visited the country that spring the papers expressed amazement that the French general was not interested in reviewing the famous Polish cavalry: the country had but two hundred very obsolete warplanes. Since none were produced in the industrially backward country, they had been acquired from France, herself, as 1940 was to reveal, just as disastrously backward in military technology. Nobody could even suspect that the great French Army, the victor in World War I, could crumble in a matter of days as it would in 1940. And then Great Britain, the country which for centuries had not known defeat in a European war! And nobody, absolutely nobody in Poland, and Poles, unlike people in the West, had no reasons to have illusions about the Soviet Union, could still imagine Stalin striking a bargain with Hitler and thus emboldening him to unleash the horrors that were to come. All in all, the atmosphere that spring of '39 was far from panicky, if anything, it was one of false confidence: should Hitler against all odds still decide on war, the Germans would have a hard time subduing Poland and of course before this could be completed, the invincible French would emerge from behind the Maginot line, and this time, unlike the last, the war would be concluded on German territory with the Nazis biting the dust.

I shall discuss later whether we have the right to consider such fantasizing as being peculiar to Polish public opinion. Belief in France's military power was shared by many others prior to May 1940, and they included Churchill, Stalin, and the German general staff. But what was inexcusable was the Polish government's unawareness that courage and martial spirit in this case could not compensate for the country's industrial and technological backwardness. Psychologically, if probably not militarily, it would have made a great deal of difference, if, upon the revelation of the German threat, the regime invited the opposition parties to join in a government of national unity. This was not done and the country entered the war under a regime not representative of the majority of the nation.

As the war clouds darkened over Europe during the summer of 1939, people could not or would not face the true implications of the coming terrible storm. Those who did actually pretended otherwise. And this practice of magical thinking beguiled ordinary citizen and statesman alike. It was certainly true throughout my native Poland and in my own family.

Oh, but how little even intelligent people unfazed by government propaganda realized that we were on the threshhold of a catastrophe. My brother chose as usual to spend his summer vacation in Poland. Once there, he and I began in a very leisurely fashion to plan our trip to the States. Freshman week at Brown was due to start the second week in September. We were planning to go by boat from Gdynia, and the date originally chosen for our departure was September 3. Though he himself did not quite believe in the imminence of war, my father, as if gripped by a premonition, urged us in the strongest terms to leave earlier. However, I had become increasingly reluctant to leave my family. My brother also was not eager to leave sooner: his academic year at Harvard also did not begin until the middle of September. He was courting a young lady, and it was a beautiful summer unlike the hot and humid ones in New England, which he hated. Ironically, the beautiful and dry weather which in Poland persisted through September, would make it all the easier for the German Panzer. And so passage had been booked for the two of us on the September 3rd sailing of the *SS Batory* for the New World. I've often wondered what might have happened had we stuck to that date. Of course, we would not have been able to sail from the Baltic!

From the standpoint of decades later, it must seem utterly amazing that anyone, especially in Poland that summer, could have been unaware, even nonchalant, about the possibility of war. While there were daily new threats and fresh demands from Hitler, my brother and I were lounging with out friends in the cafés of Lwów and Warsaw.

We took time out to spend a few days in my uncle's estate in the Carpathian mountains on the Polish-Hungarian frontier. We were joined there by my cousin Andrzej. He came from a more prosperous branch of the family and used to go there to hunt, not only for boar and stags, but also, I suspect, for local girls. There were quite a number of attractive ones in the vicinity, as a rule not too prudish and quite accessible, especially to "city gentlemen." Smorze, as the estate was called, was thirty miles from the nearest railway station, and the distance had to be traversed on one of those terrible country roads certainly not made for automobiles. On one occasion ours gave up. Oh no, there was no gas station on the road, nothing in the way of AAA (prewar Poland for a population of about 33 million could boast of some 25,000 private motor cars), no likelihood of another car appearing for hours if not days in that wilderness. Finally a horse drawn cart happened to pass by. My cousin imperiously commandeered the vehicle, ordering the peasant driver to take us to our destination. Such was the semifeudal atmosphere in that primitive corner of Poland.

*   *   *

Well, it is difficult to recapture the atmosphere of those days and recall what governed my own thoughts. There was obviously a threat of war. But this threat had been just as palpable the year before, and then it had passed. To be sure, Hitler had gotten what he wanted: Czechoslovakia bullied into accepting occupation; possession of the Sudetenland: and after misleading Prime Minister Chamberlain into saying, on his return from their meeting in Munich, "We shall have peace in our time," the prompt dismemberment of the rest of that unhappy country.

We reasoned that the Führer must know, as we all did, that the Poles would fight rather than surrender Danzig. He might be infuriated by Warsaw's rejection of his "modest" demand; he might rant and rave, but surely he would not succeed in his blackmail. And having learned how fatuous it was to try to appease him, this time Britain and France would not, as they had the year before, abandon their ally and agree to another Munich.

But my brother and I could anticipate nothing of the coming events as we left from the Polish Baltic port of Gdynia, which lay about 18 miles north of the contentious city-state of Danzig (now Gdansk) not on September 3rd, as originally planned, but barely two weeks before the last night in August even though earlier that month we had been set on keeping to the original departure date. As I have mentioned, Stan had his girlfriend in Lwów; I wanted to spend as much time as possible with my family before my new adventure began so far away from home. It was my father, in his wisdom and solicitude for his sons, who finally prevailed upon us not to wait for the September sailing, but to depart immediately. I'll never know if, indeed, he had had a clear premonition of what would happen. His reasons did not touch on the war scare: I would need a couple of weeks, he said, to adjust to an unfamiliar environment before entering college. I had never been so far from home as across the Atlantic, and possibly he did not want to add to my already considerable nervousness by invoking the danger of war and the possibility that I would never see him again.

So, we returned then to Lwów after the bracing interval in the country, during this summer of high drama. Europe was on the eve of the (then) unimaginable catastrophe. But though Hitler's anti-Polish propaganda was becoming all the more shrill, there was still the delusion that the worst would not happen: "He (Hitler) is just bluffing ... the French army ... the German generals do not want war." (The last was at least partly true.) The press kept up the bravado: if worst came to worst Poland would show the Germans. Some in the media persuaded themselves that in the initial stages of the war the Polish army would not only hold its own, but would be able to occupy East Prussia! And then, of course, the French army would strike through Germany's western frontier.

On the eve of our departure from Gdynia in the middle of August (after a six hour train trip across Poland from Lwów), none of us could free our minds of a feeling of uneasiness. A photograph taken at that time expresses this. My father and brother look thoughtful, if not troubled. I look clearly nervous; and it is only Uncle Szymon, known as an incurable optimist, who has a hint of a smile on his face.

3

Pre-War Poland: An Assessment

Some history…the role of Pilsudski…grandiose national ideas…Jozef Beck and Foreign policy…

Lwów's appearance and ambiance belied the city's tempestuous past. It bore no scars of recent conflicts. Even its occupation in 1914-1915 by the imperial Russian armies left no visible traces, the military practices of that time still light years away from the future barbarities of the Germans and the Soviets. But the city was rich in the monuments of its earlier and colorful history: ruins of the castle erected by the city's founder in the 13th century, a Russian prince who named it after his son Lev or Leo, some of the earliest examples of Latin and Eastern church architecture, houses of rich merchants dating from the 16th and 17th centuries, when the city was an important station on the trade route between the Black Sea and the Baltic. A tablet on the Castle Hill commemorated one of the high points of the martial past. It was from there that King Jan Sobieski, future savior of Vienna from the Turks, launched his heavy armored cavalry which smashed the hordes of besieging Tartars. But after such an eventful past the 18th century was for Lwów, as for Poland in general a period of political and economic decline, the once rich and vibrant commercial circle sinking into provincial insignificance.

The region came under Austrian rule. In the 1800s when the empire became a constitutional state and the province of Galicia of which Lwów was the capital was endowed with considerable autonomy amounting to home rule, the city recouped its status as a major center of Polish culture and became a haven for political exiles and refugees from the not so fortunate Polish provinces in Germany and Russia.

Much later, as the thirties advanced, neither the high school or the university could remain unaffected by the rising political tension in the country, and that in turn reflected the ever more tempestuous and ominous international atmosphere. The term "semiauthoritarian" still fails to describe precisely the Polish political system at the time. The authoritarian element originated in the military coup carried out in May 1926 by Marshal Joseph Pilsudski. From then on, athough officially just minister of war, he exercised the highest authority in the country and his followers preempted all the leadership positions in the army and in the civil administration. Yet the opposition parties and press were allowed to function, and to compete freely in the election to parliament and local legislative bodies. Pilsudski himself did not fit the usual stereotype of a military dictator. Until his forties a professional revolutionary and socialist in Russian Poland, he organized in Galicia shortly before 1914 military units which technically on the Austrian side fought in the war against the Russians. His real wager was on the simultaneous collapse of the three empires occupying Poland and when this came to pass in 1918, he was elected head of an independent Poland leading it in 1920 in the successful war against the Soviets. He eschewed totalitarian methods of repression with one conspicuous exception in 1930 when a number of opposition leaders were arbitrarily interned, and then in effect forced to leave the country. As long as the old marshal lived, the regime had no specific ideological physiognomy, its parliamentary supporters were socially and ethnically a motley crowd ranging from landed aristocrats to orthodox Jews. But the core of his partisans and office holders in the military and the government consisted of those who in 1914 had answered Pilsudski's call to arms and joined his Polish Legion.

Unlike in the case of other authoritarian rulers, the reverence for the marshal survived his death. In 1990, with the death of Communism and the birth of real if still feeble democracy in Poland, the Lenin shipyard works in Danzig, the birthplace of Solidarity, was named after Pilsudski. But, during his reign, his personal popularity did not extend to the government as a whole. Abroad it was dubbed "the Colonels' Government." In fact, though many of the officials were or had been army officers, their background had not been militaristic. Those were people who as students or young professionals had enlisted with Pilsudski in 1914, and who by the mere virtue of that fact now held high preferments. In view of that background there was at first something amateurish, even bohemian, about the regime. As time went on, like any ingrown group monopolizing power the ruling elite became increasingly prey to factionalism, corruption, and blindness to the pressing problems facing the country. And those problems would have taxed the most enlightened and selfless group of administrators. Already a poor country, Poland was hit hard by the depression. Seventy percent of the population was engaged in agriculture, the economic condition of the peasantry in the southern part of the country probably more deplorable than anywhere else in Europe outside of the Soviet Union. I occasionally visited my uncle's estate in the Carpathian Mountains on the Polish-Hungarian frontier. One had the impression of being not in Europe but in an obscure corner of what would later be called the Third World: the mostly Ukrainian population of the region lived in grinding poverty, deprived of the most basic amenities of modern civilization

Few in the press were enlightened enough to arrive at a balanced judgment: to understand that a nation which had endured so much could not have developed into an exemplary democracy in the twenty years of its recovered statehood. Such reality clashed with the image of Poland propagated by the regime. Official propaganda which did not spare the schools tried to convince young minds that their impoverished underindustrialized country situated between two military giants was virtually a great power. It is true that the long years of national humiliation were conducive, once independence was recovered, to a kind of national hubris which would at times exhibit ridiculous manifestations. Some aspects of that stultifying campaign bore a tragicomic aspect. As it was assumed at the time, one of the qualifications for being a great power was ownership of overseas colonies. But even to the limited intelligence of the propagators of such nonsense it was clear that neither Britain nor France was likely to hand over one of their colonies to satisfy the imperialist aspirations of the new great power. But why not Portugal, a small country with a surfeit of overseas possessions? It was not quite clear how Portugal was to be made to cede one of its imperial jewels: purchase? The Polish treasury was nearly bankrupt; force of arms? How and when? In any case, an officially spawned preposterously named outfit, the Polish Naval and Colonial League (in which Polish high school students were encouraged to enlist), urged, quite seriously, Poland's pretension to Angola. History at times plays funny tricks.

Many years later, the Portuguese empire did, like the others, disintegrate. Soviet intrigues and Castro's Cuban soldiers helped foist upon Angola a Marxist regime. In a strange way the idiotic phantasy of my school years came true: Angola became, not, to be sure, a Polish possession, but part of the "socialist camp" of which Communist ruled Poland was a member. And then the entire "camp" ignominiously collapsed and with it the grotesque attempt to plant Marxism Leninism in African soil.

But official megalomania also had much more serious consequences. With the death of Marshal Pilsudski in 1935, the ruling elite whose mutually incompatible elements were kept together by him, now openly split, and the country came close to being a police state. The "winds of change" over Europe, i. e., fascism, convinced some within the government camp and in the extreme right-wing opposition that Poland should move in a similar direction. The same circles, almost superfluous to say, propagated anti-Semitism and xenophobia. Some were for continuing the paternalistic non-ideological character of the regime. But fascism was on the march in Europe and was finding imitators in Poland. They wanted to be done with the caution and self-restraint of the old order. Anti-Semitism was raising its head. A few in the ruling clique felt it was high time that Poland too became a one-party state with all the usual paraphernalia, an attempt all the more foolish in a country where thirty percent of the population belonged to various national and religious minorities. With the encouragement of some in the government, there was launched the Camp of National Unity, in its muddled ideology and organizational design, a clear imitation of Italian fascism. The ideological guru of the new movement was to be a Colonel Koc, a name which in Polish means blanket and that gave rise to a widespread witticism among the young: "Male and female comrades, let us join under Koc!" (A pun that works because Polish doesn't have the definite article). As the Communists were to find out later, the national sense of humor was not the least potent of the antidotes to totalitarian propaganda in Poland. The Ozone, as the camp became known from its Polish initials, collapsed partly because of the sheer absurdity of its concept, partly because of the emphatically negative response of society.

Yet despite the failure to introduce outright fascism, the inflammatory brand of nationalism grew stronger and more raucous, both within the regime and the country at large. On the eve of the greatest challenge to its existence in history, the nation was riven by violent political crises. Divided within itself though it was, the ruling group still became more intolerant and oppressive. The death of Pilsudski had deprived it of whatever moral authority it had possessed. The country knew it as a group of bureaucrats clinging to power and its perquisites for their own sake.

With the mid-thirties the flirtation with Germany came dangerously close to becoming a love affair. Hitler flattered the national ego by delegating his deputy, Hermann Goering, to represent the Reich at the funeral rites for Pilsudski. The corpulent marshal would return to Poland supposedly just for a hunting trip; and other high-ranking Nazis, such as the incongruously titled Minister of Justice Hans Frank, also took to visiting their future victim. This man's visit, seen from the post-1939 perspective, was especially goulish. The once-honored guest became the governor of German-occupied Poland, chief official of the regime that gave currency to terms such as *holocaust* and *genocide*. It would be incorrect to believe that the majority of Poles, with its firmly Francophile intelligentsia, approved that degree of intimacy with Germany. Even on the right there were voices warning about Hitler. It was one thing for people in the West to believe the Führer's peaceful professions. History provided little reason, to put it mildly, to trust any German government's, let alone Hitler's assurances that it had no territorial claims against Poland. Yet the same fatuous arguments that were used to justify appeasement in Chamberlain's Britain found currency in Warsaw's ruling circles: Hitler saw his mission as saving Germany and Europe from Communism, hence he would not start a new conflagration of which the main beneficiary could only be the Soviet Union; he was not a Prussian, and therefore was alien to the Bismarck model of Prussian militaristic tradition. (This was certainly true but in a different sense; compared to Hitler, Bismarck appears a Gandhilike humanitarian.)

After Pilsudski's death, the main responsibility for conducting Poland's foreign policy rested in the hands of the foreign minister Joseph Beck. It is not clear to what extent his illusions about Germany were shared by other influential figures of the regime such as General, later, Marshal, Edward Rydz-Smigly, commander-in-chief, rumored to be aspiring to dictatorship. Beck cannot be absolved from being mainly responsible for the general direction of foreign policy and its style, its arrogant rhetoric reminiscent of the totalitarian leaders. To be fair, he resolutely rejected Hitler's hints about joining in an allianace against the USSR.

Warsaw did not learn anything from Hitler's rape of Austria in March 1938. Almost immediately there followed another of Hitler's attempts at conquest through blackmail: his brutal intimidation of Czechoslovakia to cede the Sudetenland. Like Poland, Czechoslovakia was "protected" by a military alliance with France. Common sense should have urged the Polish government to render at least moral support to the Czechs. Yet such was the blindness and megalomania of Beck & Co. that as French and British support for the fellow Slavic country faltered, the Warsaw government announced its own territorial demands on Czechoslovakia: i.e., the Cieszyn district which had a mixed Polish and Czech population. Brought to its knees after the Munich conference when Britain and France capitulated to Hitler, and then pressured Czechoslovakia to yield the Sudetenland, Prague had no alternative but to surrender the Cieszyn district to Poland(As the saying goes, Warsaw's behavior was more than a crime, it was a fatal error on the part of the government which in a year's time would find itself under similar German pressure as that suffered by the unfortunate Czechoslovakia.)

This scandalous exploitation of a neighboring country's misfortune, and all for the acquisition of a small and unimportant piece of territory, was touted by the regime as a great victory. But among the population at large, the ordeal of Czechoslovakia brought dire forebodings and the regime's vulture-like action provoked if not outright shame, then deep embarrassment. Even my most nationalistically minded classmates shared those feelings. The opposition press noted the sordid action with no comment, or, insofar as censorship allowed, with disapproval. One of the most persistent critics of Beck, a conservative journalist hitherto a supporter of the regime, was sent to a concentration camp the government had improvised a few years before, and where people could be sent by a mere fiat of the Minister of the Interior. Though in its size or the treatment of the inmates, the camp could not be compared to a Soviet or Nazi lager, it was a sad indication of the direction in which the government was moving.

One must keep a sense of proportion: had Poland been an exemplary democracy, its foreign policy a model of virtue, and Beck not a pompous dilettante, but a diplomat with the skills of a Talleyrand it is still unlikely the country would have escaped its wartime tragedy.

That tragedy was almost unavoidable because of Poland's position between two ruthless dictatorships. But a more honest and realistic foreign policy by the prewar regime would have made Poland's case much stronger at the end of the war. when its exile government in London strove in vain to persuade the U.S. and Britain to oppose the Soviet Union's imposition of Communism upon the country. But perhaps even that would not have availed much.

Part Two

A Polish Youth in a New Land

4

The New Country; A New Life

On the *SS Batory*...the war begins...settling in at Brown...American attitudes about the War....

With the egotism of the young, I was preoccupied with my own problems, excited yet fearful at the prospect of my forthcoming adventure abroad. How lighthearted we were is shown by the fact that there was little thought given as to how I was going to pay my way in the U.S. Some money had been deposited in a New York bank, but it would last only a few months. Did we really think that my father would be able to send me more in the course of the coming year? I had but a student visa, which would effectively bar me from earning my subsistence, even if a foreigner could find a job in unemployment-ridden America, and even more unrealistic as if a seventeen year old for the first time in the country, studying full time in a hitherto completely alien environment would have the leisure to work on the side. As it was, for two years I would have to depend entirely on my brother with his far from munificent salary as a university lecturer.

We set out from Gdynia in the middle of August The German invasion started on September 1; Poland's Baltic was occupied in the first two days. I did not give any thought to the possibility I would not see my father, sister (Stefania), nor friends, ever again. There was no party, no dramatic farewell; we were going to be returning next summer! Nor was our, in retrospect incredible, lack of concern so unusual. On shipboard we met a friend of my brother's, a well-known mathematician and logician, Alfred Tarski. He was going just to a scientific conference in the U.S. Naturally he brought only summer clothes with him; he would be going back in two weeks! His wife and children were left behind in Poland. Miraculously (they were Jewish) they would survive, but he would not see them again for six years! Another person I encountered on the Polish ship *SS Batory* was a high school teacher of mine, he was also "coming back in a few weeks!" What could we all have been thinking about as our father and uncle Szymon accompanied us to Gdynia?.

And so we boarded the *SS Batory*, one of two Polish transatlantic liners, shortly before the German battleship *Schleswig-Holstein* entered the same harbor by night on August 25th with anti-aircraft guns and 225 storm troopers aboard. Then, on September 1st, Gdynia, all the rest of the Polish seacoast, and the celebrated Polish Corridor between the main body of Germany and East Prussia were swept by Hitler's legions.

Unaware of these impending events, we settled into our rather luxurious quarters on the *Batory*. After a few days, my mood lightened. The ship, though it took all of nine days to reach New York, was comfortable, with an excellent cuisine. Sea voyage, if one is a good sailor, is conducive to a serene view of the world and its problems.

The mood did not last. On August 22, we were thunderstruck by a radio announcement: Germany's foreign minister, Joachim von Ribbentrop, was flying to Moscow to sign a non-aggression treaty between the two dictatorships. My brother, and I, and most of the Polish passengers did not have to be told what the pact implied: aggression by Hitler against Poland would be certain, now that he didn't have to worry about the Red Army throwing its weight against him. My brother and I never shared the belief, so widespread in the East among the Left, the liberals and even the Communists, that an accommodation between the two dictators was unthinkable. However, it seemed reasonable to assume that the Soviets would not wish to contribute to another conquest by Nazi Germany. We did not as yet know that this was more than accommodation: in a secret protocol to the treaty, the robber powers divided Eastern Europe between themselves. But, one did not have to know of this protocol (discovered by Western scholars after the war in the captured German diplomatic files and finally acknowledged by the Kremlin under Gorbachev's *glasnost*,) to know that Stalin would not help the Germans for free. Stan and I looked over a map of Poland, and he drew a line along which the dictators were likely to divide the country. It came close to the actual dividing line as it was established within the next few weeks. Our hometown Lwów, predominantly Polish but set within the mostly Ukrainian countryside, would very likely become part of the Soviet's spoils.

We tried not to give up hope: If Hitler expected that his tryst with Stalin would make Britain and France abandon Poland to its fate, (i.e. to him), he was to be disappointed. Both powers reaffirmed their pledge to stand by Poland if it was attacked.

We now know that Hitler postponed the date of the invasion, originally scheduled for August 26, to September 1, hoping that the Western powers would back away at the last minute. As it turned out, he would have his war. Enraged by the impudent Slavs' defiance, the Führer was no longer capable of rational consideration of the risks involved, which had enabled him to play so successfully that subtle diplomatic game that in the past had brought him so many bloodless victories. He came closest to expressing his innermost feelings when he told a foreign diplomat that he would rather wage war when he was fifty than when he was old, even though the circumstances later on might be more propitious for Germany's war machine. So much for those economic and social forces that allegedly determine nations' destinies, regardless of individuals' volition and whims!

The last slender thread of hope was to snap within one week of our arrival in America. Stan and I stayed in a New York hotel. All around me there was a new and wonderful world, but the distractions we sought failed to keep me from anxiously wondering what was happening three thousand miles away. All I remember is that it was extremely hot and humid, which only added to my intense misery.

SU: "Adam was frightened and nervous when we landed, a young boy abroad for the first time and away from familiar surroundings. Johnny [von Neumann] had come to meet us at the boat; on seeing Adam, he asked, "Who is this fellow?" He had not heard my introduction and was surprised. There is a difference of thirteen years between my brother and me, and we do not look at all alike. Adam is taller than I, blond and with a pink complexion. I am somewhat darker and stockier. In appearance he resembles some of our uncles, while I look more like our mother...We first visited cousins for a few days, the painter Zygmund Menkes and his wife (Stasia) who had given additional financial guarantees for Adam, who had a student visa (Actually the plan was that my brother would receive monthly checks from home via our uncle's bank in England...)"

"...I left Adam in New York to go with Johnny to Veblen's [Oswald Veblen, nephew of Thorstein Veblen] summer place in Maine. Though we were gone only two or three days, Adam was very unhappy with me for having left him...On the way...we mostly talked about what was going to happen in Europe. We were nervous and worried; we examined all possible courses that a war could take, how it could start, when. And (then) we drove back to New York. These were the last days of August..."

On the last day of August, Stan and I went to see the 1939 World's Fair. We visited the Soviet Pavilion, which surprisingly featured a strongly anti-Nazi Russian film depicting the suffering of a German Jewish family. Somebody in Moscow had obviously forgotten to order off the screen this libelous attack on the Soviet Union's newest ally.

After dining, we returned to our hotel. About one or two o'clock in the morning, the telephone rang, waking up my brother; while I slept the deep sleep of a sixteen-year-old. A Polish friend of his had just heard on the radio that Warsaw and other Polish cities were being bombed.

> SU: "Adam and I were staying in a hotel on Columbus Circle. It was a very hot, humid, New York night. I could not sleep very well. It must have been around one or two in the morning when the telephone rang. Dazed and perspiring, very uncomfortable, I picked up the receiver and the somber, throaty voice of my friend the topologist Witold Hurewicz began to recite the horrible tale of the start of war: "Warsaw has been bombed, the war has begun," he said. This is how I learned about the beginning of World War II. He kept describing what he had heard on the radio. Adam was asleep; I did not wake him. There would be time to tell him the news in the morning..."

As Stan would later write: "At that moment I suddenly felt as if a curtain had fallen on my past life, cutting it off from the future. There has been a different color and meaning to everything ever since."

Because I was thirteen years younger, the impact of both the news and the subsequent tragic events was to be different in my case. I had been brought up entirely in independent Poland. Stan had spent his first ten years as a subject of His Apostolic Majesty, the Emperor of Austria and King of Hungary. Long before the war, he had decided to seek his academic career abroad: Poland had a surplus of talented mathematicians and there were probably fewer chairs of mathematics in all of the Polish universities than there are today in one major American university. And in the 1930s, it emphatically did not help if one was Jewish. While he was much more grounded in Polish culture and way of life than I could have been at my age, he also had a cosmopolitan background that I at that point completely lacked. It would be harder for me to immerse myself in American ways, but once the process began, I would absorb them more thoroughly. Such reflections would come much later.

All I could feel on that fateful day at the beginning of September was shock, fear and bewilderment.

The next few days brought no relief. We groped for anything we could hold on to, only to have it disappear almost immediately, like a mirage. On September 3, France and Britain declared war on Germany. It is sad to recall the new wave of American delusion brought on by the news. Some of our American friends were thrown into a paroxysm of joy at the announcement: now the time of reckoning had come for Hitler; the vast power of the British Empire and the invincible French army would teach him a lesson in short order. I recall a headline in a New York daily paper: "The poilus (an affectionate sobriquet for French soldiers) cracked Germany's Siegfried line in thirteen places." The Siegfried line was supposed to be a line of fortifications on Germany's western frontier. In fact, it was a fabrication of German propaganda. To be sure, in a few places French troops would emerge from behind their fortifications and advance cautiously a few miles into Germany, only to scuttle back almost immediately. But perhaps those were just reconnaissance missions. With the bulk of the Wehrmacht in Poland, the Reich's western border was defended by second-line troops. We now know that the Polish-French convention obligated the French General Staff to order an attack en masse on the sixteenth day after an attack on Poland. As it happened, nothing of the kind took place, and the RAF confined itself to dropping leaflets over the territory. We also know that the proposal to drop something more substantial on the German factories, railroads, etc., was given up by the British Cabinet, some ministers protesting that it would lead to "wanton destruction of private property."

Then there was new military intervention by the enemy. On September 17, the Red Army entered eastern Poland. Moscow's official explanation did not, of course, refer to the German-Soviet non-aggression pact of August 23 with its secret protocol, but stated that in view of the disappearance of the Polish state, the Soviet Union could not remain unresponsive to the Ukrainian and Byelorussian populations' pleas to take them under Stalin's "paternal" protection. What was going to happen to my family under that "paternal" protection, to my father, a lawyer, and our relatives, among them, bankers, industrialists, and architects, considered "typical bourgeois," according to the Communist canon?

Under the circumstances, I was lucky not to realize that the situation was even worse than it appeared. Who could have imagined the unpreparedness of the British, the appalling technological weakness of the French army, the imbecility of the French commanders, and the rampant defeatism plaguing a society that had performed so heroically in World War I? An American cousin of mine, who had lived in France and had just returned from there, spoke glowingly of the high morale of the people and their determination "to be done with it," i.e., with the curse of fascism, which he encountered in Paris. I did not find preposterous a statement by a French minister who attributed the alleged superiority of his army over that of the enemy to the fact that its leaders had already held senior command posts between 1914 and 1918, while their corresponding numbers in Germany were then but junior officers. And so the consoling thought during the months of the "Phony War" was that when it came to the real one, the great French army and the equally invincible Royal Navy were bound to prevail.

Poland's ordeal made me something of a celebrity at Brown when I arrived in Providence on September 20th, the only foreign student, I believe, in a freshman class of about four hundred.

> SU: "...On the way to Cambridge (from New York), I accompanied Adam to Brown University in Providence, registered him as a freshman, and introduced him to a few of my friends, including Tamarkin and his son. His English was quite good, and he did not seem to mind being left alone in college...Early in September I saw in The Boston Globe a large photograph of Adam surrounded by other young freshmen at Brown. It was captioned, "Wonders whether his home was bombed."

I was interviewed by the campus paper and the *Providence Journal*. My teachers expressed their sympathy and tried to help me to adjust to the strange new academic environment. Fortunately, my fame lasted but briefly, and within weeks I was, both for my classmates and professors, just another freshman. Brown, now a large and distinguished institution of learning, was then a small college with some excellent teachers but without the panache and renown of Harvard, Yale, or Princeton. Student life centered around fraternities and sports. It was achievement in the latter, especially football, which brought one fame in campus life and popularity among the girls in Brown's female affiliate, Pembroke College, and invitations to join the more prestigious fraternities. Yet, unlike some other schools in those times, it was far from being part finishing school, and part club: intellectual values were fostered by the faculty and good students were respected rather than dismissed by their fellows as "grinds."

Still, there was a rather parochial atmosphere about the place. I was familiar with student life in Poland where, as elsewhere on the Continent, the passage from high school to university meant a leap from barracks-like discipline to the realm of freedom, where the student's only obligation was to take examinations at the end of the academic year. Here, a collegian's life was subject to numerous regulations: where he could reside, take his meals, when and where he could entertain friends of either sex, etc. Once a week we were expected to attend a nondenominational chapel, to listen to a nondenominational sermon, and to sing nondenominational hymns. Baptist in origin, most of the predecessors of Brown's current college president had been Baptist ministers.

Apart from the university regulations and customs, there were also some, one might call them, tribal aspects of the then college life. Freshmen were supposed to wear distinctive headgear, and if caught without it, were subject to hazing by the upperclassmen. One the eve of an especially important football game, the Brown tribe would hold evening rallies. After an inspirational harangue by a coach or a dean, the tribe would break out in wild yells and songs expressive of the determination to win, and of scorn for the next day's enemy.

Those manifestations of youthful effervescence were essentially harmless and probably preferable to what would take place during the great American university revolutions of the late 1960s and early 1970s, when students' emotions were channeled into political manifestation and havoc rather than football rallies.

At this time, in 1939, Brown was predominately Anglo-Saxon. There were few African-Americans at the university, and just a sprinkling of Jews on the faculty, a situation that also prevailed in all eastern colleges and universities. Few Jews would be asked to join the more fashionable fraternities, and unless they happened to be prominent athletes, men with non-WASP names were not welcome there either. Despite this veneer of snobbery, one did not encounter open prejudice among the student body. In my four years at Brown, I did not hear a single derogatory epithet about a racial or ethnic group. Once America was at war, the popular press did not refrain from scurrilous references to the Germans and especially to the "Japs." It is all the more remarkable, therefore, that such blanket condemnations of entire nations for their rulers' crimes were by no means common among my contemporaries, at least prior to their actually confronting the enemy in the war. For all the backwardness of society on the racial issue, and granting a certain childishness of the college mores, young Americans of my acquaintance reacted to the war in a civilized and amazingly mature way.

Also, 1939 was still a time when one could catch the atmosphere of prewar America, with its parochial preoccupations. The mood of the majority of people was overwhelmingly isolationist. With young people, it was largely a reflection of scant interest in international affairs, in fact, in politics in general, incredible as this must appear to people today. There were no Republican or Democratic clubs at Brown; before December 7, 1941, I can recall no rallies for or against U.S. intervention; and of course after that date all my contemporaries except for a few conscientious objectors soon had a more direct way of manifesting their feelings.

This indifference was grounded in the fantastic good fortune of America, free ever since its inception from any threat to its territory, and in fact practicing what might be called non-strenuous imperialism toward its neighbors to the south and in the Caribbean, as well as through FDR's "good neighbor" policies in the 1930s. A great number of Americans ascribed this happy condition to the democratic virtues of their society rather than to the two oceans. Europe's troubles were popularly ascribed to lack of such virtues in the Old World and hence to its susceptibility to constant squabbles. To many, America's intervention in World War I was still questionable. "What did we get out of the war?", I was asked more than once by young and older Americans. (It would have been tactless to point out that this country's human losses were minimal compared to those of Britain and France.) Another argument I found hugely insensitive, was the complaint that the "ungrateful British and French had refused to repay their debts to the US." Everything else aside, Britain and France forfeited much more than was due to them. Actually, what the world avoided through US intervention was probably the domination of the Continent by Germany: to be sure, a Germany some light years different from Hitler's; but still not a pleasant prospect.

In the eastern states, especially, the obfuscation soon to be called "America First" was countered by the intense Anglophilia of much of the educated class. And, needless to say, few Americans could have wished for Hitler's victory. But until the disastrous May of 1940, when the famous French army crumbled before the Germans almost as fast as Poland's did in September 1939, and the British evacuated the rest of their forces from Dunkirk, few thought that the two democracies would need America's armed help; and so for the moment, there were no "entangling alliances" and no armed intervention in "Europe's troubles." The United States was safe and would wait until the Wehrmacht broke its teeth against the impregnable Maginot Line.

On second thought, perhaps I was wrong to generalize from my impressions at Brown. Harvard, I subsequently learned, was politicized, with the isolationists and pro-British attitudes clashing among the student body and the faculty. There was a small Communist nucleus in both bodies, and for the Communists and fellow travelers this was still an imperialist war, the extreme right and the extreme left becoming allies in trying to keep the US out of the European imbroglio.

My initiation into American college life was progressing. I merged easily into the surrounding atmosphere, indistinguishable, except for my accent, among the body of freshmen. I attended football games and rallies. I sang the college songs imbued with fierce Brown patriotism, such as the one that begins "We're ever true to Brown..." I didn't reflect that Oxford or Heidelberg do not have such songs, proclaiming their superiority and calling for eternal loyalty of their alumni. The spirit of the times was conducive to the personality cult of the football coach, even though Brown's record in the sport was at the time rather mixed. The president of a college, especially a small one, was in those days accepted by the students as a benevolent dictator. Student rebellion was inconceivable. No group in the university pressed for changes in the regulations, hiring, or admission practices, unlike in the 1960s, which introduced the era of "Issues," still with us today.

Was such passivity characteristic of other campuses? In general, I think, yes. But there were exceptions. We knew that the City College of New York was heavily politicized. At Harvard, which I visited frequently to see my brother, 1939-40 witnessed a clash between its administration and the faculty over the question of tenure. Some assistant professors had stayed in that rank for five, ten years, or even longer, on term appointments, and the university, still strained by the depression, now proposed to fire them. There was considerable outcry from the faculty and several of the intended victims did get promoted to tenured positions. In general, the atmosphere at Harvard was, as we would say after the 1960s, quite "activist." Many on the faculty joined a teachers' union, which at the time found itself under strong-left wing influence. The union split and then expired when the majority of its members subscribed to the resolution that the war against Hitler was an imperialist one in nature and that

America should stick to strict neutrality, a position then held by the US Communist Party. I don't think I encountered a single Communist or advanced leftwinger in all my years at Brown.

That year of the "Phony War" was a melancholy time for me. Letters from home, from our father, ceased; and my brother and I tried not to talk about what was happening in our town, now Lviv (in Ukrainian) or Lvov (in Russian), in the Soviet Union Republic of Ukraine, from which the Soviet authorities were systematically deporting to Central Asia members of the Polish, Jewish and Ukrainian intelligentsia. But those were the lucky people, at least the ones who survived the long trip in unheated railway cars. Within a year and a half, the others who stayed would meet a more horrible fate at the hands of the German invaders. The only members of my family who managed to escape and get to the United States were my cousin Andrzej, his mother, and his stepfather. Andrzej was my favorite relative, full of joie de vivre. He could be trusted to succeed in escaping where numerous others failed. With his ingenuity and striking good looks he would have very likely made a dazzling business career in America after the war: he was a banker by profession. But, alas, within a year of his arrival he was dead, a victim of pneumonia just before the appearance of penicillin, which could have saved him. Andrzej's scintillating wit and his ability to attract charming women had bolstered Stan's and my morale. His death in his midthirties was a blow from which it took a long time for us to recover.

But the latter was still in the future. And beyond such social trivialities, this first year on American soil also made me rethink my Polish youth. Pre-World War II Poland seldom enjoyed a good reputation among the liberal circles in the West. Its regime was undemocratic; it was commonly known as the "colonels' government." Following Munich, the Warsaw government forced helpless Czechoslovakia to cede a disputed territory. The official policy toward national minorities, comprising some 30 percent of the population, was discriminatory. All in all, while condemning Hitler's and Stalin's rape of the country, many, not necessarily just leftwingers, saw Poland as having brought upon itself the cataclysm which struck in 1939 and again, in a different form, after the Second World War.

I cannot be positive that those were exactly my reflections at the time; rather, they are colored by subsequent experience and study. But I did feel the incongruity between the tumult and gaiety of college life around me and what was happening in my homeland. Here, my classmates' greatest worries were what fraternities they should join, or would Brown's injured quarterback recover before the next Saturday's game. But my heart was heavy with foreboding: what was happening over there? My father's letters having stopped arriving, where and how was my beautiful, warmhearted older sister, recently graduated from law school? And what was happening to my high school friends: not a single letter from them. I was still too young and foolish to be seriously concerned about my very personal problems: what would I live on after the money I brought with me ran out at the end of the academic year? It was hardly likely that, as we had lightheartedly projected before my departure, another check would be forthcoming from home. Being on a student visa, I was effectively barred from seeking a job. The financial burden would fall on my brother, whose Harvard stipend was modest. And with his Junior Fellowship drawing to an end, he himself had to look for a new position in the then very depressed academic market.

SU: "From the start, Adam did very well in school; a few months later, he was able to obtain a tuition waiver. Nevertheless we were finding ourselves in severe financial straits. The proposed income from Britain had been frozen; the English government stopped all outgoing money, and my salary as a lecturer at Harvard was hardly sufficient to put a younger brother (who was not allowed to work because he was on a student visa) through college. On previous trips, I had never thought of transferring funds or property from Poland. Now it could no longer be done. I went to see a dean of the College and explained my situation...I told him that if I could not get a little more assistance from the University, I would be forced to leave my academic career and look for some other means of support...He was sympathetic and was able to find two or three hundred dollars more for the year, which was a sizable help in those days...

...This was the period of my life when I was perhaps in the worst state, mentally, nervously, and materially, My world had collapsed. Prospects for the reconstitution of Poland in any recognizable form were dim indeed. There was a terrible anxiety about the fate of all those whom we had left behind, family and friends. Adam was also in a very depressed state, and this contributed to my worries..."

As my first college year was ending, the fortunes of war took a turn that pushed personal considerations even further from my mind. Was it in March that I heard on the radio Neville Chamberlain's inanely optimistic assessment of the situation, concluding with "Has Herr Hitler missed the bus?" The Führer must have heard it too, for soon afterward he caught not only the bus, but also much more; in April, German troops occupied Norway and Denmark. How frightened of the German juggernaut everyone was by now was well demonstrated by what Commissar Molotov told the German ambassador when informed of this new gambit by the Soviets' Nazi ally: he wished the

Germans "complete success in their defensive [!] measures." But that turned out to be but an hors d'oeuvre on Hitler's menu. On May 10, the Wehrmacht struck west.

So now came the moment for which all decent people in the world hoped: the invincible French army, the glorious Royal Navy, and the RAF would soon put an end to the tyrant's hitherto victorious advance. And then that last illusion crumbled. Almost as speedily as in Poland, Hitler's armies smashed their foes' resistance. On June 23, France capitulated. Now that it was safe, the jackal-like Mussolini hastened to declare war, hoping that his German fellow-dictator would spare him part of the loot. Europe now lay at Hitler's feet.

Beyond the horror and fear of the moment, I experienced what might be called culture shock. For me, as for most educated Poles, for other Europeans, and, I dare say, for many in this country, France was every civilized man's second home. And now the Nazi barbarians (today I find even this epithet insufficient; barbarians are not necessarily evil) had her in their power. Being also an Anglophile, I still could not bring myself to believe that the struggle for civilization was irretrievably lost. But, rationally speaking, how could Britain, much of its armor and other equipment abandoned before and during the evacuation of Dunkirk, withstand the forthcoming German invasion? This was the air age; and to the popular mind, the Luftwaffe and the German Panzer were invincible. One tried to bolster one's courage by recalling Britain's defiance of Napoleon. But in that period, England was an island, which from the military point of view had now ceased to be because of modern technology.

It may have been late 1940, that my brother and I were talking with two distinguished exiled German professors. Strongly anti-Nazi though they were, they saw little hope. Democracies were simply incapable of withstanding dictatorships, which had the ability to energize all sinews of power for war and to inspire fanaticism among their followers. Timidly, as behooved a youngster among such sages, I objected that the Italians were not doing so well against the British in North Africa. "Oh, that's Mussolini," said one of the professors, a distinguished physicist. "Wait until the Germans get there." And, indeed, the Italians' performance in the war came close to being the sole source of comic relief in that depressing period between the fall of France and America's entrance into the war. I recall that at one point a question was asked in the House of Commons whether it was true that each time a British naval officer in the Mediterranean shouted "waiter," an Italian submarine would surface. At the time it seemed very funny, but later on I repented my amusement at such tasteless reflections on that great nation's character. It was a sign of the Italians' rationality rather than their lack of martial prowess that they did not have their hearts in the war. Why should they have willingly suffered and died because Mussolini, "Hitler's tattered lackey," as Churchill referred to him, fancied himself another Caesar?

And then one man became the embodiment of hope for all men and women who prized freedom throughout the world. Taking over from the inept Chamberlain during those crucial months, Winston Churchill inspired not only his countrymen, but millions all over the world with the conviction that Britain would not vanish from the earth.

During the Battle of Britain, my brother and I often visited Alfred North Whitehead, the famous British philosopher and co-author with Bertrand Russell of *Principia Mathematica*. Whitehead and his wife lived in the same hotel (The Ambassador Hotel) in Cambridge as Stan, and we would often drop in to listen to broadcasts from England. The aged philosopher would manipulate the dial, and on finding the right station would sometimes say, "Dreadful music! Must be the BBC!" We would then listen to the communiqués and occasionally to Churchill's impassioned oratory. But for me, the most exalting moment came later, during the period when London was being raided relentlessly by the Luftwaffe. One day the BBC announcer, with the British penchant for understatement, began with a few words about some not very important House of Commons debate. Then in a tone almost implying "and by the way," he told the world that during the preceding day, the RAF had destroyed 185 German bombers!

Only after the war, did we learn that the figure had been somewhat padded. But in fact it had been a crucial moment in the Battle of Britain. Now German losses began to far exceed those of the British fighters. Hitler canceled Operation Sea Lion (the invasion of England) and turned his covetous eyes eastward. For Britain, it was a veritable new lease on life. Losing planes at the rate they were, the Luftwaffe bomber fleet could not last long. The German troops would never march through London, as they had done so insolently through the Arc de Triomphe in Paris. Though it was vastly premature, I felt that the forces of barbarism would somehow be defeated.

5

War Years

Visit to Stan in Wisconsin...Presidential election of 1940...Course of the War..."What if" scenarios...Hitler's mistakes and Stalin's shrewdness...Thesis writing at Brown: observations on English nation...Wartime teaching at Wisconsin in colorful company...Stan "disappears"...War nears end...Fear of Stalin in Eastern Europe looms...Warsaw uprising...Stalin's perfidy...Farewell to Madison...What Stan was up to!

Before returning to Brown for my sophomore year, I visited Stan at his new academic post in Madison, Wisconsin. Initially he'd been apprehensive about going to the University of Wisconsin. Like most Europeans new to this country, he had assumed that the Northeast was culturally close to the Old World and that the Midwest, as he wrote, was "more primitive and intellectually barren." This misconception soon yielded to a more just impression. The University of Wisconsin was a distinguished university, its faculty full of eminent and interesting people. Madison was and is a charming place, with its lakes and its semi-rural ambiance. He soon grew very fond of the place, and of the Midwest in general, and so did I. One might say the atmosphere on campus in that last prewar year was "decorously boisterous," without that certain stuffiness then characteristic of the great Eastern institutions. Politically, the community of Madison still reflected the progressive tradition associated with Senator Robert LaFollette.

Wisconsin was then, and I suppose still is, one of the principal farming states. Farmers then constituted a much larger percentage of the population than now and consequently their political clout was much stronger. If one followed the local press, one read a great deal about the farming community's problems, many of them dating from its catastrophic condition in the early days of the depression. There were thus constant attacks on the iniquities of the manufacturers of margarine and other products threatening the interests of agriculture.

Among the consequences of the state university's dependence on the largely agricultural electorate was the occasional difficulty of the two sides to find a common language. How, asked a state representative, would you explain to a farmer working from dawn to nightfall that your professors had to teach only twelve to fourteen hours a week (in fact a fairly heavy teaching load, even at that time). A legislator wise to country ways saved the situation. Your professor, he explained, is like a bull: it is what he does and not how much, that is important. The people's representatives were appeased.

The populist canon required also that professors' salaries be made public. All other state employees' remuneration was public—why not theirs? But frequently it led to embarrassing revelations, e.g., Professor X, a chemist with a national reputation, could hardly be pleased by the report that his salary for the coming year was raised from $6000 to $6050. And why, *The Capital Times*, the local organ of liberalism, would protest, was Professor X paid $200 more than his much less prominent colleague? Was it perhaps because the latter was active in local Republican politics?

For all such semi-humorous aspects, local politics was a good example of grass-roots democracy in action. The political scene that summer and fall was, however, preempted by FDR's unprecedented bid for a third term. It was a good lesson in the sometimes strange ways the Americans ran their public life. The presidential convention and the atmosphere surrounding it was then a much more festive and ritualistic affair than it has been in recent years. Once the candidate's name was pronounced—"And he is...."—his partisans on the convention floor would erupt into a kind of St. Vitus dance and amidst a wild cacophony would take a half hour or so before they would subside. Each of the states' delegation chairmen would in recounting its vote take much time and with more flourish in recounting his state's special virtues and distinctions than is done now. My memory may deceive me, but Roosevelt's announcement of his candidacy was couched in an unusual way: his spokesman gave the message, "I am not a candidate for the nomination." This seeming abdication was greeted by wild cheers: "he would run if nominated." Although Willkie, a brilliant Wall Street lawyer who had defied the federal bureaucracy, appeared a most attractive candidate on the GOP side, my sympathies lay with Roosevelt.

I absorbed eagerly the details of the conventions and then of the electoral campaign. The latter, then and even now in the TV age,

seems to me to be a cruel ordeal for the candidates, especially as one
of them was crippled. To be sure, the press was then much more
reticent than now, so that the extent of Roosevelt's infirmity was not
realized by the bulk of the voters. And that discretion of the media
was extended to other aspects of the candidates' private lives which
today would be trumpeted uninhibitedly from the day they entered
the ring. It was only later that the piquant facts about the campaign
became known. One of them was quite damning. Mr. Roosevelt's
vice-presidential running mate Henry Wallace had fallen under the
spell of a foreign guru of uncertain origins, whose counsel he sought
on political questions. The Republican standard bearer had a more
understandable failing. He had long kept company with a lady, not
his wife, and was reunited with his spouse for the campaign. If publicly known in those morbidly conventional days, that lapse would
surely have scotched his candidacy (A play on the affair written
after the war had its punch line "politics made strange bedfellows.").
Sensible men that they were, the managers of the two campaigns
struck a deal: Republicans would keep quiet about Mr. Wallace's
bad judgment (which he so lamentably was to display again after
the war) in return for the Democrats keeping mum about Willke's
peccadilloes. And so the public image of the two men remained unscathed: Mr. Wallace, a staunch New Dealer, an agronomist who
had mastered such strange arts as throwing a boomerang, and
Wendell Willkie, a brilliant executive.

I was particularly interested in the quaint customs still permeating
presidential politics. It was still customary for the candidate to be
formally notified of his nomination by a delegation, which in the
pre-telephone days would visit his home. Mr. Willkie had chosen to
be so notified in a small Indiana town, his birthplace, which earned
him the epithet of the "barefoot boy from Wall Street" by Harold
Ickes, the most acerbic of FDR's cabinet members. FDR, in his
speeches, roused the greatest applause and merriment of his audiences by criticizing a trio of Republican legislators with the eupho-
nious names of Martin, Barton, and Fish. He would, in his inimitable
voice, come to a crucial passage, and the audience would follow
him with the chant of the three names.

Willkie appeared a most attractive candidate, but my sympathies
and vote, as was true of the majority, went to Roosevelt. To a democratic European, he was then close to being an idol. Willkie, despite
his oft-expressed sympathy for the anti-fascist cause, had to be a bit

suspect to a Pole because of his German ancestry. Later on, I regretted my unworthy suspicions: no one had proved more wholehearted in favor of smashing Nazism as he, and his premature death was a great loss to this country. I still had to learn a lot about America.

Had the candidates been able to afford to speak frankly, both undoubtedly would have urged much greater help for the Allies, especially for Britain. But this was election time, and they pledged repeatedly to keep America out of the war. As it was, FDR took much risk in alienating the hard-core isolationists with steps such as providing over-age destroyers and other war supplies to the besieged island. Well, no one could really blame the American people for their reluctance to expose their young men to carnage, least of all someone in my situation(But in retrospect it is still amazing that the bulk of the electorate did not understand what Britain's conquest by Germany would have meant:)

Europe completely under Hitler's boot, America's trade and communications paralyzed, and fascist coups all over Latin America. And for all of the miracles performed by the RAF, would Britain have really been immune to a determined Nazi effort at invasion? At the time I believed it was, but the facts we learned after the war showed how fragile such hopes had been. Had Hitler chosen to bomb airfields and ancillary facilities, rather than reveling in the burning of London and other cities, he would have destroyed Fighter Command. Once on British soil, that summer of 1940, the Wehrmacht would have encountered the still relatively small and poorly equipped British army and the Home Guard, armed mostly with pikes and cudgels. Our hopes were a byproduct of despair, rather than of rational calculations. How close the world came to seeing Reich commissars in London and Manchester!

In my memory, the 1940-41 school year at Brown remains quite blurred by world events. I worked arduously under excellent teachers in all my four courses. This was especially true of my United States history course, in which the senior lecturer was the late Carl Bridenbough, a fierce partisan of the New Deal. From my course in psychology I can recall only one somewhat bizarre datum: "a warning about an excessive reliance on statistics, one example touching on the inexplicable strict correspondence between variations in the size of the American College of Ophthalmologists and that of the population of the Indian state of Hyderabad!" Political philosophy was taught by a young instructor fresh from Harvard, where he had studied under the great medievalist Charles McIlwain, whose course would be one of my delights in my own graduate work there. And my great debt is to my instructor in English composition. He took special care of my work in his course and was a rare example of a teacher who without pedantry and with infinite patience could impart a feeling for the rhythm and style of a language to one who, in some ways, was still a stranger to it.

*   *   *

But my attention was riveted to the radio and newspapers. The British were holding out: more than that, they were scoring sensational successes in North Africa. But then the picture changed. The ill-advised British intervention in Greece brought another disaster inflicted by the still-invincible Wehrmacht. The Germans, led by Rommel, appeared in North Africa to save Mussolini's crumbling empire. I could not understand, and still cannot, how the Royal Navy could have allowed the German Panzer corps to be transported there through the Mediterranean. But those German victories in the Balkans and Africa turned out eventually to be a poisoned gift to Hitler. What if those few divisions and a commander with the drive of Rommel had been available to him in Russia in late fall of 1941? Even without those advantages, his armies came quite close to capturing Moscow. With them, the course of history might well have changed and the war been prolonged.

Fortune, so long perversely favoring the Führer, now was turning against him; or more properly put, the tyrant once so cunning began to make one mistake after another. What was the point of conquering Yugoslavia, for example, just because the Serbs refused to join the Axis? Here again, several of his divisions were immobilized far away from what soon became the main theater of war. And if he had to fight in Africa to help his "tattered lackey" Mussolini, why didn't he force Franco to let the German armor race through Spain and seize Gibraltar? With the Mediterranean closed, Britain's entire Near East position would have crumbled. The Nazis could have seized Egypt and Iran, and could then have attacked the USSR from the south. As the proverb has it, "Whom the gods would destroy, they first drive mad." It was high time for the gods to intervene. Their most decisive intervention came when they inspired Hitler to attack the Soviet Union. Ever since the Germans had conquered France, the Soviet tyrant lived in fear of his German ally preparing an unpleasant surprise for him, as well. Stalin, at least when it came to international affairs, was a highly rational man. Knowing what he had done to his own people, he had to tremble at the thought of how they would react if the world's most powerful army entered Soviet territory. But in Hitler's place, surely he, Stalin, would not have opened another front without first finishing off Britain. Stalin had been warned about the German plans by the US and by his own spies in Germany and Japan, but he still could not believe that his fellow tyrant could be so irrational. Surely all those rumors were the work of London. For Stalin to prepare the USSR as ready for war could have enabled those German generals itching to invade Russia to persuade Hitler to attack.

Torn between hope and fear, the "genius leader of progressive mankind" left his country morally and militarily unprepared when at dawn, on June 22, 1941, three million German and satellite soldiers struck at his virtually undefended borders.

At the time the momentous news broke, I was a counselor in a boys' camp, a job for which I was quite unprepared. One of the senior counselors, a man of irreproachable democratic convictions, nonetheless delivered the opinion that perhaps Europe should be united to be done with wars, etc., and that perhaps Hitler was the man to bring this about! Indeed, the violent end of the romance between the two dictators brought some strange reactions from Americans. The junior Senator from Missouri, Harry Truman, was quoted as saying that we should watch with satisfaction as the two sides destroyed each other. This was perhaps morally justifiable but under the circumstances very poor advice; and after the war, the Soviet authorities never let their people forget about President Truman's old lapse of judgment. I myself, to tell the truth, partly shared Truman's sentiments, the difference being that I wished Hitler and his regime to be destroyed first. And then, though not sentimental about the Russians, I did not feel that they were responsible for the horrors of Stalin's rule. I sympathized with the ordinary people who had suffered so much under their own system and who were now threatened with being subjected to a different, yet equally lethal, brand of barbarism. But how could the Soviet army stop "the Huns," as Mr. Churchill called them.

A prewar schoolboy in Poland often learned more about the USSR than many experts in the West. We knew Stalin had purged the officer corps of the Red Army. Now that I've learned much more about the Soviet recovery outside of Moscow in December 1941, the achievement appears even more amazing. The officer corps had not merely been purged, it had been massacred just a few years earlier. Not even in the subsequent four years of cruel warfare were so many Soviet officers, especially in the higher ranks, killed by the enemy as had been killed by Stalin between 1936-39.

By the winter of 1941-42, the Germans had taken three million prisoners. In many places in the Ukraine and Byelorussia, the inhabitants greeted the invader's units with flowers. Had they been humane and clever, the Germans could have secured many more collaborators than they actually did. But with their mind-set, how could the Nazis even pretend to be humane? In their view, the inhabitants were not normal people, even if uncorrupted by democracy. These were Slavs-"Untermenschen". And so the initial welcome or passivity of the population turned to bitter hatred. Many a Red Army warrior, even a man whose father had been been killed and his land seized during collectivization, would fight valiantly "for Mother Russia," and, alas, "for Stalin."

But for the first few weeks it appeared that the Wehrmacht was going through the Red Army like a knife through butter. In places the Russian troops fought with bravery typical of their nation, but elsewhere they were unprepared enough to make the German advance appear a parade march. "The greatest genius of all ages" kept issuing contradictory orders, and between June 28 and July 1, as we learned from Khrushchev, he was disabled by a nervous shock. "We fucked up all that Lenin built," was Stalin's own elegant formulation of the situation.

Like Mr. Churchill at the news of the invasion, I would have been willing to embrace Satan if he would only help defeat the Germans, but few in those summer months were willing to bet on the Russians. Writing about Ireland in the nineteenth century, a British statesman complained: "What all the wise men promised has not come to pass; what all the goddamned fools prophesied is happening before our eyes." Well, against the almost unanimous voice of the experts, there was one man in the very beginning who expressed faith in a Soviet victory: Joseph E. Davies, who through connections and his wife's wealth had served as the US ambassador in Moscow. He was the author of an extremely silly book, *Mission to Moscow*, which was then made into an unwittingly hilarious movie. Stalin and his gang are represented there as wise and honorable statesmen, while victims of his purges were, as charged, German, Japanese, etc., agents. Speaking to American newspapermen after attending one of the infamous Moscow trials, this incredible ambassador proclaimed, "Believe me, boys, as a lawyer I can tell these men are guilty." So much for the experts and fools!

For the rest of the war, I had to cheer for the Russians. Their patriotism and valor in defending their native soil made one occasionally forget about Stalin, just as those brave people must have pushed out of their own minds how cruelly their own government had used them. Alas, one cannot fight a war without developing illusions about one's allies, at least Americans can't. Once the Soviet Union became our ally, and after the siege of Stalingrad the Russians began to push back the Wehrmacht, Stalin became, for the American public, one of the three great leaders of the Free World, and at the level of popular legend, the benevolent "Uncle Joe."

But I get ahead of my story. In the fall, I returned to what was to be my junior year at Brown. My roommate at that time was Fred Heck, an excellent companion, full of gaiety and mischief. Fred came from a small town in Illinois, close to the epicenter of "Americanism," as it was then understood, Peoria, and, as such, subject of many jokes about its being the quintessence of provinciality. But, after my visit to Fred's family, the jokes, good-natured as most of them were, appeared to me unfair. The neat and orderly midwestern town had a special charm of its own. It was snobbery and ignorance on the part of so many Europeans to speak of the Midwest as if it were some woebegone primitive land, the Lower Slobbovia of that comic strip then so popular, Al Capp's *Li'l Abner*. In fact, a visitor was received with genuine hospitality. The general tenor of life as well as interpersonal relations seemed more natural and relaxed than the hectic pace of the big cities in the East.

Isolationism, however, was stronger in the Midwest than in other parts of the country and was ponderously proclaimed so by *The Chicago Tribune*, the dominant journal of the area. I read the paper avidly, not because of its editorials, but because it had a splendid collection of comic strips. I admired *L'il Abner*, undoubtedly the funniest masterpiece of the genre, and Dick Tracy, a close second, insofar as humor was concerned. Some other comics were unwittingly humorous. *Little Orphan Annie*, an impossible brat, was probably closest to the Republican philosophy of the *Tribune*. One of its key characters was Daddy Warbucks, a prototype of the benevolent capitalist. At one point in the strip he lost half of his fortune of $2 billion. In those days that was a lot of money. The newspaper's owner was Col. Robert McCormick, ferociously hostile toward FDR and an Anglophobe. In addition to printing his virulent editorials, the colonel was often on the radio, and in his sepulchral voice berated the President for his un-American partiality to imperialist Britain and for his dark design to bring this country into the war on her side.

Thank God the crusty old colonel was not too wrong on that point, though there was nothing "dark" in the President's designs. The President made it quite clear that a victory for Hitler would be catastrophic for this country and the world. And insofar as it was within his power, he tried to steer the public mind toward the same conclusion. It was not easy. Britain had ceased being an island, but America was still protected by the two oceans, though not for long—until that flash in the New Mexico desert followed by Hiroshima. The "America First" arguments had to be seductive to those who were, or had sons, of draft age. But the healthy instinct of a democracy was slowly prevailing. Many political leaders, including the defeated Republican candidate Willkie, would have felt the same in Roosevelt's place. But it was his almost infallible political skill that made possible the ever more extensive aid to the anti-Hitler forces, while America was formally still at peace. The transfer of destroyers to Britain, Lend-Lease, cooperation with the Royal Navy in fighting German submarines, and the extension of Lend-Lease to the USSR: all those measures quite possibly enabled the anti-fascist camp to endure until this country could throw its full power onto the scales. Having taken courses in American government, it crossed my mind even then that some of those steps might have transgressed the President's constitutional power. But who in retrospect would deny that they were necessary and salutary?

*   *   *

As I've indicated, the fall of 1941 was a nerve-wracking time with the Wehrmacht moving inexorably closer to Moscow, while in North Africa, Rommel was now pushing the British towards Cairo. By this time though, there was a general feeling everywhere that the US was going to enter the war. But when, and how? And would it happen before Moscow fell and the Mediterranean became a German-Italian lake? Thank God, we were spared the knowledge of the dreadful advances in military technology. Imagine if the Germans had put in production their V1 and V2 missiles about the time of the Allied invasion of France in 1944, one year earlier than they actually did, Britain would have been devastated and the invasion rendered impossible or incredibly costly in American and British casualties. Or suppose that they had been the first to develop the A-bomb. Truly, at one point Providence blinded Hitler and belatedly began to favor the anti-fascist cause.

And this providential blindness now also struck the Japanese. I remember when, years later, I was working on the German diplomatic documents and read a conversation which took place between Hitler and Ribbentrop, his gangsterish foreign minister, sometime in 1941. He asked, shouldn't they press Japan harder to attack the Russians, rather than to go after the US? No, said the Führer, whose armies were then trouncing Moscow's; the Japanese then would claim the main credit for the Axis victory!

Then on a December afternoon in 1941, I was listening to a football game broadcast with one of my roommates, Bob Radway, when the announcement came. The Japanese had bombed Pearl Harbor. We were at war.

Now Hitler gave way to another one of his idiotic impulses. He instantly declared war on the US—it is true that we would have been at war with Germany before too long; but without Berlin jumping in immediately after Pearl Harbor, it would have been difficult for FDR to make victory over Nazism this country's first priority. Let us do justice to Hitler, however. He believed in honor among thieves. By helping Mussolini, and by declaring himself on Japan's side, thus weakening his forces, he hastened his own doom. Stalin, on the other hand, would not have hesitated a minute to betray his allies if it was to his advantage. He might well have been disappointed that, during the Korean War, the US did not drop a few A-bombs on his Chinese comrades!

*   *   *

With difficulty, we went on with our studies; but now football games, fraternities, and other sidelights of college life receded in importance. Most of us wished and expected to be called. My own situation was a bit complicated. I was still on a student visa and had to change my status to that of an immigrant (so-called first papers), before I could be drafted. Eventually, I went to Canada (one had to go abroad to change a visa), obtained immigration papers, and reported to the Providence, RI draft board. Some months later, I received not a ritual "Greetings," but a baffling and absurd communication: I could not serve in the US armed forces because I had relatives living in enemy territory. It took a whole year, by which time I had graduated from Brown, before I succeeded in reversing that bizarre ruling and was summoned for a physical.

In the meantime, I had to watch my friends planning their military futures. Some, indeed, would not wait for the slow working of the draft and volunteered for various branches of the armed forces. Two of my roommates, John Roberts and Bob Calhoun, went into the Air Corps and, alas, did not survive the war. Bob Radway applied to the Naval Reserve training school, which required perfect sight. He was a trifle near-sighted but had recourse to an excusable patriotic deception. Contact lenses were just coming into use and having inserted them, he appeared for his physical examination. Amazingly enough his ruse was not detected. He went on to a distinguished naval career. Fred Heck was drafted in our senior year. I waited to be certified as not being an "enemy alien." How different was the attitude of young people then than during the Vietnam imbroglio! But who in those days could doubt that if there was such a thing as a just war, this was it?

                           *   *   *

I continued my college existence, as the sounds of war grew ever louder. There was the Battle of Midway (1942), where the Americans destroyed the main force of the Japanese aircraft carriers, thus predetermining Tokyo's doom. In retrospect, it appeared a fantastic piece of luck that there were no American carriers at Pearl Harbor when the Japanese struck. We all bewailed the loss of the US battleship fleet, but it was a hollow victory for Yamamoto. The battleship turned out to play a very secondary role in the war. Had the Japanese sunk or disabled the four carriers of the Pacific fleet, the war in the East would have dragged on for many more years than it did. Then came El Alamein, Rommel's signal defeat, followed by the Allied invasion of North Africa: yes, the tide of the war was definitely turning against the Axis.

All through the summer of 1942, the press agonized about the German offensive pushing the Red Army back to the Volga and the foothills of the Caucasus. Though critical, the situation was not as grave as it had been the preceding fall, when the Germans had been advancing along the entire front (not just in the south) until they were thrown back by the Soviet counter-offensive in December. Still, in that summer of 1942, the Germans seemed on the way toward conquering the Caucasus and spilling into the Near East.

Then came that extraordinary event that was to be central in the turnabout of the war: (though again, an infuriating piece of luck for the Soviet tyrant) the epic of Stalingrad. Never had the Russian soldier fought so indomitably, defending house by house the city bearing his name. The credit belonged squarely to the Russian people, and to their gallant commanders, some of whom, like Konstantine Rokossovsky, had spent years in Stalin's jails before the war. But in the West it was Stalin who became the main beneficiary of his people's heroism, and his stature came to rival Churchill's and Roosevelt's.)

There was relief, then exultation, when in November the Soviets surrounded the Sixth Wehrmacht army. The Führer could still have saved some 200,000 soldiers by authorizing their breaking out and retreating. But no, if he could not have a victory, then he must have a kind of Wagnerian Götterdämmerung instead—with the last soldier dying bravely at his post. To ensure this, he made the Stalingrad commander Paulus a field marshal. A German marshal surrendering? Inconceivable! But the next day, after his promotion, the shaken Paulus was photographed surrendering the remnants of his troops to Rokossovsky. His field marshal's ingratitude shocked Hitler. As he told his intimates, the least a decent man in Paulus' situation should have done was to shoot himself. He then tried to barter Stalin's son Jacob, a German prisoner of war, for the marshal; this time, he obviously had in mind a different kind of elevation for the unfortunate commander. Stalin rejected the deal. Jacob would eventually commit suicide, and Paulus compounded his ingratitude by joining the Communist-sponsored Free Germany committee in Moscow.

*   *   *

In comparison with those momentous events, I found various trivialities composing my college days. The draft had not yet scooped up most of the young manhood of America, but some people were already beginning to look questioningly at clearly able-bodied twenty-year-old men not in uniforms. I could do nothing but wait. Scholastically, my senior year at Brown was most rewarding. I took a course in modern European history, excellently taught by Professor Hans Rothfels. He was a German exile and a veteran of World War I, where he had lost a leg. People like him offered the then much needed reminder that there was another Germany, not merely that of Hitler and the Nazis. Whatever grievances he must have had against his native country, he returned to it after the war's end to help rebuild the older, civilized Germany.

To be frank, a balanced view of the German question was not easy to entertain in the midst of the wartime fever. We greeted with glee mass bombings of the German cities as a deserved retribution for Warsaw, Rotterdam, London, etc., etc. It was only when, with the war practically won, the RAF devastated lovely Dresden, that I began to share the doubts which more thoughtful people on the Allied side had long entertained about "carpet bombing." Indeed, after the end of the war, special surveys established that indiscriminate bombing of the cities, as against that of military targets, did little, if anything, to speed up the victory.

My last term at Brown was largely devoted to writing my honors thesis. The subject I chose was the British Utilitarians, those early nineteenth century reformers, in many ways pioneers of modern liberalism. At the time they were considered to be the main current of liberalism in the early and middle Victorian era, being closely associated with economic laissez faire, while many philosophers and reformers were proponents of government action to lift the masses from their ignorance and poverty. The patriarch of the sect, Jeremy Bentham, was one with the makers of our constitution in believing that the right kind of institutional setting was of primary importance in steering societies toward freedom and prosperity, thus assuring "the greatest happiness of the greatest number." Many of his followers adopted a less mechanistic outlook on politics, and the most notable of them, John Stuart Mill, came close toward the end of his life to a non-Marxian kind of socialism. My interest in the subject reflected my long-standing fascination with British history and politics. Here was a society that was transforming itself peacefully— though at times a close thing—from oligarchy to a democracy, while growing in power and wealth. What was the secret of the country's good fortune, of that, at the time unique, combination of world power and freedom. In my later studies of Britain, I was to discover that the picture, impressive as it had been for me, was not as blissful as it had appeared to me while an undergraduate. There was Ireland, a festering sore in the body of British politics. In the last quarter of the nineteenth century, England began to fall behind the US and Germany, not only because of their larger populations and economies, but also because of Britain's antiquated and class-ridden educational system. The Pax Britannica was largely an illusion. And then there was the disheartening picture of politics between the wars, complacency in the face of the dictatorships that led to Munich and then to the tragic first years of the war. Still, how much of the history of freedom under law has its roots in the British experience, and how much does our modern ideal of civilized politics, instructed by tolerance, practicality, and humor, owe to the same source!

My college career concluded in the spring of 1943. I retain fond memories of Brown, and in retrospect agree with my brother's view that going through a small college of quality was a better introduction to American life than I would have had attending, straight from Europe, a large university like Harvard or Wisconsin. After the war, I watched with pleasure as Brown grew into a full-scale university with an enviable reputation that has made it one of the most attractive schools in the country. It prospered greatly under the presidency of Barnaby Keeney, a medievalist and former student of Harvard's C. H. McIlwain. My ties with Brown became strengthened when my former graduate student, Howard Swearer, came to head the university. Witty, elegant, full of joie-de-vivre, Howard had none of the stuffiness so often found in our college presidents. Sadly, he died very, very prematurely.

I received my B.A. in the summer of 1943. With my future still unclear, I continued to wait for resolution of my draft status. I did not have a home to go to and had to await the decision of my "neighbors," as the draft boards were euphemistically described in the summons to serve, that though having come from Poland, I would not become a threat to the security of the US if drafted. (A friend of mine in a similar situation was asked by an official of his board whether Poland was an allied country!) So I went to join my brother in Madison, Wisconsin, and wait.

Stan had just married a charming French girl, Françoise, whose situation had been somewhat similar to mine. An exchange student from Paris, she was caught at Mt. Holyoke College by the collapse of France. Just as Stan and I would never again see our father, Françoise, having lost contact with her mother in Paris, would learn after the war that she had died in a Nazi camp.

The long-awaited "greetings" from the President finally reached me in Madison, and I was instructed to present myself for a physical examination. We all were sure I would be accepted. I was 6 ft. 2, in perfect physical condition, except ... To my amazement, the "except," my extreme near-sightedness, kept me from being drafted. My disappointment, after such a long wait, was great. The war was coming to a crescendo, and here I was, IV-F.

Fortunately, shortly afterwards, another opportunity to help with the war effort materialized. Wisconsin was one of the very few universities to have a chair of Slavic studies: even Harvard did not have a regular chair then. And so the army chose the school for one of its special training programs in Russian and Polish. Ed Zawacki, the chairman of the Slavic department and director of the program, asked me to join as one of the instructors. We had as students sixty or seventy army privates and non-commissioned officers, most of whom applied for special training in the belief that they would be taught French or German! Teaching languages can be a harrowing business, especially and paradoxically if one is a native speaker without pedagogical experience. What seems so natural to you as to not require an explanation is often an indecipherable puzzle to a neophyte. At first I was frequently stumped instructing my students in the oddities of Slavic grammar; almost to a man, they were ignorant of any foreign language. (In the usual army way those with special linguistic ability were very likely to be assigned for training, say, in electronics, and vice-versa.) A British philosopher with strong Marxist convictions once wrote a book extolling the Soviet Union for all the wonderful things Communism had done. But how, he lamented, that this beacon of hope for mankind should have such an unprogressive language, with all those superfluous conjugations, declensions, and other peculiarities which make it difficult to learn by the working masses of the world. I believe he was subsequently thrown out of the Communist Party of Great Britain for denigrating the language of Lenin and Stalin.

I owe my recruitment mainly to the fact that at the time even a major academic center was desperately short of people who knew the relevant languages. As it was, we were in age and occupation a rather bizarre group of "teachers." Our senior was an aged ex-Tsarist general who for some reason had settled down in Wisconsin. The old Russian immigration was also represented by a baroness, the wife of a professor who had fought with the White armies after the Revolution. Then, there was my very close friend, George Szpinalski, a high-spirited and talented violinist who as a boy had studied in the Moscow Conservatory; his father, though Polish, had been the bandmaster in a Cossack regiment. And of course, then there was Ed Zawacki, also of Polish descent but born in this country. Actually, he was the only trained linguist among us.

Our pedagogical shortcomings were more than made up for by our students' eagerness to learn. It was a very intensive course, six hours of lessons every day, throughout the week. My students struck me as almost always good humored and tolerant of their teacher's occasional slips and bewilderment in explaining the mysteries of Russian and Polish grammar(I don't know how many of my students were able afterwards to put their language skill to good use: those with whom I kept in contact after the war admitted they had all been assigned after graduation to the Pacific theater of operations!)

Only a short time after I started teaching, my brother and sister-in-law disappeared from Madison. "Disappeared" is the correct word, even if it does not imply flight or a kidnapping; for I had no idea where Stan was going and for what purpose. With a discretion exemplary even for wartime, Stan did not even hint to his own brother that he was going to work on what we have known since 1945 as the Manhattan Project. All I was told was a post office address where I could send letters, and that it was a government project radar, or something like it, I speculated. Only after Hiroshima would I recall a conversation of Stan's with a visiting scientist, when to his visitor's remark, incomprehensible to me, he said, "But it might blow up the world," and then changed the subject.

SU: "...Finally I learned that we were going to New Mexico, to a place not far from Santa Fe. Never having heard about New Mexico, I went to the library and borrowed the Federal Writers' Project Guide to New Mexico. At the back of the book, on the slip of paper on which borrowers signed their names, I read the names of Joan Hinton, David Frisch, Joseph McKibben, and all of the other people who had been mysteriously disappearing from Madison to hush-hush war jobs without saying where. I had uncovered their destination in a simple and unexpected fashion. It is next to impossible to maintain absolute secrecy and security in wartime!...Upon my arrival at Los Alamos, Johnny (von Neumann) took me aside and told me of all the possibilities which had been considered of the problems relating to the assembling of fissionable materials,... about plutonium (which did not yet physically exist even in the most microscopic quantities at Los Alamos). I remember very well, when a couple of months later I saw Robert Oppenheimer running excitedly down a corridor holding a small vial in his hand, with Victor Weisskopf trailing after him. He was showing some mysterious drops of something at the bottom of the vial. Doors opened, people were summoned, whispered conversations ensued... there was great excitement. The first quantity of plutonium had just arrived in the lab..."

After the war, when I visited Los Alamos on several occasions—of which more later—I would wonder how with all the people assembled there the secret could have been so well kept from the Americans (if not from the Soviet spies), given the garrulity of most scientists, and our inquisitive press. After all, early in the war, *The Chicago Tribune* clearly implied that we had broken the Japanese naval code JN-25.

My sister-in-law was to give birth in Los Alamos, and my niece Claire has the rare distinction of being born about the same time and in the same place as the dreadful weapon. I never teased her with the fact, probably showing better taste than when after my brother's co-fatherhood of the H-bomb was revealed in the press, I would gravely inform my small sons that they were first cousins of this even more cataclysmic device.

With my brother and Françoise gone, my main companion during the next year and a half in Madison was George Szpinalski. George, who made a joke even of his last name ("don't forget the 'z' between my 's' and 'p'," he would inform receptionists and telephone operators), embodied the proverbial Slavic joie de vivre, talent for revelry, and contagious sense of humor. His personal charm would break down the Anglo-Saxon reserve of even the stuffiest Madison citizens, bringing cheer to the depressed. For all his twenty years or so in America, his English was colorful and vigorous rather than grammatical. All such gifts and his undoubted talent as a violinist were, alas, not reflected in material rewards. One had to be at the level of a Heifetz or a Serkin to earn a comfortable living as a performing artist. And though he was probably the most popular person on campus, his Polish exuberance and small regard for the formal rules and regulations did not endear him to the university bureaucrats. Thus, despite long service, he was still only an instructor in the music department.

We decided to pool our meager resources and share an apartment. The one we settled on, i.e., we could afford, while not a slum was not much above that classification: two small bedrooms, living room, and a primitive kitchenette in a basement next to a boiler room! Still we initiated our stay with a grand party, crowding our tiny quarters with some fifteen people. The main and only course was that mainstay of Slavic cuisine, cabbage soup. This sounds simple to make, but a real cabbage soup requires elaborate preparations, as hinted at in that crude Russian peasant saying, "Beat your wife, your cabbage soup will be tastier." And, indeed, it was a very laborious enterprise: for several hours, at prescribed intervals, we tossed various viands into a huge kettle. Then for the next few hours, one of us had to be present to prevent the thing from boiling over and to periodically remove the scum. While there was only one course, the accompanying drinks were plentiful, varied and strong. The party was acknowledged a great social and culinary success.

Through George, I was to learn a great deal about music and musicians, hitherto a closed book to me. He himself had studied his art in Moscow, Warsaw, and Paris. With meager opportunities in Poland, he came to the States in the 1920s and had difficulties in getting a residency permit. He appealed for help to Ignacy Paderewski, his brother then being one of the master's very few students. Paderewski's telegram to a Wisconsin congressman did the trick, but also showed how even the greatest and most acclaimed artists are not free from such ordinary human foibles as vanity. George obtained it and kept the telegram. In it the great man asked the congressman's help for his countryman, and thought it fit to add that George had studied at a musical academy where he, Paderewski, had become professor at the age of eighteen. A rare achievement, but why mention it when one is universally acknowledged as one of the greatest pianists of all time?

To my subsequent regret, my overindulgent parents had never forced me, as were so many of my childhood contemporaries in Poland, to become literate in music, i.e., to play an instrument. Now I greedily embraced every opportunity to take advantage of Madison's frequent musical events. There were occasional concerts by the Chicago and Minneapolis symphony orchestras and visits by soloists. I took special delight in the performances of the then well-known Pro Arte Quartet, which was attached to the university, and which contributed to a love for chamber music that never left me.

The British philosopher A.N. Whitehead considered music and mathematics as the two highest achievements of mankind. Without being more than a dilettante in both fields, I was fortunate to make the acquaintance of practitioners of both arts (for such is mathematics as well as being a science). Both are rich in interesting, if not to say eccentric, personalities. George's boon companion Germain, the cellist with the Quartet, was a good example. A Belgian, he combined that nation's practicality with a French speaker's frequent unwillingness to recognize other languages. Though in this country for thirty years, his English was of the most limited kind, but his linguistic shortcoming did not hamper him either in this artistic career or in his love life. A short man, bald in his sixties, he still enjoyed considerable success in the latter sphere. But how, George once asked him, did he manage to procure a certain article that would protect him from untoward consequences of his trysts. Quite simple, explained Germain. He would walk into a pharmacy and declare to the salesman, "Want to fook, no children." He never had any difficulty in getting what he wanted.

As against that representative of Gallic culture, our other friend, Alexander Alexandrovich Vasiliev, embodied the best characteristics of the pre-revolutionary Russian intelligentsia. A retired professor and a world authority on Byzantine history, Vasiliev was at the same time a great connoisseur of music. Born in 1867, he was full of stories about the scintillating artistic scene of St. Petersburg of his youth and mature age. He had known Tchaikovsky personally. He used to tell an anecdote about him: the great composer was evidently a bad conductor, even of his own works. On one occasion, when Tchaikovsky was conducting a symphony orchestra, a prominent music critic could not stand it any longer and, jumping to his feet and exasperatedly shouted: "again a wrong beat, Pyotr Ilyich!"

The three of us would often dine together: an incongruous trio of the old professor in his late seventies, George, about forty, and myself, twenty-two. There was a small Italian restaurant in an unfashionable part of town, dispensing meatballs and spaghetti to its usual customers. But when we three appeared, Niccolò, the proprietor, would lay out a veritable feast, very largely, I believe, because of his reverence for Vasiliev, who spoke fluent Italian. But such pleasures could not dismiss the war from our minds, nor the gnawing worry about what was happening to our families in Poland, mine as well as George's much-loved brother.

To be sure, as mentioned previously, by the summer of 1943, the course of the war had definitely turned against the Axis. But as the Nazi forces were being pushed back in the East after the battles of Stalingrad and Kursk, and as the British and Americans, having triumphed in Africa, were now advancing in Italy, a new and somber shadow loomed over the entire scene the Soviet Union's policy and its post-war intentions.)

The epic of Stalingrad almost quieted my suspicion of the Soviet Union, but the events that followed revived and intensified that fear. One of my great friends after the war was Alexander Erlich, professor of economics at Columbia, a rare case of a true political idealist. Brought up in the socialist tradition in Russia and Poland, Alex remained faithful to it until his death. I loved to tell my acquaintances that they did not have to read books to find out what the Mensheviks (the anti-Communist Russian revolutionaries) were like; they should just get to know Alex; except that few of them equaled his integrity and intellect. Well, Alex's father Henryk and his cousin Viktor Alter were imprisoned by the Soviets at the beginning of the war. Released after the Nazi attack, they worked for a while for the Polish embassy in the USSR. Then in December 1941 they disappeared. Nothing was heard of them until the winter of 1942-43, when probably counting on America's public opinion being distracted by the jubilation over Stalingrad, the Soviets saw fit to release information that these two Jews, socialists throughout their lives, had been shot for working for the Germans. The Kremlin's calculation proved correct: no one in the West made much of a fuss over the murder and slander of these two honest and distinguished people. They were done away with most likely because once in the US, they could have deconstructed the idealized propaganda version of Russia and Uncle Joe. Yes, there was one protest meeting over these executions at which if I remember correctly, Mayor La Guardia of New York brought himself to say, addressing the Soviets: "Don't ever do it again."

The Kremlin would and did, again and again. Shortly afterwards, at Katyn, the Germans discovered mass graves of thousands of Polish officers captured by the Russians in 1939. For once, the Nazis could afford to tell the truth: the victims had been murdered by the Soviet secret police. Not so, said the Soviets, when the Red Army soon reoccupied the area: they had been shot by the Gestapo in the summer of 1941. We know that for years the Polish government-in-exile had been searching for an answer to what happened to some 15,000 Polish officers seized by the Russians. Stalin, usually a skillful liar, had faltered on that question: they may have escaped to Manchuria (!), he told the Polish Prime Minister. And now the Soviet government became a beneficiary of its crime. When the Polish government asked for an investigation of Katyn by the Red Cross, the Kremlin had an excellent reason to break its diplomatic relations with the Polish government-in-exile. Much of the Western press shared Moscow's indignation: how typical of these Polish reactionaries (in fact the government-in-exile contained socialists and peasants' party representatives) to fall for German propaganda and try to disrupt the unity of the Grand Alliance! I now began to hear how the Red Army units, when entering the areas where Polish resistance forces were active against the retreating Germans, would first welcome their collaboration, feast them as brothers-in-arms, and then proceed to disarm them, send them to the rear as prisoners, and often liquidate their commanders. As for Katyn, only with perestroika did the Soviet Union admit that the thousands had been shot by the NKVD (the secret police). And after the "Evil Empire" had crumbled, out of its secret archives came a copy of the Politburo memorandum authorizing the deed. On it was found the signatures of the Politburo members, beginning with that of Stalin—Well, he had ordered the death of even more Soviet officers between 1936 and 1940.

It is an unanswerable question: could the Western public have been presented with a realistic view of the Soviet Union and "Uncle Joe" while the main burden of the war was still being carried by the Soviet Army? Certainly the first priority had to be the smashing of the German and Japanese war machines. And suppose our leaders had known the full truth (which they, even Churchill, had not known), they couldn't have escaped the conclusion that "after the war, it will be different." After all, the millions of Soviet citizens, Communism's and Stalin's victims, shared that delusion. Millions of his subjects perished in the prewar purges, yet the overwhelming majority of Soviet people stuck loyally by their government, something which greatly surprised the tyrant. Wouldn't he then reward them for that unexpected and unearned loyalty, at least by discontinuing government by murder?

It was in my basement apartment in Madison that I heard by radio the exhilarating news that the Allies had landed at Normandy on June 6, 1944. It was a glorious but fearful moment: will the landing succeed, shall we see casualties on the scale of those of World War I? Again, luck abandoned Hitler, so long and outrageously its beneficiary. Had he rushed his Panzer divisions to Normandy, the invasion, fiercely resisted as it was, could have been foiled, and then his V-1 and V-2 rockets, just then coming into mass production, might have devastated more than they in fact did. But the Führer assumed that Normandy was a feint, and that the real blow would come elsewhere. German defenses of the beachheads buckled, and "Festung Europa" (Fortress Europe) began to crumble.

For me, a Francophile, there was one jarring episode in the glorious venture. General de Gaulle was initially prevented from taking his place on French soil, largely because of FDR's personal antipathy toward this very stylized male version of Joan of Arc. Luckily for the West, this ban was soon lifted, for without this indomitable if impossible man, the Communist-dominated French resistance might well have taken over France.

Recalled from today, the events of the next months seem to have cascaded toward that final scene in Hitler's bunker and the Reich's fall in May 1945. But at the time, the progress of the Western allies after the June euphoria seemed agonizingly slow. There were anxious moments with the German counter-offensive in the Ardennes in December 1944, famous as the "Battle of the Bulge." A friend of mine was one of those who at the time came close to being shot by their fellow Americans. The Germans had been dropping English-speaking infiltrators in American uniform behind the front lines, and in the near panic, stray soldiers separated from their units were being subjected by suspicious GI's to a rigorous examination about things only a real American would know. My friend, who retained a trace of a foreign accent, was stopped by the Military Police and at the point of a gun was asked who played second base for the Brooklyn Dodgers. It was with great difficulty that he persuaded his interrogators that though he did not know much about baseball, he was not an enemy agent.

As VE day grew nearer, so did the prospect of the Soviet Union emerging as the master of Central and Eastern Europe. The future of that part of the world could be previewed through the tragedy of Warsaw. With the Soviet armies just across the Vistula, the Polish government in London exercised the unpardonable foolishness of asking the Warsaw underground to rise against the Germans. At least some of its members should have been better able to take the true measure of Stalin. Now Stalin would take advantage of the fateful blunder. Even if he had originally planned to have his armies cross the river, he would now hold back, letting the Germans destroy the underground army so as to make it easier for Poland to be turned into a Soviet satellite. And indeed no appeals from Roosevelt and Churchill could persuade him to help, even with military supplies, the gallant but doomed Polish fighters who were combating German guns and tanks mostly with rifles and grenades. The unequal struggle lasted from the first of August until early October, when the remnants of the insurgents surrendered to the enemy, who then proceeded to complete the destruction of the city. The proximity and certainty of their military defeat did not abate the Nazis' savagery in carrying out the "final solution;" if anything, it was intensified. The news of what would come to be described as the Holocaust began to emerge in the American press. Initial descriptions were skimpy, partly because the full horror of it could hardly be conceived until the Allies seized Auschwitz and the other concentration camps at war's end. And shocking and hard as it is to believe, continual efforts by the Polish resistance to inform the Western capitals about the massacres perpetrated on the territory of the "General Gouvernement," (that elegant name, with French origins, which the Nazis bestowed on the bulk of occupied Poland) fell on deaf ears. Washington and London's insensitivity to the news drove a Jewish member of the Polish parliament-in-exile to suicide. Even loud rhetoric and warnings by the West might have alerted those Germans who were not Nazi fanatics to the retribution that awaited them for complicity in the mass murder and reduced the number of victims. As it was, the final count of Polish citizens erased by the Holocaust would stand at six million, half of them Jews.

And so with such somber accompaniments, the European war was winding down. At Yalta in the Crimea, the three supreme leaders of what was described as the Free World gathered to tidy up the postwar settlement. The crippled President of the United States, already harboring an ailment that would eventually kill him, had to travel thousands of miles; for Stalin would not go anywhere but to Soviet-controlled territory (Teheran, where they met in 1943, was then under joint British-Soviet military occupation). Of course, at the time all these facts, as well as the details of the Big Three negotiations, were shrouded in wartime secrecy.

There will be more on Yalta when I come to Soviet foreign policy. But it's important to note here and now that the general view of agreements arrived at in Yalta as signifying that Churchill and Roosevelt had agreed to divide Europe into two spheres of domination, the US and Britain taking the West and the Soviet Union absorbing the East is grossly over-simplified. What did emerge in February 1945, and was understood as such by the rest of the world, was that Poland's goose was cooked: not only were the Russians to retain their loot from the Molotov-Ribbentrop agreement of 1939; but Poland itself would almost inevitably become a satellite of Moscow, and almost as surely have a Communist system imposed upon its people. FDR tried feebly and ineffectively to soften Stalin's territorial demands. Wouldn't his partner allow Poland to retain Lwów, a bastion of Polish culture for over 700 years? He was sorry, replied the dictator, but his Ukrainian subjects would create political trouble for him if he renounced the city so dear to them. A dictator mindful of his subjects' feelings that sensitivity had to disarm his American interlocutors. No one on the Western side was impolite enough to remind the tyrant that he did not show much concern for Ukrainian feelings in 1932-33 when he let five million of them starve to death in a great famine, while his government exported two million tons of grain.

The Yalta agreement, in fact, de-legitimized the London government-in-exile, which Stalin characterized as composed of fascists and reactionaries. No one thought to object to that scurrilous characterization of people, many of whom, had suffered persecution in prewar Poland for their democratic views. The Polish underground under London's command performed countless acts of sabotage against the German war machine, greatly helping the Allies, the USSR included. It provided invaluable information to the common cause, e.g. identifying places where the Germans produced heavy water (for nuclear development) and the V-1 and V-2 rockets. They were and would be replaced by Polish Communists and fellow travelers, many of them brought from the USSR, plus a few "London Poles" acceptable to Moscow. To Churchill was left the humiliating task of browbeating the exile government into committing political suicide.

As the Red Army occupied the bulk of Poland, its underground leaders were called upon by the Soviet command to identify themselves and to confer with their Soviet allies. Sixteen of them did so and "disappeared." Appropriately enough, it was at the United Nations founding conference in San Francisco that Molotov revealed that the sixteen had been arrested and accused of hostile acts against Soviet forces. Asked by a Western diplomat what was going to happen to them, the Soviet foreign minister gave an answer which may serve as the quintessence of Soviet justice: "The guilty ones will be tried." Stalin would later say that he could not interfere with the judicial branch of the government.

*   *   *

Because the Wisconsin language program was to end in late 1944, I applied to the Harvard Graduate School of Arts and Sciences. Early in 1945, I would begin my studies in politics and history. With the political picture of the world undergoing great changes, I was attracted to the Harvard Government Department; and part of the attraction lay in the name. In other universities, the study of politics, international affairs, and the like lay under the rubric of political science(I did not and do not consider the study of politics to be a science.) At the same time, most of the history departments at that distant time still concentrated on strictly diplomatic and political history, and what had been happening since 1914 was rarely if ever treated. In college, two of my teachers had studied government at Harvard, and from them I got the picture of its department as being much broader in scope: mainly an historical approach to modern politics enlarged by philosophical analysis and political and economic considerations. That was what I wanted, along with some of the strictly historical courses, which had been so praised by my teachers. I was offered what was for those days a magnificent scholarship, $900, with tuition then being but $400.

My departure from Madison coincided with that of two of my close friends. George Szpinalski was leaving to join the Chicago Symphony. He had long resisted offers from symphony orchestras, because he believed that playing in them led to the attrition of an artist's individual style. But at forty, he simply could not continue at the meager salary of an instructor and his stuffy department would not promote him. Vasiliev had just been offered a research professorship at the newly established center for Byzantine studies at Dumbarton Oaks in Washington

The three of us were given a party by our common Russian friend Sergei Wilde who, as behooved a Baltic baron and former officer in the Imperial Guard (Baltic aristocrats, descendants of the medieval Teutonic knights who had ruled over what is now Estonia and Latvia, served as the bulwark of the old Russian regime, while retaining much of their traditional German culture), entertained us magnificently. At a late hour we set out for our quarters, but soon heard the frantic voice of Wilde summoning us back. He had found another bottle of rare brandy!

This chapter in my life really concluded with another event, which took place after several months at Harvard. The news of Hiroshima and Nagasaki astounded the world. I finally understood where my brother had been all that time.

6

A Fugitive Stays with Józef Ulam: George Volsky's Tale

An escaped prisoner-of-war meets Jozef Ulam

MU: In 1963, Adam received a telephone call from Miami, Florida, from a man who identified himself as George Volsky. He had seen one of Adam's books in a bookstore and was calling to ask if he was any relation to a Jozef Ulam. Adam replied that his father was named Jozef Ulam, whereupon Volsky said that he had spent the winter of 1939 with him and that a letter would follow, telling how that had come about. Shortly afterward, it arrived.

Miami, December 22, 1963
"Drogi Panie,
"Yes, you are so right in reminding me (on the telephone) that it is almost 25 years since those unforgettable days of the summer of 1939. My reflections of Lwów are naturally hazy and, as I come to think of it, unreal. I had never been to your town before, just passed by it, several times, I think, on the way to, Pkzernyl, but Lwów was always surrounded in my mind with an aura of its fierce pride and courage and peculiar stubborn individualism...

*　　*　　*

...I entered the Ulam apartment house in Lwów on a cool, misty and very gray morning in the early days of October 1939. The house was situated near the university on a narrow street in the city's old town. Both the house and the street seemed devoid of warmth, or at least so I thought at the time. I carried with me a small suitcase with a few personal belongings, including a heavy sweater and a blanket that my aunt, providentially, insisted I take with me when I left my Krakow home eight weeks earlier. It was my third day in Lwów, where I arrived via a train full of refugees from the also Soviet-occupied city of Rowno, some 200 kilometers distant. In my pocket, I hid a golden watch and about 350 zlotys, also given to me by my aunt, my only possessions of value. On the trip to the Ulam house, by tramway and on foot, I was accompanied be a middle-aged attractive woman - a relative of a friend - whom I had met on my first day in the city. Disregarding the watchful glance of the concierge, we walked up to the first floor apartment, the best one in the building, where my companion introduced me to the owner of the house who she said was a prominent Lwów lawyer, named Jozef Ulam.

My first impression of Pan Ulam was his reserve, gentleness and what appeared to me infinite sadness. Not more than 5'5" in height, he wore a dark, three-piece woolen suit. He looked at me and, without asking any questions, said with kindness that I could stay and sleep in one of the apartment's rooms. He exchanged a few words with the woman, whom he knew well, and who had contacted him before to ask if he could give shelter for a few days to a boy (I was 18 at the time) who in effect was an escaped war prisoner. Almost immediately, the woman waved goodbye to me and left. I barely had time to thank her for letting me stay in her place for the two previous nights and for finding me a new place to stay. I never learned her name and I never saw her again. Pan Ulam then took me to "my" room, a small, dark study, where on a mattress I was to sleep for a week that stretched to more than three months. He told me, almost apologetically, to stay there for now; we would talk in the afternoon as he had to go out to run some errands. So there I sat on the mattress with my gloomy thoughts, alone for the first time in weeks during which I had been constantly on the move. I ate a piece of bread and a sausage that I had brought in my suitcase. I felt overwhelmed and dazed by the events that had taken place in my life in the last several weeks. So as not to think about the past and even less about the foreboding future, or not to cry, I forced myself to sleep.

Eight weeks earlier in Krakow, I was preparing, albeit with some apprehension, for my second year at the Jagellonian University's medical school. Hitler's threats against Poland were commented on by all but were not taken with the utmost seriousness they deserved. We were led to believe by our government that he would not dare to attack Poland and face not only what we were assured was a very brave and powerful Polish army, but also the even the mightier armadas of France and Great Britain. Then in the middle of August events darkened. My father, then a 43-year-old reserve artillery Lt.

Colonel who lived in Warsaw, was ordered to report to his unit in the field, and so was my uncle, his older brother, who was a reserve colonel in the medical corps and with whom I lived in Krakow. (My mother died when I was 12; my father subsequently married and moved to Warsaw; I remained in Krakow with my uncle, a physician and a university professor, and his wife, who were childless and lived in a very large, elegant house in the best residential district of the city.) Then, on August 30, like many young university students who were cadet-officers, I was instructed to report to Krakow's military barracks to be given uniforms and weapons in order to be later posted to various units, in my case, to the air squadron outside the city. On September 1, 1939, when the Nazis invaded Poland, our group, still without uniforms, was ordered to move to Kielce, north of Krakow. We never got there. It became immediately apparent that the Germans had broken through the Polish defenses in the west, and we received information that Nazi tanks were thrusting deep into the countryside near Kielce to encircle Warsaw. It was a glorious September - warm weather day and night, with cloudless skies. We prayed for rain to slow the Nazi armor, but the heavens did not cooperate. Our small unit found itself adrift and almost leaderless. Without precise orders, by train, trucks, and sometimes on foot, we were withdrawing eastward where, we were told, our army was reorganizing for a counteroffensive. That never happened. Instead, in a few days the Polish Army and the Polish state disintegrated; so did my theretofore pleasant, carefree life and secure future.

By September 17, fleeing from the Germans, our ragtag unit of some 200 youngsters wearing Polish army caps but without uniforms or weapons, was in a territory occupied by the Soviet troops which, under a secret Hitler-Stalin treaty, were to control the eastern part of the divided Poland, including Lwów. In no time, we were seized by the Soviets. At the beginning, the Russian officers did not know what to do with the bunch of boys. Some said we would be sent to a prisoner-of-war camp in the Ukraine, or the far north. (That's where I found myself later on.) Others told us we would be let go home. The Soviet commanders had more important things to do: to rapidly reach the river Bug, their demarcation line, across from the Nazis. Thus, taking advantage of the confusion, of a temporary disinterest of the Soviet military, and of the presence of civilian refugees in the area, with a Krakow friend of mine, I escaped from the lightly guarded Russian compound. We discarded our military caps and became civilians, hoping to avoid re-capture. He headed for Lwów where he had distant family and friends, and I, by foot, to Rowno, a town not too far away where my family as I recalled had acquaintances. I stayed in Rowno, a small town of about 10,000 people, for only about 10 days, changing abodes almost every night. The NKVD, the Soviet secret police, which arrived in town en masse on the heels of the military, seized control and jailed Polish policemen and other officials. The NKVD's first action was to order all non-Rowno residents to report to a special "census" office. The presence of young "outsiders" (I became friendly with a number of refugees of my age, some from Lwów), who dressed more fashionably than the locals, became very conspicuous and it was difficult to find places to stay.

Some of my new friends were returning home to Lwów and suggested that I do the same and become submerged in a larger population of refugees from Western Poland who fleeing the Germans by the tens of thousands sought refuge in that city of 350,000. As soon as I arrived in Lwów, I got in touch with my Krakow friend. He introduced me to the woman in whose apartment I stayed until she contacted Pan Ulam and guided me to his house. In the afternoon of my first day in his house, Pan Ulam woke me up gently and explained the rules of my stay even though it was going to be a short one. He said he would mention casually to the concierge (who probably would spread the news to other tenants) that I was the son of a good friend who came to enroll in the University of Lwów as soon as it inaugurated its classes and, as a student, I would then move to a university dormitory. He introduced me to a housemaid, an older woman, whom I later helped to wash dishes. The kitchen, rather large, had a window that overlooked a U-shaped patio of the two-story house. From the kitchen window I could look at other apartments. There was one in particular which caught my attention because I saw that an attractive young woman lived there. The woman, wife of a tailor, saw me and apparently liked me from afar. Later, on several occasions when her husband was away, she signaled me to come up to her apartment, visits that proved to be rather pleasant for both of us. I told Pan Ulam that I would be away most of the time because I had friends in the city. I also said I would try to contact my aunt to seek her advice about whether I should return home. In October 1939 there was no mail between the two occupied parts of Poland. But the border dividing the Soviet and German zones was still very porous, which permitted enterprising and—I must say—honest individuals, to move, for a price, people, letters and even packages to and from virtually all parts of Poland. (By January 1941, because of that year's very cold winter and increased German and Soviet vigilance, this traffic practically ceased.) One event I recall that took place during my first week in the Ulam house was that when I came back in the evening, I found another young man whom Pan Jozef had also invited to stay, which he did for one night only.

After the first 10 days in the house, I told Pan Ulam that I could not immediately find another sleeping place. He replied that I should not worry and that I could stay as long as I believed it was safe. He was slowly warming up to me, abandoning some of his somewhat shy reserve. Most of all, he came to like me, I think, because I reminded him of you two and the fact that you were safe warmed his aging heart in spite of the cold. One day he asked me to come home earlier and dine with him. (I would usually have a cup of tea at the apartment and a slice of bread). Then I would go out and, weather permitting, would meet friends at some place in town, or in my Lwów friends' houses, if it rained. A university medical school, to which I was planning to transfer and which was scheduled to reopen by early December, was offering free lunches to regular students and transfer applicants. So several of us who were in the latter category were able to eat at least one good meal a day. Unfortunately, in late November the University under new Communist leaders decided that only residents of the Soviet-occupied part of Poland were eligible for university admittance; consequently, there were no more free lunches for me and my colleagues.

At our first dinner together—Pan Ulam, who was a light eater and usually had only a bowl of soup at night—asked me about my family and told me a little about his. I learned that his wife had died the year before, and that he had two sons, Stanislaw, then about 23 and Adam, who was my age, who were in America. He was extremely proud of his sons, especially Stan who by that time had already two science doctoral degrees. He also said that Adam was an extremely bright young man, and that he was sure that his older brother would help him to chose a right career. During the meal, and even more so later because he alluded to the subject several times, he would express, as though speaking to himself, a feeling of sadness at being left alone. But at the same time he was happy, and convinced of the righteousness of his decision, because he had sent his sons abroad to escape the calamity of war which he wisely foresaw coming.

Oh, the resilience of youth! My initial gloom at being alone in the world and left to my own devices was beginning to dissipate. And it was assuaged by a letter from my aunt who practically saved my life. She ordered me to stay put in Lwów to await further developments and, bless her heart, sent me a large package with winter clothing, including two suits, my sturdy shoes and, most important, a heavy overcoat which I urgently needed, as well as 200 zlotys. (On many days in October I shivered going out dressed in a light suit and my heavy sweater.) How did she manage to send me such a large package I never found out, but she was always a very resourceful person. I owe much to her. An extremely beautiful, poised—almost regal—and very well-educated woman of only 45, she had taught me, by her example, manners and savoir-faire. I sent her the most loving letter of thanks that I had ever written, and later, when I knew my free days in Lwów were numbered, another one. I hope she received them both and was proud of me. I never got a reply. She died during the war in Krakow of an unknown ailment, as I was informed by my relatives after the war. Her—our—house was commandeered by the Gestapo, and was destroyed beyond repair by the SS troops when they abandoned the city in 1945. As time wore on, my relations with Pan Ulam became more friendly, or rather he took a more paternal, though still reserved, interest in me perhaps because, by age at least, I reminded him of Adam. Our age difference aside, we were alike because both of us were lonely. I had no mother and did not know where my father was, indeed if he was alive. (He survived the Soviet captivity to fight with the Polish Army and died as a result of serious wounds he suffered in the Monte casino battle. My uncle died in a Soviet prison.) Pan Ulam knew his sons were in America, but I think he had few hopes of seeing them any time soon, if ever. One day he introduced me to his nephew, a banker who came to visit several times. I do not remember the nephew's name). The only recollection that I have of him is that he was about 40, with sparse blond hair, a round pleasant face and a cheerful demeanor. The three of us discussed politics, a gloomy subject at the time. The southeastern part of Poland, with Lwów as its center, was incorporated into the Soviet Ukraine. The Ukrainian language was rapidly displacing Polish in the city, which had a sizeable Ukrainian population, although not a majority like in the surrounding countryside. On one or two occasions when the weather was nice, Pan Ulam and I would take a stroll along the Lwów streets. He would tell me stories about the city's past, some of which I knew from my history lessons, and about its buildings, plazas and avenues. Until then I had not realized how attractive Lwów really was, having always thought that Krakow was Poland's most beautiful and pleasant city. I still see Pan Ulam in my mind's eye. Even during a few warm October days, he always went out wearing a heavy dark fur-lined coat with an Astrakhan collar. He wore a black derby hat angled to the left side (somehow I remember that detail) that gave him a slightly rakish look.

In early November, the weather was becoming inclement and I was spending more time at home with my host. The apartment was cold as there was very little coal and wood for the stoves. One day I asked Pan Ulam if he had any old useless papers we could burn to warm ourselves even for a while. He produced legal briefs, but they were gone in no time. He and I looked at the heavy books in his legal library and after a moment of hesitation he picked up one volume at random and gave it to me. It took much longer for the book's pages to be consumed by fire and we felt warmer for a longer time, too. From that day on, we sat together many mornings and evenings, as though mesmerized, looking at the fire of his legal volumes, each with his own thoughts. I am sure he was remembering his past life that the burning books were witnesses of. He did not bemoan their loss; on the contrary, he seemed to enjoy their non-legal usefulness. At the same time, losing the past, he was probably giving up on the future. Bleak as my present was, with youthful unreason, I was hoping that I would survive, although I did not know how.

My situation, which I shared with Pan Ulam, was becoming more precarious as 1939 was coming to an end. It was clear that it would be not be possible for me to transfer to the Lwów medical school, which would mean receiving free housing, meals and a small stipend. It was because the Soviet authorities started to differentiate between the permanent population of its Polish provinces and that from Poland's German side. A population census by the Lwów Communist authorities provided the former with valid Soviet residence documents. People like myself (I had only my Krakow university identity card and a mobilization order) could not apply for them and in effect I became stateless. In early December, the omnipresent

NKVD began rounding up refugee families for deportation to Siberia, or other far eastern regions. Rumors that trains full of Polish refugees (and some locals whom the Soviets regarded as politically suspect) were leaving the Lwów railway yard were soon confirmed. Once or twice, Ukrainian paramilitary officials visited our house to inquire if any outsiders lived there, adding that it was illegal to give shelter or lease space to people without proper documents. The concierge, who knew me by sight said there were no strangers in the apartment house, and later told Pan Ulam about the visits. His concern was not so much that the woman, who was a trusted long-time employee, would denounce me, but that it could be done by some tenants who were either nursing an old grudge against the landlord, or wanted to ingratiate themselves politically with the Ukrainian Communists.

I knew then that I would have to look for another place to stay. I did not want to compromise Pan Ulam, of whom I have become very fond and who never told me, or even suggested, that I leave. Before we parted, he gave me one piece of advice, which I followed. If I were to be detained by the NKVD, he said, I should tell my captors that I was an escaped prisoner-of-war and as such, under international law, I had the right to be turned over to the military authorities.

Christmas and New Year came and went. In vain, I sought a solution that would keep me legally in Lwów. Finally a local friend told me he would arrange for me to have a bed at a university dormitory where a few other young men like myself were trying to "pass" as legitimate students. After a week of considering the offer, I realized there was nothing for me to do but to take it. So on a chilly night in early January I left furtively the apartment. I said goodbye to Pan Ulam, thanking him with as much emotion as I could express for the kindness and affection he had showed me during the preceding months. I walked away with my small suitcase and cried because I was sure I would not see him again. When we parted, I think he shed a tear too; he knew he would be left alone again with only remembrances of the past and nothing to look forward to. In hindsight, I am glad thinking that I had brightened his lonely life even though it was only for a short time.

Ten days later, the NKVD, apparently tipped by informers, arrived late at night to inspect the papers of the students in the three-story dormitory. Wakened in my tiny cubicle, I immediately knew my game was up. I quickly packed my belongings, went to the ground floor where the Russian political police set up its check point and turned myself in, presenting my military papers. I was arrested, and the next day I was sent to the military police headquarters. I was interrogated for several hours by two officers who inquired about my life since my September escape. Even though they wanted to know where I stayed in Lwów, I said that I had always slept in various university establishments.

I was not treated too badly. Several days later, with other former Polish soldiers, I was sent under guard to a prisoner-of-war camp located between Kiev and Kharkov, and a year later to another camp north of Leningrad. We were liberated in July 1941, after Germany attacked the Soviet Union. I became attached to a Polish division being organized in Uzbekistan, where I met my father, also freed from a similar camp. My father continued with his Polish Army division that eventually fought in Italy. I was transferred to a Polish Air Force squadron in England, and later to the Royal Air Force. But that is part of another story of my long life...

"...As I write these lines, I remember many things which I did not know were stored in my memory. And it is because hitherto I thought myself the one and only actor of those memorable days. Now my figure diminishes and other figures appear on the scene, more defined and more tragic than the senseless youth that I then was.

I hope I have been able to translate into words the atmosphere of those months. I am told it is generally a forlorn hope. Nevertheless during these Christmas and New Year's days, do remember, as I stated, that 24 years ago, I spent them with your father.

Best regards,
George Volsky

MU:George Volsky is a retired journalist who wrote for The New York Times. *He now lives in Florida*

7

Echoes of the Holocaust

Three letters tell of tragedy

No major war has ever ended without the victors encountering disappointment, new fears, and troubles after the initial euphoria has passed. For Stan and me, the end brought the confirmation of our worst fears that most of our relatives had shared the terrible fate of the Jewish bourgeoisie under the Soviet, and especially the Nazi, occupation. Also, with very few exceptions, our friends and acquaintances from Lwów, as well as my brother's fellow mathematicians, whether Jewish or Aryan, did not survive those hellish six years.

Julius Ulam to Stanislaw Ulam, Lwow, 16 March 1945

Dear Cousin!

It is for the first time during the war, that I have the possibility of sending you some news. Alas, these news are without exception sorrowful, as can be the news from the theatre of war.

From our whole family, I and my mother are the only alive. Your father and mine, your sister(Stefania) and her husband fell from the hands of Nazis; and these five years of war, from the very beginning, are for us a story of constant terror and persecution. It would have no purpose to relate this story with details; I shall do it, when we meet again.

As to myself, I am still in Lwów, but not for long. After the flight of Germans from here, I got a post on the University, owing to the help of Stephan, and I was accepted to the IIIrd course of mathematics, after having passed all necessary examinations. My incessant study of mathematics, which I continued in spite of most unfavourable conditions, enabled me to do it. Stephen left for Moscow in January, and got perhaps a contact with you already. I leave in the nearest days for Cracow, where I shall enter the University, most probably the IVth course, if my material conditions, very heavy now, will allow me to study.

I am wearing now my mother's maiden name;(MU:Julek's mother was gentile) and if you would like to write to me, write to the University of Cracow, for Julius Flondor. If you could make the departure from here possible for me, I would be most grateful to you.

With kindest regards for you and Adam, I remain

Yours faithfully,

Julius

MU: Julius Ulam was Adam and Stan's paternal first cousin. His father was Szymon Ulam

Julius Ulam to Stanislaw Ulam, Cracow, 14 June 1946

Kochany Staszku!

Because I was not sure whether my last letter, sent to Harvard, would reach you, I am sending the current one to the Annals of Mathematics, where they probably know your address.

It may be that you may have learned indirectly from relatives and friends some details of the wartime events in Lwów. As I wrote you in my previous letter, only Mother and I were saved out of our family. Everyone else perished between 1942 and 1944, in various circumstances at the German hands. It would take up too much space if I were to describe everything for you. Our experiences throughout these 6 years, 1939-45, would provide enough raw data for an entire library of adventure stories, thrillers, and, unfortunately, macabre tales. One emerged from that period intact and healthy only because of some extraordinary accident. [I can say so] as a member of a small handfull of those who were saved. Each of us lived throughout the period with an unpleasant perspective of sudden death at any time and in a constant struggle for life that gave us laughable small chances for survival. Therefore I am not even attempting to describe for you the incidents which directly caused the deaths of our closest relatives. I shall tell you about them when we meet. My greatest wish is that we meet as soon as possible.

I left Lwów a year ago; I am about to finish my studies in Kraków but, overall, I have no idea what I will do upon my graduation. I would leave here most gladly. If there are any possibilities that could allow you to help me achieve that, I beg you let me know about that. Even more importantly, take advantage of those opportunities as soon as possible. Many of my acquaintances have already left and I see no wiser way than to follow into their footsteps. I would have done it last year already but being a senior (majoring in mathematics of course!), I wanted absolutely to graduate here first.

I really care to get in touch with you as soon as possible. I still know nothing about both of you. I have not had any news, even indirectly. I believe that this is because you were looking for someone in Lwów. I beg you, when you receive this letter, write to me to the address as indicated on the envelope. I am awaiting your reply with great impatience.

Give my cordial best to Adas and accept my firm handshake and kisses.

Yours,
Julek

A letter, by a relative of the Ulams, addressed to Mary H.B. Ulam, 20 February 2001

I have long hesitated before bringing myself to put on paper the memories of a sad time of my life. This was the period when, together with Stefania Ulam, and her little child, we lived secreted in the house of a loose, but indeed generous, [Christian] woman who gave us hospitality without any compensation. There were three adults in the hideout: my mother, her father (an attorney) and Stefania, together with two children, myself (11 years [old]) and Stefania's little child. This toddler was about 1 year old, but I can't remember whether a girl or a boy, while my reminiscence of Stefania is that of a young lady in her early thirties.

I remember it was early spring when our neighbors betrayed us. We were arrested by the Gestapo and brought to the "Janowski Lager" in Lwów, the same concentration camp where my father was shot.

Our generous [Christian] benefactress was shot and our group brought to a small detention centre called the "bunker," waiting to be gunshot the following morning at dawn. But the evening before, the commanding officer, Hauptsturmfuehrer Warzog came to interrogate us. During the inquisition it appeared quite plain that he was open to bribery and that, against compensation, he would carry us to a camp instead of shooting us. Accordingly, my mother took him to a hideaway in Lwów, where she had hidden jewellery and valuable carpets, after recovering which, he decided that the valuables were not of an adequate amount to save everybody's lives. He would only save two individuals from being killed and gave my mother a few hours to make the tremendous choice on who he would save from certain death and be taken, instead, to a concentration camp.

I have no memory of the following hours, thanks God I have repressed it from my reminiscence. Only I remember that at dawn my mother and myself were brought to the camp, while Stefania, her baby and my grandfather were killed.

Afterwards, while the Red Army moved forward, in September 1944, my mother and myself were taken to Plaszów concentration camp [near Cracow] and next, in October, we were moved to Auschwitz-Birkenau. We were parted away, my mother and I, but, luckily, I managed to get away with the "selection" by Dr. Mengele and, after many misadventures, I was rescued and set free by the Russians, at the end of January 1945.

Please excuse my poor and very condensed picture of such a tragic occurrence, hard to even imagine nowadays. I have searched my memory intensely but there must be a sort of biological self-defense of the organism that clouds terrifying and upsetting events, besides my unconscious has probably just switched off this tough time of my life.

Part Three

The Professor

8

Early Harvard Years

Instructor in the Government Department...Three years with the British Empire...Goof re Henry Kissinger...A famous anthropologist at the helm of the RCC...Course on Marx...Eliot House colleagues...Harvard anecdotes...

To my overwhelming grief was added vivid apprehensions about the future. I could not share in the general, though short-lived, optimism in this country about the possibility of the democracies and the USSR co-existing peacefully for very long. What the Soviets were doing in Eastern Europe was a sinister omen for the future. Not that unlike most Westerners, I overestimated the power of the Soviets. At that moment of victory, the US was the most powerful state in recorded history. Those countless millions of Soviet soldiers, which in the imagination of some in Washington would very soon be sweeping to the English Channel, were more than countered by America's industrial strength (and in fact at the war's end, the US had more men under arms than the USSR: no one at that time in the West came close to realizing how many lives the war had cost the Soviet Union). Nor, as was the conventional early Cold War thinking, was it the A-bomb that kept Stalin from sending his armies West. With or without the wretched bomb, it was America's fantastic production record that had to awe any potential enemy: the sheer numbers of ships, planes, and munitions provided not only for America's forces on several fronts, but also for those of its allies. There were equally impressive figures in food production and other necessities of life. Had the United States been ruled by a dictator, and had he been bent upon creating a world empire, he would have been capable of frightening Stalin away from grabbing Eastern Europe, and into making all kinds of other concessions.

But America was a democracy. The idea of world domination, or of threatening "Uncle Joe," was far from the minds of the millions

99

who after V-J day just wanted to go home and resume civilian life. Few cared whether one man with an unpronounceable name rather than another was called upon to govern Poland or Czechoslovakia, or that the dynamics of international relations would change so that the era of American omnipotence would pass, Russia would repair her wounds, and in five to ten years, she would have the A-bomb (and most scientists with whom I talked at the time favored the latter date). A few bombs in a dictator's hands have stronger psychological impact than the much greater nuclear arsenal of a democracy. Would the American people be able to withstand a war of nerves with a dictator, one not as foolhardy as the late Hitler, but who was as cunning and patient as Stalin had already proven to be? Should we in a few years see repeated in the West what was then happening in Eastern Europe?

Fortunately, my fears about American democracy's powers of resolution and endurance were to be dissipated by the brilliant improvisations of the Marshall Plan and NATO. (At Yalta, FDR had incautiously said that American troops could not be expected to remain in Europe for more than two years after V-E day. As late as the 1980s, the Soviets would persistently complain about that broken "promise"). Eventually, of course, it was the Soviet system, with its rulers demoralized, that collapsed. But it has been a "damned close thing," as Wellington said of Waterloo, and we have had some close calls.

The one great concern that marred that jubilation of 1945 touched on the economy. For all of the reforms of the New Deal and the psychological boost of Roosevelt's oratory, it had really been the war that had put an end to the Great Depression. Now, true to the tradition of the "dismal science," most economists saw the swift return of those hardships of the 1930s. There would be two to three years of grace; the pent-up consumer demand would maintain a high level of employment; but then, alas, our English friends looked at us with compassion. They had just installed a socialist government, which through wise planning would avoid "the anarchy of the marketplace," high unemployment, etc. Poor Americans, stuck on their capitalism! Planning was the big word in those days. Look at the Russians, who with their scientific planning had performed miracles of industrialization. My economics teacher at Harvard, Joseph Schumpeter, himself a staunch conservative, did not believe that a democracy could retain a free-enterprise system for long. He professed not to understand how his fellow Austrian, Fredrich Hayek, could, in his *Road to Serfdom*, denounce the fallacies of socialism, whether democratic or not. Of course, Schumpeter believed that socialism did not make sense economically. But it was the wave of the future. It was Sumner Slichter, another star among Harvard economists, who, almost alone among the "experts," resolutely maintained that capitalism was here to stay, that America's economy would get bigger and stronger. Hayek had the satisfaction of living into the time when Mrs. Thatcher clobbered the Labour Party, and the Soviet economists and other believers in "scientific socialism" became almost overnight advocates of free enterprise, condemning what until quite recently had been extolled as the "Soviet model of development."

Perhaps today we have turned too much in the other direction. But in 1945-1946, as a dilettante in economics, I was impressed by all the "wise men's" prophesies of gloom unless we adopted "planning." I sympathized with those in Congress who wanted to retain rationing and other wartime regulations for an indefinite time. Fortunately, the common sense and hedonism of the American people prevailed against the "experts" and bureaucrats, and those elaborate schemes of government control were ended. Unfortunate Britain, after all her wartime sacrifice, had to put up with those controls until, I think, 1951.

The economic situation and prospects had, of course, direct relevance to academic life. During the Depression, academic jobs were scarce, and, as we had seen, badly paid (though as I used to remind Harvard's President Bok, in 1945 the average salary of a full professor here was slightly above that of a baseball major-leaguer. Perhaps in the seventies and eighties, such reminders were not so tactful). There were graduate students at Harvard who intentionally delayed finishing their doctoral theses. As students, they could earn a few hundred dollars assisting in the courses. As a Ph.D., they faced a high risk of unemployment. Now what if a similar situation would return? Some at war's end gloomily speculated about the gradual decline of private universities. How would even Harvard be able to compete with the state-financed universities of New York or California?—Such prognostications were soon belied by the growth of the economy and the masses of veterans with their college education financed under the GI Bill of Rights. Universities of all kinds flourished, salaries went up, and all went well until the Great American University Revolution of the late sixties and seventies.

In my first years at Harvard, I was too busy learning about the place to give much thought to my eventual professional career. And the enjoyment of my daily routine and new surroundings tempered my concern about the state of the world, scandalous as it may appear today when the young are endlessly harangued to be activists, to work "for a change," and otherwise to make a nuisance of themselves. Why not allow a few years for learning, and then let them try to do everything that those heckling them evidently forgot to do themselves or botched up in the attempt?

Harvard of those days was a much leaner and simpler institution than the one into which it would evolve in the next two decades, not to mention by today. The staff of the Graduate School of Arts and Sciences consisted of a dean and secretary, both active teachers, and two clerical assistants! Now it has a profusion of deans, directors, coordinators and the like, the great majority of them full-time administrators. Though President Conant had instituted a program of national scholarships just before the war, the undergraduate student body was still recruited mainly from New England and the Atlantic seaboard. In two or three years, this would all change with the flood of veterans, and a little later, Harvard would begin to assume the cosmopolitan character that it has today.

The faculty, on the other hand, included already a number of scholars who had come from abroad, and the same was true of the graduate schools. In general, all the leading American universities would undergo vast changes in the immediate postwar years. Those ancient seats of learning, Oxford, Paris, Heidelberg, etc., had in various ways been devastated by the war; and with Europe's economy in the doldrums; they would not recover for some time. Especially in the sciences would America assume primacy, as can be seen by comparing the number of American Nobel prize winners before the war with those since 1945.

Socially, the changes would be equally great. Until the war, Harvard, Yale, and Princeton were mainly schools for privileged undergraduates, though in Cambridge there was mixture of boys from poor Boston area families who mostly lived at home or were on scholarships. In 1945, it began to change, and very rapidly. The air of exclusiveness, however, hovered around some of the departments. One of my brother's colleagues in Harvard's Society of Fellows (special fellowships for talented young scholars, which freed them from any formal requirements for a degree and allowed them to study and research what they wanted) was a brilliant economist; in a few years one of the leaders in his profession. On finishing his fellowship, he was not offered a faculty appointment, apparently because he was Jewish. Years later, he would be wooed by a repentant Harvard, but understandably to no avail. It was my impression then and for some years afterward, that in some branches of the university, practicing Catholics, also, were not particularly welcome. By the 1950s, such prejudices were a thing of the past.

My own department, Government, contained several distinguished professors who in addition to their eminence as scholars represented a fascinating variety of personalities and temperaments. The senior member of the department, Arthur N. Holcombe, Harvard class of 1906, was a delightful old gentleman. He was full of stories of Harvard of the previous decades, when the majestic A. Lawrence Lowell presided over the university. Holcombe, an intimate of the president, would be sometimes summoned to his office when he needed advice or wanted to relieve his mind after a stressful incident. On one such occasion, on arriving in Massachusetts Hall, Arthur passed an elegant black gentleman who was just leaving. Did he know what this man wanted, burst out Lowell, with a mixture of amazement and indignation? His son was going to be a freshman and the visitor wanted him to live in one of the dormitories. "Mr. President," said Arthur after a pause, "you have four freshmen dormitories. Can't you run one of them on a Northern principle?"

Later, my first years as a tenured member of the department coincided with Holcombe's last before his retirement. We were discussing some junior appointments. One candidate evidently did not meet with my senior colleague's approval. Finally, he asked, undoubtedly knowing the answer, "Is Mr. X. married?" "He is not." "If no woman wanted the man," he gravely intoned, "I don't see why we should." Being older and still a bachelor, I wondered how I made the grade. For all such foibles, Holcombe was a kind-hearted man. A friend of mine, Peter B., was a grader in one of the sections of Holcombe's course. What befell him was the teacher's ultimate disaster: he lost his section's final examinations. Instead of confessing his sin, he resorted to a laborious and clumsy subterfuge. He interviewed his students and from the impressions he received, plus their records at mid-semester, he concocted their grades. Holcombe uncovered the deception. As Peter sat facing the professor, Holcombe sat smiling and finally said: "I am not as old and stupid as you thought, am I?" Difficult as the question was, the answer still could have been more tactful: "I guess not."—A stickler for the rules would have fired Peter from his teaching position, if not worse, but Holcombe not only forgave his errant assistant, he remained fond of and helpful to my friend.

If Holcombe in many respects epitomized the "old Harvard," Charles Howard McIlwain stood for the old scholarly tradition that transcended individual institutions, being entirely detached from the passions, fads, and other troublesome reminders of contemporaneity. One could imagine him in an Oxford college in the mid-nineteenth century, or in an obscure provincial American academic institution doing exactly what he had been doing at Princeton and Harvard, teaching in the same chaotic and inspired way, shunning any administrative posts and tasks.

The trite saying "bringing the past to life" for once fitted McIlwain perfectly. I recall a whole lecture devoted to the question whether the Latin *vel* in the 39th article of the *Magna Carta* was meant to be "or," which is its literal translation, or should be more loosely translated as "and." On the face of it, this appears sheer pedantry, but it became in fact the search for clues in an intriguing mystery story. Who among modern historians would put so much weight on arguing whether the American colonists, in contemporaneous British law, were right in opposing George III and the British Parliament? McIlwain did, and again this seeming scholasticism made a fascinating tale. His enthusiasm for the new materials of history was disarming: "They are doing a fine job," he said once about the Rolls Society, which, since the beginning of the 19th century, had been publishing English legal documents, "they are already all the way up to 1400!"

For all his absorption in the Middle Ages, there was nothing impractical or otherworldly about the man. Solicitous about his students, I believe that it was on his recommendation that Ralph Bunche became the first high-ranking black official in Washington, who then went on to a distinguished career at the United Nations.

Great teachers and scholars often have the faults of their virtues. While McIlwain's course on English constitutional history was a masterpiece, his lectures on the history of political theory were just very good. It was difficult for him to establish a rapport with modern political thought after Rousseau.

After he retired, I had the pleasure of attending parties organized by his students and colleagues on his eightieth and ninetieth birthdays. The first one was a cheerful affair enlivened by such antics as a future president of Brown partaking too enthusiastically in the toasts, breaking several glasses, and fleeing into the night. The latter occasion was understandably rather melancholy: though still strong physically, McIlwain confessed to me that he could no longer work. If there is a posthumous life, he has undoubtedly by now found out whether his interpretation of the *Magna Carta* was correct, even though it is most unlikely that King John and the rebellious barons have gone to the same place as my old teacher.

The recent and, on the whole, undesirable fashion of offering professorships to "celebrities," i.e., public figures currently unemployed, had not as yet taken root. But in the thirties, Harvard saw fit to appoint Heinrich Bruning, the former Chancellor of Germany, then in exile from his Nazi-controlled homeland. His name drew to his seminar unsuspecting graduate students, largely from abroad, despite other professors' hints that the course would turn out to be a waste of time. My curiosity also prevailed over good advice. It was difficult to visualize this good and democratically minded man as a leader of a great country, coping with the Depression, and standing up to the intrigues that eventually persuaded the senile octogenarian president Hindenburg to turn over power to Hitler (one story had Hindenburg during a parade gazing wonderingly at Hitler, already Chancellor, and whispering to an aide "since when has Herr Bruning grown a mustache?"). As a teacher, the ex-chancellor was no more successful. But what could one expect? From my talks with him, I got a strong impression that he was painfully reliving his failures to stem the fascist tide in Germany and the devastation brought by Hitler upon the Fatherland, for which he had fought bravely during World War I and, as a result, was awarded the Iron Cross.

The two teachers with whom I had the closest contacts, and who became my friends and colleagues, were Bill Elliot and Merle Fainsod. Huge in stature, Bill's massive bulk loomed over the lecture room, his stentorian voice dominating the discussion. He was a southerner of courtly manner, tempered by Oxford, where he had been a Rhodes scholar, a combination often conducive to a special type of personality. And indeed, his oratory partook of something of the politician's: at times, a free-flow of consciousness with occasional bombast, diverting from the subject under discussion to topics like the Soviet threat, his own various experiences as a vice-president of the War

Production Board, and general reflections on life. Yet to those who knew him more closely, such initial impressions were soon dispelled by an appreciation of Bill's keen mind and his analytic powers when it came both to political theory and practical politics. He was a master at getting the best out of his doctoral students and most solicitous in promoting their careers, among others, that of Henry Kissinger, who always acknowledged his great debt to Elliot. In fact it was Bill who pioneered that double lifestyle which later became the rule for so many Harvard political scientists, economists, etc.: residing and working partly in Cambridge and partly in Washington (not to mention the more permanent migration from Cambridge to the corridors of power that began with John F. Kennedy, something that has not ceased to this day.)

My association with Merle Fainsod, which began in 1945, lasted until his untimely death in 1972. Nothing could be more instructive in learning the canons of scholarship than to participate in his seminars. They provided a model of orderliness and of a search for authenticity in dealing with the sources. Merle, in addition to great erudition, possessed that necessary quality for a great seminar teacher: patience (I must confess to being somewhat deficient on that count, myself). First of all, there is the discipline of group discussion: you must not let one or two students monopolize the session, but instead draw out the timid and the apathetic. The teacher should refrain from trying to dominate the discussion and giving all the answers, and make it appear more of a conversation rather than an academic exercise. A fairly obvious prescription, but how difficult in practice! Merle was a master at it.

He was eloquent as well as fastidious in his lectures and writings. Merle was an early visitor to the land of the Soviets, having gone there in the thirties in connection with his thesis on the Comintern. He then served his apprenticeship as instructor and assistant professor, teaching courses on government and business. At that time Soviet government was taught by Bruce Hopper. Bruce, a veteran of the Lafayette Escadrille, had impressed Lowell with his student oration at a post World War I commencement. In the twenties he served as America's only member of the intelligence service in Moscow. American correspondents' account of their travels in the USSR of that period have occasionally a passage like "I suspected that I was being followed by the OGPU (the KGB of the day) and asked Bruce to meet me at the bar at the Metropol."

From that location, Hopper moved to the safer environs of Harvard. On passing the presidency to James Conant, Lowell extracted from him the promise that he would appoint the gallant former pilot to a tenured spot on the faculty. Conant did so despite strong opposition by the Government Department, which afterward in a heartless manner kept refusing to recommend him for further promotion. He remained for thirty years and retired as an associate professor.

To be sure, his lectures tended to be more colorful than enlightening. The most famous of these, and very popular among the undergraduates, sought to epitomize Russian history as alternating between violent popular excitement (revolution) and apathy. You have a Russian moujik (peasant) drowsing on the stove (for most of the audience, this was both titillating and incomprehensible: how can one sleep on a stove?). Suddenly he is seized by an irresistible impulse, jumps down, and launches into a frantic dance. Then, as time goes by, his energy oozes away, a few last steps, and then back onto the stove. There you have the sense of Russian history!

Merle's course on the USSR, which he started after the war, was cast in a more serious vein. Merle's original views must have been, I would guess, left of center. Among the books assigned for the course was Sir John Maynard's *Russia in Flux*. Though the author was far from being a Communist—he was a Fabian socialist, and in fact an old Russia hand—it still continued the nonsense about Stalin as a benevolent father of his people, and other misconceptions quite popular in the thirties among the British Labour Party. But Merle's scholarly integrity and meticulousness soon led him to arrive at a true assessment of the Soviet system. No one else I have known has come as close to being an ideal combination of teacher, scholar and a good citizen of the academic community as Merle Fainsod; and it is strange that up to now he has not been commemorated at Harvard by the naming of a professorship or an institute after him. While I wrote my dissertation with Bill Elliot, it was Merle who guided my first steps as a teacher; and my debt to him is great.

And then there were my colleagues and contemporaries: Louis Hartz, with whose brilliance and tragedy I will deal later, and Bob McCloskey, my closest friend, whose premature death, I am strongly convinced, was at least partly caused by his agitation over what was happening to the university in the late sixties and seventies. There was also Sam Beer, a dashing and athletic figure, a sky diver well into his fifties and now in his eighties, still the leading connoisseur of British politics in this country; all splendid companions and colleagues.

SB: When I first met Adam shortly after WWII, I said to myself: Who is this fellow—this arrogant, unfriendly German with the thick glasses. I could not have been more wrong on all counts. Yes, perhaps Adam's eyes were weak. Yet I remember his reminiscing that once he had received a prize, a silver star, I think it was, for marksmanship with a rifle! At any rate, Adam became and remained for half-a-century, one of my closest and wisest friends. I do not, however, put all the blame on myself for those first impressions. Adam was not a person to exert the slightest effort to make a good first impression. He would not lift a little finger in that sort of self-advancement, and, here is the puzzle, indeed, the paradox of Adam. On the one hand, he was something of a genius when it came to understanding the human motivations displayed in his great works—for instance, in his *Lenin* and *Stalin*, and of their associated barbarians, to use his characterization. Nor would I want to exclude that extraordinary novel on the Kirov affair. He also was no less penetrating in his assessments of people, unfavorable, or favorable...He was not a constant naysayer of colleagues and other candidates for promotion on the academic ladder...On the other hand, he refused to use these powers of empathy to exploit or to manipulate or even simply to assuage the feelings of persons who could harm or help him. In his behavior, in short, he was just not there, as a politician or a courtier. He was a supremely penetrating observer and severe moral judge of human conduct. But—he was not an activist—he was not a participant. He could not be drawn into the battles, petty or grand, inevitable in academic politics. The same aloofness led him, while still untenured, repeatedly, to pass by the chairman of the Government Department with no salutation – no sign of recognition –Nor would he write and publish simply to get into print. For instance, there was a gap in time between his earlier and his later publications. The then dean of the faculty, in an act of bureaucratic insolence, made this an occasion to call in Adam and wonder brusquely why he was not publishing. Adam was not one to explain or complain. He simply continued on his way, writing and publishing a few years later...his greatest works...

One exception to Ulam's aloofness (there were others) was personal. He had good friends, and as a man of hearty appetite, he enjoyed their camaraderie. In the early postwar years, a half-dozen or so of the young and untenured members of the department would, from time-to-time, get together for a night of overindulgence in steak, whiskey, and disputation. Our favorite spot was deep in the woods not far from Walden Pond, where we could make an unholy spectacle of ourselves without fear of observation or interruption. We would sit around a campfire and eat, drink, and argue violently about politics – German rearmament in the 1950s, whether totalitarianism had any meaning; did Mirabeau cause the French Revolution...until far into the night..."

Samuel H. Beer, Eaton Professor of the Science of Government, Emeritus, Harvard University

My non-professional friendships also flourished. The first year as a graduate student, I resided in Claverly Hall. Its main janitor, who always wore a derby hat and a pince-nez, told stories about a young student who lived there around the turn of the century: Franklin D. Roosevelt. The building at the time was a veritable United Nations in miniature. There were several Chinese students. One clearly was not the typical student: the middle-aged and somewhat mysterious

Mr. Wu, reputed to be a high official in Chiang Kai-shek's regime. At times he could be seen bringing into his quarters, with what's usually described as the inscrutable Oriental smile, mature and elegant ladies, obviously from the upper strata of Boston society. My immediate neighbor on the other side of an especially thin wall, a Frenchman, was less mysterious; he used to bring in young boys.

It was with the Chinese students that I developed friendly contacts. One also named Wu (how with that scarcity of last names do they make telephone directories in China?) was a frequent companion. He taught me a lot about his country, though as of 1945 he did not in the slightest anticipate the victory of the Communists. One of the three brothers Pu, also in Claverly, would subsequently become a dignitary under Mao. "My" Wu was eager to go back to his homeland and to put his knowledge at the service of his people. The fall of the Nationalist regime evidently changed his plans. A talented architect, he was to become a professor at Yale.

My circle of friends and acquaintances was enlarged in the second year of my graduate work. From a largely Chinese milieu, I entered upon what might be called my Greek phase. My conduit to it were Andreas Papandreou and his charming wife Christina, he studying for a Ph.D. in economics, she for an M.D. Through them I was then introduced to a number of their compatriots in Cambridge, almost all of them children of former ministers and other officials in their country. They also shared two other characteristics: fairly radical views and skill at table tennis, both activities evidently quite widespread in the American School in Athens that they all had attended. Andreas was a delightful companion, "both for prayer and for dance," as the Polish proverb has it, i.e., both for serious intellectual discussion and for fun-seeking. His company assured one special treatment in the Greek restaurants (his father was a very important politician), and he was an enthusiastic attendee of Boston's then meager array of nightclubs.

How difficult it is to predict young people's future careers! None of the Greek phalanx in Cambridge seemed to be so thoroughly Americanized as Andreas, who had served in the U.S. Navy during the war. The next twenty years or so seemed to confirm that impression. He advanced in his profession, becoming a professor of economics, first at Minnesota and then at Berkeley, California. But then his aged father summoned him home to be his political aide and Andreas abandoned an established career for the vicissitudes of

Balkan politics. When Greece fell under a rightist dictatorship, he found himself in jail, possibly facing something worse until rescued through the intercession of President Johnson.

With the military regime overthrown, Papandreou soon found himself Prime Minister of a leftist government, its ostentatiously anti-American rhetoric causing occasional trouble for the State Department. And, after an interlude in opposition and after having endured a dangerous operation, evidently resuscitated by marriage to a much younger lady, my erstwhile companion became Prime Minister of Greece, and died only recently.

Most of my other Greek acquaintances disappeared after graduate school, the majority of them jettisoning their radicalism and reverting to the norm of the native country as important businessmen and officials. One who had chosen an academic career in America and remained my lifelong friend was Roy Macridis. A student of French politics, Roy embodied worthily the French tradition of "gauchisme," i.e., opposition to any authority in power, be it in government, at home or abroad, one's university, etc. Small and pugnacious, prone to violent denunciation of whoever at the moment was his target, whether in the academic or political establishment, Roy, who eventually landed at Brandeis, had a devoted circle of friends in Cambridge. They enjoyed his philippics, even when, as not infrequently, they were directed against themselves. I witnessed at times some very heated disputes between Roy and our common Turkish friend Lahoute Uzman, whose brilliant career in research and as a professor at Harvard Medical School was sadly cut off by his death in his middle thirties. "How can you take all those attacks from Roy," I once asked Lahoute semi-seriously. "Never mind, my fathers used to flog his fathers," replied the descendent of the long-time masters of the Balkans.

Among other unusual personalities whom I got to know well among my fellow-students was Pierre Trudeau, a handsome, finely featured French Canadian. Pierre is another example of how difficult it is to predict a young man's future political inclinations and views (and he was, in his late twenties, not that young). Delivered with an aristocratic air, his opinions on government, rarely voiced, evinced a vague sort of Christian anarchism. He was about the last person I could envision engaging in the hurly-burly of democratic politics. He left Harvard in 1947, intending to travel extensively, if I recall, in the Far East. For all the occasional reports about his subsequent activities, I was astounded many years later to read of him becoming the leader of the Liberal Party and the Prime Minister of Canada, not only a skillful but also a tough-minded politician who coped with separatist terror and kept his native Quebec from seceding.

Because of Pierre's good looks and air of mystery, it was understandable that I found myself under pressure from my women acquaintances to be introduced to him. But to their disappointment, his behavior on such occasions, though invariably charming, was rather distant, something that I understood was also to change in his later years. After a long interval, I did have the pleasure of seeing Pierre again, the last time a few years ago after I gave some lectures in Montreal. His charm and good looks have persisted.

Yes, there's the suggestion here that my life in Cambridge was not limited to studies and male companionship. Nearby Radcliffe College was, in practical fact, an integral part of Harvard. The silly tradition of having separate lectures for (undergraduate) men and women was given up by 1945. For a few more years, the final examinations were still segregated; if allowed to learn together, the two genders were still not supposed to sweat together. Gone by my time was also the social and sexual snobbery that dictated that Harvard boys seek dates in remote Vassar or Smith rather than next door among the alleged bluestockings of Radcliffe. That "tradition," I suspect, was more honored in the breach than in the reality and if there was anything to it, it resulted from the numerical disproportion between male and female contingents, of three or four to one. No one as yet dreamed that coeducation should imply cohabitation— not, God forbid!—in the literal sense, but simply in the sense of joint housing. Radcliffe dorms were much inferior to the Harvard Houses. And what would today's feminist say to the arrangement that also would persist for some years: ladies were supposed to enter the Faculty Club by the back entrance and were confined to a separate room. There were still parietal rules that limited inter-gender visiting hours and were based on a dubious proposition that sexual passion was unlikely to be aroused between 2 and 7 p.m. rather than, possibly, during the hours before or the hours after.

All such barriers to progress were of course completely ineffective in achieving their purpose, especially in view of the mass appearance of the veterans, often quite a bit older than the usual run of undergraduates. I doubt that even today in the era of no rules and of sexual liberation, male-female contacts of all kinds are any more frequent than they were in 1945-48. Difficulties put in the way of such contacts made them only more exciting and aesthetically satisfying.

My own great romance began fittingly enough in the reading room of Widener Library. There was an undergraduate of Anglo-Irish background. Her passion for horses and dogs led me to attend innumerable exhibitions of those two species, as well as the racetrack. At one dog show in 1946, there was a special cage enclosing a perfectly ordinary looking German shepherd, an inscription informing the public that the dog had been captured from the Japanese forces in the Pacific. "He even looks Japanese," I heard one young girl say. But we attended also more culturally elevated events: the theater, the Boston Symphony, then in its glory under Serge Koussevitzky. The romance lasted two years and though it ended tempestuously, we have remained good friends to this day. My graduate studies concluded at exactly the same time: this was the Harvard Commencement (1947) at which General Marshall announced his great plan to save democratic Europe.

I entered upon my teaching career in an appropriately monastic mood.

SU: "...At that time, Adam was brilliantly concluding his studies at Harvard, and came to visit us in Los Alamos. I, who had been conditioned by the pre-war scarcity of jobs, was pessimistic about his chances of finding one. When I asked him what his plans were, he answered, "I'll get an instructorship, of course." I felt dubious. He must have read the skepticism in the expression on my face, because I saw in his eyes that he took me for a pessimistic old dodo. He was right, because he immediately obtained an instructor's position at Harvard and has remained there ever since..."

9

A Young Instructor

Harvard personalities Instructor in the Government Dept....Goof re Henry Kissinger...Three years with the British Empire. A famous anthropologist at the helm of the RCC...Course on Marx...Eliot House colleagues...Harvard anecdotes...Kennan in Russia...Stan's illness...Climbing mountains with Edward Teller...

Before I taught a course of my own as an instructor in Government, I went through an apprenticeship conducting a section of an introductory survey. The undergraduate newspaper, *The Crimson*, published every fall the "Confidential (obviously a misnomer) Guide," evaluating the previous year's courses and their teachers. Its judgment on my performance was succinct and severe: "Ulam: a dull man and a hard grader." I may well have had a disgruntled editor of the paper among my students. Such was my self-confidence that the censure did not shake me. But as I started teaching my own course, I wondered whether the wretched "evaluation" would indeed ruin my reputation among the undergraduates. At the first session of my class I counted twelve people in attendance, at the second, seven, the third, four. I was seized by panic. What do I do if nobody at all turns up? Do I pretend that I am still teaching a course or do I resign my instructorship and seek some other employment? Harvard students have a week or two to shop for courses before they make their final choices. Great was my relief when at the next session some twenty appeared, and the attendance stabilized around that figure. Still, it was hardly an accolade; my friend Louis Hartz would have hundreds in his classes. Other young colleagues like Sam Beer were also among the most popular teachers.

My morale would have been bolstered had I realized that at least one of those in my course on the British Empire was slated for greatness. Henry Kissinger, though about my age, was then a senior, but already endowed with that self-assertiveness that would help his future dazzling career. According to an old custom, the students enclosed in their final examination a self-addressed postcard, on which the instructor or his assistant would write their grade for the course. I must have performed that task somewhat absent-mindedly, for one afternoon my telephone rang and a deep, Teutonically accented voice interrupted my reverie: "Dr. Ulam, I do not know whether this is a joke, but my card says D minus." I was tempted to say something impolite, but being a conscientious teacher, I checked Henry's name in a copy of the official grade sheet I had sent to the Registrar. It was with some embarrassment that I had to explain to my future colleague and good friend that it had been a slip of the pen, and that his grade was indeed an A. In fact, he had an excellent record and graduated from Harvard with highest honors.

After teaching my British Empire course for three years, I felt that it was time for a change. "I will not preside over the liquidation of the British Empire," Mr. Churchill had said indignantly during the war. Well, pedagogically that was what I was doing; for every few months a piece of my course would, so to speak, fall off, the name of the Empire changing first to the British Commonwealth and then simply to the Commonwealth. I decided, I told my friends, to shift to an expanding rather than to a contracting subject, and to teach about the Soviet Union. I added that I expected its fall to coincide with my retirement from teaching, which I calculated to come about 1992. The Soviet Empire did not let me down. It imploded in 1991. But with my reputation as a destroyer of imperialism, my friends were begging me by the late eighties not to start teaching about the United States.

On the serious side, I bewailed Britain's loss of power and prestige. For all of its inherent flaws, e.g., the case of Ireland, the anachronism of colonialism, Great Britain's policies had for a long time promoted the cause of freedom and world peace. I was irritated by those Americans who, during and after the war, equated British imperialism with that of the Soviet Union, with the United States supposed to remain impartial in dealings with both. FDR's enormous merits and achievements cannot entirely excuse his giving currency to this obsolete image of the British holding on greedily and oppressively to other nations. In the first place, it should have been obvious to anyone studying the subject that no democracy would be either able or willing to hold on to such rule in the postwar era of growing literacy among colonial peoples, and vastly advanced international communication and television. Some colonial possessions, notably India, should have been emancipated much sooner than they actually were. Others, judging by the oppression and political and economic chaos that succeeded colonial rule and have endured ever since, would have profited by a longer apprenticeship in self-government.

In the case of Britain itself, I felt that while the Labour Party should be given its due for initiating much needed social reforms, its puritanical anti-capitalism, its mania for nationalizing industry, and its narrow class view had blocked what might have been a British economic "miracle," similar to that which regenerated postwar Germany and Japan. My basic Anglophilia remains unchanged despite my experiences with English cuisine and heating systems.

My secession from the Commonwealth was facilitated by the establishment at Harvard in 1948 of the Russian Research Center. That and Columbia's Russian Institute, inaugurated some time before, contributed enormously to creating in this country what was missing before: a critical mass of students of politics, economics and history, etc., of that country and culture. The first director of the Center, and the man who set it on the right course, was Clyde Kluckhohn, a man of great intensity and a renowned anthropologist and specialist on the life of the Navajo Indians. The fact that back then he did not know much about Russia was, in the opinion of the directors of the foundation which financed the Center, Kluckhohn's primary qualification for the job: he was unbiased. My first meeting with him left me with mixed feelings. Despite his thoroughly un-Slavic Midwestern roots, there was something "Russian" about him: he bore a striking resemblance to the actor who in the Soviet film Peter the Great played the role of Peter's unbalanced son Tsarevich Alexis, whom his father ordered strangled because of his unfitness to rule.

My misgivings were almost immediately dissipated. Kluckhohn revealed himself as a masterful administrator and a delightful colleague. Like all successful managers of academic enterprises, he knew how to choose the right people, allow them complete freedom in their pursuits, and bolster their morale whenever any difficulties or personal problems interfered with their work. He could inspire deep affection in his collaborators. Again, it is sad that Harvard has not suitably memorialized this man, who though a stranger to the field, helped raise Soviet and Russian studies to a notably high level.

My new teaching duties centered on lectures and a seminar on Soviet foreign policy, though occasionally I would teach the course on Russian domestic politics usually given by Fainsod. From my initial interest in English Socialism, on which I wrote my dissertation and first book, I progressed to the study of socialism in general. This led to my course on Marxism, hitherto not given in my department.

My approach touched on the question of Marxist doctrine, which J.M. Keynes, the great English economist, branded somewhat unfairly "illogical and dull," and how it succeeded in influencing mass movements, not, as Marx had thought, in highly industrialized countries like his second homeland, England, but on the contrary, in countries just undergoing intensive industrialization, like Germany in the last quarter of the 19th century and Russia early in the 20th. I sketched an answer in my *Unfinished Revolution*, published in 1960. Its main point was that Marxism is attuned to the mentality of a peasant or craftsman compelled by economic factors to become an industrial worker, and whose hitherto stable if primitive existence becomes subject to the capricious forces of the market and changing technology. Hence his susceptibility to anti-capitalism; while in a mature industrial economy the factory worker works to improve his lot not through revolution, but through labor unions and the ballot. Marxism is thus not wrong, but simply anachronistic in trying to superimpose on the modern social welfare state the atmosphere of the early Industrial Revolution, when there was no democracy, no union power, and hardly any social legislation. And Marxism actually is an intricate intellectual doctrine; notwithstanding Lord Keynes, it certainly is not dull. Its character explains the seductiveness to intellectuals of its main current—Communism—despite its moral and by now also economic and political bankruptcy.

Unlike my course on the liquidation of the British Empire, the topics of Soviet foreign policy and socialism both drew a respectable clientele. I like lecturing to an audience of between 80-120 students. A much larger class often becomes unmanageable. A smaller group, unless it is a very specialized course, does not provide enough boost to the lecturer's ego. Personalized student-teacher contact, which is sometimes excessively extolled, was at Harvard provided by seminars at the graduate level and, for the undergraduates, by the group and individual tutorials. To promote student-teacher rapprochement, Harvard and Yale in the early thirties instituted a residence system modeled after that of Oxford and Cambridge.The Houses (called Colleges at Yale) shelter and feed students, as well as a number of faculty members and graduate students, usually acting as tutors. There are also non-resident tutors and senior faculty members attached to each House.

In a probably apocryphal story, President Lowell was asked during the planning phase of the new system whether the faculty should not be provided with parking spaces near each house. No, said Lowell, the tutors' chauffeurs would bring their cars when needed. Such fantasies aside, the Houses did provide fairly luxurious amenities, but, alas, only until the war. There were spacious quarters, table service in the dining room, and maid service. After the war, overcrowding and rising costs put an end to the earlier gentility. Cafeteria-style dining, with meals placed directly on plastic trays, and gradual elimination of the cleaning personnel became the rule.

In other respects, the Houses still differed from the general run of dormitories when I moved into one of them in 1946. In 1950 came a transaction similar to that of two baseball teams: I moved from Winthrop House to Eliot House in a trade for McGeorge Bundy of future fame as Security Advisor to Presidents Kennedy and Johnson. Bundy went to Winthrop as Senior Tutor.

Several things drew me to Eliot. My close friend John Conway, a handsome, dark-eyed Canadian of sturdy build and sterling character who had lost an arm in the war, was currently a resident tutor there. Sam Beer, the distinguished specialist in British government and popular teacher of Social Sciences II was also on the staff. In addition, the House had among its faculty several people specializing in Russian and Soviet subjects.

Once settled there, I found other reasons to congratulate myself on my choice. Eliot then had an atmosphere unique among the Houses, approximating the original purpose of the system, that is, to temper mass education inevitable in a big university with closer-knit communities of students and scholars created within. This happy result was largely the achievement of Eliot's extraordinary housemaster, John Finley, professor of Greek, famous throughout the student community for his popular course known among the undergraduates as "Hum.II," the Epic and the Novel, of which he taught the first half. Whereas other housemasters required their resident tutors to "interact" with their students, lunch with them, etc., Finley gave his staff complete freedom. The result was that while elsewhere, faculty members avoided frequent appearances in the dining halls and at other functions, Eliot hosted each day a large number of faculty, including the most renowned figures in the university, who, free of pressure, did in fact commune often with the undergraduates. John himself knew each of his three hundred or so flock by name, and without slackening his scholarly pursuits was indefatigable in helping them to gain admission to graduate schools or pursue other career paths.

The esprit de corps extended to the House employees, some of who had come to resemble old retainers of an Oxford college. The American spirit was, however, worthily maintained during my seven years' residence by the superintendent, a retired chief petty officer. By analogy to the Navy, he tended to consider the undergraduates as the swabbies, and the tutors as officers. One spring day after the end of the academic year, I saw him supervising his crew in policing the courtyard for broken glass. The tutors, as he put it to me, "have their women folk here in the summer and some of them like to run around barefoot."

One may have already deduced that for all of its numerous merits, Eliot House did not quite resemble an egalitarian democracy. Indeed, while at the time about half of the Harvard students came from private schools, at Eliot House, the proportion was usually higher. But so was the number of those interested mostly in the humanities and so-called social sciences. Each House in those days attracted a somewhat different clientele: one, the budding scientists; another, the athletes; but without being entirely monopolized by a given type. Along with the scions of plutocracy, Eliot also housed occasional representatives of European aristocracy: a Count Potocki, a Prince Lobkowitz. One suite of rooms in 1953 or 1954 epitomized what today would probably be considered the elitism of the place. Three young men living there had famous names: the son of James Joyce, the grandson of Matisse, and a younger son of the Aga Khan. There were also more exotic notables, e.g. a descendent of Indonesian rajas whom I once happened to embarrass. His family, he told me, had been in politics for eight hundred years. "And what did they do before?" I asked. He didn't know.

It was, however, intellectual achievement rather than social snobbery that was the outstanding achievement of the House. Almost every year the highest proportion of those graduating with the highest honors, especially in history and literature, were resident there;

and at times, more Rhodes scholars came out of Eliot than were selected from any of several prestigious universities.

LB: "I met Adam soon after I came to Harvard College, in the fall of 1950, as a sixteen-year-old freshman. The reason for our meeting was not any passion I had at the time for modern Russian history, although eventually, in the spring of my senior year I did take his course on the Russian revolution and its aftermath. I sought out Adam because Stasia Menkes, the wife of the painter Zygmund Menkes, originally from Lwów like Adam, his brother Stas, and his parents, was Adam's first cousin. The Menkeses were my parents' best friends. They sent me to see him.

Of course, Adam intimidated me. But I stood my ground. I really wanted to know this blond, blue-eyed, good-natured giant, decked out in his perennial J. Press suits and striped bow ties. He struck me as ineffably dashing. And I admired his wit, his willingness to say anything that came into his mind, which was seldom similar to what came into the minds of other people, and, of course, his luminous intelligence. The only somewhat encouraging human failing I could discern in Adam was his Polish accent, thicker than mine although he had lived in the United States much longer.

By the time I moved into Eliot House, Adam and I were friends and had lunch there quite often, and sometimes dinner. Years later, when I was in the Law School, our lunches moved to a restaurant off Harvard Square called, I believe, the Oxford Grill. I remember vividly and with some embarrassment my efforts on those occasions to keep up with Adam's consumption of martinis..."

Louis Begley, a writer and lawyer, lives in New York City.

The high quality and sociability of the students was matched by that of the faculty. Three world-famous economists were frequent visitors: Edward Chamberlain, Gottfried von Haberler, and Alexander Gershchenkron. The last-named, an old-fashioned intellectual of wiry stature, who wore thick steel-rimmed glasses, was born in Russia in 1904. Viennese-educated, he was probably the outstanding economic historian of his generation, a man of enormous erudition and great personal charm. Occasionally, as the following story shows, he allowed his thirst for knowledge to prevail over his Viennese upbringing. While on a plane, he was engrossed in a Bulgarian text. When presented with a box of chocolates by his neighbor, he chose one with a mechanical "thank-you," without taking his eyes off Bulgarian agriculture at the end of the 19th century. It was only when he heard, in a low throaty voice, "Didn't your mother warn you not to take candy from strangers?" that he looked at the woman in the next seat. It was Marlene Dietrich.

A great admirer of America, Alex carried his admiration to the point of praising our pre-college education as free from Continental formality, though even at that time the American high school was not a particular credit to this country. And as will be seen, he was greatly shaken by what transpired at the universities in the late sixties.

Equally colorful in a different way was an ebullient, dark-eyed professor of Italian origin, Renato Poggioli, who was professor of Russian literature. His was a rather unusual case: while able to discern—in print—the slightest nuances in the writings of Tolstoy or Dostoevsky, he simply could not speak Russian. That complicated his life in the Slavic Department, some of whose members did not know English, of which Renato had full, if heavily Italian-accented command. His pronunciation could be described as sui generis, often making it hard for his students to understand him. He himself sometimes prefaced his remarks by saying, with a characteristically flamboyant Italian gesture, "Excuse my Eliot House accent."

As he adhered to the Continental radical tradition, authority of all kinds was suspect in Poggioli's mind. At the lunches on Friday, the students at this pre-Vatican II time were offered the choice of a fish or a meat course. The food in general was rather bad, but Renato would choose even the most unappetizing-appearing meat. To eat fish on Friday would give the impression of his yielding to "il clericalismo." At a general faculty meeting of the university, it was once discussed whether Harvard should abide by some federal regulation. It was the McCarthy era, and a few members discoursed eloquently about the threat to freedom inherent in complying with any government rule. But it is a trivial thing, President Pusey tried to explain: all it required was for a university clerk to lick a stamp for some documents. The gravity of the discussion was then shaken when Professor Poggioli got up, raising his finger in admonition: "Let me point out, Mr. President—you begin by leeking ze stamps—you end up by leeking something else."

It is hard today to realize that it was virtually impossible for a private American citizen to travel within the Soviet domain, i.e., not only in the USSR, but in most of Eastern Europe as well, as long as Stalin lived and for several years afterwards. Even those going there on official business were subject to chicaneries. I recall vividly meeting with George Kennan in 1952. He had just been appointed ambassador to Moscow. In his talk with a group of Russian specialists at Harvard, this brilliant man, the author of the strategy of containment in the Cold War, was not without hope about his mission. He had been there before and during the Second World War, was quite at home in Russian culture, and had a genuine affection for the Russian people. It was only reasonable for him to assume that he would do some good, perhaps change a bit that posture of isolation and hostility to the West adopted by the Kremlin. When I saw him again one year later he appeared to have aged by at least ten years. As he described in his memoirs, he had been made virtually a prisoner in the American embassy, his every step outside followed by the security police; contact with individual Russians, possible if difficult on previous missions, now utterly out of the question. Hopes of putting his great knowledge of and sympathy for the people to use in improving at least the communication between the two countries was frustrated: he was barred access not only to Stalin but also to anyone except quite inferior officials. To crown such indignities, the Soviets used a remark made by Kennan, while outside the USSR, an understandable if rather undiplomatic criticism, to demand his recall as ambassador. His resumé of his experiences and views on the future of Soviet-American relations, given in a talk at Harvard, was quite depressing. Kennan was not to recover his optimism on the latter count for some years.

Well, I cannot say that my inability to visit the objects of my studies in those years caused me great sorrow, since I could and did travel with clear conscience in Western Europe. England and France, though still suffering from the postwar economic hardships at that time, furnished fresh cultural and recreational delights.

I would meet my brother in Paris when he and Françoise visited with those few members of her family who survived the war. But I also made regular trips to Los Alamos, N. M., to which Stan had returned in 1946.Wishing to go back to teaching, he had left the birthplace of the Bomb at the war's end, and taken a professorship at Southern California. But his stay there was short and unhappy. One day—was it the fall of 1945?—I received a call from Françoise telling me that Stan had been unconscious for two days, and the doctors could not diagnose his life-threatening condition. Then another call: still in a coma; and surgery on the brain did not ameliorate the illness; the doctors would try again. I was about to fly to be at his side when wonderful news arrived: he recovered consciousness and was getting well. It had been West Coast encephalitis, often fatal or completely debilitating, but in this case, thank God, the recovery was complete, and Stan was not to suffer any after-effects. Southern California then became associated for them with the near-tragedy, and he accepted the urgings of his colleagues to return to Los Alamos.

I went there first in 1946 or 47. That celebrated place has since then taken on the appearance of a typical Southwestern town, but in those early years it looked to me, coming from the East, quite exotic. The living facilities were still rather primitive. When J. Robert Oppenheimer had chosen the New Mexico mesa for the laboratory, the only housing there had been a small private school; and the new quarters had to be constructed in a hurry. There were thus those strange paradoxes: a primitive-looking village housing the most modern technology for the construction of history's deadliest weapon, the "villagers" being a distinguished group of scientists, many speaking with a variety of accents, living in the neighborhood of the pueblos inhabited by the descendants of this continent's earliest settlers.

The access to Los Alamos was not only restricted (my brother had to get special permission for me), but along a dangerously narrow thirty-mile-long road from Santa Fe, which wound up through the mountains with sheer rock on one side and a horrifying precipice on the other. Incautiously, my brother entrusted the task of chauffeuring me on my initial visit to a friend of his, notorious for driving on the serpentine path as if he were on a four-lane highway. The terror I experienced on this trip, plus the high altitude (7500 ft.), had an immediate and unfortunate effect. Even before I unpacked, we went to a cocktail party; and there, after merely two highballs, I became ill, the only time such a negligible quantity of alcohol had this effect on me.

That initial disgrace was followed by a very pleasant stay amid New Mexico scenery, imposing in its severe beauty. I made the acquaintance of my little niece. The eminent scientists' social gifts did not always match their fame, but still I was gratified by talking with men whose names would always figure prominently in the annals of physics and mathematics, such as John von Neumann, a giant of the science, and—rather unusual for a mathematician—very conversant with political and social problems.

Like every small boy in Poland, I had devoured the novels of Karl May, the most exciting of them dealing with the Wild West and the author-hero's extravagant adventures among the native American tribes (in fact, May never left his native Germany, and my enthusiasm for him also unreasonably evaporated on learning that he was a favorite author of young Hitler). Alas, the Indian settlements one saw in New Mexico were striking mainly for their poverty and were quite different from the romantic visions of my boyhood.

Perhaps one exception was a venerable Indian who lived in a house down in the valley with an equally aged lady, who had come,

I was told, from one of the prominent families of Philadelphia. Their live-in romance had been of very long-standing. They ran a little tea shop, frequented by people from the "Hill," i.e. Los Alamos. Once on a visit there, I was baffled when our host, upon learning that I had just returned from France, asked, "How was Paris?" It turned out that he had been there about fifty years earlier while traveling with the Buffalo Bill circus.

My sister-in-law has a passion for hiking and climbing mountains. Stan, as he confessed in his autobiography, was less than fond of that form of athleticism; and I share his weakness. Yet there was no escape when she and other ladies of similar inclination commandeered their men folk for an expedition to some towering heights. On one such march, Johnny von Neumann, who also shared the Ulam aversion to the sport, dropped out soon after the start, followed shortly afterwards by my brother. Being the youngest in the group, I felt I had to go on, but then the conviction of the uselessness of such exercises grew upon me; and I gave up, while the rest of the company marched on. Alone in the wilderness, I pondered the chances of being assaulted by rattlers or bears, but somehow instinct guided me down the right path until I came upon Johnny and Stan sitting on a rock, discussing theories of probability.

In view of the above, I still cannot imagine what possessed me on another visit to offer actually to climb a mountain. This time there were just two companions: Ed Teller, of future hydrogen bomb fame, and his ten or twelve-year-old son. Set in a public park, the mountain was reputedly the place to which Indian elders had repaired to discuss issues of the day away from their wives and lesser citizens. Since the modern tourist is not likely to possess the mountain goat agility of the Indians, the park administration had installed ladders to facilitate the ascent. There would be a short wooden ladder that creaked under my weight, then a few more steps on the rock, and then another ladder, and so on. Having arrived at the summit, I realized the folly of my enterprise: there seemed no way I could climb down; they would have had to call a helicopter! Then a feeling of shame overcame my fear. Here was Teller, who had lost a foot in an accident, and a mere child. If they could get down, so must I; and I did.

Perhaps it was twenty-five years or so later, in the late seventies, that I participated in a seminar organized by Nelson Rockefeller, then Vice-President, on what is usually described as the burning issues of the day. The question came up of what to do when confronted with imminent danger of a nuclear attack. How could our cities be evacuated? An elderly man got up to speak. He looked familiar, but at first I couldn't identify him, nor his accent. Then it dawned on me that it was Ed Teller, my companion in the mountaineering expedition. The evacuation, he was saying, would not be that complicated: at a signal, you turn all the traffic lights green along the routes leading out of the cities. I couldn't believe my ears!

After 1950, my visits to Los Alamos became less frequent. Stan now traveled more; on two occasions he was a visiting professor at Harvard and MIT, and in 1957 he took a professorship at Colorado. One time we had plans to get together in Washington. We were to meet at the Cosmos Club, where George Gamow was staying. He was a Russian-born physicist whom I hadn't met but who was Stan's great friend. At about ten in the morning., I knocked on Gamow's door. A huge man, about six-foot six, met me with just the word "Gamow." He then filled to the brim two water glasses of dubious cleanliness with bourbon, offered me one, and began: "Let me tell you about the troubles I have with my wife." Fortunately, my brother arrived before I had to listen to the full story of my host's unhappy marriage.

On his retirement, Stan and Françoise moved to Santa Fe. Stan not only continued to work, belying the legend that mathematicians exhaust their inventiveness after thirty or so, but he developed new interests in biology; wrote his autobiography; hosted mathematicians from all over the world, especially enjoying visits from Polish scientists, which now became possible; and still acted as a consultant on the "Hill." His charisma and joie de vivre stayed with him, and he remained young in appearance and spirit. I last saw him in April 1984 in New York, when he joined my friends Anka and Louis Begley for dinner just before going to England for a brief visit. He was in a very good mood, full of energy and his usual effervescent charm. It was at the end of his return trip, having just arrived back at his house in Santa Fe, when he complained to Françoise of a headache and then collapsed, dying almost instantaneously.

Some of his papers are still to be published. His many contributions to science have been acclaimed in numerous publications and places throughout the world. What he meant to me as a brother, friend, and mentor in loco parentis in my youth, cannot be put into words.

10

Implications of the Cold War

Early Cold War...the anxious 50s...An event in the Cold War with momentous future implications...Insights on Stalin..Significance of the "loss" of China...Krushchev: his policies of bluff and bluster

Whatever the joys and sorrows of the postwar decade, I kept at work writing and teaching. Much of my work focused on the early period of the Cold War. For a democracy, that first phase posed an almost intractable dilemma: how do you deal with an enemy who without being reckless is almost nonchalant about provoking you and seems to believe, as Stalin put it, that the A-bomb can scare only those with weak nerves. In the US there was Mr. Kennan's doctrine of containment, which advised patience as well as alertness in the face of the Soviet threat. But outside Western Europe, containment did not seem to be working. Communism, which at that time was believed (correctly) to be just an extension of Soviet power, was on the march: China in 1948-49, the Communist insurrection in Greece, etc. And even in the West, the blockade of West Berlin, though lifted after a year by the Soviets, revealed an exposed nerve of the West, which could and would be pinched again and again. Neither Western Europe, recovering from the war's devastation, nor the Americans, enjoying their unexpected prosperity, wanted to risk a Third World War. Hence no ultimatum to the Kremlin and no armored train sent through to test the Berlin blockade, as some in Washington wanted.

Such was the awe of the ominous posture assumed by the Soviet Union that neither our leaders nor the public noticed those occasions when tough rhetoric by the West did discourage the Kremlin from new outrages. In March 1946, Mr. Churchill made his famous "Iron Curtain" speech in the presence of Harry Truman: the West

125

must unite to bar further aggression. The *London Times*, in the tradition of appeasement, criticized the former Prime Minister: Why talk so much about things that divide us from the USSR? The West had things to learn from the USSR when it came to social and economic planning. This shabby and by now comic-sounding view was still shared by many in this country. But was it just a coincidence that a month after Churchill's speech the Soviets announced that they would pull their troops from Northern Iran, where they had been installing two puppet regimes in a repetition of their East European scenario?

Mr. Truman did not take up the *Times*'s challenge: instead, there was the Truman Doctrine to protect Greece and Turkey and the miracle of the Marshall Plan, the almost equally momentous American commitment to defend democracy under NATO. But in 1948, with the election ahead, the plucky man from Missouri faltered. His party was torn apart, on the left by Henry Wallace, and from the right by that indestructible figure of American politics, Strom Thurmond; both were to challenge him and virtually assure, as everybody believed, the election of Tom Dewey. In that predicament, the President thought he must make some conciliatory gestures to the Russians. He let slip out that it was not Stalin, but the men around him who were creating all those international troubles. Then, worse, he proposed to send Fred Vinson to Moscow to find out what was on Stalin's mind. The Chief Justice of the United States is the closest this country has ever come to having a High Priest, and presumably the Soviet potentate would find him an appropriate father confessor. It took the threat of resignation by Secretary of State George Marshall to make the President desist from his bizarre idea.

I saw Truman's campaign train in 1948 when it stopped in a little New Mexico town. The President spoke briefly about the mischief wrought by the Republican Congress, and then with "Do you want to meet the Boss?" he introduced his wife. It was quite touching; perhaps he might win after all, I thought.

To this day I cannot understand the tactics of the American Communists (i.e. ultimately, Moscow), in spurring the Progressive Party, which lured Henry Wallace into running. It would have been insane to think he could win; and Tom Dewey, had he won, certainly would not have been any easier on the Soviets than Truman. Well, in any case, all the "experts" were proved wrong. Truman won and went on to demonstrate that if not always fortunate in his public statements, he was not only a skillful politician, but also a great statesman.) Under the circumstances, it was a high compliment when the Soviet press with that social snobbery so frequent with the Communists, dubbed him a "mad haberdasher." Here was a simple citizen, unprepared for his job, rising to the great historical occasion.

Today, the 1950s are often viewed as the time when the US was not only a superpower, but could afford to be one, and that the Americans were much more self-confident than they are now after the end of the Cold War. In fact, it was a nail-chewing time: the Soviets acquired the A-bomb in 1949, we "lost" China, and there were fears about WWIII.

Yet, amazingly enough, all those developments marked the beginning of the process that could not of course be discerned at the time, that of the decline of Communism and the eventual downfall of the Soviet Union. Few in the West placed great importance on the dramatic break between the USSR and Yugoslavia, between Stalin and Tito. So what if a small country broke away from the Kremlin's sway (and did it really matter?), or was it again one of those Communist charades? What was the "gain" of some 18 million Yugoslavs against the "loss" of 400-500 million Chinese by the Free World?

To me, the break between the USSR and Yugoslavia was a momentous event, and putting away for the time being my research on the Soviet Union proper, I undertook a study of the break and of what it might portend for the entire Soviet Bloc and Communism. This study led to the publication in 1952 of my book *Titoism and the Cominform*.

For me, the Soviet-Yugoslav crisis brought out two very significant propositions about Communism, which transcended the importance of the break itself. One was that the old Kremlin despot was losing his grip. Until 1948, no foreign Communist party anywhere else had been so loyal to Moscow and so fanatical in its allegiance to Stalin as the Communist Party of Yugoslavia. It seemed sheer lunacy, or the advent of senility in Stalin, to alienate his most faithful followers; and if he really wanted to get rid of Tito, why try to do so by public denunciation rather than by a slowly unfolding intrigue, as he would have done five or ten years earlier.

The other revelation was how power transformed the psychology of Communists, and not just in the way it affects other breeds of politicians. Here were the Yugoslav acolytes of Moscow, who during the war had had to be told that they should concentrate on fighting the Germans, never mind demonstrating their love for the Fatherland of Socialism, which was only making trouble with Britain and the US. And after the war, Moscow also warned them not to imitate in a hurry everything done in Russia: don't shoot the opposition leaders or improvise collectivization, wait! But here was Stalin now demanding that Tito meekly confess his errors and thus put his head into a noose that the Kremlin would pull tight at a convenient moment. However, the masterful Balkan dictator, who had hitherto readily complied with Moscow's every wish, was not about to comply. And so here was the rub: Stalin did not really want allies or even junior partners in other communist states, just slaves. And now those previously humble agents of his were becoming fond of their own power, perhaps helped by stirrings of nationalism, and did not enjoy being bossed and economically exploited by the Soviets. In fact, Stalinism and true "proletarian internationalism" were incompatible. In 1995, this was quite clear; but in 1952 when my book appeared, I must say, immodestly, it was still dimly perceived in the West, if at all.

When the walls of Yugoslavia failed to crumble after Moscow's trumpeting, Stalin's reaction was ferocious. I mentioned before that it is an over-simplification to interpret Yalta as the surrender of Eastern Europe by Churchill and Roosevelt to Communism. They assumed that Eastern Europe would be a Soviet sphere of interest, but in an old-fashioned pre-World War I sense: namely, those countries would have to defer to Moscow in their foreign and defense policies; but as was the case of Finland, they would be free in their internal politics. And, the Soviets would have let some of them (perhaps with the exception of Yugoslavia) enjoy the precarious but not slavish condition of Finland with its internal democracy. But now those lands had to be Sovietized in a hurry. The heads that rolled were those of the Communist leaders who appeared to depart even slightly from the Moscow line. No more gradual approach to socialism. Nightmarish "trials" followed the pattern of the Moscow trials of the thirties: veteran former sufferers for Communism now confessed ties to Wall Street, Zionism, and Tito. Land had to be collectivized, the churches and democratic parties suppressed.

Still, the "lap-dog of Wall Street," as Tito was elegantly referred to in the Soviet press, held firm. His stand earned him popularity in the nation, while he dealt with Moscow's agents within his party in an efficient Stalinist manner. The Communist regime became more tolerant without ceasing to be authoritarian. One of his closest lieutenants would have gone much further. Milovan Djilas, a fervent Communist in his youth, became gradually converted to democracy. From being Tito's heir-apparent, he became a dissident and political outcast. Years later, I had the pleasure of meeting and becoming friends with this truly noble and idealistic man, to my knowledge, the only Communist official who abandoned his high position and suffered imprisonment, not because he lost out in a struggle for power, but because of his genuine conversion to democracy.

I am writing this chapter against the barrage of news about Bosnia and other tragic developments in what used to be Yugoslavia. Nobody could write about it then without realizing the deep ethnic and religious divisions, which ever since its foundation after WWI, have shaken that unhappy land. In the Second World War, in addition to the brutal German-Italian occupation, there were several civil wars going on at the same time. No other country, with the exception of Poland and possibly the USSR, lost such a large proportion of its population. I have been very fond of my Serbian friends: almost without exception handsome men and women, lively, with a sense of humor. For all the criminality of those in the nineties who provoked a war with the Croats and the Bosnian Muslims, I can't bring myself to believe that the nation as a whole deserves the obloquy then heaped upon it in the US.

When I worked on my book and for years afterward, one could almost believe that for all the negative sides of his rule, Tito had succeeded in forging a Yugoslav national identity. I discussed this with Vladimir Dedijer, also a former Partisan, the official biographer of Tito who later fell out of favor. A huge and powerfully built Montenegrin with an almost childlike zest for adventure, Dedijer gave one a good idea of what the Germans faced in fighting the Partisans. Unlike Djilas, Dedijer was spared by a premature death from witnessing his beloved country's tragedy.

But my contacts with him and Djilas came later; the Serbs and Croats who helped me in my research were not Communist notables but exiles from the Communist regime, who provided me from time to time with assistance in translation.

Titoism was my first book to attract wide attention. Most of the reviews were favorable, but three critical ones stick in my mind. One was a vitriolic attack by a journalist who accused me of being "soft on Communism," as the phrase then went. Another, on the contrary, accused me of being too critical of Tito, who by 1952, for obvious reasons, was becoming quite friendly with the West. The third was by a professor, a specialist on pre-war Yugoslavia, who obviously felt that here was a layman, a mere youth, intruding into his field! Well, it was a good preparation for future experiences of appearing in print.

In the meantime, Korea brought the Cold War to the edge of turning hot. I was to be engaged in a dispute in 1994 with a researcher who maintained that I had been wrong in attributing to Stalin the decision for the invasion of South Korea, her alleged evidence being the discovery in the previously secret Soviet archives of several pleas to the Kremlin by the North's dictator Kim Il Sung for permission to invade the South; thus, according to the researcher, establishing that Stalin was forced to authorize the enterprise. The argument was on its face nonsensical: imagine Stalin being compelled by a minor Communist satrap to do something he hadn't planned, then dutifully furnishing the North Koreans with up-to-date military equipment and Soviet advisors!

It is probably true that the Kremlin had not anticipated the US reaction and full-scale intervention in the war. Once it happened, however, the "genius leader of the World Proletariat" was quite content to let the Chinese Communists pull his chestnuts out of the fire and save the North from conquest by MacArthur. The full cynicism of the Big Brother about its Chinese Younger Brother, the terms used by Beijing during its honeymoon with Moscow, is also well illustrated by recently revealed Soviet and Chinese documents. Here was Mao, with his country still in disarray after forty years of civil wars and foreign intervention, being urged to challenge the world's greatest power, possibly risking nuclear devastation. As usual (except in Tito's case), Stalin was devious in his communications with the Chinese comrades: if Mao did not mind having the American troops on his border, that would be all right with the Russians.

The destruction of North Korea might give the Americans second thoughts about what to do on the Chinese mainland, but if Beijing wasn't worried, neither was Moscow. However, if the Chinese intervened, the Russians would help, a promise on which Stalin at first reneged. When the USSR finally felt constrained to assist the Chinese "volunteers," it did so by selling to the People's Republic of China modern war equipment and providing some air units whose pilots wore Chinese uniforms.

The "loss" of China was, at the time, a bitterly disputed issue in American politics. We should not worry about Mao's followers conquering their country, the old "China hands" were saying in the 1940s; they would be different from the Soviets. And different they turned out to be: fanatical and much more anti-Western in the 1950s and 1960s than the more prudent Soviets. They were to become "agrarian reformers," but only after their insane "Great Leap Forward" and the creation of rural communes had led to the greatest famine in history. (If we treat them right, it was said, they will turn to the United States for help—And so they did, but not until the 1970s, and not out of great trust in American democracy, but because Mao and his colleagues were by now scared of their "Big Brother.")

And the final irony: by "losing" China, we may well have saved the American economy. Imagine capitalism prevailing in China in 1950: we would have Taiwan multiplied by fifty by now. Who would buy American or Japanese automobiles rather than those produced by those hard-working millions? And so we must not be complacent: that big country may yet produce new surprises.

When I came to write my history of Soviet foreign policy in the 1960s, the Sino-Soviet split was already a fact. I could thus speculate whether the greatest victory of Communism since 1917, China, would not ultimately turn out to be not only an embarrassment for the USSR, but a truly disastrous setback. (There was no way in which the two Communist giants could harmoniously coexist or remain allies. The Soviet Union would not acquiesce in the existence of a Communist regime it did not control.) And China was not Bulgaria. The ideological veneer of international Communism was visibly wearing off, and behind it, not only the West but now Mao and other Communists would clearly see naked Soviet imperialism.

On March 5, 1953, Joseph Stalin died. I shall deal later with the complex personality of one of the two greatest mass murderers in history (Genghis Khan and Tamerlane I don't count, because they simply followed the cruel customs of their times). Much as they hated and feared him, his henchmen and putative successors were thrown into a panic. Two facts illustrate their alarm. He died in his country villa, but the official communiqué lied and placed his fatal stroke in his Kremlin residence, where he had almost never spent the night after the war. To specify the right place might have suggested to the grieving nation, which had never been told about his daily routine, that the Greatest Leader of All Times had been victim of a plot.

Another and this time transparent deception was that soon all the Soviet newspapers carried a picture of the late despot in the company just of Mao and Georgi Malenkov, the two leaders seemingly conferring their blessing on Stalin's successor. But how many Soviet citizens failed to realize that the three figures were cropped out of an image taken just three years before, when Stalin and Mao were photographed amid a large number of Soviet and Chinese dignitaries?

There were other signs that the leaders were afraid of each other as well as of their people. Under an amnesty for a range of crimes, the enormous Gulag, the network of concentrations camps, began to release its victims; and there was friendlier official rhetoric about the West. The rulers could no longer afford to treat China in Stalin's haughty fashion. The hitherto endless negotiations about a truce in Korea, in which the Soviets were a behind-the-scene partner on the Communist side, were accelerated. With an end to the fighting, Mao could turn to reconstructing China in the Communist image.

In *The New Face of Soviet Totalitarianism*, which appeared in 1957, I summarized the vast changes which followed Stalin's death, as transforming Soviet society from something for which there is no term in the lexicon of politics into an "ordinary" totalitarian one. Before, terror was a regular phenomenon, a random threat used impartially on the supporters and opponents of the regime: it could and would claim a member of the Politburo, maidservants, Stalin's brother-in-law, and relatives of Trotsky, to name just a few categories. Under Stalin there had been no room for defiance of the regime; no one of sane mind would raise a finger or protest when he knew that his act or words would bring terrible punishments not merely upon himself, but also upon his parents, children, and friends. In post-Stalin years, you could "afford" civic courage and become a dissenter: all you risked were a few years in jail; perhaps your wife might lose her job; and the children might be banned from university admission. Compared to 1937-38, or to the last years of Stalin's reign, this seemed the height of liberalism.

At the time, I incurred criticism from some of my colleagues in Soviet studies by suggesting in an article that in order to understand the current political game in the USSR, it was less instructive to study Marx and Lenin than to reread the accounts of Al Capone's struggles with rival gangs in Prohibition-era Chicago, and of Murder Inc. And indeed, reassured by passivity from the Russian people and from the West, the oligarchs after Stalin's death proceeded to settle their scores with each other. The most sinister of them was Lavrenti Beria, long-time head of the secret police and its auxiliary forces. This man, who personally supervised the torture of more prominent victims, now alarmed his colleagues by pushing the new "liberalism" to an impermissible extent: "socialist legality," more government jobs for non-Russians, relaxation of the collective farm system, and a deal on Germany with the West. Stalin also had begun his bid for supreme power by playing the role of moderate; and Beria's fellow oligarchs were possibly right when they assumed that Beria proposed to emulate his fellow Georgian's career.

There is a similarity between Beria's fall and how Capone's rival gangsters were deceived and then massacred. Several military men were smuggled into the Kremlin past Beria's guards, and in the midst of a Politburo meeting they seized the arch-executioner turned harbinger-of-perestroika.

While he languished in a secret military bunker, his former pals treated the Party's Central Committee to a colorful catalogue of his crimes. No, it was not about his murderous role as Stalin's high executioner, for the dead dictator's reputation must still be preserved, but about his other sins. He mocked and disparaged loyal Communists, wanted reconciliation with Tito, and proposed to cede East Germany to the West. Beria's sexual excesses merited prominent attention. He did in fact already have a reputation as a pervert and rapist, but his accusers could not resist gilding the lily: an examination of the files of Beria's security ministry that were in his personal office (!) revealed drawers full of feminine underwear, stockings, and other articles confirming his bestial lust. Shaken, the Central Committee voted unanimously to condemn the man who had been, until a few days before, the number two man in the regime. But since it was now the era of socialist legalism, the monster and his main accomplices had to be judged by a court of law, superfluous as that might appear to an outsider, before which they duly appeared in December 1953, the verdict being what might have been expected.

Less dramatic and Mafia-like was Nikita Khrushchev's 1955 demotion of Malenkov as the leader. Malenkov's alleged sins were not as colorful as those of Beria, consisting merely of so-called errors of judgment such as neglect of the principle that under socialism, heavy industry must be given priority in the economy, and undue reassurance given to the West by his public statements that an all-out nuclear war would be catastrophic everywhere and not just to the capitalist world. The admission did not square with the policy of bluff and bluster and nuclear-missile rattling that would be pursued under Khrushchev.

In 1956, Khrushchev dropped the other shoe: his "secret" speech condemning Stalin. Though the condemnation was still limited and hardly did justice to the enormity of the despot's crimes, it brought about what might be described as a collective nervous breakdown of world Communism, from which never quite recovered. Like many of Khrushchev's colleagues, as well as Mao Zedong, I wondered whether the Soviet system could afford such—even though limited—frankness about the horrors of the past. Could you pull Stalinism out of the Soviet edifice and yet leave the whole thing standing?

One still must give old Nikita the credit for trying. He didn't do it out of purely humanitarian reasons: it enabled him to beat more strongly on his diehard rivals like Molotov. (But he could not avoid the irrepressible Soviet impulse to fib.One could come to believe all kinds of things about Stalin, but not that he planned World War II operations on a library-sized world globe!) Still, the stage was now set for Solzhenitsyn and other representatives, and forms of dissent, unforeseen, and certainly unwished for by Khrushchev when he let the winds of change sweep, though briefly, through the musty verities of Communism.

Life became easier for Soviet citizens, and to some extent, for the Kremlin's satellite states also. They could pursue their own "roads to socialism," i.e., their rulers could do pretty much what they wanted at home, provided that on important issues they still obeyed Moscow and preserved the monopoly of power of the Communist Party. When those boundaries were transgressed, as in Hungary in 1956, the Soviets' intervention and the punishments inflicted on the recalcitrant nation were swift and brutal. The non-ruling parties also gained some freedom of maneuvering, though none chose to cut its umbilical cord to Moscow. As a French socialist said of his country's Communists: "They are not on the left or the right, they are in the East!"

But for the West, Khrushchev's reign (1955-64) did not bring much relief. True, the USSR was no longer hermetically sealed off from the rest of the world. The Soviet leaders embarked on their tours abroad; and with some qualifications, foreign visitors were now welcome in the USSR. But in many ways Khrushchev's "peaceful coexistence" would prove harder on the nerves of the Western statesmen than Russia's ominous isolation under Stalin.

The trouble was that though Nikita meant well, i.e., wanted to avoid war, he was essentially a bully, and, as his colleagues mercilessly characterized him when they kicked him out, "full of hare-brained ideas." Here he was chummy with Eisenhower—then the next day threatening the West with nuclear devastation. It was as if someone would gently knock on your door, arousing expectations of affability, and then all of a sudden start banging on it, or appear at the window grimacing ferociously. Did he really want America's friendship, or was he ready to risk WWIII over Berlin? And the Soviets' nuclear arsenal was growing, while their deadly potential was immensely increased by the appearance of the long-range missile.

In the good old pre-Soviet, pre-A-bomb days, the foreign policies of the US were usually designed by men whose qualifications consisted in their Yale or Harvard diplomas, supplemented by apprenticeships in a prestigious law firm. But now those people, though still in the seats of power, were hardly qualified by such training to decipher the mysteries of the Kremlin, or, to put it in practical terms, to make a reasonable guess about what the Russians would do next. Hence the government's increasing dependence on that hitherto scorned class: the professors. Physicists led the way, although the alleged "Russian enigma" resulted in the flourishing of a new class of specialists serving as government consultants and guides of public opinion: the Kremlinologists.

Practitioners of that erratic science were drawn from the ranks of the Russia and Eastern Europe scholars, hitherto quietly ensconced in their libraries and studies. These people, be their specialty as apolitical as Ivan the Terrible or the aorist in Church Slavonic, would parade before Congressional Committees, advise the State Department, and appear on TV news and talk shows. Nor did many scholars resist this call of duty or regret the loss of their academic privacy, with the consequent danger of bearing the burden of celebrity status. I certainly did not resist, and fell in step with my fellow students of Soviet affairs.

11

On Being an "Expert"

Beware of quacks...A courageous Communist...Soviet constraints on writers

"Expert" is undoubtedly one of the most abused terms in American usage. Basically, that description fits those who can fix or correct some things, e.g., a plumber or an electrician. In the social sciences, strictly speaking there can be no experts. A scholar may have amassed extensive knowledge of Russian history, economics, etc., and yet it doesn't follow that his advice on American policies about the USSR would be necessarily more perspicacious or valuable than that of a layman guided just by common sense. Because of insistent media use of the term, I've acquiesced in being identified as an expert in Soviet of Russian affairs. But I must protest those aspects of the expert game that approach being a racket. Often enough there is a mismatch between the "expert" and his/her credentials. I have known people who could not put a Russian sentence together, or worse, did not know the language at all, and who yet would babble, or before the TV era, scribble, about Stalin, Gorbachev, and of course, "what the Russians will do next." There are also knowledgeable people whose thirst for public exposure leads them to sheer foolishness. One such person devoted much time and energy to studying election results under the pre-perestroika Soviet system. Why did the government's list of candidates to the Supreme Soviet (the only list) obtain 99.1 percent of the vote in Byelorussia, and only 98.6 in Kirgizia? A prodigious waste of paper!

Exiles from the Soviet Union would at times be equally playful. A former Soviet diplomat who defected and set about enlightening the West about the "Evil Empire" must have logged some kind of record when he published such "inside" stories of Soviet politics as *I was*

Stalin's Nephew and the *Litvinov Memoirs*, written allegedly by the former commissar of foreign affairs. They were interesting, their author being an intelligent observer, but completely phony. I would be asked occasionally by publishers to vet various manuscripts bearing on the USSR, some of them similar in character to the above. One was particularly entertaining. It was the story of Stalin's marriage to the sister of one of his henchmen, Lazar Kaganovich, as told by the brother-in-law, and was full of interesting revelations on the dictator's sexual habits. Unfortunately for its promoter, Kaganovich's only sister died in the 1920s and Stalin never remarried after his second wife's suicide in 1932.

Let me not be misunderstood. Most of the works by Western academics do represent honest scholarship, and émigrés from the USSR both before and after perestroika did contribute valuable information. And we owe a special debt to a handful of dissenters who without leaving their country when repression was still rife smuggled abroad books with data then unavailable to us.

Perhaps outstanding among them is Roy Medvedev, the author of that veritable encyclopedia of Stalinist horror, *Before the Court of History*. I met this courageous man in Moscow, where he tried to convince me that no foreigner could really ever understand Soviet reality, something which for obvious and not entirely personal reasons I could not admit. A Soviet patriot and by his sympathies a Communist, Medvedev held equally unrealistically that the Soviet system could be purified of its flaws and that one-party rule might be reconciled with democracy. What happened after 1991 must have been a severe blow to him.

What were some of my deeds as an expert? Here and there I would be asked to do a short memorandum for somebody in the seats or corridors of power. Occasionally, I would testify before a congressional committee. At one such hearing, the congressmen were interested in a question that can be discussed as interminably as who started the Cold War? My fellow witnesses were Arthur Schlesinger and William Appleman Williams, the latter an early exponent of "revisionism." As such, he brought up the argument that the real motivation for dropping the A-bomb on Japan was Washington's intention to frighten Moscow into complying with America's demands. I pointed out that if such had been the case, we were singularly ineffective: Stalin went on to swallow Eastern Europe. In the second place, the Russians were obviously unaware that we were trying to scare them: they never made the connection between the A-bomb and our alleged blackmail until illuminated on the subject by American revisionist historians. He remained unconvinced.

Another hearing stands out in my memory, before the Senate Foreign Relations Committee, presided over by the late William Fulbright. As I talked, other senators, one by one, tiptoed out, and the public also began to leave. Fulbright stopped and said: "Mr. Ulam, you and I have been right on many issues. And here, people are not listening to you, and I have been defeated in the primary in Arkansas."

I did not seek government jobs, partly because no one ever persuaded me to come to Washington, but also because I do not fancy myself a policy maker. When the position of special assistant to the President was first thought of under FDR, those in the job were supposed to be endowed with a "passion for anonymity," something which can hardly be said of such recent Presidential assistants as Henry Kissinger or Zbigniew Brzezinski. As a matter of fact, I cannot think of any who displayed that passion to a high degree, much as some must have wished they had after their terms in office. More realistic was the maxim that the expert should be "on tap rather than on top." Decision-making requires a certain type of temperament as well as knowledge: one ought to be able to sleep well at night, not to be a worrier, and possess great patience in dealing with knotty issues and foolish people, traits with which I am not particularly well endowed. Politicians are more likely to acquire them than professors, which does not mean that an occasional professor, e.g. Kissinger, cannot do an outstanding job as a policy maker.

At a certain point in my career, I began to attract the attention of the Soviets, which at that time—well before glasnost—suggested that they knew something I did not: perhaps I was slated for a Washington job. But it was infrequently that a book of mine would be reviewed in the Soviet Union. Certainly not my biography of Lenin: how could a bourgeois writer do justice to that sublime genius? In general, the rulers of the Soviet Union cared little for books written in the West about the USSR. But my History of Soviet Foreign Policy was noticed in the official press. Indeed, the first sentence of the review by Israelian, then the USSR's representative in the UN Security Council, might well have been used as a publicity blurb: "Mr. Ulam's history is the outstanding book on the subject published abroad." But the second was less complimentary: "It contains all the old and new fables about our country."

Starting in the late 1950s, a steady stream of Soviet visitors passed through my office: professors, diplomats, "Americanologists," and journalists. Depending on the condition of "peaceful coexistence" at the moment, they were censorious, flattering or just plain curious. "How could you write such things about the USSR?" or, conversely, when Khrushchev was smiling on America, "How come you know so much about us?" At one time, I must have been judged to be quite close to ascending to the antechamber of power, for I would receive repeated visits from two who seemed particularly suited to appeal to somebody of my background: Petrovsky, the future deputy minister of foreign affairs, first of the USSR and then, after 1991, of Russia; and Vladimir Gantman. The former informed me that he was of Polish descent; the latter was one of the few Jews still retained in the Soviet nomenklatura (the upper ranks of state service, i.e. government, press, etc.) Both were exceedingly polite and pleasant gentlemen. As the moment of my near-greatness passed, they ceased their visits. I would meet them many years later, Gantman in Moscow, already very ill, but pleased to see me again.

For all the surliness of many of my other visitors, it was becoming clear that the more time elapsed since Stalin's death, the more it became possible to have a civilized talk, even a dialogue, with my guests. Despite strenuous efforts to restore some of the Stalinist practices following Khrushchev's ouster, the fear that had benumbed the nation in the old days was visibly dissipating. Dissent, and later glasnost, were made possible by Khrushchev's opening the Pandora's box of the past, and nothing Brezhnev and his colleagues could do was really going to close it up again.

Curiously, my difficulty sleeping at night greatly enhanced my credentials as a Russian expert. I have to read myself to sleep. Though I am a great devotee of mystery stories, they do not serve that purpose. If a story is intriguing, I have to finish it, thus not sleeping; if it is bad, I feel something like indigestion, and again, no sleep. Therefore I have to look for something that is interesting and yet not too exciting. I found the ideal reading for that purpose in Soloviev's magisterial *History of Russia*, covering the beginning through the late 18th century. Though written more than a hundred years ago, it still remains irreplaceable in many respects, especially since one could not write a dependable history even of the Middle Ages during the Soviet period. Its seventeen volumes, each of 800 pages, greatly contributed to my knowledge, while dependably promoting sleep.

The same cannot be said of the works of Soviet historians, though there are some honorable exceptions. But even for them, writing history, especially under Stalin, involved hazardous balancing between historical truth and "the class point-of-view." The lucky ones got away with a few citations from Lenin and Stalin in their otherwise scholarly texts. But unfortunately, the "greatest genius of all time" was also an avid reader, and should he spot some unorthodox passage while browsing a book, the consequences would be much worse than an unfavorable review. My late friend, Sasha Nekrich, for many years a highly esteemed and much loved member of our Russian Research Center, is an example of how even after Stalin's death, the historian's lot was not a happy one. He wrote an excellent book on what occurred following the 1941 German attack on the USSR. Had Khrushchev stayed in power another year, Nekrich's book would probably have gotten the Lenin prize, and he, deservedly, would have become a member of the Academy of Sciences. Alas, with the change in leadership, what had been the historical truth between 1956 and 1964, i.e., that Stalin, despite all warnings, had left the country seriously unprepared for war, became "unworthy libel." The book was roundly condemned; Sasha was expelled from the Party and practically barred from publishing. Eventually, he emigrated and came to us.

Soviet fiction suffered from similar constraints: Stalin was the chief literary critic and would often modestly suggest who might get the literary prize bearing his name. Yet, one must not be condescending about Soviet cultural life. Amidst the desert of socialist realism, one would find oases of real creativity. Certainly Sholokhov's *And Quiet Flows the Don* is not only a masterpiece, but remarkably objective in portraying the struggle between the Reds and the Whites during the Civil War. As behooves a whimsical deity, Stalin chose to overlook the writer's ideological deviation, though insisting himself on editing and changing some particularly ticklish passages. He was repaid by Sholokhov's disgusting behavior in his later years, when he sank into drunkenness, and would call for severe penalties for literary dissenters. Another talented writer, Alexei Tolstoy, played the role of jester at the dictator's court. Such great poets as Mandelstam and Akhmatova were less fortunate, the first dying in a concentration camp where he was sent for composing and reading to a few "friends" (at least one of whom denounced him) a scorching poem about Stalin. Akhmatova, who survived, was publicly denounced by a henchman of the despot as a "part whore, part nun." Stalin's successors, though less cruel, still would not tolerate departures from socialist realism (in plain English, glorification of Soviet life), or even apolitical works such as Pasternak's *Dr. Zhivago*. But to get the sense of the era, one has to read the works not only of the rebels, but of the run-of-the-mill Soviet writers as well. Prior to 1930, they still were not regimented, but from then until the 1950s, they had to kowtow to the Leader; after that, they were kept on a bit longer leash. I developed a perverse taste for the very bad novels; the not so bad ones are just boring, but the former are very often very funny. Outstanding in this genre are the scribblings of Vsevolod Kochetov. Most amusing among them is the novel whose title freely translated would be *What the Hell Do You Want?* It contains an unforgettable portrait of an American woman journalist, who to corrupt Soviet youth, instructs innocent boys and maidens in such Western practices as the strip tease.

An apologist for Soviet literature might claim that the picture I've drawn is not really worse than what could be described as capitalist realism of the contemporary American cultural scene, its main preoccupation being kinky sex and violence—I leave the verdict to the experts, i.e., students of comparative literature.

12

Lenin

One cannot begin to understand the tragic and complex history of the Soviet people without a knowledge of Communism. And that in turn is impossible without studying in depth the life of the man who virtually single-handedly fathered Bolshevism, the original name of modern Communism. For us, whether in the West or in Russia, Lenin is perhaps more difficult to understand than Stalin. There are still people in what used to be the USSR who worship Lenin's memory. For all his "errors," Stalin built the Soviet Union into a superpower feared throughout the world; and his cynical lust for domination, frightening and repellent, is still understandable. But Lenin was a cultivated Russian gentleman; the Party that he joined as a youth bore the name Social Democratic, and until 1914, he never repudiated what was meant by the second part of the name. It is thus not easy now to explain his fanaticism, and what made him, from the first moment that power was his, trample on everything that was meant by democracy. Personally not a sadist like Stalin, his delectation—there is no other word for it—in terror laid the foundation for the horrors to come and legitimized his party's acceptance of his terrible successor.

At the same time, this impractical fanatic, sometimes suspected even by his followers of being mentally deranged, once in power showed himself again and again to be a shrewd leader and statesman. He beat his party into accepting the catastrophic Brest-Litovsk treaty, which, had Germany won the First World War, would have turned Russia into the Kaiser's puppet. He steered the infant, seemingly impotent Soviet state through the Civil War, dominating such unruly lieutenants as Trotsky and Stalin. Lenin insisted that the Civil War could not be won by the Bolsheviks without enlisting former Tsarist officers, and that the economy could not be rebuilt without employing the former bourgeois industrialists and managers.

In my biography *The Bolsheviks* (the British edition bears the more appropriate title *Lenin and the Bolsheviks*), I address those questions, as well as the nineteenth-century Russian revolutionary background that inspired the hereditary nobleman and lawyer Vladimir Ulyanov to become Lenin, and the master of much of 20th century politics.

His penchant for terror had its source in the intense hatred of his own class, which regardless of the official classification of its members is usually defined as the intelligentsia. In the customary Russian use of the term, it stood not only for the educated part of society, but also for a specific political attitude, largely critical of the autocracy. Even when he was formally adhering to the Social Democratic dogma, Lenin's fury was often aroused by any concept or postulate that could reflect the mentality of the intelligentsia: liberalism, independence of the judiciary, or parliamentarianism. Even when seeking a political alliance between the liberals and his own faction, Lenin would burst out into intemperate abuse of those he sought as temporary allies.

Perhaps his violent feelings against his own social and intellectual milieu had been triggered by the fate of his elder brother, Alexander, hanged in 1887 for his participation in a plot to assassinate Tsar Alexander III. Most acquaintances of the Ulyanov family described the relations between the brothers as not particularly close, and the revolutionary group to which Alexander belonged was Populist: semi-anarchist in its ideology, rather than Marxist. But the effect of the blow must have been telling on seventeen-year-old Vladimir, perhaps even more so if he regretted his previous coldness toward his brother.

It was this perverse revulsion against his own class and all its "nice" conventions that also fed Lenin's naive faith in the inherent virtues of the "simple proletariat." And since few of them qualified for a leading role in the Bolshevik clandestine organization, it is not surprising that in 1912 he chose for its Central Committee the son of a Georgian cobbler, the little-known Joseph Djugashvili—Stalin.

Glasnost and then the fall of the Soviet Union have led to a partial opening of the previously closed archives, as well as to revelations about previously super-secret subjects. Yet for all the mass of new materials, the picture of Lenin remains very much the same as I tried to paint him thirty years ago. There are two biographical items on which I speculated, and on which we have now more information. One, about his ancestry, a subject on which the official Soviet line discouraged discussion: it was always accepted that his father, Ilya Ulyanov, was the son of a tailor of Kalmyk descent. More problematic was the ancestry of his mother, her maiden name Blank clearly being non-Slavic and leading to rumors that her father, Dr. Blank, was Jewish. We now have documents proving that such in fact was the case, Dr. Blank having converted in his youth. The father of the international revolutionary movement was appropriately of mixed Russian, Mongol, Jewish, and German ancestry.

Another biographical problem, on which, given the Soviet prudishness, we were never enlightened, was Lenin's love life. His marriage to Nadya Krupskaya, while childless, was extolled as an exemplary union of two revolutionaries. A love affair on the side was unimaginable! Yet we also knew that he had a close personal relationship and political ties with a fellow revolutionary and an early feminist, Inessa Armand, who, unlike poor Nadyezhda, was described as capable of arousing male passions. For all the gossip transmitted by some women revolutionaries of the period, I remained skeptical about the Lenin-Inessa romance. His all-engrossing passion for revolution seemed to preclude the possibility, perhaps the ability, to respond to the temptation of the flesh. But now, some of the newly published letters appear to rebut my skepticism and suggest that he indeed had an affair with Inessa while Nadya, as behooved a good comrade, accepted the liaison.

It would not have pleased Lenin to be accused of straying from the straight and narrow path. He was rather Victorian in his views on the subject. Alexandra Kollontay, who enlivened the rather grim Bolshevik leadership after the Revolution, advocated and practiced free love, writing that the sexual act should be considered as of no more consequence than drinking a glass of water. Lenin's reaction would have pleased today's Christian Coalition: "Who wants to drink from a dirty glass?"

His posthumous fate would have further embittered this personally modest man. The cult of his personality was the foundation on which Stalin built his own. Lenin's mausoleum, formerly the Mecca of the Communist movement, now serves as just another tourist attraction in a city where the reading of the Stock Exchange news and the latest edicts of the International Monetary Fund have replaced Karl Marx's and Lenin's own writings. *"Lenin Lives"* was a song composed by a Soviet bard after the leader's death. Today his lyrics sound pathetic.

NT: It was Lenin who first brought us together as professor and student. Thirty years ago I began work on a thesis about the cult of Lenin. And I naturally gravitated toward the author of "The Bolsheviks." He was magisterial and intimidating at first, with his booming voice and huge size and a peculiar gait that seemed to be simultaneously stiff and slightly uncontrolled. But his graduate students called him by his first name, very unusual in those days, and he treated them—including women graduate students—with a respect that was rare in the bad old days of Harvard University. Also rare was his famed wit, and even before Adam and I were acquainted, I had enjoyed the "Adam stories" that circulated among students.

I had come to Harvard in the fall of 1966. The following October of 1967 marked the fiftieth anniversary of the Bolshevik Revolution....The Russian Research Center feted the event with some occasion I no longer remember, although I do recall that Adam brought down the house by expressing the wish that in the Soviet Union one of Karl Marx's great prediction for socialism should be realized: the withering away of the state!

I believe that Adam and I first met formally at the Russian Research Center's event marking the second Brezhnevite megaholiday: the April 1970 centennial of Lenin's birth. Our librarian, Susan Gardos, held a fanciful party in the library, a marvelous place with multi-paned old windows, nooks and crannies of all sorts, and a row of huge old microfilm readers. There was an immense sheet birthday cake onto which someone had drawn Lenin's profile in icing, and onehundred and one (the last for good luck) candles were lit. I believe that Adam (as author of "The Bolsheviks") and I (as a student beginning her research for a thesis on the Lenin cult) were jointly given the honor of blowing out the candles, with a little spontaneous help from others. The librarian had also distributed a questionnaire about Lenin that we were all invited to fill out and submit in a Lenin trivia contest. Of course everyone thought it unfair that Adam got to fill one out along with students. Naturally he won the contest. To one, the question, "At what age did Lenin become bald?" Adam had replied: "at birth."

We all knew that Adam hated the dull aspects of teaching, but I didn't know him as well then. Only later did I realize how tiresome he must have found all the questions I asked him about Lenin and even worse, about obscure bibliographical references to Lenin. But he never let on, year after year, inviting me into his office or staying late after everyone else had left our famous daily coffee hour, allowing me to ply him with questions.

When the thesis came out as a book, I dedicated it to Adam in gratitude for the enormous support and encouragement he had given me over the years. Adam had such a terrific sense of self-mockery! He loved to be honored and praised, and at the same time made fun of himself for it. When I presented him with a copy of my book and showed him the dedication "To Adam Ulam," he looked at me and said: "why is my name in such small letters?" Some years earlier, after he had read my dissertation, he handed it back to me (with a book mark about one-third into it) and said: "This is very good. I only have one criticism. In your annotated bibliography, you call *"The Bolsheviks* the most useful of the biographies of Lenin." "Well it was terrifically useful," I replied. What's wrong with that?" "Isn't this a bit like calling Michelangelo the most useful of the Renaissance artists?" he boomed.......

Adam took enormous comfort in predictability, sameness, routine. To write at the same time and in the same place every day, our long mid-morning coffee hour of chitchat (we were not allowed to talk about anything serious), a civilized lunch with friends or at the long table with what he called the "Old Crocks." And if encounters had a certain sameness, for him their ritualized nature was soothing and bonding. For how many years did Adam ask me, every time he saw me, "How's Lenin?"

Nina Tumarkin
Professor of History
Wellesley College

13

Turbulent Foreign Relations

"Myth" in foreign policy...Khrushchev gambles and the world shudders....Cuba...The "Swan of Simbirsk"...The Cold War warms (a little)

When I was working on my book, the system Lenin had built was very much alive. One could not become, I felt, totally engrossed in the distant past of pre-1924. Never was the Soviet challenge and danger felt more acutely in this country than in the late 1950s and early 1960s. This challenge now also touched the field in which Americans had always complacently assumed their superiority: technology. The Soviet Sputnik, earth's first space satellite, made its debut in 1957. Soon afterwards, Yuri Gagarin made his pioneer space flight. Where was the American celebrated "know-how?" We were currently persuaded (incorrectly) about the "missile gap." The Atlantic Ocean had become a narrow stream, with Moscow's ICBMs half an hour away. Khrushchev intermittently smiled benignly or ranted about Berlin. President Eisenhower was about to return Nikita's visit and celebrate "peaceful coexistence" in Russia. And then Francis Powers and his U-2 spy plane dropped in uninvited and inconveniently, ending the "spirit of Camp David." The tentacles of Soviet power reached to within ninety miles of Florida's coast. Following the 1961 Cuban crisis, the 1962 crisis brought us, it is still believed today, closest to an actual nuclear catastrophe.

An expert could not remain oblivious to all those developments and concentrate on some ancient quarrels between Lenin and the Mensheviks. Not when many Americans began fatuously to prepare private shelters to protect themselves from those missiles. Was it really West Berlin the Soviets were after? Why did they put land-to-land missiles in Cuba? Why then did they pull them out? I embarked on a study of Soviet foreign policy. Perhaps it would help to provide the answers. "Of consuming interest to me in the years from 1958 to 1965 were the turbulent relations between East and West, as well as what was going on inside Soviet politics. My reflections resulted in the book *Expansion and Coexistence: Soviet Foreign Policy 1917-67*. A later edition extended the period covered to 1973.

If the author is at all objective, most studies of foreign policies of great powers deal not only with the facts but also with the attending myths. It will not do for a student of America's foreign relations to represent them as based always on democratic virtue, regard for other nations' rights, and international law. In democratic societies you will always find writers who criticize national self-adulation and self-righteousness, and provide a necessary corrective to the conventional and biased views of such events as the Mexican War of 1846, or the US acquisition of the Panama Canal. (It is another matter that at times, as in this country following the Vietnam drama, such critiques may turn into unintentional masochism.)

In the case of the USSR, virtually no Russian source between 1917 and 1988 criticized the government's policies or chose to report them as in the slightest departing from the straight and narrow path of proletarian internationalism and love of peace; the only exception being Khrushchev's criticism of Stalin's policy toward Tito. (It should be noted, however, that beginning in 1988, highly critical articles appeared in the Soviet press.) Some of the official "myths" about Moscow's foreign policy from 1917 on have found some acceptance in the West. I have already dealt with two such myths, one about Britain and France in 1939 leaving Stalin no other option but to sign a pact with Hitler, and about Washington's use of the A-bomb on Japan being influenced by the desire to blackmail the Kremlin. Let me add that on a few issues, I find the Soviet version credible. For example, it is widely believed the USSR would not have entered the Pacific War, or would have delayed its intervention indefinitely, except for the Kremlin's fear that after Hiroshima and Nagasaki, Japan's prompt capitulation would prevent Russia from sharing in the spoils. Yet such was not the case. All the data indicate that Stalin was ready to enter the war as he had promised, three months after the German surrender, which he did to the day. In general, however, I always found the frequent Soviet declarations that no other country can match the USSR's record in fulfilling its international obligations to be correct—but not in the sense meant by the Kremlin.

But my aim in the book was not to "catch" the Soviets at this or that dereliction, or to provide a chronological record of their foreign policy. First of all I took it as my task to give the reader a "feel' for the subject, something that is not possible without understanding both Communism and the internal politics of the Soviet Union. Now that the previously closed Soviet archives are being opened, such caution is still vitally necessary for the Russian and Western scholars who work on them. Otherwise they are likely to find themselves in the same predicament as the researcher whom I mentioned before, who persuaded herself that it was not Stalin but his North Korean vassal who masterminded the invasion of the South. The notion of the latter pestering the despot to the point when in exasperation he finally said in effect, "Oh, I guess I'll have to let you do it. Go ahead and invade!" could not be seriously entertained by anyone who had studied Stalin's ways of operating.

Even less excusable than such naiveté is misinterpretation of Soviet policies in the face of abundant factual evidence to the contrary. Ask the great majority of the people who have written on the subject of the two Berlin crises of 1948-49 and 1958-62, and they would say the answer is self-evident. The USSR tried to force the West out of West Berlin and to grab it for its East German puppet. In 1948 it tried to do it through land blockade, in 1958-62 through constant threats and pressure. But aside from the illogic of such a risky course just for the sake of gaining 1.5 to 2 million new subjects, the Soviets' own diplomatic notes and public statements during both crises make it quite plain that the conquest of West Berlin was far from being the Kremlin's objective in starting those dangerous games. Yes, West Berlin was a huge inconvenience, the main route for escape from the Communist East, and some three million Germans availed themselves of the opportunity. But this hemorrhaging could always be stopped; and was, in 1961, by the erection of the Wall. Yet cutting off the escape route did not bring to an end the Berlin crisis; it continued and took on its most ominous form during 1961-62.

By exerting pressure on West Berlin, the exposed nerve of the West, Moscow hoped to compel it to give up something else. In 1949 its objective was to prevent or delay the creation of the Federal Republic of Germany. In 1958, the latter being a fact of life, the USSR deemed it of the highest importance to make the West agree to a German peace treaty which would not only legitimize its East

German satellite but, and this was more important to the Soviets, would also preclude any possibility of Bonn obtaining nuclear weapons, or having any say in their potential use by NATO.

It is the latter point that would provoke objections by the critics of my interpretation of the 1958 crisis. With the US owning a vast quantity of strategic nuclear weapons, and with NATO (read its American commander) having at its disposal a large quantity of tactical ones, why should the Kremlin worry so much about the possibility of West Germany having a few A-bombs of its own? The answer is that the Kremlin had learned to live with American nuclear power, and in its actions if not its propaganda, displayed considerable confidence that without extreme provocation the US would not use that power. For very understandable reasons the Russians had no such trust in the West Germans. For them, certainly for Khrushchev, the Germans were "revanchists;" Chancellor Adenauer and his successors always scheming to bring the West into a confrontation, perhaps even war, with the USSR, so that Germany could be reunited. And thus the possibility, discussed in the NATO Council in 1958, of giving Bonn some sort of access to nuclear power struck Moscow as a grave danger, justifying serious risks and leading to hazardous gambles.

The Berlin crisis festered for four years. Since for many of the present generation in the US, modern history begins with the Vietnam War, it is not surprising that our worries during that period have been largely forgotten. The impossible Nikita was at his worst, trying intermittently to cajole and scare us. But he had an excuse: it was infuriating for him that we did not understand what he was after, and took him at his word that it was Berlin! But how could he tell us what he was really afraid of: West Germany's finger on the nuclear button? Washington would have undoubtedly said: "Ah, but what's it worth to you? How about a united and democratic Germany?" And so Khrushchev bluffed and blustered. The Soviets, he announced, had a transcontinental missile of such accuracy it could hit a fly in space. He broke up a summit conference because Eisenhower would not apologize for the Americans about the U-2 flights. He would turn over the access to Berlin to his East German commanders, and this time when the blockade was mounted, they would also prevent flights to West Berlin. Then he would relieve our anxiety by announcing that he would give the West a period of grace; but if there were no settlement within six months, then the blockade!—and, if the West tried to break it the rockets might start flying! He was both amiable and threatening on his 1959 visit to the US. What remained constant was his penchant for telling fibs. You should not believe, he told Eisenhower, all those stories about the estrangement between the USSR and China; why he and Mao were the best of friends! But on his subsequent trip to Beijing, not only Mao but also subordinate Chinese officials scolded him for trying to appease the American imperialists.

John Kennedy inherited the so-called Berlin Crisis. I had met the future president a few times when he was US Senator. A loyal alumnus, he would come fairly often to Harvard. For all his personal charm and intelligence he didn't strike me then as a future leader. He appeared too young and without that gravity of demeanor which I mistakenly considered to be among the necessary elements of a Chief Executive. A good part of the Harvard faculty migrated to Washington after his inauguration, and at the time I was unconvinced that a Harvard connection led automatically to one's being among "the best and the brightest." (I still have my doubts about it.)

The first years of the new administration did not dispel my concerns. There was the Bay of Pigs fiasco. John F. Kennedy's formula "Never fear to negotiate, never negotiate from fear" did not appear to me to be a particularly apt precept for diplomacy. If you are not scared even a little bit, then there is no need for negotiation. And he should have been apprehensive about seeking negotiations with the USSR right after his administration had stumbled so badly over Cuba. But then all American presidents since FDR, with the exception of Truman, have believed that a personal encounter with the Soviet chief might work wonders. And so he rushed to Vienna to meet Khrushchev. His biographer's statement that both men emerged from that session with increased respect for each other is somewhat questionable. Nikita's subsequent behavior suggests strongly that he saw Kennedy as a likeable but politically inexperienced young man, who could be bullied. And so then came in quick succession the Berlin Wall, and then the Soviets breaking the nuclear tests moratorium by exploding a 56-megaton bomb. It was a weapon that could have no particular use; but it certainly scared us, and the Russians, too. And so tension built up in the West and reached its climax in October 1962.

Memories of my anxieties about the Cuban missile crisis are mixed incongruously with recollections of my trying to master billiards. My colleague Bob McClosky had introduced me to the game, of which he had been the intercollegiate champion while an under-graduate at Michigan. Several of us appropriated a basement room in Lowell House and turned it into our private gambling den. Poker at night, billiards in the daytime. And so during those nerve-wracking October days, and especially after Kennedy's speech revealing the presence of medium and intermediate missile sites in Castro's realm, I tried to dismiss black thoughts from my mind by playing a game which requires that one concentrate to the point of becoming oblivious—at least for the moment—to the possibility that the world might end the next day.

But one could not play billiards all day. My agitation increased with the arrival from England of an old friend, Leo Labedz. Editor of a strongly anti-Communist journal *Survey*, Leo was the epitome of the cold warrior. Of Polish nationality though born appropriately in Simbirsk, Russia, also the birthplace of V.I. Lenin and Alexander Kerensky (I liked to call him the swan of Simbirsk, his last name meaning swan in Polish), he was a vigilant critic of any writer, historian, etc. who in his eyes was an apologist for Moscow's past or present actions. No, he was not a reactionary; he was a very fair and enormously erudite man, but endowed with a powerful temper. He would often tax me for all the sins of omission and commission of American foreign policy as if I were indeed one of its framers. And now Leo was in his element: why did we, meaning the Washington establishment and I, allow the Soviets and Castro to land this country in such a predicament? If memory serves, Leo along with Dick Pipes, professor of history, and Zbig Brzezinski, then still an assistant professor in my department, sent a message to one of the powers-that-be in Washington urging no retreat on the blockade of Cuba. It would be interesting to know which government official in those feverish days took the time to notice and ponder this message from three Polish-born scholars.

Well, thank God the crisis passed, and the US went on coexisting with the USSR, though not always happily; certainly a better outcome than had they both been "nuked."

(Later researches led me to believe that the possibility of war in 1962 had not been as great as believed at the time by everybody from the mighty in Washington to some of my colleagues and me in Cambridge)

Generally for there to be a war, one of the parties must wish it. In 1914 it was the Austrian and German General Staffs, which pushed for it; in 1939, Hitler. In 1962 both sides wanted to avoid a disaster. Still, the presence of nuclear weapons made chances of a misjudgment vastly more frightening than before 1945. There is this ominous term "escalation." What if, as some in Washington urged, we had bombed the missile sites right away? What if, as I greatly feared that October, the Soviets had answered our "quarantine" (euphemism for blockade) of Cuba, by a complete blockade of Berlin? Rigging missile sites ninety miles from US soil was a most dangerous gamble by Khrushchev and one that his fellow oligarchs undoubtedly had in mind when following his dismissal two years later they heartlessly upbraided him for his "harebrained schemes."

Why did he do it? The official version given by Nikita after the missile sites were dismantled, and those missiles already in Cuba removed, was simple: They did it to protect a fellow socialist country from Yankee invasion.

Since then scholars have been able to consult a number of previously secret documents on the crisis, retrieved from the Soviet archives. There have been conferences at which the surviving American and Soviet officials active during the crisis exchanged their recollections and reflections. Fidel Castro himself graced one such conference. There has been a lot of information about how both sides handled the crisis, how the Cubans bitterly resented and protested Khrushchev's alleged capitulation to the US. But have we learned more about the Soviets' motivation behind their risky gambit? No. The official Soviet, now Russian, version, remains what it had been in 1962: "We did it to protect Cuba from an invasion. When Kennedy pledged not to invade in exchange for removing the missiles, we were glad to comply." As an additional incentive for the USSR, the US also dismantled its missile sites in Turkey, a move then presented to the American public as scrapping obsolete missiles. And on the American side, such key actors in the drama as the then Secretary of Defense, Robert McNamara, still accept that version.

Even in 1962 I felt that the Soviet explanation would not do. There are obvious common-sense objections to it. 1) There was absolutely no sign prior to the aerial discovery of the missiles that the US was preparing an invasion. John F. Kennedy's mind was on the fall Congressional elections. 2) How could nuclear bombardment of American cities protect Cuba from an invasion? (Remember: those missile sites and rockets were being installed in secrecy). Moscow must have known that were its rockets to be used, the US would reply in kind.

Whatever happened subsequently between the US and the USSR, Cuba or at least its population would be utterly annihilated—some protection against invasion! 3) Up to that time, and in general, the Soviets never liked to have their missiles and nuclear warheads outside their own territory. True, the Cuban sites were guarded by a considerable contingent of Soviet troops. Still this was less than 100% security. 4) It defied everything we know about the Kremlin to believe that just to save "socialism in Cuba" it was willing to risk a nuclear war, especially with the "missile gap," which really existed at the time—but in favor of the US. In my *Expansion and Coexistence*, and subsequently in some other works, I adduced considerable if circumstantial evidence leading to the only hypothesis about the crisis that makes sense: the missiles were installed (we now know that warheads had been slipped aboard the Soviet freighter *Indigirka*, but had not yet been deployed on the missiles) in order to be withdrawn...at a price! But not just for an American pledge not to invade. Nikita was after much bigger fish: the resolution of the "Berlin" crisis, i.e., a German peace treaty containing iron-bound guarantees against West Germany obtaining nuclear weapons or having such weapons stationed on DBR territory. Having despaired after four years of any other way of obtaining what he thought essential for the Soviet Union's security, Khrushchev thought up the Cuban gambit. Before October it had been officially announced that he would be coming to the US in late November to address the UN. This was going to be the setting for that historical drama that was so much in his style. Surprise! We do have nuclear missiles in Cuba! But the Americans' *frisson* of horror would be instantly followed by a vast exhalation of relief: We'll pull them out if you pledge not to give nuclear weapons to the West German "revanchists," who want to embroil you in a confrontation with us. He did not come to the US in November; after the whole scenario collapsed in October; there was no longer any point in his coming.

There was also another big fish Khrushchev hoped to catch with the Cuban gambit. With Soviet-China relations clearly growing worse, the Kremlin had second thoughts about the possibility of nuclear weapons in Mao's hands. In 1959, in violation of a previous recent agreement, the USSR refused to deliver to Beijing a sample A-bomb. All Soviet nuclear specialists and advisers, and soon experts in other fields, left China, taking with them the blueprints and other relevant materials. Rather comically, the Kremlin at the same time tried to convince the Chinese that building nuclear facilities and acquiring nuclear weapons was not in their own best interest. They didn't need them! Since the USSR provides a nuclear shield for China, its leaders ought not to waste their resources on the bombs, but rather should concentrate on their economy. Protect us for a few more years until we have our own nuclear weapons, was Mao's grave reply. But, wouldn't a theatrical coup with the Cuban missiles incline Beijing to see the wisdom of the Soviets' advice? And the whole deal might have been more attractive to Mao if Khrushchev also obtained an American quid pro quo in the form of the US removing its nuclear weapons from the Pacific Theater.

Looking back from the present moment, we barely remember that in the 1950s and early 1960s the prospect of China acquiring nuclear weapons was viewed by the American public with an alarm almost surpassing that over the Soviet Union's actual possession of them. The Russian leaders were prudent, was the general US view; Mao and his people were fanatics and possibly mentally unhinged, as the insanities of the "Great Leap Forward" made one suspect

All in all, Khrushchev may have thought he was doing the Americans a favor and that they would agree after studying the Soviet proposals. They did not really want West Germany to have those weapons, and were deathly afraid of the Chinese Communists acquiring them. At the same time, at one blow, he would be solving the Soviet Union's major foreign policy problems. And then the whole beautiful scheme collapsed because some vigilant American pilot photographed a suspicious-looking plot of land.

When my book on Soviet foreign policy came out, it enjoyed a quite favorable reception in this country and in Britain and Italy, where it was published in 1968. But practically none of the reviews as much as mentioned what is one of its central points: the hypothesis of the missile crisis. My only tentative explanation (authors do not ask reviewers to open their hearts, at least I don't) would be that most of those who wrote about it thought my thesis too far-fetched, though the circumstantial evidence was too strong for an outright rejection.

As late as mid-1995 my guess as to the fateful clash of the two superpowers had still not been confirmed. I discussed it with some Russians, once perestroika loosened their tongues and opened some of the previously secret Soviet archives. Khrushchev's son, a most amiable gentleman and now a US citizen located at Brown University, was skeptical: as far as he knew, the missile crisis was not connected with the "Berlin" issue. A former Soviet official, he based his skepticism on his belief that the old man was not smart enough to think up such a complicated scheme. But the children of political leaders are not often privy to their fathers' secrets. Sergei Khrushchev, for all his connections and perspicacity, missed some important details even in describing the intrigues that brought his father's downfall. As to the Soviet authorities under glasnost and their Russian successors, their unwillingness to reveal the entire story of what had led to the October 1962 crisis can be easily understood. My version would dispose of the myth that the Soviet Union was ready to risk a war to defend a small allied country and "socialism in Cuba." One must hope that sooner rather than later the Russian guardians of the Soviet past will come clean!

One place where Khrushchev's lame explanation of his adventure found no credibility at all was Beijing. The Chinese Communists openly laughed at his excuse. Why did he put those missiles in Cuba when there was no danger of the United States invading the island? It must be sheer adventurism! But once there why did he pull them out, thus humiliatingly capitulating to the imperialists? The split between the two Communist superpowers worsened. The erstwhile Elder Brother became for Beijing a renegade state led by "capitalist roaders," as it was elegantly put in the English translation of the Chinese epithet. (Or in plain English: Those Communists who allegedly would follow the capitalist road.) And for the Kremlin what was once the Great People's Republic was now led by the "left-wing sectarians and dogmatists," trying to push the US and Russia into a nuclear war that would reduce both countries to ashes.

Another infuriated party was Castro. Perhaps he now understood what had been Khrushchev's real game, and in any case he was outraged that the whole crisis was settled without the Kremlin even pretending that he was in on the negotiations. The Soviet chief troubleshooter Anastas Mikoyan had to abandon the bedside of his dying wife to go and try to appease the temperamental Fidel.

But elsewhere there was general relief (epitomized by a couple I knew who had packed up and were ready to fly to New Zealand but then relented and gave coexistence another chance). Hardly anyone noticed that the "Berlin crisis" had suddenly vanished. Khrushchev now realized that the man he had to deal with in the White House was a person of some mettle, and not just an inexperienced youngster who got where he was by being the son of a multi-millionaire.

The new "coexistential" attitude of the Soviet leaders was demonstrated in 1963 in their signing a treaty with Britain and the US which banned above-ground and underwater atomic tests. The Cold War was not over, but it entered a new and less nerve-wracking phase, even though Vietnam would soon open another front in it, which then would grow into a real shooting war.

14

Vietnam

US missteps and the beginning of Vietnam...US misunderstanding of USSR-China relations...Why we failed in Vietnam

I was lunching in the Faculty Club that November day in 1963 when the news came of the fatal shot in Dallas. I rushed home to monitor the unfolding story on TV. When Oswald was stupidly being paraded for the newsmen, I observed to my wife that it was an imprudent thing to do, and indeed within seconds the assassin was killed. Although many people are firmly convinced about there being only one assassin, and that Oswald's deed must be explained simply in terms of his warped personality, I still have doubts on both points. No alternative theories, but just doubts, based perhaps on my addiction to detective stories and hence the conviction that there must be something beyond the obvious about a murder.

*　　*　　*

For all the great merits of his domestic legislation, Lyndon Johnson lacked a feel for international relations. Kennedy acquired it, not only because of his varied experiences with the Soviet Union, but also because his mind was more attuned to world events. In contrast, Johnson had built his entire career on his skill in manipulating American politics. That is not to say Kennedy would have avoided the Vietnam imbroglio, the initial phases of which took place on his watch. But one suspects that once the Southeastern Asia situation reached the critical stage he would have addressed the problem more nimbly than did his successor

*　　*　　*

In the summer of 1961, I was in Geneva attending a conference on the Soviet Union's relations with other Communist states.

But also going on in Geneva at the same time was a much more important international conference. Delegates of the Western powers were meeting with those of the USSR and China about the knotty problem of Laos. This part of what used to be French Indochina was witnessing a preview of the Vietnam mess, the pro-Western forces battling the Communist and allegedly neutral ones, each faction presided over by a prince of the royal house. The conference settled on a neutralist regime, which eventually gave way to a Communist one following the fall of South Vietnam.

One evening, I went to a nightclub with my Polish friend Leo Labedz, who frequently attended such conferences. The place had a reputation which belied the Calvinist tradition of this allegedly puritanical Swiss city. We were astounded to see among the customers a number of Chinese, obviously relaxing from deciding the fate of Laos. One of them especially could not take his eyes off a very good-looking and most uninhibited stripper. Later on, after putting on some clothes, she mixed with the public; and our Chinese diplomat took her to the dance floor. What would Comrade Mao think? What if she were a CIA agent? One could take this indulgence in decadent bourgeois amusements as a hopeful sign for future China-West relations.

But the Great Cultural Revolution was just around the corner. It was China, I believe, rather than the problem of Communism at large, which prompted our eventually unhappy intervention in Vietnam. President Eisenhower formulated the "domino theory:" if one Southeast Asian state falls to Communism, then others will follow. Then Kennedy put a special Chinese spin on that theory. He and his advisers were intrigued and alarmed by the problem of "brushfire wars," more particularly about Communist China promoting such wars where American power supposedly could not be applied. This was thought in Washington to be much more dangerous than the Soviets' very largely rhetorical support of the wars of "national liberation," some of them, e.g. in Algeria, being clearly nationalist rebellions against the colonial power, and as such, not regarded by the US as threatening to the free world. The French understandably disagreed: the Americans were ready to go to war to preserve West Berlin, but France was supposed to resign itself to the loss of what was legally a province of the Republic with its population of ten million, one million of them Frenchmen. But in South Vietnam the rebellion against the native pro-Western regime was clearly Communist led and cheered on by Beijing. Here then, in South Vietnam, was the place to show Mao that brushfire wars do not pay off. And in view of the Sino-Soviet conflict, some in Washington had convinced themselves that the Soviet Union could not but look favorably, if secretly so, upon the US crushing this largely China-inspired rebellion.

That was a very basic misreading of the implications of the Sino-Soviet quarrels. Much as they may have disliked the prospect of the then pro-Chinese North Vietnamese Communists creating troubles in the South, the Soviet Union could not have afforded to remain indifferent to what was going on there. Such indifference, especially after the US began aerial attacks, would have definitely endangered the Soviet Union's leadership and control of the international Communist movement, already shaken by Mao's defiance. Stalin could afford to sacrifice foreign Communists if it was in his interests, because he would still retain his power over the world movement. Neither Khrushchev nor his successors could afford such games.

With bombing raids beginning in 1965, the US's undeclared war on North Vietnam in fact carried the risk of bringing about a reconciliation between the two Communist giants. Fortunately, that did not happen, because each of them suspected the other of having ulterior motives in helping Hanoi: Moscow of China, trying to push it into a confrontation with the US; Beijing of the USSR helping North Vietnam to make it dependent on itself, so it could "sell" it later to the US in exchange for concessions elsewhere. The massive US intervention turned out to be a great boon for the Soviets. It helped them to regain greater influence over the Ho Chi Minh regime: China could help it mostly with rhetoric; the USSR did so with vitally needed supplies and munitions. Russia gained diplomatically by US prestige and image being hurt worldwide. And so Moscow would help America to extricate itself from the Indo-China morass, but only after its failure there became irrevocable.

I write failure rather than defeat, because militarily the American forces were not defeated. The ill-conceived and badly managed war had to come to an end, because public opinion in this country turned decisively against it. While I believe that the massive American intervention should never have started, and the decision to end it was overdue, I do not embrace the notion that what went on in Vietnam was just a civil war in which this country should not have taken sides. North Vietnam was a ruthless totalitarian regime, which had the advantage of discipline and of fixed purpose over the admittedly corrupt and inefficient autocrats of the South. The hundreds of thousands of refugees who fled the South after its conquest by Hanoi offer a sufficient refutation of the notion that this had been a people's war against the tyrannical masters imposed upon them by the American imperialists. And what can one say of the leaders of the Khmer Rouge, who after seizing Cambodia with China's support surpassed Stalin's records in massacring their own countrymen? No one can say with assurance that there was another way of preserving a non-Communist south. But the goal did not justify expending thousands of American lives and devastating the Vietnamese and their country.

Many of the above doubts and questions about US policies in Vietnam appear in my treatment of Soviet foreign policy, and in my *Rivals*, a study of US-Soviet relations since World War II. Both came out while the war was still going on, its domestic repercussions having such sad effects on American society. But in retrospect I still wonder how we avoided something even more disastrous: say a sizable mutiny on the part of our troops in Vietnam. Thousands of miles from home, our soldiers could read about racial riots, of the assassinations of Robert Kennedy and Martin Luther King, of how the unfortunate war had aggravated every ailment of American society.

As to the war's rationale, the celebrated domino theory, I tried to point out that it was being refuted at the very time Washington was stepping up its military efforts. It is largely forgotten that prior to 1965 the danger of Communist takeover in Indonesia was very real, and that would have dealt a greater blow to US interests than the fall of South Vietnam. Indonesia, the most populous Moslem country in the world, with vast natural resources, had the largest and best-organized Communist party, second only to the ruling ones in Asia.

President Sukarno did more than merely flirt, first with the USSR and then increasingly with China. Under his leadership Indonesia engaged in an undeclared war against pro-Western Malaysia. One obstacle to a complete Communist ascendance remained, and that was the country's army. On September 30, 1965, the Indonesian Communists with the complicity of Sukarno attempted a coup against the armed forces. The coup failed and was followed by savage retribution by the army chiefs. More than 100,000 people are alleged to have been killed. Sukarno was reduced to a figurehead with the military taking over. The most important country in that region escaped Communist domination.

The events in Indonesia demonstrated another reason why the US government should have thought twice about intensifying the war in Vietnam: the ever-increasing hostility between China and the USSR. The latter's leaders could hardly conceal their satisfaction that the Indonesian Communists in the Chinese camp suffered a shattering defeat. The Soviet Union did not even make the gesture of breaking diplomatic relations with the new Djakarta regime, which had slaughtered tens of thousands of its at least nominally ideological comrades. The United States derived obvious benefits from the split between the two Communist powers. But both the rapprochement with China, and detente with the USSR, initiated in 1972, might have taken place earlier, had the turn of events in Vietnam been different.

15

The Fall of the American University

1960s: Era of the "Issues"...The Harvard Faculty: "a rowdy Balkan Parliament"...My angelic-faced student pushes a dean down the stairs of University Hall

The Vietnam drama is very widely blamed for the turbulence that swept our cities and college campuses in the sixties and seventies. About the race riots and related phenomena I could add very little to what is generally known. I was appalled by what I saw on TV and read in the papers. But during the university crisis, I was right in the middle of what was one of its major battlegrounds.

But was it all because of Vietnam? The war greatly aggravated tensions already vibrating on the university campuses. The guilt feelings produced by the undergraduates' draft exemptions, plus the mixture of fear and of moral revulsion due to the war all undoubtedly played a major role in what was in a way the American Cultural Revolution. Yet elsewhere at the same time student unrest reached its height in France, spread to West Germany, and was noticeable in other lands. Did this vortex of energy also have anything to do with the real Cultural Revolution in China, the clash between the regime and the young in Poland? No: those occurrences in the Communist world had completely different roots and just happened to coincide with the crisis in the West.

Why such troubles afflicted the West, at the time more prosperous than ever before, is still open to conjecture. France, with the economic crisis and the Algerian war behind it experienced in 1968 a veritable student revolution. President de Gaulle previously fearless in the face of several assassination attempts on him when he was ending the Algerian war, this time faltered to the extent of fleeing to French army posts in Western Germany and contemplating a refuge for his family in the Federal Republic. Well, the general was only human and seventy-eight. Perhaps part of the answer to the problem of the student revolt epidemics came from a middle-aged Frenchman witnessing a Paris riot: "They haven't had a war for twenty years." In the French case, it was not literally true; draftees were used in the Algerian War. During my trips to France I would see their obituaries in the papers, each preceded by the Napoleonic: "Died on the field of honor." But perhaps there is something perverse about man's psychology when young that makes for impatience with physical and material security and leads to trouble. One reads, and not only in Rupert Brooke, how the coming of the War of 1914 was eagerly welcomed by the middle and upper class youths in all the states drawn into it.

My first awareness of the youth revolution came in 1964 during a visit to Stanford, California. Martin Malia rushed into my room announcing that there was a student rebellion at Berkeley: the city or the university had enclosed a plot of ground previously used for political meetings, and the undergraduates were taking to the streets! (Such excitability is typical of Martin: during the Cuban crisis he was in Moscow and burst in upon Anna Akhmatova exclaiming, how could she be working calmly when the world might blow up? She explained to him, as she would relate to her friends, that the fate of the world was not going to be affected by whether she worked or not. And the great poetess added that the Americans were very peculiar!) No, it was not just student caprice, it was the beginning of a revolution.

And so it was. Within a few years the American social scene would be drastically altered. Feminism would become a mighty force. Rock-and-roll music would expand its reach to become a national cult. "Alternative life-styles" heretofore persecuted would become protected by the law. The contrast with the past was stark. When I came to Harvard in 1946, a student caught in a homosexual act would be expelled within twenty-four hours. During the US national tennis, championships in 1950, a disgruntled player grabbed a microphone and shouted a four-letter word. He was banned from tournament tennis for life. Now such words would appear regularly in print, and even the most venerable magazines, especially in England, would not be above their use.

Public attitude toward sexual mores underwent the most drastic change. During my first years in New England, newspapers were vigilant guardians of morality. If it happened to be a lean season for news, they would send teams of male and female reporters to try to register in various motels for a few hours, and then would print startling revelations of how illicit and criminal activities found some havens. As late as 1967, *Life* magazine thought it worthwhile to print a story about something supposedly unheard of: a Harvard graduate student was sharing an apartment with a young lady student, without their being married.(Was it only a year or two before this that the president of Vassar admonished its students that they were expected to preserve their virginity throughout their college careers?)By 1970 all such maxims and cautions could have been the stuff of film comedy.

During his 1964 presidential campaign Lyndon Johnson, who was going to win by a landslide, knew that he must greatly enlarge the scope of American intervention in Vietnam. He still thought it proper to conceal it by the awkward declaration that Asian wars should be fought by "Asian boys." The government's lack of candor would greatly magnify the future troubles and resentment of the young. At Harvard I watched the rising tide of that resentment affecting the student body. Looking back from today, I cannot refrain from a selfish reflection that observing what turned out to be a local mock revolution was highly instructive for those like me who were students of real revolutions.

But at the time, the growing unrest looked much too serious to be just a subject for dispassionate study. The first harbinger of the coming troubles was the appearance in Cambridge in 1966 of the Secretary of Defense Robert McNamara. After he delivered a talk, a mob of students in an ugly mood surrounded his car, and eventually he had to leave the scene by an underground tunnel. From then on the number of incidents grew at an increasing rate. Classes of professors thought to be government consultants were interrupted. The student paper *The Crimson*, previously a somewhat jocular reporter of local events, now specialized in revolutionary diatribes. A colleague of mine believed to have justified US policy in Vietnam as conducive to "nation building" was not once, but twice, called a murderer in *The Crimson*. Those institutions within the university that appeared to the "activists" to be associated with the military-industrial complex were continuous targets of verbal abuse and in a few cases of actual violence.

We entered the era of Issues. Practically all the elements of university life: the social and gender composition of the student body, the curriculum, the power of the faculty and the governing boards were now the subject of student attacks and constant demonstrations. Then of course there was The Issue: the university's complicity in the War. As I arrived in Harvard Yard on my way to a lecture or my office I grew accustomed to the frequent morning scenes of a sizeable crowd sometimes filling the large space in front of the library and an orator with a microphone denouncing violently some special iniquity of the university and/or of the bourgeois world.

The university administration, which previously had to cope with crises on the order of a raid by some jokesters on a Radcliffe dormitory to secure female underwear, or a "riot" by those opposed to changing the Latin in the diplomas to English, was understandably handicapped in dealing with a revolution. Appeals to the good sense of the student body met with the response that might have been expected. Then a number of committees were set up to consider soberly various grievances, and again as might have been expected they mostly conceded to the radicals' demands. But by then there were new Issues. One of the most persistent concerned the ROTC program, under which hundreds of students received military training and upon graduation commissions in the Army and Navy reserves. Incidentally the program was helpful to poor students because the government paid their tuition. Yes, despite its obvious benefits, and the fact that the armed forces would not collapse if deprived of a few Harvard-trained officers, the ROTC had to go! A faculty meeting, where some professors achieved rhetorical heights in denouncing America's menacing imperialism, sanctioned its ejection from the campus.

What was happening at Harvard was reproduced at numerous other campuses; at some, e.g. Berkeley, Columbia, and Wisconsin, the situation was both more serious and more grotesque. But, to repeat, at the time we could not appreciate the latter. In addition to the growing divisiveness over the war, several currents of disaffection and rebelliousness united to threaten the basic social order. The flowering of the drug culture was an important element in the whole mess. Cambridge Common became an official gathering place for the potheads, and even from my home a half-mile away I could smell the collective aroma wafting eastward.

Some of the causes of the national turmoil had their source in real grievances: to some extent the war, certainly the extent of racial inequality. But even so, violence was inexcusable. The attack upon the universities was not only irrelevant to the real issues of the day, but also especially destructive; for it struck at a most vulnerable institution. I still grow impatient when I hear people express nostalgia for the "idealism" (probably the most abused term in contemporary speech) and "activism" of the 1960s. It is a huge oversimplification to hold that young rebels are always prompted by idealism. As a boy in Poland, I witnessed how the right-wing student extremists tried to bar Jews from the universities. And on a much wider scale this also happened after Hitler's coming to power in Germany. Youthful passion and combativeness are just not synonymous with idealism. Students and other young people have played an honorable role in the struggle for democracy in many continental countries, and in America in the fight for racial equality. But the university in a democratic country is not the proper place for political struggle. It is noteworthy that the two most successful democratic societies of modern times, Great Britain and the US, arrived where they are without any appreciable contribution by university students. Contrasting is the mixed record of Germany and France, where in the past, the young, including the students, massively and frequently responded to the call of Fascism and Communism.

Issues proliferated and so did the varieties of student radicalism. The most conspicuous of them was the SDS (Students for a Democratic Society), which, in the late sixties, appeared to be the wave of the future for the radical movement, despite or maybe because of its chaotic ideology. Then there were other more ideologically rigorous factions, but hardly any pro-Moscow Communists, because that variety had by the 1960s faded out among the young. We did have a small detachment of Maoists. At Harvard they could be distinguished from the other protesters by their jackets and ties, the incongruously retro bourgeois habit being evidently a sign of discipline, or perhaps a consequence of the unavailability of the Mao tunics in the local clothing stores. Conspicuous among those followers of the Great Helmsman was a well-known Harvard professor. A few years later this zealot radically changed his view, abandoned the group house where he had dwelt and which in 1968 bore the proud name The East is Red Commune after the anthem of the Cultural Revolution, and so came back to earth.

As at other universities, Harvard faculty were deeply divided in their reactions to the crisis. Many viewed the whole surrealistic scene with wonder and dismay. Among them were not only people with conservative views, but also of the left, who still could not stomach the notion of the university as a playground for manifestations, interruption of classes, and bomb threats. Yet there was a considerable number who were reliving their youth, or rather thought they were, and who eagerly sought the young rebels' approval. Others were influenced by their own children, and some unabashedly saw the mini-revolution as an opportunity to gain fame and advancement. All in all, one must admit the behavior of the faculty as a whole was unheroic. Most of the levelheaded professors must have felt that what was going on could not be justified, and represented an intolerable threat to basic academic values. There was hardly any physical danger in making it clear to one's colleagues and the students. Not many did so.

I knew quite well the man who had seemed at the time to be the spiritual guide of the revolution, and of what was known as the New Left. In temperament, Herbert Marcuse was very far from being a revolutionary. Then a professor at Brandeis, he was a rather bookish scholar of the German professorial type, with a good sense of humor. Very modest, too; at one learned meeting we attended he told me he was surprised to have been invited. He must have been astounded at being propelled to fame during the brief flowering of the New Left. Few who invoked his name could have read his books through; for while most erudite, they are virtually unreadable. But they are seeded with phrases that suited the mood of the late 1960s. The most famous one was "repressive tolerance," standing for the villainy of the capitalist democracy that deludes and enslaves man through elections, bills of rights, etc. And then there was "liberty can be made into a powerful instrument of domination."

Having criticized my colleagues for their attitude in the face of the assaults on the university, I confess with some regret that I myself was far from being an active defender of it. I did not go to the mass meetings where some professors extolled the young for their courage in tearing the mask of hypocrisy from the face of American society and the Harvard administration; while others plaintively appealed for moderation. My conservative friends had to drag me to the faculty meetings where measures against the disorder were lengthily and ineffectively discussed. I went on cultivating my garden, in the sense of focusing on teaching and writing. I have said that there was no physical danger to the faculty in those days, but perhaps that thought merits a qualification. The building containing the Russian

Research Center also housed another institute, which for some reason aroused the hostility of the radicals. From time to time an anonymous caller would warn that the building would be bombed. At first the university police would clear the premises and look for explosives. After a few such false alarms, the university let stay those who wished to, and then adopted another to me incomprehensible method of warding off the danger. After a bomb-threat call, Professor Archibald Cox of the Law School, who gained fame later on as the special prosecutor in the Watergate investigation, would hasten to the scene and stand in front of the menaced building. Whether by his personal magic or no, Harvard escaped bombings, except for the destruction of the ROTC building, fortunately empty at the time. At Columbia in 1968 and 1969 such threats were daily occurrences. I remember once being a guest lecturer at Zbig Brzezinski's seminar, which was held on the 13th floor of the School of International Affairs. Sure enough, the bomb-warning bell rang and, under instructions not to use elevators, we started down the stairs. After three floors Zbig said, "To hell with it," and we went back to complete the class, with few defections among the students.

Some but not many Harvard classes were similarly threatened. Mine never were. But the classroom in which I gave lectures was also used for a chemistry course, and was therefore full of lab equipment. This coincidence of dual use suggested the possibility of a chemical explosion in the midst of a lecture. One of my teaching assistants was an SDS member who nervously absented herself from my classes. She finally declared that she felt that grading papers, etc., was not creative, at which point I asked her to seek creativity elsewhere.

In 1968 Columbia had its great crisis, complete with the trashing of the administration offices. One year later, there were ominous signs that something similar might take place at Harvard. There had been strange portents the year before. For the first time in living memory the outdoor Commencement rites were rained out, and the ceremony had to be held in cramped indoor quarters. Some divinity evidently disapproved of Harvard bestowing an honorary degree on the Shah of Iran. In the spring of 1969 the deans prayed for rain. But it was a rainless, beautiful New England spring day like those that had smiled upon countless Commencements. Outdoor radical rallies proliferated; tension was visible.

In my socialism course I happened to be lecturing on Tkachev, a noted Russian revolutionary of the 19th century whose motto was

"A revolutionary does not prepare a revolution, he makes it!" It happened to be an appropriate sermon for the day. As soon as the class ended, many of its members rushed out to join the large crowd besieging University Hall, the seat of Harvard's administration. There were the usual speeches, pleas by the deans for moderation and dispersal. Then there followed a facsimile of the storming of the Winter Palace during the Bolshevik Revolution: the crowd rushed in, evicting the deans and taking over the hall. Later on I saw a photograph of an angelic-looking student from my socialism class pushing a dean down the stairs. Fortunately, the similarity with the great historical event extended to the fact that no one was injured (contrary to legend, the Winter Palace was not really stormed; the Bolshevik mob just seeped in, encountering no real resistance).

The university authorities held hasty conferences on how to deal with the occupation. Later on, President Pusey was criticized for not waiting out the rebels. University Hall is hardly a place where a large number of people can stay indefinitely. Even revolutionary fervor could hardly sustain them in the face of such realities as the scarcity of toilet facilities. Then the occupiers soon were quarreling among themselves: the puritanical factions insisting on banning pot smoking, the libertarians incensed by such deprivation of personal freedom. A prolonged siege of the conquered bastion, on the other hand, would have carried obvious risks. Harvard Yard is in the center of a bustling, populous city. Students from a neighboring high school pass daily right by University Hall. What if the urban masses, belonging to what President Nixon called "the silent majority" chose to express in a very unsilent manner their resentment at Harvard students, whom they saw as both pampered brats and troublemakers? I don't know whether this was a concern of the president and his advisers. It certainly would have been one of mine. Whatever the reasons, the powers that be decided to counterattack. As I was shaving the next morning, I heard on the radio that the building had been recaptured by Cambridge police and several of its recent residents arrested. I hastened to the Yard, but though untidy it did not appear to have been the scene of a battle. But I was told that University Hall was in a shambles, the invaders having rifled the cabinets and files, in search of secret documents attesting to the university's sinister ties with the CIA or the like. None such had been discovered.

The invasion put an end to the attitude that "It can't happen here" and to the idle boasts that Harvard was not Columbia, that students were having close relations with the faculty, etc. There was a hastily called faculty meeting held in Sanders Theater, normally used for concerts and lectures, while the profaned building was being purified. I felt it appropriate that the first four speakers were all Russian-born, and had emigrated after the Revolution. Theirs were discordant voices, also suggesting the atmosphere of the Petrograd Soviet in 1917. The eminent chemist Bohday Kistiakovski pleaded for the condemnation of the invaders. Equally renowned as an economist, Vassily Leontiev asked for leniency for the students and censored the administration for summoning the police. Professor George Hanfman and Alexander Gerschenkron voiced their outrage. I forget what was decided after a very tempestuous debate, but it was clear that the faculty would not sanction any punishment for most of the invaders. The university proceeded to quash legal action against all of them. A few, very few, were eventually expelled.

And now our little Harvard world took on the appearance of a rowdy Balkan parliament. The faculty certainly did. Those scholarly men (at this time there were hardly any tenured faculty women), largely without prior interest in politics, split up into combating factions in the now almost daily faculty meetings. Two were represented by regular caucuses: one which stood for the restoration of college discipline, the other taking a benign view of the radical students activities and a critical one of the administration. But there were other groupings, as well as what might be called freelance followers of the New Left. Was it the department of philosophy or of Romance languages that declared itself to be a commune? I am not sure what this was supposed to mean, but it obviously implied a blow against the American Establishment and the reactionary governance of Harvard.

For the students, Issues were paramount. The radicals addressed an ultimatum to the university in the form of "eleven non-negotiable demands." This was truly a diplomatic innovation. Even Hitler and Stalin lured their victims to their doom by pretending that their demands were negotiable. One such point was an amnesty for the perpetrators of the seizure; probably a psychological mistake, for if the authority being threatened is illegitimate, why ask it to rescind its rulings? Another was that the governing bodies of Harvard were to be transformed. Instead of all those Establishment figures, there was to be a nine-member body, three members elected by the students, three by the faculty, and the rest by the maids, cooks, janitors, and other servitors of the university. There was also something on the list specifying that ten percent of the university's endowment or annual income, I forget which, be devoted to social work in the depressed areas of Boston.

Why have I described at such length a tempest on one campus? There were at the time far more important issues threatening to tear apart American society: Vietnam, and the civil rights. And should one not be more charitable anyway about the student rebels? For all the grotesque features of the rebellion, wasn't there some justification for the young people's anger?

Experts much more qualified than I have written at length about those more important problems. And the university drama did have its own importance. Harvard's ordeal was one of many. The cause and consequences of the crisis in Cambridge influenced developments elsewhere.

As for being charitable, I personally find it difficult to excuse uncivilized behavior on the scale and in the form it assumed here. And if we indulge the young, I wonder, should we also indulge their elders who thought fit to abet it?

As in many revolutionary situations, the actual troublemakers among the students and the faculty were clearly a minority. But the great majority of either group while uneasy about the disruptions was, again typically, afraid or embarrassed to express disapproval.

Then there were people who regardless of their political views were emotionally deeply distressed by what was happening to "their" Harvard. Interestingly enough, many so affected had not been undergraduates here but had come as graduate students or faculty. Alex Gershchenkron, who admired American institutions as could only a refugee from central Europe, lost his jovial mien. Merle Fainsod was indefatigable as chairman and member of various committees trying to handle the crisis, and indeed his efforts probably helped avoid even more serious troubles. But none was more involved both emotionally and actively in trying to stem the forces of disorder than my close friend Bob McCloskey. His voice growing hoarse, he spoke at every faculty meeting, was constantly in touch with others trying to restore the university to something like its normal condition. His hands shook, he smoked immoderately. About a year or so later, he died of a sudden heart attack.

The explosive situation continued through the balance of the school year. There were other student sit-ins. At one point there was a threat to bomb Widener library, the largest and most valuable collection of books of any institution of higher learning in the world. The threat was thought serious enough for several professors to keep an all-night vigil there. Teaching in some courses had virtually ceased. On the other hand several radical "courses" unsanctioned by the university sprang up; one was led by a graduate student and had an attendance of about seven hundred.

In retrospect, I find it amazing that so much of the regular university work continued. My own course proceeded undisturbed, even though I had a reputation as a reactionary on the Issues. But the atmosphere was hardly favorable to scholarly pursuits. The police guarded many buildings, rebel students urging boycott of the classes stood in front of the lecture halls. As I lectured, I could sometimes hear loudspeakers bellowing in the neighboring Yard. TV vans and crews could often be found near certain places like the Russian Research Center, where there seemed fair promise of a riot taking place. Once on leaving my office I heard the TV crewmen cursing, complaining that they had waited all afternoon and nothing had happened! Harvard also began to attract visiting non-student troublemakers. One such group, which specialized in stripping naked, put on guest appearances in several locations, including Eliot House. I was glad that John Finley, the master of my old House, had resigned the year before and was spared the performance.

As I have mentioned, my own role during the episode was distinctly unheroic. I went dutifully to the faculty meetings and gave my proxy to the "conservative" caucus. But in view of the general attitude of the faculty, I concluded that the unpleasant business, like much else that was happening in the country, was the product of a wrong idea whose time has come; and while one had to make clear where one stood, for the time being one could not do much more. I recalled a Chinese sage's advice on how to preserve peace of mind: sit under a tree in your garden and drink tea. I did not have a garden, only a small yard in front of my house, but with some trees. I sat under one of them drinking iced tea or occasionally something stronger, and played with my two small sons. And then came Commencement and the end of that academic year. The revolution went on vacation and never regained its momentum. True, there were to be some serious troubles during subsequent years; on one occasion, several shops in Harvard Square were vandalized. President Pusey, who undeservedly incurred the hostility of the radicals, and criticisms among the faculty, resigned after a face-saving interval. There were other changes in the administration. The dean of the faculty, who had suffered a stroke in the spring of 1969, also quit after another year. Somehow the feverish campus atmosphere of 1969 never quite recurred. The smell of *Cannabis Indica* emanating from the Cambridge Common, which I had been convinced would endure for years, gradually subsided. It seemed that normalcy had returned.

But, as in the case of every other institution of higher learning in the country, it was now a different university. A great proliferation of bureaucracy follows every revolution, and Harvard was no exception. Until the time of troubles, teaching and research had been the main features of university life. Now the academic scene would be overshadowed by the Issues.

16

The Tyrant's Shadow

Khrushchev opened Pandora's box and Brezhnev and Co. can't get it shut again...How they bullied the old man at the end

The 1968 Paris student revolution which came so close to toppling the mighty De Gaulle (and probably influenced his decision to retire soon afterwards) inspired a well-known French writer to hail it as the dawn of a new age—nothing would remain the same. But in the daylight hours of politics, this proved to be a wrong prophecy. De Gaulle departed, but the system he had installed, surprisingly enough, went on (who could have imagined that without him, France would not revert to having a new government every six months or so). In this country, Richard Nixon became president like a Phoenix rising out of the ashes. Those who had jumped on the bandwagon of change were discovering that its former occupants were now getting off it. Many of the erstwhile radicals among the students would as alumni turn to pursue traditional career paths. The New Left expired in the middle seventies. How many of today's college students have heard of Herbert Marcuse? Perhaps the same fate—oblivion—will in due time overtake the New Right, born largely out of the premature relief at the end of the Cold War. Will there be then some other fashionable extremism that will engage the passion of the young and the middle-aged in the West? Quite possibly.

The Soviets looked with less than enthusiasm at the New Left, though in their eyes it was a welcome symptom of the decadence of the West. Its chaotic ideology was much closer to anarchism than to Marxism. By the same token many representatives of new radicalism disapproved of the current condition of Soviet society. By their standards it had undergone an embourgeoisement: its puritanical code, especially when it came to sex, its bureaucratization, and in-

179

equality not much of an improvement over capitalism. China was closer to the heart of the short-lived cult, and Castro's Cuba probably closest.

But the Communist world was too much involved in its own troubles to pay much attention to the intellectual fashions in the West. Another disadvantage of the Vietnam folly was that it obscured the progressive disintegration of "proletarian internationalism" i.e., of world Communism. The Soviet system itself was losing its ruthlessness, which much as it was desirable from the humanitarian point of view was loosening the grip of the authoritarian oligarchy on its society. Our own distress did not keep me from following on a daily basis what was happening in the Fatherland of Socialism. Khrushchev's brusque dismissal in 1964 could have been anticipated if not precisely timed. His garrulity about Stalin's crimes was clearly undermining the myth on which the edifice of Soviet authoritarianism was based. And equally important, he roused his colleagues' fears about their own power. Meetings even of the Party's highest organs were packed by Nikita with outsiders, so as to overcome his fellow oligarchs, growing opposition to his "hare-brained schemes." He was improvidently taking a vacation while in Moscow the plot against him ripened; his last words spoken in public having been a message to the Soviet astronauts traveling in space, promising to meet them upon their return to earth. Instead, he was packed on a plane and escorted by the KGB and transported to the oligarchs' meeting which pronounced his political doom. A man who for ten years shook the world with his threats and bluster became, overnight, an obscure pensioner.

When under perestroika scholars could obtain some details about old Nikita's fall, I realized how far my understanding of the event lagged behind the changing Soviet reality. I had imagined the intrigue to have been conceived in absolute secrecy, and the coup, carried out suddenly and resolutely, somewhat in the way that Khrushchev himself had cut short Beria's career in 1953. But as the old man's son Sergei Nikitich related in his memoirs, the agitation against Khrushchev among the Party hierarchy had been carried out almost openly for some time before the actual blow was struck. Yet the First Secretary, who was vaguely aware what was going on, took no countersteps. Age (seventy) and weariness combined to make him a different man from the one he had been in 1957 when, confronted with a similar intrigue, he defied the majority of the Presidium (as the Politburo was then called) and brought about his enemies' downfall. What is rather pathetic was his reliance to the last on his closest friend Mikoyan, who had all along been in on the plot.

To King Stork there succeeded King Log; to the irascible Nikita prone to violent outbursts against his colleagues and others, the rather indolent and pleasure-loving Brezhnev. In retrospect, I have often felt that in what remained essentially a Stalinist system, a single leader could not firmly establish his authority without having something of a Stalin in his character. Khrushchev could fire his colleagues in a fit of temper, but since he would not periodically have some of them shot, he was not sufficiently feared by his fellow potentates. With Brezhnev there ensued a Golden Age, or rather two decades for the Party and government bigwigs. No longer terrorized as under Stalin or bullied, as under Khrushchev, they could cling to their offices and privileges well into senility, sometimes beyond. At the beginning of perestroika, the minister in charge of the nuclear industry was eighty-eight years old. Their chief himself was during the last few years of his reign physically debilitated. "Come, grow old along with me!" appears to have been Brezhnev's message to his Politburo colleagues. And they did and not only chronologically. His two immediate successors were already seriously ill when they were elected to the world's most exacting political position. I cannot help reflecting on the parallel to today's American university, where because of the legislation against "ageism" professors are no longer required to retire. But what made all those prudent oldsters elect in 1985 a mere youngster of fifty-four to the Politburo? They should have known that he, Gorbachev, would make trouble.

For Soviet society at large the change at the top in 1964 meant the tightening of discipline. Whatever their behavior in the high Party circles the new leaders, Brezhnev, as the General Secretary and Alexis Kosygin, as Prime Minister would try to avoid their predecessor's great mistake, i.e. his quasi-liberalism. Nikita was usually photographed smiling. Now Brezhnev's stern expression in public and Kosygin's bilious one, both in their appearance reminiscent of masters in a reform school, conveyed the message to their subjects "Now now, there will be no more nonsense."

It was especially in the 1960s that I felt a certain incongruity in being an analyst of Soviet affairs. Here I was in America in the midst of a society pulsating with strong emotions on a whole variety of issues. Public opinion polls, whatever one thinks of their relevance, still brought us valuable information about how people felt on a variety of issues. The political game was being played openly in the Congress and elsewhere; the media brought us contrasting views on problems ranging from Vietnam to the civil rights. I was right in the middle of the university crisis and could write about it from first-hand knowledge (I did. My little book *The Fall of the American University* came out here and in England after being refused by my regular publishers, who said it was not consistent with the "political correctness" of the times. But when it came to Soviet affairs, I could write only about politics that transpired on the surface of society.

A joke current in the pre-glasnost era posed the problem. An expert was asked how he could know what was really happening in the Soviet Union, in view of the fact that most of his information came from the official sources. Well, he replied, self-consciously, one could learn a great deal by reading between the lines in Pravda. I see, said the non-expert, that one does not have to know Russian to be an expert, what is between the lines is blank! Indeed, how could we know what the millions of Russians, Ukrainians, etc. really felt? And in other fields, e.g. the economy, the official statistics had been regularly falsified under Stalin, as his successors admitted, and were hardly reliable afterwards. There had to be developed a special art for trying to find out what the Soviets spent on defense, the official figure being grotesquely unrealistic. To many in the West, therefore, the study of Soviet politics, Kremlinology as it was dubbed, appeared of questionable validity, something akin to an occult art, or worse, tendentious writing sponsored by the Cold War. I never let myself be intimidated by such arguments. Recognizing the obvious limitations in obtaining information about the USSR, I felt then as I do now, that there was enough of it to reach important and interesting conclusions. When it came to ascertaining public opinion, the analogies with the West did not hold, or to put it more bluntly, public opinion in our sense didn't exist in Stalin's time.

Russian society was anesthetized by terror. Most people, including even many victims of the terror, believed in what official propaganda fed them, and if they did not, were afraid to think even about what might be an alternative to the terrible reality. Weird as it must sound, Soviet society came close between 1935 and 1953 to extirpating individual consciousness of public affairs. Compare it with another tyranny—that of Hitler. There you could find an occasional individual, a Catholic prelate like the Bishop of Speyer, a Protestant pastor like Martin Niemöeller, even a general, like Ludwig Beck, who would protest against what was going on. And one could be reputed to be an opponent of the regime, like Konrad Adenauer, and survive if one remained silent. But in the Soviet Union during those terrible years, a majority of political prisoners in the Gulag remained supporters of Communism and believers in Stalin's genius.

After Stalin's death this self-abasement of society began to dissipate. But still, until the coming of glasnost most Russians would remain afraid to criticize the Soviet reality, and many remained incapable of thinking of it in critical terms. Dissent grew, and would become extremely important both by teaching people to think for themselves and by undermining their leaders' self-confidence. But the actual dissenters remained for long few in numbers and drawn almost exclusively from the intelligentsia.

All of the above lends weight to the argument that the most practical and important approach to the study of the Soviet Union was through its politics, which in its turn had to be an inquiry into what was going on within the political leadership. It would have been impractical in 1945 and fairly useless in 1980 to ask the man in the street in Moscow what he thought of his government. By 1987 or so it became both practical and important. However unnatural and repugnant it may seem to the Western mind, the fact remains that the destiny of the Soviet state was for most of its existence determined not by its people, not by impersonal social and economic forces, but by the decisions, first of a despot, then by that of a small oligarchy only slowly and gradually affected by the rise of political consciousness within the intellectual elite.

I have written here and elsewhere how the neurosis that afflicted the Soviet people began to abate after the middle fifties and how the Great Fear in which they had lived (along with the faith in their system) began to recede. Yet the past cast a long shadow. Along with the contemporaneous scene I was studying the Stalin era. And compared with it what was happening under Khrushchev and Brezhnev seemed in a different world. But objectively it still remained a cruel and repressive one. Literary dissidents were hounded, and if they published abroad they were sent to jail or the Gulag. (Pasternak because of his world reputation, escaped that fate but he was publicly vilified and his mistress sent to a camp.). For others who would not keep silent, the KGB devised a new refined form of punishment, for which the 19th Century held a few precedents: perfectly sane people were certified as unbalanced and locked up in psychiatric institutions where their "cure" was likely to bring about the condition for which they had been falsely diagnosed. I remember meeting one such martyr, Petro Grigorenko. That strapping once vigorous man, former general in the Red Army, was released and allowed to go abroad after several years in the psikhushka, the name for such torture chambers. The consequences of his "treatment" with harmful drugs undoubtedly shortened the life of this gallant officer and courageous defender of human rights. When at Harvard in 1983, he inscribed for me his memoirs. A few sentences from the preface deserve to be quoted: "Born into a working family, from my childhood onward I believed in Communist ideas and later served them fanatically. I took a leading place among the ruling hierarchy...I had bright prospects. And all of a sudden embarked on a road of a struggle..."

Not quite "all of a sudden"—a diligent reader of his memoirs would correct the author. The psychological roots of his rebellion must have been accumulating ever since as a young man he witnessed the fearful famine of 1932-1933 in his native Ukraine. Later on, Grigorenko had to stop his wife from denouncing him to the political police. She held no grudge against him but as a loyal Soviet citizen was responding to the authorities' appeal for "vigilance against the enemies of the people." Her husband had just received a letter from his brother describing the pitiful conditions in their native village. Still Grigorenko, a demolition expert, went on fulfilling his duties, which included blowing up orthodox churches; and he served valiantly in the war. It was only in his fifties, and after Khrushchev's "secret" speech that he realized what kind of system he had been serving. You could not be a Red Army general without at least an outward patina of "russification." But in his trauma, General Grigorenko rediscovered his Ukrainian nationality.

Here then is the story of one dissident, but also, in a way, a preview of the various impulses and other factions which were to make the dissident movement a social force, help to bring about perestroika and glasnost, and finally lead to the implosion of the whole system and of the Soviet Union.

But we are still in the late 1960s, and the Soviet ship of state was still fully afloat, though encountering ever-rougher waters. If by firing Khrushchev, his colleagues thought they could turn the clock backward, they were in for a great disappointment. True, the revelations about Stalin's crimes abruptly ceased with Nikita's exit. (Stalin was not restored to his pedestal but if referred to at all, which was discouraged, was no longer an object of abuse, but an "outstanding Marxist-Leninist" who made some errors.)

Unfortunately for the rulers, modern technology and the rise of dissidence thwarted such attempts at Stalin's partial rehabilitation. Dissident literature kept dwelling on the Stalinist past, and on the Stalinist features persisting in the Soviet system. The end of hopes associated with Khrushchev had the effect of transforming former critics of the status quo, notably Alexander Solzhenitsyn into its open enemies, no longer satisfied with being tolerated by the regime but began attacking Communism itself.

The great writer's *One Day in the Life of Ivan Denisovich*, incautiously authorized for publication by Khrushchev, and his other works, disappeared from the book shops and libraries, and the authorities would not permit his new novels, now explicitly anti-regime, to be set in print. The writer's now worldwide fame made it awkward for the Kremlin to try to silence him in a more drastic way, much as such restraint was publicly deplored by the regime's literary lackeys, such as the old Sholokhov.

(Another powerful enemy of the official orthodoxy was the xerox machine)or, as the primitive Russian variant of the sinister device was called, shapirograph. (This name fitted in nicely with the rulers' anti-Jewish orientation.) Through its use, the dissidents could and would outflank the authorities' ban on subversive and non-conformist literature and tracts. Samizdat, or illegal literature, would perplex and torment the regime till its very fall. And with the USSR no longer sealed off from the outside world, there were now foreign visitors, newsmen, even an occasional foreign communist who would snatch the forbidden fruit and carry it abroad where it would be enjoyed by the Western readers to the humiliation and fury of the Kremlin.

Not being able to resort to terror, the Brezhnev team tried to repress dissent through chicanery. But its clumsy efforts in that direction were to prove ultimately counterproductive. Take the trials of the dissidents. In the bad old times, the "guilty ones" were condemned either without any legal niceties, or, if before the court, then readily confessed their real or imaginary crimes.(But now a novelty developed: the accused often denied guilt or even impudently assailed the Soviet system, and occasionally lawyers appeared who really defended the accused.)The old judicial system was epitomized by Counselor Broido in the notorious Moscow Trial of 1938 who began his "defense" by "Comrade judges, I am appalled by my client's crimes." The only thing which remained unchanged from the pattern of the old tragic spectacles (so-called trials) was that the verdict was fixed before the trial by an appropriate Party agency. Unfortunate for the victims but hardly effective from the propaganda viewpoint. Unwittingly, the regime was educating the public about the fraudulence of the judicial system. The authorities tried various remedies to correct this shocking state of affairs. The accused were promised more lenient verdicts if they adhered to the old custom. (He was all ready to confess, said one, but he was not able to memorize the complex tale of his fictitious crime. He should write its main points on his shirt cuffs, suggested a helpful KGB agent.). The uncooperative lawyers were disbarred. Still it did not quite work. The once well-oiled machinery of repression would at times emit grinding noises, and they would be heard also outside the Soviet Union.

I was in on an analysis of one of the most jarring of such sounds. None other than Nikita Khrushchev had his memoirs smuggled out and published in the West. In 1970, when the first volume appeared, I was not sure that they were genuine. There were factual errors in the text; they contained no special revelations about the inner mechanics and personalities of Soviet politics. Then along with several other students of the Soviet scene, I was invited by Time magazine, which had serialized parts of the book, to a conference to determine its genuiness and significance. My doubts about the former were dispelled. We heard several tapes on which old Nikita perpetuated his tales and reflections. It was undoubtedly his familiar voice, occasionally enlivened it seemed, by an appropriate potation. More important than my opinion was that of the specialists in voice analysis who assured us of the authenticity of the recordings.

The story of how his father came to write his memoirs is contained in Sergei Nikitch's 1990 book about Khrushchev's last years. Those years were not kind to the former leader who from his political fall until his death was practically under house arrest, his apartment and villa bugged by the KGB. His former friends and protégés now shunned him. There was nothing in his recollections that touched on state secrets, nothing really that could be taken as a criticism of the Communist system as such—to the end he remained a believer. Yet his successors treated the old and infirm man as if he represented a major danger to the state. Men who had owed their advancement to him continued to bully Khrushchev until the end about his memoirs and their publication abroad.

In 1960, the poet Alexander Tvardovsky, the unofficial poet laureate of the post-war Soviet Union, sought the sense of the terrible pre-1953 past: "Though alive, cut off from life by the Kremlin walls he stood over us like a dread spirit." And the refrain of his poem: "What can you add, what can you put differently. Such things did happen on this our earth." Proponent of liberalization, friend of Solzhenitsyn, yet a believer in Communism, the poet was driven by these inner contradictions to alcoholism, which probably contributed to his premature death. For all the reforms and past denunciations of the "cult of personality," Stalin's ghost still hovered over Soviet society of the 1960s and 1970s. In some ways it still does over Russia.

17

Stalin

Writing about Stalin...not a pleasant subject...His use of Terror...Stan's condescension toward his younger brother's profession

In 1970 I undertook the difficult task of writing a biography of Stalin. The only worthwhile biography extant at the time was by Boris Souvarine, a Russian-born French writer who in the 1920s was read out of the French Communist Party for a variety of deviations. Written in the 1930s, it was understandably not complimentary to Stalin, and as such did not find an American publisher during the war. One presumably could not print such a libelous tract about the man who was our ally, *Time* magazine's "Man of the Year;" perhaps a bit undemocratic; but still "Uncle Joe."

I met Souvarine after the war. He was then the editor of the strongly anti-Soviet French journal, East-West. Small and nervous looking (he was convinced that the Soviets might try to do him in), it seemed incongruous that at one time he had been one of the leaders of the French Communists, so many of them tough, boisterous characters. I was even more amazed at his reaction to the evidence (presented among other places in my book) that after the February Revolution Lenin took money from Imperial Germany. The facts are incontrovertible. I found their confirmation even in Lenin's own correspondence published in the Soviet Union. But suddenly and momentarily an old Communist reawakened in Souvarine. Stalin was capable of every villainy, to be sure; the Soviet system was rotten, but he could not accept that Lenin, his one-time idol, would have stooped to such a thing.

My own biography came out in 1972. The subject was in many ways more difficult than Lenin's life. Lenin was primarily a revolutionary; the period of his actual power until struck by a paralytic stroke, just five years. In contrast, Stalin, at first the revolutionary, then the politician groping for power, and mostly Stalin the dictator, was in fact three different persons, something which many who write about him overlook. One has to rub off several layers of legend to try to get at the basic Stalin. Then, also as when restoring an ancient painting, one has to scrape off a variety of the different versions to get at the facts. There was the superhuman Stalin of Soviet propaganda during his rule. Khrushchev described the man who until 1934 did useful work, but then gave way to criminal impulses. The Brezhnev era saw a great though occasionally fallible leader. Dissent and especially glasnost gave rise to a veritable explosion of books, articles, and even plays unmasking the tyrant, but do they add up to the real Stalin? I wrote my biography without the benefit of what glasnost was to reveal by the opening of the hitherto secret archives and files. Yet there was little to change or add in the new editions of the book that appeared from the late 1980s until the early 1990s.

Much that was newsworthy was withheld from the Soviet citizen until the collapse of Communism was known in the West. But here again one had to scrutinize the nuances carefully, because of the bias of the defectors and of some dissidents. One had to steer clear of the fantasies propagated by renovation seekers among the Western writers. The myth of Rosa Kaganovich, Stalin's non-existent third wife, was found not only in completely spurious works, but was also endorsed by a fairly respectable British biographer. Moreover, since Stalin was a villain and murderer, why not make him also an agent of the Tsarist secret police before 1914 as did a former CIA agent in his book? But that charge is completely false, much as it would be psychologically satisfying, especially to a disillusioned Communist.

Was he a paranoiac? One is tempted to assert that a degree of paranoia is necessary to a tyrant who wants to preserve at least his political health. Stalin didn't have to look far back in history to note a cautionary finale to a dictatorship, namely the fate of a "normal" politician like Mussolini. One day he walked into a meeting of the Grand Fascist Council, all of its members until then his obedient tools—and was sacked. After he was toppled from power, his once adoring countrymen jeered and celebrated when his bullet-riddled body was hung by the heels from a balcony in the village of Dongo, on Lake Como.

Every successful politician has to be to some extent an actor. In Stalin that ability was highly developed. In studying his career I was struck by how in its course he could fool even such great connoisseurs of human nature as FDR and Churchill. To Roosevelt he was a much larger version of the city boss who had been a familiar figure on the American political scene during the president's career. For Churchill, he was a great national leader, impressive for sharing his own gift for the quick mot juste. (He replied to Churchill's compliment that the Russians were good soldiers by saying that, yes, in the Red Army one had to be foolhardy not to be a good soldier.) Neither of the Westerners realized the extent of their partner's depravity.

And so that "morbid suspiciousness," which no Soviet official writing or talking about Stalin after his death failed to note, was largely acting! It served to frighten his subordinates, and inhibited them from even thinking of how to get rid of the monstrous man who could read their minds. It served to obscure his cruelty and sadism: it was obviously some others who exploited that weakness of the Boss, as he was known in the higher Party circles, for destroying innocent people. With age, what had been acting may well have become a real character trait. Certainly his savage fury about Tito, the preparations for a new purge, and, if rumors are to be trusted, the strong anti-Jewish measures contemplated in his last years suggest irrational behavior.

The mind behind the façade shows in the extremely skillful political game he played before power was fully his, from the time of Lenin's stroke in 1922 to the end of the decade. He conspired with Zinoviev, and Kamenev to defeat Trotsky, and then with the help of Bukharin and Rykov, turned upon those two former closest collaborators of Lenin's, later destroying the latter two themselves. It was only when those real or potential rivals were rendered impotent that he gave free rein to his savage temper and struck at the millions of peasants, and then physically annihilated his erstwhile closest collaborators. Cordell Hull, Roosevelt's Secretary of State who was once sent to Moscow, reported in his memoirs, "I thought to myself that any American having Stalin's personality and approach might well reach high public office in my own country." Of course, the old gentleman was fantasizing, but it is apt testimony of Stalin's ability to act out roles deceptively.

After the first edition of my biography was published, I unexpectedly received a fan letter from Svetlana Alliluyeva. Having fled the USSR, first to India, Stalin's daughter was helped by George Kennan to settle in this country. I visited her in Princeton where she was living after the breakup of her marriage to an American architect. I was then very much impressed with her quick intelligence and dignified bearing. For someone with her parentage and stormy background she seemed to be remarkably well balanced, though it struck me as odd when she told me she would not let her little daughter learn Russian. We corresponded for a couple of years. But, as it is also evident from her books, for all his affection for her (or maybe because of it) she had never been privy to her father's political life. Still she could tell me interesting things about her mother (who died when Svetlana was six) and about her family life. Then, for no apparent reason, she put an end to our correspondence. I heard from quite a few of her other acquaintances that establishing warm relations with people, then abruptly breaking them off, was a habit with Svetlana. Years later, in the late 1970s, I received a friendly letter from her. Her son in the Soviet Union had just married a Pole, and she said that had made her think of me. Very soon afterwards she left the States, first for England, then for the Soviet Union, then after some time spent there, to return to America with the permission of the Soviet government. I was surprised to learn that while in the USSR she had on one occasion shouted vulgar abuse at some Western correspondents who were pestering her. The psychological burden which she bore must have been very heavy.

What one could glean from our correspondence and her books were scraps of information about Stalin's personal life. For once he was not acting when he exploded on learning of his teenage daughter's romance with a much older man, who was Jewish to boot. The all-powerful dictator was for the moment transformed into a very ordinary old-fashioned father, who yelled at and struck his daughter, and kept repeating "You could not find yourself a Russian?" But unlike other fathers, he had an expeditious way of terminating the romance. The reckless wooer was sent to a hard labor camp. In view of the above it is difficult to say what is more astounding, Svetlana finding other suitors, and marrying one, who also happened to be Jewish, or her father acquiescing in her choice. To be sure he was pleased when she divorced her first husband and married the son of a high Party official. More surprising, nothing happened to Stalin's former son-in-law, even after the divorce. For a man who had his two brothers-in-law shot and his wife's sister locked up, it showed considerable restraint.

Much as a biographer must strive for a balanced portrait of his subject, it is indeed difficult to find Stalin responding to a normal human emotion. He was a bad father, despite his affection for young Svetlana. He mocked and executed his oldest friends and collaborators. Seldom have even the worst despots of ancient times shown themselves so incapable of the slightest sign of compassion or generosity.

But there is one incident, that is of considerable psychological interest. All the reports agree that his marriage to Nadyezhda Alliluyeva, Svetlana's mother, was an unhappy one. Whether it was Stalin's treatment of her, the depressing tales of the terrible things happening in the countryside as a result of his policies, or a combination of the two, the unfortunate woman was driven in 1932 to commit suicide. Understandably, some writers abroad and in Russia after glasnost, would question the suicide and conjecture that the tyrant, in a moment of fury, killed his wife.

A tale from October 16, 1941 at his sense of connection to her. Only weak Soviet forces stood between Moscow and the advancing German Panzer divisions. Most government ministries and officials were evacuated from the capital. Many buildings and the Moscow subway were mined to blow up as the enemy entered the city. It is still debatable whether Stalin himself left the capital, to return three days later after the immediate danger had passed. For a man as single-minded in his passion for power, every minute should have been occupied with devising means to avoid the ultimate disaster. Yet at that moment when panic and near anarchy gripped Moscow—no one thought of proclaiming a state of siege until the 19th of October—Stalin, as reported in a little-noticed source, found time to visit the grave of Nadyezhda, possibly fearing that he would never see it again.

AS: "...Adam's gifts as a historian and writer were manifold. But perhaps the most important was his ability to put himself in other peoples' shoes, to imagine how people would have acted under the particular circumstances in which they found themselves. He could penetrate the mind of a Stalin or Lenin and explain how and why they acted very convincingly. The opening of the Communist archives have not altered his basic arguments, even though he wrote them long before the fall of Communism..."

Angela Stent
Professor of Government
Georgetown University

*   *   *

My brother Stan wrote in his autobiography rather disparagingly of what we call the social sciences. For him, a mathematician, they represented no intellectual challenge comparable to that of the real sciences. A social scientist was for him not much different from a mere bibliographer—his work consisting in the accumulation of data. Political analysis and speculation could be done just as well by reading *The New York Times* as by a more laborious examination of primary sources. I never discussed with him this dismissive view of what, along with others, his younger brother was doing. I have little patience myself with those professional colleagues who attempt to present the study of politics and history as analogous to theoretical physics, or who think that by dragging in mathematical formulas and quasi-mathematical jargon they add very much beyond unreadability to their work. But the study of history and politics can be as intellectually challenging and rigorous as the search for scientific proofs and systems. In some ways it can be likened to the work of a criminal investigator, in others to that of an artist. We try to accumulate evidence, examine it with tools much as in psychology and statistics, and apply special insight to present a convincing likeness of this kind of reality.

The complex story of Stalinism is a good example of the intellectual challenge confronting a genuine historian and political analyst. Beyond sheer chronological narrative, there are intriguing questions, which cannot be answered just by diligent reading of *The New York Times*, or by consulting the works of Marx and Freud.

One such overreaching question is the nature of the terrors practiced under Stalin. Terror has been used by tyrants throughout the ages. What made the Soviet Union's variety different was both its massive and universal extent. Hitler applied terror to the enemies of the regime and specific ethnic groups, but Stalin subjected all nationalities of the USSR at all levels of society. Once in my class I said that I supposed that at the height of the purges in 1937 only somebody like a cleaning woman could feel safe. Much later in 1990, I read about the so-called Kremlin conspiracy; among the hundred or so condemned were two cleaning women.

Even more unusual was the customary practice of having the doomed formally charged, even though their "trial" might last but ten minutes, and pressuring them to confess to fictitious crimes even when the "trials" in most cases were not in public. At a Party consultation in 1938 deciding the fate of the two former allies of Stalin,

Bukharin and Rykov, the formula for which the majority of the participants voted was "Arrest, judge, shoot." Stalin's moderate proposal was for the secret police to investigate their crimes—which in the end led to the same result.

Why then this weird and time-consuming ritual? And the really basic question: were those millions of people destroyed who were innocent of any real or even potential opposition to the regime, because of the dictator's genuine conviction that treason was widespread or was it the result of his cynical conclusion that the safety of his power required periodic sacrificial offerings of multitudes of innocent people in addition to those he really distrusted? I believe there is no question that it is the latter. In 1937-1938, every regional office of the secret police in the vast country was assigned quotas of people who were to be physically liquidated.

Another question: did Stalin believe in the preposterous charges that the old companions of Lenin's, army generals, even his own relatives, were guilty of previous charges of being foreign agents, and other nonsense, for which they were sent to their deaths? In most cases, no, his "morbid suspiciousness" being, as argued here, mostly a pose. After the Soviet armies in western Russia collapsed at the beginning of the German invasion, Stalin ordered its commander General Pavlov and his staff officers to be shot. His chief executioner in such matters, Vassili Ulrich (who probably should be in the Guinness Book of Records, having pronounced more death sentences than any other judge in history) presented for the dictator's approval a routine verdict: Pavlov was found guilty of anti-Soviet plots plus all the other customary embellishments. Ulrich was then told to forget all that nonsense: Pavlov was to be shot for incompetence and dereliction of duty. This was no time for elaborate scenarios.

Why were such fantasies employed in the Great Moscow trials of 1936-1938, as well as in other trials? Trotsky "unmasked" as Hitler's agent, people formerly in charge of agriculture and industry confessing to organizing systematic destruction of cattle, and to blowing up factories and avowing all kinds of other absurdities? Had not human lives and not only of the accused been forfeited, those spectacles could be seen as hilarious black comedies. But again, there was a cold-blooded decision behind the farce. Society was not only to be numbed by fear, but also energized into hysteria with everyone looking for traitors and saboteurs, with only one man, Stalin, standing entirely above suspicion, infallible and invulnerable, protecting the state and the people from internal and foreign enemies.

Today an average Russian reading the stenographic reports of the trials would be abashed at the thought that his father or grandfather could stomach all that mishmash of nonsense and lies. But in the hectic atmosphere of the 1930s, people believed. To think otherwise would have been to see the Soviet Union as a madhouse. And weren't Hitler and the Japanese militarists capable of any degree of clever treachery toward the USSR? Less excusably, there were Westerners who fell for that very unsubtle propaganda. I mentioned Ambassador Davies. But even Winston Churchill came to believe that there had been a military plot against Stalin, and that the eight high military commanders "judged" and executed on June 12, 1937 were guilty as charged.

Perhaps we should not be too condescending toward the Russians of the 1930s. How many people in this country in the 1950s swallowed McCarthy's fantasies about a huge Communist conspiracy? And how contrived and preposterous the fabrications about the background of John Kennedy's assassination! Still, let us not equate those occasional lapses from rationality in our society with the phantasmagoric enslavement of the minds of the Soviet people under the greatest tyranny in modern history!

What made such tyranny possible? Certainly not just one man. Those who constituted the core of the Nazi party were for the most part thugs and social misfits. Though being a Bolshevik was not as dangerous in pre-Revolutionary Russia as is usually believed (in fact, the Tsarist police were much more fearful and hard on the semi-anarchist Socialist Revolutionaries who engaged in terrorism), still membership in any illegal party was a risky business which required an ideological commitment. How can one then explain that in the Soviet period some courageous people would acquiesce in herd-like obedience to the dictator, and to the martyrdom of an independent peasantry, euphemized as collectivization, and later on, until they themselves were repressed, would serve as police, informers, inquisitors, and torturers of their comrades?

Part of the explanation lies in the ideology. For one indoctrinated in Marxism-Leninism, there is a gray area lying between reality and fiction—the "objective reality." A small peasant proprietor is "objectively" a class enemy even though he may never have thought of active opposition to the regime. "Objectively," Stalin's Russia was moving toward socialism and a classless society, even if it was through the sacrifice of millions of innocent lives.

Clearly this is not a complete explanation of the despicable or suicidal behavior of so many Communists during those terrible times. But for some it was a convincing rationalization of their servility and refusal to see the Soviet world as it really was. And for most, that world had to be reinforced by fear and career considerations. Where Arthur Koestler errs in his otherwise penetrating *Darkness at Noon*, in my opinion, is in placing excessive emphasis on the ideological motif. His hero, modeled on Bukharin, confesses to false accusations and goes to his death believing that he owes this self-sacrifice to the Party. In this the author is completely unrealistic. Those who played their roles as prescribed by the prosecution did so for very human reasons. They were unable to endure physical torture and lack of sleep or, like most in the great public trials that sent the Bolshevik Old Guard to death, they had been promised (falsely) that in return for their confessions their own lives might be spared, or that their families would not suffer unduly. Bukharin had a young wife and a baby. Years later, after the Soviet state had passed into history, I met his widow. She had been through trials and camps, but still professed to be a believer in Communism.

For some readers of Dostoyevsky, the spectacle of Moscow trials spectacles, especially the phenomenon of elaborate confession by the accused, was explained by the existence of the "Russian soul," that alleged particular need of the Russians to indulge in self-flagellation and submissiveness to authority.

But the same pattern of purge trials reappeared in Communist-ruled Eastern European states between the end of the war and Stalin's death. In Hungary, Czechoslovakia, and Bulgaria the accused, some of them former Party potentates, and others, opponents of Communism, including a Roman Catholic bishop, were all compelled to confess in the manner of their victimized Soviet predecessors. So much for the "Russian soul."

Isaac Deutscher in his quite partisan biography credits Stalin, for all his peccadilloes, with making Russian an industrial and military power. But a Tsarist Russian country, which before World War I was already modernizing and industrializing at a faster pace than the United States, undoubtedly would have reached a higher level of development by 1941, and without paying such a terrible price for it. If under Communist rule Stalin's inhumanity was instrumental in the Soviet Union emerging from World War II as an awesome giant, by the same token, Stalinism, once glasnost revealed its full picture to the people, was the prime cause of Communism's and the Soviet Union's downfall.

Today, in the disheveled and frantic condition of Russian society, the memories of the past horrors have faded. Some unthinking Russians, when contemplating the rampant crime and corruption of today's scene, may foolishly romanticize the past when the iron hand of the Boss enforced order and his country was a superpower. But although there may be another form of authoritarianism on the horizon, the Russian people as a whole will not tolerate a second Stalin.

I have considered this grim subject at length because, like the Holocaust in Hitler's Germany, so is Stalinism the defining characteristic of Soviet Communism. There have been those who argued that it was not true Socialism, but that by an accident of history a humane and liberating creed was distorted by Stalin. Some would use in regard to Communism an analog to the saying that the trouble with Christianity is that it has never been practiced. Be that as it may, we must judge political ideas by their consequences.

Working on Stalin, as I suppose on Hitler, is not a pleasant job. One cannot help becoming depressed by recounting the stories of human depravity and mass suffering. Yet a historian must not allow himself to be reduced to the role of moralist. To be sure, I found occasional distraction in trying to resolve the intriguing historical puzzles of the period. Was Stalin mentally incapacitated for several days following the shock of the German invasion? Did he arrange the murder of Sergei Kirov, his then close collaborator? Here is a mystery that would challenge the ingenuity of Agatha Christie's Hercule Poirot and other famous fictional detectives.

Sifting through so many instances of horror and brutality, I encountered now and then passages of weird "comic relief." Tyrants like ordinary mortals, have their humorous side. We have read of Hitler babbling incessantly over coffee and cakes with his entourage, and his monologues inducing drowsiness in his most fervent admirers. Stalin had a coarse sense of humor. Alexis Tolstoy, a distant relative of the great writer, returned to Soviet Russia after spending some time abroad following the war. A talented writer, he became a shameless flatterer of the dictator, who was not displeased to have an aristocratic courtier. As with most of his attendants, even those in favor, Stalin could not refrain from a joke at Tolstoy's expense. One day at a Kremlin reception, emboldened by alcohol, Tolstoy approached the dictator and proposed that they drink a *brüderschaft*, a kind of "bonding" toast. The leader of the world proletariat stepped back: "you must be joking, Count." More unkind was Stalin's joshing of Fedorenko, a distinguished Sinologist who was his interpreter in the talks with Mao. When Fedorenko would pause while trying to decipher some Hunan-accented phrase of Mao's, Stalin would ask with a serious expression "what are you plotting?" At a buffet supper, which followed a conference, recounts the interpreter, the dictator indicated to him one dish, which he said would taste like nothing Fedorenko had ever eaten before or would ever eat again. Both must have thought of Ivan the Terrible, who indeed would occasionally treat his guests to poisoned delicacies which they had to consume. Hard as it is to believe, this story was told by the Academician Fedorenko in all seriousness. I met the scholar many years later when he gave a lecture on what happened to Chinese intellectuals during what is weirdly known as Mao's Cultural Revolution, but at the time I had not read his article and could not ask how the unusual delicacy tasted.

Stalin was favorably reviewed in this country. Those who adhered to Marxism would of course prefer Deutscher's biography which, despite the author's devotion to Trotsky, eulogizes the man who ordered Trotsky's murder. One could not expect Stalin to be published in the USSR, but as I was told, it was translated clandestinely into Russian, on the one hand by the government for the use of officials, and on the other, by the dissidents. Under perestroika, the Russian reader finally got, in Dmitri Volkogonov's *Triumph and Tragedy*, something like a realistic picture of the despot. But though Volkogonov, as a former high official, enjoyed access to the archives and other sources still not open to a foreigner, his book, written from a Leninist point of view (which the author completely repudiated in his subsequent biography of Lenin), does not bring much that we did not know in the West, except for the grim statistics showing that the victims of Stalinism were much more numerous than I dared to assume.

18

The Surprising 70s

....It's all ruined by CREEP....Moscow takes advantage....Yom Kippur war doesn't help...Soviets dance in Africa and Asia..Angolan adventure...precarious condition of world Communism....Russian nationalism keeps things together at home.

It was hard to be optimistic about what the decade of the 1970s would bring. There appeared to be no easy way out of the Vietnam mess. And as long as the war continued it was bound to increase tensions and divisions within American society. With the political hypochondria that comes so easily to one born in Eastern Europe, I could not see how the Soviet Union would stand idly by while American society was tearing itself apart, thereby tempting the Kremlin to make mischief. Would it be Berlin again, Cuba, or the Middle East that would witness another dangerous confrontation between the two superpowers? And when it came, could one still count on that national consensus on foreign policy, which helped the country sustain the Korean War and respond to the Cuban missile crisis? And would not our own kind of cultural revolution encourage Mao's China, just emerging from follies of its own, to try this time a mad adventure outside its borders, for example an invasion of Taiwan? Thank God, my worst fears did not materialize. But instead of the troubles we expected, the 1970s presented us with some that no one would have foreseen.

What moderated my apprehensions about future developments in the international field was mainly the continuing conflict between the two potential troublemakers: China and the USSR. This conflict was enhanced rather than diminished by the Vietnam War. For all their rhetoric about "proletarian internationalism," and satisfaction over America's discomfiture, both Communist powers suspected each other of dark designs to exploit for their own purposes the struggle of the Vietnamese comrades. Beijing feared that Moscow would use Hanoi's growing dependence on Soviet help for war materials to strike a bargain with the US. It would pressure Hanoi for an accommodation with the US and in return might expect the US to help it in an intrigue against China. By the same token, the Kremlin believed China was eager to use the war to make any détente between the two superpowers impossible, if not indeed, to push them into a confrontation and war.

Here then was a situation American diplomacy could have exploited—but not in the naive way attempted by President Johnson's administration, which having plunged into the mess, expected that the USSR would virtually help America preserve South Vietnam, and thus discredit China's propagation of "wars of national liberation." It wasn't sensible to believe that Moscow would be ready to assist America to extricate itself before it had drawn the maximum advantage from the war, and besides, had pressing reasons to think that its continuation could indeed benefit China.

Few would have thought that Mr. Nixon would be capable of a more subtle policy than his predecessor. Anatoly Dobrynin, the Soviet Ambassador, revealed in his memoirs published in 1995 that the Kremlin shared the American Left's view of Nixon as a diehard right-winger. Indeed such was the Soviet apprehension of the Republican candidate that Dobrynin was instructed to contact the Humphrey camp, to inquire what Moscow could do to advance the Democratic candidate's chances, including an offer of financial help! The latter point is hard to believe, but had the Soviet offer (which of course was rejected) become known, Nixon would have beaten Senator Humphrey by a landslide rather than by a narrow margin.

There are no books about the latter phase of the Cold War as informative as Ambassador Dobrynin's *In Confidence*. Dobrynin was the USSR's long-time (1962-86) ambassador to the United States. Unlike similar exercises by many former Soviet officials with their sensational but often unreliable revelations, Dobrynin's memoirs display the very un-Russian quality of understatement, yet are most instructive and reliable. The length of his service in the US is a testimony to how highly his bosses from Khrushchev to Gorbachev appreciated his skill. In fact his very appearance was a great diplomatic asset. Unlike the dour expression of foreign minister Gromyko, and the thug-like visages of other Soviet diplomats, Dobrynin's pudgy face, which might have been taken from a Norman Rockwell *Satur-*

day Evening Post cover, was bound to impress Americans: could the state represented by such an amiable man really be the "Evil Empire"? And to be sure, he was a skillful and urbane diplomat, well suited to correct his bosses' misconceptions about American politics, and to soothe his hosts' fears about Moscow's actions.

His is a convincing testimony about the disheveled state of American foreign policy prior to Nixon's presidency and again after Watergate(In talking with Lyndon Johnson after the Soviet invasion of Czechoslovakia in 1968 Dobrynin was astounded to find out how ignorant Johnson was of the background and significance of Moscow's suppression of the "Prague Spring." The ambassador thought Nixon, on the other hand, had considerable sophistication about international affairs.) Brezhnev & Co. soon became convinced that the President and his chief foreign policy advisor, Henry Kissinger, genuinely sought an amelioration of Soviet-American relations.

Nixon's insight lay in the realization that the path of détente with the USSR lay through Beijing. His achievement is not lessened by the fact that he did not have to court China too strenuously. China was eager to open up to America, in order to protect it from the "Elder Brother." Whether Beijing was actually justified in thinking that the Soviets, if guaranteed America's non-interference, were seriously considering an attack on the People's Republic, we still don't know. I personally think it was very unlikely, but we must wait for the further opening of still secret Soviet archives to speak with assurance on the question.

And so, from the position of unremitting hostility to the "American imperialists" Beijing became open to American entreaties. And then of course Moscow had to make sure that this new friendship would not go too far. In February 1972, Nixon went to China; and in May, though American planes were at the time intensifying the bombing of North Vietnam, and several Soviet ships were hit in the process, he was welcomed in Moscow. And so was born the short-lived détente.

(The aspects of détente that attracted the greatest attention at the time (and violent debate later on) were the strategic arms agreement and the agreement limiting both sides' anti-missile defenses.) The Soviet Union was granted a quantitative advantage in total megatonnage, which the Americans believed was offset by the US technological advance in multi-targeting ("MIRV-ing") their missiles. At the time this was generally hailed as the first step to an eventual reduction and control of the dreaded weapons. Then the Soviets solemnly pledged not to interfere with access to West Berlin.

As I saw it those agreements were indeed important, even though both sides preserved their capability to destroy each other several times over. But what I thought was of greater long-run significance was the Kremlin's willingness to declare publicly its intention to liberalize their procedures for allowing Soviet Jews to emigrate. Apart from its humanitarian aspect, here was the first time that the Soviet government agreed to alter its domestic policies at the intercession of the US, something unthinkable under Stalin, and not much less so under Khrushchev. And indeed many more Jews were to be allowed to leave the Soviet Union during the next two years, even though the Kremlin balked at formally specifying numbers.

There was a plethora of other agreements and informal understandings, ranging from trade to the plan for a joint space shot. But the guarantee about emigration, though later largely repudiated, was for me a sign that the masters of the Soviet Union were beginning to lose that self-assurance that in the past made them refuse even to discuss with a foreign power their internal and oppressive policies. The cracks in the once impregnable fortress began to let in a breath of freedom for many in their own country; not just for Jews. One could express openly one's dissatisfaction with life in the Fatherland of Socialism, and it would not inevitably lead to jail. The voice of dissent would grow stronger. It was a brief but tantalizing glimpse of the perestroika to come.

Of course, Nixon and Kissinger could no more than anyone else look so far into the future. What they immediately expected from détente was Soviet help to extricate the US from Vietnam. The Kremlin could not, and would not, transform the Vietnam stalemate into an American victory. But it undoubtedly did assist American diplomacy in reaching the Paris agreements of 1973 and the subsequent ceasefire. It was not exactly "peace with honor;" no one could realistically believe that with the Communist forces remaining in part of the South, the Saigon government could long survive. But the US troops would leave; American prisoners of war would be freed, and to some extent it was a face-saving transaction.

To me the significance of the events of 1972 went far beyond the importance of the actual agreements. They demonstrated that for all practical purposes Communism as an international movement was finished. The Sino-Soviet dispute had been previously rationalized by both sides in ideological terms. They accused each other of departing from Marxism-Leninism. Now even that pretense could no longer be maintained, Both sides sought accommodation with the chief capitalist power(And with China in the late 1970s, that accommodation came close to an informal alliance, so great was Beijing's fear of being attacked militarily by the USSR.)What was the point or practicality of propagating an ideology that far from influencing its adherents, exacerbated their differences and led to hostility?

American-Soviet détente in 1972 promised to be long-lasting, and held out the hope of bringing about a salutary change in the relations between the two superpowers. Both sides reaffirmed the common-sense proposition that in the nuclear age there could be no alternative to conducting mutual relations on the basis of peaceful coexistence. To be sure, not even states bound by the closest ties of friendship could have lived up to another pledge of the Nixon-Brezhnev declaration: "efforts to obtain unilateral advantages at the expense of the other directly or indirectly must be eschewed." But such extravagant promises apart, there were sound indications that for quite a while the Cold War would be in remission. The Soviet establishment developed considerable respect for the President and his agile foreign policy advisor. Nixon addressed the Soviet people on television, an honor unprecedented for a capitalist leader. As usual, the Kremlin appreciated dealing with a foreign statesman whom it deemed resolute but predictable in his actions.

What led détente to falter within two years, and to the Soviet Union's open resumption of the pursuit of those "unilateral advantages" which it had so piously abjured in 1972?

X The main reason must be sought in a series of events that followed a failed burglary at the Watergate office-apartment complex in Washington. Seldom had a petty criminal act such far-reaching consequences. It is still not clear what led some members of CREEP (an appropriate acronym for the Committee to Re-Elect the President) to authorize an action even more idiotic than criminal. What could they have hoped to find in the files of the Democratic National Committee? Here was Mr. Nixon virtually assured of a triumphant reelection after his foreign successes and with the pressures from the late 1960s calming down.(To paraphrase Talleyrand's dictum: it was worse than a crime; it was an act of gross stupidity.)

Soon after his reelection, the President was confronted with a televised investigation by the Senate Judiciary Committee which bared not only the truth of the Watergate caper, but also threw light on other not exactly decorous aspects of the office of the President. A follower of Dr. Freud would discern clear signs of political masochism in Mr. Nixon's behavior: why make those compromising voice-activated tapes; why not destroy them at the first stirrings of the scandal?

The Kremlin beheld the American fiasco first with incomprehension and then with incredulity: how could a renowned political leader get into trouble by doing something so trivial and natural as a little spying on his opponents? Or was Nixon victim of an intrigue by the enemies of his policy of rapprochement with the USSR? The Soviets believed they had a friend in Nixon, and if Ambassador Dobrynin is to be believed, Brezhnev's feelings toward him bordered on affection. As the President's political fortunes were rapidly sinking, he sought political salvation by emphasizing his foreign policy expertise and successes. The Soviets were cooperating; Brezhnev arrived in June 1973 and took special care to praise the embattled president.

And the following June, with his position crumbling, Nixon was warmly welcomed in Moscow, and cordially entertained by the Soviet leader at his Crimean villa.

But Soviet sentimentality had its limits. The Kremlin could not overlook the fact that the Watergate affair not only led to Nixon's resignation, but also weakened the presidency, hence incapacitating this country's foreign policy. If the Americans chose to mess up their government, did the Soviet Union still have to adhere scrupulously to the engagements it undertook in 1972 when the situation was quite different? A Russian proverb freely translated proclaims, "Friendship is precious, but must not interfere with one's duty." And the Kremlin's "duty" if conditions warranted, was to seize every opportunity to expand the Soviet Union's power and influence.

And then came another crisis, which further weakened the position of the West and increased Moscow's temptations to seek those "unilateral advantages" which it had so pointedly promised to abandon. The 1973 Yom Kippur war pitted Egypt and Syria against Israel, the Arab states seeking revenge for the 1967 humiliation and loss of territory to the Jewish state. The attack caught both Tel Aviv and Washington by surprise, which contributed to the Arabs' initial military successes. Moscow, though becoming increasingly estranged from Sadat's Egypt, and having advised the Arabs against the venture, still felt bound once the fighting began to continue its long-lasting policy of supporting them.

To Washington, the Kremlin's attitude represented a violation of the 1972 understanding, which by definition obliged both parties to communicate in the face of an impending crisis. And the Egyptians-Syrians did inform the USSR of their impending attack.

Here, for once, there are good grounds for believing that the Soviets sought to live up to their commitment and at least indirectly to signal the US about the war. On October 1st or 2nd, the Soviets were informed by Egypt about their forthcoming attack. On October 4th and 5th, the USSR openly carried out the evacuation from Egypt of their diplomats' families and civilian advisors. Such solicitude for their civilians was hardly characteristic of Moscow, and a hurried airlift of some 2,000 Soviet personnel was bound to alert the outside world to what was coming. Incredibly, not only their diplomats but also the intelligence services of Israel and the US ignored the clear warning, and both countries were caught entirely by surprise when the Egyptians and Syrians struck on the sixth of the month. I believe my book *Dangerous Relations* was the only treatment of the crisis that stressed the intent and significance of the Soviets' betraying the secret Sadat had entrusted to them. Needless to say Sadat was to draw appropriate conclusions from the incident and despite the subsequent Soviet attempt to compensate for their double game by supplying Egypt with war materiel, the Soviet alliance with the chief Arab state would soon come to an abrupt end.

Even so, the Soviet Union achieved substantial if indirect benefits from the conflict during the initial Israeli setbacks. Moscow pleaded with its allies that having made their point they should halt the military action. The Kremlin believed, correctly, that Egypt's successes, the result of a surprise attack, could not continue. But Sadat wanted a full victory; he was not satisfied just to cross the Suez Canal and push the enemy a few miles back.

And then the fortunes of war began to change. In Washington, Vice President Agnew had just been forced to resign, and there was open talk of Nixon's impeachment. The USSR felt encouraged to take publicly a strong pro-Arab stand and carry on a massive airlift of war supplies to its clients.

What emboldened the USSR was the Arab states' blow to the economy of the Western world. Arab members of OPEC cut off oil shipments to the US and proclaimed their intentions to continue to use this weapon until Israel gave up its territorial conquests in the 1967 war. The European allies of the US, their own economies threatened, now pressed Washington to moderate its support of Israel. Some frantic shuttle diplomacy by Kissinger, now Secretary of State, and Prime Minister Kosygin, led the two superpowers to agree to seek a cease-fire. But with their troops now surrounding the Egyptian Third Army, the Israelis had no wish to lose their advantage. Then came the critical moment. After being rebuffed in his pleas to Nixon that the USSR and the US jointly enforce the truce with their military contingents, Brezhnev announced that the Soviet Union would be compelled to act unilaterally to stop the Israelis. American intelligence allegedly had information about six Soviet parachute divisions ready to be dispatched to the Middle East. In response, the United States proclaimed a worldwide nuclear alert.

Was this a confrontation as dangerous in its potential consequences as that of October 1962? Not quite. There were good reasons to believe that both sides were bluffing—and both bluffs worked. The US pressured Tel Aviv to stop fighting, and instead of six parachute divisions, some seventy Soviet military observers descended on the battlefield to monitor the cease-fire. Was Mr. Nixon, then in desperate straits, trying to distract public opinion from his plight? Rather unlikely. But in the nuclear age even bluffs of this kind carry the danger of escalating accidentally into a real horror. On October 26, the Middle Eastern crisis relapsed from its violent phase into its "normal" festering condition. Détente, though shaken, held.

But what happened during the crisis evidently inspired OPEC, the oil cartel, with the happy thought that they could control the oil market. And in December they raised the price for their product fourfold. This was the most severe crisis for the entire West's economy since World War II. One would have thought that this conglomeration of shaky authoritarian regimes, feudal monarchies, and petty sheikdoms could have been restrained in their greed. They were all dependent on the West for industrial and military supplies, and where else could they invest their vast income? Fearful of Communism, Saudi Arabia and Iran, two of the main producers, depended on the United States for the security of their regimes. But with Washington unable to offer leadership, the Western industrial powers proved incapable of concerted action, and were thrown into an energy crisis leading to inflation and the stunting of economic growth.

The USSR, itself a major oil producer and exporter, benefited greatly from the rise in prices. Moreover, the weakening of the West's economic position and America's obvious helplessness in grappling with OPEC's exactions provided yet another reason for the Kremlin to feel free from the constraints of détente. (There was no reason why friendly relations and expanded trade with the United States should not continue; but surely the Americans ought to understand that the correlation of forces in the world had changed in the Soviet Union's favor, and hence Moscow could not follow the same path of virtue in its foreign policy to which it had committed itself two years before, under greatly different conditions.)

Without Watergate and the Yom Kippur War, it is quite likely that the Paris agreement on Vietnam, providing for Saigon to hold on to power but with NVA and Viet Cong military enclaves in the South, would have endured for several more years. But under the new alignment of forces there was no reason for Moscow to restrain Hanoi when it decided to take over the South. A North Vietnamese general offered post facto a very candid explanation of why his government embarked in 1975 on the massive invasion that rendered the coup-de-grâce to the inept Saigon government. As I quoted in *Dangerous Relations*, "The internal contradictions within the US political parties had intensified. The Watergate scandal had seriously affected the entire situation of the US.... [it] faced economic recession, mounting inflation, serious unemployment, and an oil crisis."

And indeed President Ford's and Secretary Kissinger's pleas to Congress to help General Thieu's regime fell on deaf ears, even their request for military supplies for Saigon. Indochina fell under Communist rule. Even though preserving the outward forms of détente, Moscow could not help gloating over "this lesson to the American imperialists."

In a short time, events in the Indochina peninsula would vividly illustrate the "internal contradictions" within the Communist world itself, following the horrendous genocide by the Khmer Rouge in Cambodia. But for the moment, the fall of the regime which the US expended tens of thousands of lives and billions of dollars to help was a telling blow to America's prestige and to its credibility as an ally.

I was engrossed at the time in my *Stalin*, but still functioning as an "expert," being called upon to give TV and radio interviews and writing an occasional paper for a Congressional committee. But no amount of expertise on the Soviet Union, no brilliant idea for a diplomatic stratagem could affect the fact that the domestic situation rendered this country's foreign policy ineffective in countering Soviet moves. True, Washington now had "the China card," but no one quite knew how this card could be played. With the important exception of Egypt, American influence in the Third World was eroding. The Sino-Soviet conflict, which seemed so momentous in the mid-1970s, was of little consequence in stemming the Soviet advance in the various regions of Africa and Asia. Enfeebled by the idiocy of the Cultural Revolution, China was unable to help Pakistan, its sole Asian friend, when India fell upon it and scored a rapid victory. India's move was applauded by the Soviet Union. The war led to the secession of Pakistan's eastern component, now Bangladesh. At the time, one could not discount the possibility that with Mao's imminent disappearance from the scene, his successors might seek a reconciliation with Moscow.

The soon to be shattered Soviet empire was in the heyday of its influence in the non-European world. A Filipino Communist speaking at the 25th Party Congress of the Soviet Party in 1976 declared that the confrontation between socialism and imperialism in Vietnam demonstrated that, "With the help of the Soviet Union one can achieve national liberation without threatening either peace or détente."

His hosts in Moscow had indeed been acting upon that premise. They were in the process of acquiring new clients in Africa. And the Kremlin brought an innovative element into the process. Cuban troops installed in power the pro-Soviet faction in Angola, and soon, were put to the same use in Ethiopia, bolstering perhaps the most bloodstained regime in all Africa. Ambassador Dobrynin is at his least convincing when he asserts in his memoirs that the Angolan venture was at its conception and execution entirely Castro's doing. Who could have transported the Cuban troops, and then continued to supply them? And even Moscow had to admit that the military operations were directed by Soviet officers.

I had an amusing experience in connection with a very serious civil war in Ethiopia. One day, I received in my office a phone call from a man who gave no name but said he was an American volunteer with the Eritrean Liberation Front, a Marxist force fighting the murderous Mengistu regime. He called me because I had written on Stalin. He was disturbed that his comrades still worshipped the late despot, and could I think of a way to get them away from that mis-placed idolatry? But surely, I said, they must know that the Russians had turned against the Eritreans and were now supporting and di-recting their Ethiopian oppressors. Yes, he said, but my comrades believe that it would have never happened were Stalin still directing world Communism. I advised him to find another cause.

As Ambassador Dobrynin noted, the Soviets had scant respect for President Ford's grasp of international affairs or his ability to carry Congress with him on more resolute foreign policies. And even to-ward Kissinger, still in the State Department, their attitude was quite different from that during the brief honeymoon of détente. When the Secretary of State on a visit to Moscow announced that he pro-posed to discuss Angola, the once affable Gromyko announced pub-licly that indeed Mr. Kissinger was welcome to discuss it—but only with his American aides. Angola was a sovereign state; its internal and external affairs were its own business, in which the USSR did not propose to interfere. Gromyko would live to see the day when his own government would seek American help with its domestic economy, and indeed help to preserve the Soviet Union.

How ephemeral would those Soviet "conquests" look, hardly more than a decade later! The pro-Moscow regimes collapsed like a house of cards once the Soviet Union itself began to crumble. In the mean-time, Soviet resources were being poured into those fatuous enter-prises. Like other empires before it the USSR was discovering that imperialism, at least economically, was a losing venture. When the USSR actually went bankrupt in its last years, it was, ironically, a creditor nation. A host of Third World countries owed vast sums for the Soviets' "selfless fraternal help," their weapons, advisors, and surrogate troops provided by Moscow.

But did those foreign acquisitions accomplish their goal, i.e., im-press the world and the Soviet people itself, that the regime was still powerful and dynamic? Did they sufficiently obscure the fact that the country's economic growth was slowing down and that the Soviet Union was falling still farther behind the West in new technology?

Domestically, the gambit did not work. Few Soviet citizens could be impressed by the accession to the socialist camp of countries which most of them could not locate on a map. Even a convinced Marxist must have looked askance at trying to bring socialism to societies decades away from possessing the first prerequisite of an industrial economy and riven by tribal divisions.

But then there were few real believers in Marxism-Leninism left in the Fatherland of Socialism. A sociologist friend of mine profited by détente by being allowed to give a few lectures to university students on a visit to Russia. A kind of Trotskyite in his youth, he was now a social democrat, which eased his efforts to explain to his audiences that true Marxism was somewhat distorted in its Soviet version. On his return, he expressed to me his puzzlement over the fact that his listeners, while invariably polite, would suddenly titter once he began to dwell on the complexities and various interpretations of Marxian dialectic. I did not have the heart to explain to him that for most of the Soviet people, Marxism-Leninism with all of its subtleties belonged to a never-never land, as distant from their everyday cares and problems as the old belief in Tsarist autocracy.

Comparisons between the Stalin times and the 1970s led to some unexpected conclusions. The period of the Great Fear had also been one of great ideological fervor. Often even those closest to the victims kept their faith in the Leader and the Idea. Perhaps psychologically it was understandable. One is reminded of the frantic religiosity that swept Europe during the Great Plague in the 14th Century. People would not admit the thought that all that mass slaughter and the Gulag had their origin in one man's obsession, and that the security service was like a vast Murder Inc., rather than a defender of the revolution against the plots of the capitalists and the Trotskyites. By contrast, Brezhnev's Russia was a prosaic police state incapable of evoking either the fear or ideological fervor of the terrible time.

It is only fair to admit that, like the great majority of the observers of the Soviet scene, I could not definitely foresee any basic change in the system in the near future. Dissent was spreading, but it was confined to fairly narrow, still mostly intellectual circles. Since Khrushchev's time there had been occasional local riots, work stoppages, and demonstrations, but any notion of a mass uprising was totally unrealistic. (Nowhere in his writings did a man as sensitive to his society as Alexander Solzhenitsyn indicate that he expected an imminent overthrow of the system he loathed.)

Whence then could a basic change come in the near future? Only from the top. But why should the leaders wish to change the system, which provided them with power and privileges?

Khrushchev did not want to change the system, but only to make it more humane and responsive to the people's needs. But even that ambition went too far for his colleagues on the Politburo So would

anyone else be allowed to try to steer his country away from dictatorship and the police state, and reach out for real peaceful coexistence with the West? As I wrote at the time, "It is easy to imagine a
Politburo member arguing that the USSR could not afford to become less feared abroad and more liberal internally. It would then
be exposed to much greater pressures from both the outside and at
home, [like] growth of political dissidence, claims for real autonomy
. . . for the non-Russian ethnic groups, in fact, reforms, incompatible
with the survival of the Soviet state and system. In brief, no sensible observer could have or did predict the Gorbachev phenomenon.

And yet, no student of history should underestimate the influence
of snobbery as a political factor. Brezhnev & Co. did not dream of
giving up their power, but they wanted to be considered by the outside world to be "respectable," civilized leaders of a civilized nation, and not rulers in the style of Stalin and Beria. They expelled
from the Soviet Union prominent dissenters, notably Solzhenitsyn,
rather than deal with them in the old summary way. At the assembly
of thirty-four heads of state from East and West, the Conference on
Security and Cooperation in Europe, Brezhnev solemnly signed the
Helsinki Final Act, which was a ringing reaffirmation of human rights.
The signatory states pledged to "respect human rights and fundamental freedoms including freedom of thought, conscience, and religion which derive from the inherent dignity of the human person."

Undoubtedly, the Kremlin believed that such rhetoric was harmless, just like the charter of the UN or the Soviet constitution. Who in
the real world could expect the regime to abide by rules that would
spell its suicide? But this was 1975, and Stalin, who had gravely
assented to the other two documents, was long gone. The Act became immediately a source of repeated embarrassment to the regime. In theory it opened a way for foreigners to pry into Soviet
domestic affairs. It seemed also to legitimize the dissidents' protests
and other activities. It was a different era from that when during an
audience with Stalin, Lady Astor shrieked, "When will you stop killing people?" to which the dictator replied composedly, "When it is
no longer necessary."

By the 1970s, mass terror was no longer practical, even though
had Stalin been in charge, he would have deemed it more necessary
than ever before. But the Soviet oligarchs would no longer permit
the emergence of another Stalin, any more than they would tolerate

any steps toward a law-abiding democracy. They wanted security for their own lives and privileges, as well as for their state.

Moderate repression at home and moderate expansion abroad were the methods the Kremlin proposed to follow to perpetuate the regime. The new spirit at the Soviet Olympus is well illustrated in the memoirs of a Soviet security official who went to Brezhnev to complain that he had been denied the promotion Brezhnev himself had promised him. Can one imagine a similar complaint being lodged under Stalin or even under Khrushchev? But instead of dispatching the disgruntled official to some prison or worse, the General Secretary was all amiability, assuring the unfortunate office-seeker that his services were highly appreciated, and in fact he had been just appointed to the important position of Soviet Ambassador to Upper Volta! In brief, no longer Murder Inc., but a kind of cross between the Mafia and Boss Tweed's Tammany Hall.

And indeed, as we can now verify from the records of the period, the 1970s were for the USSR not only a time of economic and technological stagnation, but also, especially among the elite, of vast material corruption. The Party boss of Uzbekistan required the local Party secretaries in his fiefdom to pay him regular tribute. The minister of the interior of the Soviet Union, an old crony of Brezhnev stole money to finance his and his family's luxurious life on such a scale that after Brezhnev's death, the government, which usually hushed up the crimes of cronies of the higher- ups, felt compelled to make his public, and the malefactor and his wife committed suicide.

Corruption permeated not only the higher circles. It was notorious that entrance to the more prestigious teaching institutions, or positions in the administrative ranks, etc. were often facilitated by bribes. From mass terror the system was evolving into mass thievery. This phenomenon could not be concealed from the West, even though the full details were to become known only under perestroika. To be sure, violent crime in the street was nowhere near present levels. But the Mafia infecting Russia has its roots in the recent Soviet past.

All in all, I could not take seriously the assertion of some Western Sovietologists that the system was developing toward an eventual social democratic transformation. Some such prognosticators had themselves leftist backgrounds and/or convictions, and just as they had minimized the extent of savagery under Stalin, could not now abandon the illusion that one day a true socialism in the Soviet Union would vindicate the dreams of their youth. For a few short years perestroika seemed to justify their hopes; but then they had to face the stark reality that the new Russia, though groping, and not very successfully, toward democracy, had certainly and absolutely renounced not only Communism, but also socialism, and that the capitalism that was emerging was more like that of the robber barons in post-Civil War America than the current Western variety.

In thinking about the future, I distinguished the problem of the Cold War from that of the character of the Soviet system. The two, obviously, were organically connected. Yet there were cogent reasons to believe that the regime might grow more accommodating in international affairs, even though remaining authoritarian and repressive at home. The logic of the nuclear age, the experience of the Cuban missile crisis, and the Yom Kippur War urged the Politburo toward a prudent and pacific foreign policy.

How did this square with the USSR's African adventures? The Kremlin was not going to bypass opportunities for easy and painless expansion if America's internal disarray and inept policies made such expansion risk-free. But if Washington could overcome the after-effects of Vietnam and Watergate and show an understanding of the precarious condition of world Communism, and if China remained united and irrevocably anti-Soviet after Mao's death, the logic of the situation would constrain the prudent men of the Kremlin to follow pacific policies, expand SALT I, and in general cease being a destabilizing force on the international scene.

To be sure, it was a big "if." Mr. Ford's administration inspired the Kremlin with little of the respect they had for Nixon before his fall. The new President reached his position due to a series of accidents. The Soviets have always paid attention to the personality and political strength of the Chief Executive and shaped their policies toward the US accordingly. And the first unelected president of the US was hardly in a position to dominate the American political scene. Nor was Ford's grasp of international politics equal to that of his predecessor. In the presidential campaign of 1976, he was to assert on TV that Poland was a fully independent state, showing a lack of basic familiarity with the facts of life in Eastern Europe. But even so, the Soviets let his Presidency pass without a major crisis.

The problem of stability of the Soviet system was of greater complexity. Obviously, it was becoming less feared at home and losing control over world Communism. But did it add up to the possibility of its early demise? At the time nothing indicated what was in the cards. Russian nationalism had long replaced ideology as supplying the cohesion through which the ruling oligarchy maintained its rule. One heard occasionally of dissent inspired by national aspirations among the other ethnic groups, notably the Ukrainians; but it came from individuals rather than from organized groups. And it expressed itself for the most part in demands for greater cultural, rather than political, freedom for the non-Russians.

No, from the perspective of the middle 1970s, I seldom contemplated the possibility of a collapse of the Soviet system or a basic change in it before some twenty years to come or when a complete generational change would take place in the leadership. And even so, it would take a very unusual set of circumstances for a regime that had survived massive famines, unbridled terror, and catastrophic military defeats to pass into history.

I was wrong by quite a few years; but it did take the most unusual circumstances to bring down a mighty empire and a worldwide movement, and that without a war or violent revolution.

19

Mystery Novels & The Kirov Affair

Mystery and history....Tangled nuclear talks...Balance of terror...Solzhenitsyn

My passion for mystery stories started very early. The genre was completely unknown in the Polish literature of my youth, and for that matter still is today. Perhaps, it requires a very stable and law-abiding society for murder to be presented as a fit subject for intellectual pursuit and the reader's enjoyment. The immortal work of Conan Doyle was of course translated into Polish. But it was only after I learned English that I could plunge into the delights of the novels of Dorothy Sayers and Agatha Christie.

The detective story is one of the arts whose female practitioners tend to be superior to their male counterparts. True, the aficionados of Raymond Chandler and Dashiell Hammett would challenge such judgments, but theirs is a different though equally intriguing variety of the art. Their stories reflect the turbulent and populist American environment as against the decorous and aristocratic setting of Sayers' and Christie's pre-World War II England. Can one imagine Hercule Poirot or Lord Peter Wimsey being roughed up by some lower class characters or conversely beating them up, scorning or submitting to sexual advances by loose women as is intermittently endured and enjoyed by Philip Marlowe and Sam Spade, the hero detectives of Chandler and Hammett?

But then having become addicted to detective fiction, one cannot afford to be too selective in one's reading. On occasion as before a flight, train journey, or trying to induce sleep in an unfamiliar surrounding, the addiction drives you to pick up what is at hand. Along with the masters of the craft I would read the works of such journeymen as Earle Stanley Gardner of the Perry Mason fame. I recall that when I moved into the fifties I left behind a treasure of some 200 paperbacks. They sold in those happy days for something like twenty-five cents. I did not foresee the periods of inflation, or, that from the seventies on the real mystery story would become increasingly rare, the books passing as such being for the most part trashy sex and violence "thrillers."

Reviewing the suspense stories became my avocation. On occasion I was moved to defend the genre against those who would demean it as vulgar, and the reading of it as a waste of time. How could we have endured all the tensions of the modern age without the relaxation and solace of that delightful branch of literature? Some indeed would still make us feel guilty for spending a few hours with a mystery. Look here, say those killjoys, the world is threatened by the Bomb, overpopulation, and exhaustion of natural resources and it behooves every citizen to become thoroughly alarmed about the horrible dilemmas confronting us rather than to waste time enjoying oneself—indeed, our reading matter should enhance our anxieties. If you grow weary of those endless and repetitive books, as I do, on these issues; then you should relax constructively by reading the revelations about horrible misdeeds of our current and past politicians or sexual transgressions of the famous in all fields. But how does it help us to readjust for pleasure?

The above paraphrases part of an article I wrote in 1976 on Agatha Christie for the *New Republic*. In a way it was also a response to the challenge issued by the late Edmund Wilson in his essay *Who Cares Who Killed Roger Ackroyd*. Possibly the great critic's attack on the detective genre was written with a tongue in cheek. If he despised the whole lot why did he read *Who Killed Roger Ackroyd*, Dame Agatha's masterpiece? Still one could not leave unanswered his provocative statement: "Friends we represent a minority but literature is on our side. There is no need to bore ourselves with this rubbish." As I pointed out isn't it so that ordinary people don't buy, certainly don't read boring books unless they've been certified as literature by eminent critics?

The subject certainly lends itself to jocularity. I chose to represent Dame Agatha (she was deservedly given an order by the Queen) as an apostle of the welfare state, democracy, and feminism. Didn't she fight British insularity of her period by making her hero detective a Belgian? Wasn't her other master pursuer of crime an aged lady—this striking a blow for women's rights and "ageism?" Aren't Christie's villains for the most part upper or upper middle class men—yet another affirmation of her belief in democracy and a strike against male chauvinism? At times, to be sure, her writing is, well, flat, but that in itself is a testimony to the profound democratic feeling of the author. It makes her books accessible to the masses who would not take to a tale of crime clothed in the prose of a Joyce or Proust. All in all, I concluded, this fiction as represented by Christie provides us, besieged as we are daily by stories of senseless violence, with an oasis of sensible mayhem, fictional, orderly and intellectually stimulating. There are few ways of whiling away our time as delightfully and innocently by trying to find out who killed Roger Ackroyd.

My article brought some rather unexpected reactions. Didn't I realize, wrote some humorless individuals to the magazines or to me personally, that Christie novels are permeated by rank snobbery? That a typical one is usually woven around country house tittle-tattle interrupted only by servants bringing in brandy and soda and the thud of falling corpses? And someone even found hints of anti-Semitism in her earlier productions. There is no way of arguing with killjoys.

My further ventures in reviewing the mystery scene became infrequent with the demise of what might be called its classical form. There is something to the argument that the latter depends on the class system. Christie's Poirot and Miss Marple are amateur sleuths catering to the aristocrats' troubles and scandals. Chandler's Philip Marlowe works mostly for plutocrats. In contrast, today's "democratic" suspense stories are often as unappetizing and sordid as real crime.

The Cold War brought new popularity to another variety of the genre, the spy novel. I have occasionally reviewed the works of the acknowledged master of the craft John Le Carré. Much as I enjoyed his earlier works, I cannot quite say the same for his later productions, e.g. *The Russia House*. It seems to me that there the author has encumbered his stories with an attempt to endow them with political and philosophic matter which detracts from their value as entertainment. Some other greats of the genre have suffered from the quite unnecessary feeling that what they were superbly good at was not what Edmund Wilson and the academe would recognize as Literature. Conan Doyle attempted to kill Sherlock Holmes to free himself to write a Great Historical Novel. Dorothy Sayers jettisoned the delightful, if slightly absurd, Lord Peter Wimsey to undertake translations of Dante. Alas, in both cases their "serious" literary efforts turned out to be quite mediocre.

A first-class mystery writer would probably do better doubling as a historian rather than aspiring to the laurels of Stendhal or Tolstoy. There is a kind of natural affinity between the two crafts. Unless he is a mere chronicler, your historian has to analyze the evidence, spot the clues. To be sure, his is not only an art but also a discipline; unlike a fiction writer, he must not give free rein to his imagination. But in a way, the search of the solution of all interesting problems of history does partake of detective work.

In no other field is it as apparent as in Soviet history. Already the Tsars' regime had the reputation of conducting its affairs in greater secrecy than was the case with any other government in 19th Century Europe. Secrecy as much as terror was the staple of Stalin's rule, and while terror was attenuated under his successors, secrecy continued unabated, and did not disappear entirely even with perestroika and glasnost of the eighties. No nation lived in greater ignorance of how its government really operated and how and why the most important and sometimes even minor decisions on foreign and domestic policies were arrived at than the people of the Soviet Union between 1917 and 1991. Today, even with the formerly secret archives opened, many of the critical events, from the first days of the Soviet power to the unsuccessful putsch of August 1991 that led to its collapse, have still retained an aura of mystery.

Undoubtedly the most mysterious (and contentious) of those events was the murder on December 1, 1934 of Sergei Kirov, the Communist boss of Leningrad, one of the closest henchmen of Joseph Stalin.

The assassin was one Leonid Nikolayev, a Party member, driven to his deed allegedly because of his wife's affair with Kirov. The location of the crime was the Communist Party headquarters, the famous Smolny Institute in Leningrad.

Stalin used the crime to launch a wave of terror that reached its climax in 1937-8. The assassination was presented as part of a vast plot to overthrow the Soviet regime, the plot planned and engineered by the former opponents of Stalin, i.e., practically all the former members of Lenin's old guard, the makers of the 1917 revolution. The most prominent figures among the old Bolsheviks were publicly paraded in the infamous Moscow Trials of 1936, 1937 and 1938, forced to confess to a huge variety of fictitious crimes, convicted and shot. Nikolayev, who had been executed within days of his deed, was barely mentioned in the trials nor was a single sentence of his presumed testimony introduced in the proceedings.

The absurd lies of the Moscow trials (e.g. Trotsky having been an agent of the German and Japanese general staff) were not officially repudiated until well into the Gorbachev rule. But in his attacks on Stalin's reputation, Khrushchev hinted though never stated so explicitly that the murder of Kirov had been engineered by Stalin. That his secret police knew of Nikolayev's homicidal intentions actually assisted him to corner the victim.

Though the archives opened after the Soviet Union's fall did not yield any new substantive materials relating to the case, Stalin's guilt has been accepted by most Sovietologists both in Russia and in the West. What would have prompted him to order the deed? Does one have to ask that question about a man who had licensed murders of his closest collaborators and his two brothers-in-law? But in addition some scholars have claimed that the tyrant was apprehensive of Kirov's popularity in the Party and that in 1934 there were high-ranking Communists who discussed the possibility of having Stalin replaced by Kirov.

The case against Stalin, even if based on circumstantial evidence, appears thus very strong. Yet, as I studied the story, I developed doubts. Would it have been in Stalin's interest to have the Soviet people told about a successful terrorist attack perpetrated against one of his lieutenants? Terrorism, if successful is highly contagious, and for all the hypnotic spell the tyrant held over his society, how many Russians must have wished for his death! If he did want to dispose of Kirov, his agents could have easily arranged a traffic accident or a fatal "heart attack."

Was Kirov's popularity threatening Stalin's power? There is no convincing evidence to that effect. It was in the interest of Stalin's successors, his former accomplices, to try to show that even as late as 1934 the Communist party was not entirely enslaved by him, and instead why there were people ready to try to replace him.

My tentative conclusion in my biography of Stalin was that the act was conceived solely and for personal reasons by its perpetrator Nikolayev. And then the death offered the tyrant a pretext to launch the bloody purge that in all likelihood he must have been contemplating for some time It seemed that all the persons even vaguely connected with the whole affair had by 1939 been physically liquidated. Nikolayev's mother, brother, sister, and wife were all shot in

1935. Between 1937-39 the same fate befell all the security and Party officials in Leningrad. This again must not necessarily be taken as evidence of Stalin's complicity; what happened in Leningrad was not much different from what was going on in Moscow and all over the vast country.

Yet miraculously (or possibly because 1934 was before the computer age) one witness to the crime survived. He was Mikhail Roslyakov, an official of the Leningrad city administration. Imprisoned during the purges, he emerged from the Gulag in 1955. He wrote down his reminiscences and after Khrushchev's denunciation of Stalin tried to interest Party authorities in his recollection about Kirov's end. Not surprisingly he was then told to thank his lucky stars and to keep silent. Roslyakov died in 1985. The manuscript he left behind was published in what was still the Soviet press in January 1991, and it throws new light on the momentous event.

The official communiqué issued after the murder stated that Kirov was not at the entrance to his office in Smolny and that the culprit was seized while trying to escape. Roslyakov's testimony shows that the account was false. At the time, the witness was in the office of Mikhail Chudov, Kirov's deputy. They did not expect their boss. That evening Kirov was scheduled to deliver a speech in the Tauride Palace to the Party activists and had informed Chudov by phone that he would go from home directly to the Palace and not to expect him in Smolny the meeting being scheduled for six o'clock.

Around five o'clock, as the officials were chatting about the forthcoming session, two shots rang out. They ran out. There Roslyakov remembers "lying in the corridor was Kirov, his body to the left of the door pointed in the direction of (Chudov's) office...To the right of the door some fifteen or twenty centimeters away lay another man on his back, arms spread out, a revolver in his right hand. Between his feet and Kirov's there was a distance of about a meter." Far from trying to escape, Nikolayev had fainted and was lying unconscious close to his presumed victim.

But was it his bullet that lodged in the back of Kirov's head? Roslyakov again reveals a crucial detail unmentioned in the official account of the murder: There had been two shots: the other bullet was found in the cornice of the wall to the right and behind Nikolayev. Was the second shot discharged by Nikolayev's gun as he was falling down?

Yet there is another possibility: as Kirov and his pursuer turned into the small corridor, someone else observed them from behind the corner. He saw Nikolayev raise his gun, and fire, but then fall in a faint, the bullet hitting the wall. The third man then completed the job Nikolayev messed up.

Who could be the third man? Like all other Soviet potentates, Kirov was never supposed to go out without being accompanied by bodyguards. On the fateful day, the bodyguard, one Borisov, arrived at the scene of the murder, Roslyakakov tells us, after a few minutes. Once in Smolny, he explained that Kirov simply ran upstairs and he could not catch up. He was not able to enlarge upon his explanations. Next day he was brought before Stalin who, having hurried to Leningrad, was personally conducting the investigation. Under arrest, Borisov was being driven in an open truck (!) to Smolny. It ran into a wall and Borisov fell out, killed on the spot. Was he the man who had fired the second and fatal shot? And it was only someone in attendance on Kirov who could have primed Nikolayev that his prey would be in Smolny at the time rather than going directly to the Party meeting in the Tauride palace where the would-be assassin planned originally to shoot him (a ticket to the meeting was found in Nikolayev's pocket).

Does the above make it more credible that it was Stalin who through his secret police had arranged the death of his "comrade in arms?" Not necessarily. Kirov had rather difficult relations with the local heads of the NKVD (the then equivalent of the KGB). They were certainly the kind of people capable of doing murderous plotting on their own.

And so the mystery still awaits a solution. What is not in dispute is that the former communist greats accused and convicted of complicity in the crime were, whatever their other transgressions, entirely innocent, and that the tyrant and his henchmen cynically exploited the murder to throw a cloak of fear over the entire society.

One other explanation of the Kirov affair must be mentioned. It was late in perestroika; for six years now Gorbachev had been trying to eradicate the traces of Stalinism from Soviet life and to introduce if not democracy then the rule of law. And here in March 1991 the official journal of the Ministry of the Interior carried an article by one Skuratov. The author grants complacently that Stalin may have had a hand in the murder. But then as in his other peccadilloes he had good and patriotic reasons. Kirov and five other members of the

Politburo in 1934 had Jewish wives. And among the eight high Red Army commanders tried in 1938, found guilty of working for Hitler were two Jews and four other non-Russians. Never mind whether the charges were true or not—you had to protect the Soviet state from being taken over by alien elements. And so all in all, regrettable as it is that some innocent people might have been shot, "the undeniable result of the events of 1934-39 was the cleaning of the Party, state and military apparatus of the alien elements, and the turn to patriotism...in view of the approaching war such cleansing was absolutely necessary." No wonder that with people like that in his officialdom poor Gorbachev was soon to be victimized by the coûp of August 1991. And the sheer idiocy of Skuratov's argument helps explain why the coûp carried out by people with a mentality similar to his proved to be an abject failure.

In the 1980s I took the Leningrad murder as the starting point of my novel *The Kirov Affair*. There using the license of fiction, I presented yet another version of the event but one more attuned to the theme of the book rather than to the exact historical facts. Why as a historian this time I still hesitate to accept the hypothesis of Stalin's guilt, thus being reprimanded by some of my colleagues for being "soft on Stalin." Perhaps this is due to some contrariness in my nature. But I also feel that what might be called guilt by reputation ought not be uncritically accepted by historian any more than it is by a judge.

20

The Curse of the Bomb

Diplomacy in the 1970s..How to control "IT"...spying may have saved the world....The Soviet's "concealed weapon."...How are they gonna keep 'em (Solzhenitsyn China, & Eastern Europe) down on the farm?..Kremlin mellows but still on the make.

My historian-detective work did not keep me from writing on current Soviet-American relations. During the 1970s, my writing was primarily centered on those of the USSR and the US, and the grim realities and unspeakable potentialities of the nuclear arms question. SALT I and the Nixon-Brezhnev détente brought a temporary lessening of the fear of a nuclear holocaust. But as détente became frayed, those fears intensified again, and the Strategic Arms agreement itself became subject to criticism for conceding to the Soviets undue advantage in nuclear weapons. Few will recall today those agitated arguments which insisted that by agreeing to the Soviets' superiority in the mega-tonnage of their land missiles we were enabling them at any given moment to resort to nuclear blackmail of this country. At some point, one argument ran, a "nuclear window of opportunity" would tempt the Kremlin. A Soviet first strike would be capable of destroying most of our long-range missiles. Should the US decide to reciprocate with what was left in its arsenal, it would be able to inflict only a superficial wound on the USSR, killing merely some 20-30 million people, while the Soviet second strike reprisal would totally destroy this country.

I tended to discount such horrifying calculations. To my mind the Brezhnev team was composed of prudent bureaucrats, unlikely to resort to such pyrotechnics. They had denounced Mao when he had fantasized about a nuclear war that would destroy capitalism but leave socialism victorious. Their allocation of the deadly weapons reflected their prudence: the nuclear warheads were stored separately from the missiles, the former in the custody of the KGB rather than the military. Perhaps Hitler, if he had the Bomb and was faced with the crash of the Third Reich, would have improvised such a Götterdämmerung, but not those cautious men attached to their power and its luxurious perquisites.

And yet how could one be sure? Though the current occupants of the Kremlin eschewed Khrushchev's threats, they still adhered to his maxim that they must not tell the West that they were as much scared of a nuclear confrontation as we were. They were spending large sums of money on building shelters and other measures of civil defense ridiculously obsolete in the age of the hydrogen bomb. Not until 1978 would Brezhnev admit in a public speech that a nuclear war would know no victor, and it would take Gorbachev after the disaster of Chernobyl to spell out this truth clearly and uncompromisingly.

I've mentioned before, the nuclear age confers an unfair advantage on a dictatorial regime which has even a small number of such weapons at its disposal. America's monopoly of the A-bomb for five years or so gained it little in terms of political or diplomatic advantage over the Soviet Union. I have already referred to the thesis that Stalin would have invaded Western Europe except for the A-bomb. Totalitarian rulers can, on the contrary, resort to nuclear bluff, and if they don't overdo it, as did Khrushchev, may paralyze the resolve of a democracy.

One could not therefore reject out of hand the argument about the "missile gap" and the "window of opportunity." We could not put all our trust in the rationality of the men in the Kremlin. And even if we did, the nuclear horror could be triggered by an accident. Or by a third party: an unidentified submarine (China's?) lobbing an atomic missile at an American or Soviet target and prompting a massive attack on Moscow or New York. The latter possibility was particularly feared by the Kremlin, and for some time they believed not only the People's Republic but also West Germany capable of such horrendous provocation.

These fears were behind the idea of the hot line established by the two superpowers during détente, which enabled them to communicate instantaneously should a deadly danger arrive or in any other case of emergency.

In retrospect, it must be acknowledged that our avoidance of a catastrophe during the four decades or so of the Cold War was due not only to Washington and Moscow's prudence, but as well to good luck. This was probably the only period in history in which spying played a benevolent role and may have saved the world. The U-2 flights over the USSR showed Washington that there was indeed a missile gap, but it was in America's favor. After they ended with Gary Powers unintentionally dropping in uninvited on the Soviet Union, the spy satellites took over. This time both countries had the means of spotting the missile sites on each other's territory and establishing that no preemptive strike was being prepared.

Apart from warding off an ultimate catastrophe, American statesmanship faced what might be called the arithmetical-psychological aspect of the nuclear arms question. For the five years of the treaty's duration, SALT I sanctioned the Soviets' quantitative superiority in land-based missile mega-tonnage. The most formidable weapon in the Soviets' armory, and hence the main element in Washington's fears, was the SS-18 missile, capable of carrying ten megaton warheads that could be MIRV-ed, i.e. independently targeted. The United States' acceptance of inferiority in land-based strategic weapons was based on the sensible assumption that its overall position in nuclear weapons was adequate to deter a Soviet nuclear strike, and that beyond a certain number, quantitative superiority in strategic weapons was meaningless. What if we had "only" 1,054 fixed ICBM launchers against some 1,600 for the USSR; they were sufficient to destroy the Soviet Union many times over. But such reasoning, while convincing to a statesman or a scientist, was not necessarily so to the man in the street. To him the numbers meant that the USSR was stronger; and why should the U.S. accept inferiority to another power?

Your average citizen's apprehensions were echoed by many West Europeans. NATO had been founded on the premise of America's "nuclear umbrella" over the West. NATO's conventional forces, it was assumed, might not be adequate to stop a Soviet land invasion. But with the Soviet nuclear power superior to that of the United States, would the latter risk a Soviet Union's counterblow if its tanks and soldiers overran West Germany?

Control of nuclear arms became the main topic of the two superpowers' diplomacy in the 1970s. There was an element of paradox in the exercise. Both sides knew that no agreement on limiting their nuclear arsenals could preclude the possibility of disaster. The curse of the Bomb made the absolute national security that the United States possessed in being protected by two great oceans a thing of the past. It also became a frighteningly equalizing factor in international relations. A third-rate power, Iraq, Iran, or North Korea, by acquiring a few of those weapons, could pose a grave danger to the mightiest state, and have the capability of literally obliterating a small one such as Israel or South Korea. In contrast, the small number of nuclear weapons and missiles now possessed by Great Britain and France did not appear to increase their influence on the international scene. As before, and much as it would not be admitted by General De Gaulle, their national security depended on the might and protection of the United States. Despite all the earlier appearances to the contrary, the invention of nuclear fission was not a gain for the cause of democracy and world peace.

It is then to the credit of the American people that they could live for four decades with the fear that a misstep in foreign relations, whether by Washington or Moscow, or an accident, might have released universal destruction, and yet did not panic. It also warrants a tribute to our Presidents of the period, from Truman to Reagan, that for all the vicissitudes and near disasters that afflicted this country's fortunes in dealing with Communism, they never resorted to the use of nuclear weapons after Hiroshima and Nagasaki. There were moments when this country seemed close to undertaking such a fateful step: in the winter of 1950, when our armies in Korea were being apparently overwhelmed by the Chinese "volunteers;" in 1954, when the French in Vietnam were in a similar situation with the Viet-Minh; in the first flush of the Cuban missile crisis; probably at some critical points of the Vietnam War. But in each case the President in office had the statesmanship and humanity to resist the pressure from his military advisers and to refrain from what would have been a terrifying gamble.

To be sure, the above picture has to be qualified. President Truman did not contribute to the nation's enlightenment on the nuclear question when in 1953, after numerous reports of the Soviet experiments with the A or H-bomb must have reached him, he stated that the USSR had not developed nuclear weapons. Then, while crediting the good sense of the American people in not panicking, we must not forget the high level of anxiety during the second Berlin Crisis of 1959-1961, which led to a boom in building private shelters and when ministers, rabbis, and Professor Galbraith engaged in a public debate over whether the owner of such a refuge should have the right to limit access to it.

The Soviet Union entered nuclear arms control negotiations only after it had accumulated a considerable arsenal of the weapons, and after its rulers, in strained relations with China, had an obvious incentive to seek détente with the West. Until perestroika, the nuclear danger could not be the subject of a public debate in the Soviet Union, or rather: wherever such debate existed it was strictly within the limits imposed by the regime. It is only from the dissident circles, most notably from Andrei Sakharov, the architect of the Soviet H-bomb, that there came appeals for the superpowers to compose their differences. Modern weapons had rendered an all-out war suicidal to both sides.

(I always believed that the main effect of the tangled nuclear arms control negotiations was therapeutic, especially for the American public.) Once let out of the bottle in 1945 the genie of possible universal destruction could not be pushed back in. Measures like the Nuclear Test Ban Treaty in 1963, the Nuclear Nonproliferation Treaty of 1969, which shut the barn door after the most valuable horse— China— had escaped, and even SALT I were but palliatives that could not restore that sense of security which had existed before the appearance of the H-bomb and long-range missiles. But the awareness of the Soviet and American officials putting their heads together to proscribe or to reduce the ultimate danger had a profoundly calming effect on both societies. All those treaties and negotiations served a useful purpose: they exorcised fears that the unthinkable was just around the corner. Hence the illogical but understandable reaction of the American public: we were considerably less scared about what the Soviets might do in the 1970s when they had a huge arsenal of nuclear weapons and the missiles to deliver them, than in the 1950s, when Moscow had relatively few of those weapons and their long-distance missile system was not yet functional.

For some this balance of terror failed to be reassuring. They saw the concept of deterrence as both immoral and ineffective. To avoid a holocaust the democracies must give up their strategic weapons. "Better red than dead," as the extreme version of the pacifist view became known, had been propounded by Bertrand Russell. The great logician found nothing illogical in his argument that it was US nuclear power that presented the greatest danger to peace. And there were others in the Western scientific and intellectual community who pleaded for the democracies to give up their strategic weapons, even if the USSR would not follow their example.

Russell was hardly an admirer of the USSR; shortly after the Revolution, Russell wrote a very penetrating and damning critique of the Communist system. Rather his views and those of the like-minded, I felt, reflected a resentment of Britain's decline on the world stage, now dominated by those bumptious Yankees.

At the other end of the political-strategic spectrum were many Americans who viewed the negotiations with the Russians and SALT I as a snare and delusion. The situation for them warranted not further agreements with the Kremlin but, first of all, the US overcoming its supposed inferiority to the USSR in nuclear weapons, and then developing an effective anti-ballistic missile system. This view was especially strongly argued by The Committee on Present Danger, a body of academic and public figures, many of whom were subsequently to serve in the Reagan administration.

I could not endorse the more alarmist arguments of the committee, e.g., that the Soviet quantitative superiority in land-based nuclear weapons was creating that celebrated "window of opportunity" through which the Kremlin would blackmail this country with the threat of a preemptive strike. But in the atmosphere of post-Vietnam malaise and breast-beating about our foreign policy, much of the Committee's activity and publication served as a useful antidote to what came to be known as the revisionist view of the Cold War.

This view was quite widespread in the 1970s. How far inner doubt and guilt feelings had then invaded the once self-confident American society we can judge from the fact that a committee of the House of Representatives chose to hold hearings about how and why the United States had entered the Cold War.

One spring day, I was testifying before that committee. The other witnesses at the session included Professor William Appleman Williams, a long-time revisionist critic of U.S. foreign policy, and Arthur Schlesinger. There was also an elderly retired professor from Tennessee named Fleming, in whose opinion all of Washington's moves since World War II had been dictated by big business. He was not a Marxist but a populist in the style of William Jennings Bryan; even his physical appearance reminded one of the photograph of the great orator. Schlesinger expressed his doubts about the revisionist thesis, but found its injection into the public debate desirable: both policymaking and scholarship benefited from questioning traditional assumptions.

I could not be equally charitable. For me, I told the congressmen, that revisionism was based on bad history, and on the inappropriate assumption that there must be two sides to every political argument. Whatever the sins of omission or the commission of America's foreign policy, they could not morally or politically justify the steady course of expansion and repression followed since World War II by the Soviet Union. Professor Williams chose to repeat one of the cardinal points of the revisionists' argument about Washington's policies: that we dropped the A-bomb on Japan not to speed the end of the Pacific war, but to frighten, really to blackmail, the USSR. I never knew or heard such charges from the Soviet side until after they had been voiced by some Westerners. Did our monopoly of the nuclear weapons restrain Stalin from taking over Eastern Europe? Or from imposing the Berlin blockade of 1948-1949? What more might have the Russians demanded and taken had not the "bad" US frightened them with the Bomb?

Needless to say, Williams did not concede the point. His response was: that Moscow did not accuse America of nuclear blackmail demonstrates, in fact, how much they were scared of it. It was regrettable, of course that the Soviets dealt so brutally with Poland, Czechoslovakia, etc. But it was the threat to their security posed by Washington's foreign policy, the Truman doctrine, and NATO that led the Soviets to seek a barrier of Communist states between the USSR and the West.

Since the fall of the Soviet Union, many Russians have criticized its foreign policy in terms much sharper than those employed by the American "cold warriors" of the 1970s, and today the revisionist argument would find few defenders. The most astonishing thing about it is that it was often advanced by people with no sympathy for Communism. True, there should be no taboos in discussing democracy's policies, foreign no less than domestic. But by distorting the facts of America's troublesome co-existence with the USSR, revisionism can hardly qualify as constructive criticism.

My rejection of the revisionist thesis and my conviction that it was an obstacle to clear-headed thinking about the Soviet Union did not mean that I viewed the Communist State as "the Evil Empire" of Mr. Reagan's famous metaphor. To be sure, Stalin had been the very personification of evil. But his successors were run-of-the-mill bureaucrats whose main concern was the preservation of their power and privileges. Solzhenitsyn may have put it too strongly when he wrote that they did not believe in the ideology they kept continuously and tediously proclaiming; yet the notion of conquering the world for Communism was far from their minds. They were having no end of trouble with China. Would they want to have to deal with a Communist US, or for that matter France or Great Britain? As I've written elsewhere, they were trapped by their system; its legitimacy was based on the myth of Communism inheriting the world. Hence without much conviction Brezhnev and company had to strive to register new successes against capitalism on the world arena, even though the Yemens, Ethiopias, etc., meant no additional power for the USSR but only more trouble and expense.(And already by the late 1960s, the Kremlin knew, though it could hardly state so publicly, the greatest danger to Soviet security was posed not by the "imperialist West" but by that huge Communist neighbor state, now armed with nuclear weapons and making no secret of its claims to huge areas of USSR territory.)

Even the job of standing armed guard over some 100 million people in Eastern Europe was proving taxing to the USSR. Except perhaps for Bulgaria, the local Communist regimes were widely unpopular with their people, and it was only the memory of what happened in Hungary in 1956 and Czechoslovakia in 1968 that kept the regions in subjugation. Putting down local "troubles" like the Prague Spring required not only the intervention of Soviet tanks and soldiers but also a considerable infusion of Soviet economic help.

So at a time when the Soviet economy was beginning to experience stagnation, Russia's imperial role was proving to be an additional burden. "That which stops growing begins to rot," was an explanation given by Catherine the Great's Foreign Minister to an ambassador's query why the immense Russian Empire still sought more conquests. Well, social and economic stagnation could not be offset by territorial successes in the Horn of Africa and Southeast Asia.

It was still well-nigh inconceivable to me that the regime that had survived so many catastrophic situations would within a few years start tottering. Where was the force or movement that could overthrow it? Active dissent was confined to a relative handful of intellectuals, with the vast majority of the population passive and submissive. As stated before, I did see the regime losing some of its previous self-confidence, paying some attention to world public opinion, trying to appear "respectable" to the outside world. But would the rulers carry this self-restraint to the point when the heavy lid of repression lifted, and dictatorship and the unity of the Soviet

Union might be put in jeopardy. The ruling oligarchs were the very same people who had decided that even Khrushchev's very qualified criticism of the Stalinist past had posed an intolerable threat to the regime. Where among those cynical and elderly bureaucrats was a man naive or idealistic enough to believe that you could lift the burden of fear from the people and keep the system going? And if there was one poised to succeed Brezhnev, would not his colleagues deal with him as they had dealt with Khrushchev? The latter's fate was a good illustration of the immobilization of popular will that was the concealed weapon of the Soviet system. Was there a single popular demonstration against the ouster of the man who for all of his many faults, told some truths at least about the past and tried to make life easier for his fellow-countrymen?

Thus I had no expectation that the Soviet system could evolve peacefully into "socialism with a human face." There were some in the West who entertained such dreams; as, for that matter, did such prominent dissidents in the USSR as Academician Andrei Sakharov and Roy Medvedev. Leninism and Stalinism, they believed, had prevailed because of Russia's backward and ruined condition after the Revolution and the Civil War. But now, in the USSR, you had a modernized society and universal literacy; and so in the not too distant future authoritarianism would have to give way to genuine social democracy. I, on the contrary, believed that any attempt at a basic reform would lead not to democracy but to the collapse of the Soviet Union, anarchy, and possibly civil war. The Soviet Union was not only a police state, but also an empire with the Russians as the dominant nation. If the veil of fear were lifted from society, would Ukrainians, Balts, and other ethnic groups continue to acquiesce in Russian domination? It would take a leader of genius to preserve the Soviet state and yet to turn it into the democratic path. And I did not see a Russian De Gaulle on the horizon.

Though in retrospect, the events of the 1980s and 1990s were largely to confirm my gloomy prognosis, I fault myself for having overlooked the signs of weakness in the Soviet regime. Its Stalinist structure required Stalin's methods to preserve its authoritarian character. But the leaders no longer could or would resort to mass terror. In its absence the ordinary police state methods of repression were not sufficient to eradicate dissent in the form of actions and writings of courageous men and women who felt it their moral duty to oppose the oppressive state. Though not many, and their numbers regularly thinned by arrests, they made dissent a permanent feature of the Soviet Union's social landscape.

The rank and file of the dissenters could expect for their efforts a penal colony, or the infamous psykhushka, the penal mental hospitals. But the Brezhnev regime was hesitant to apply such measures to people of world renown whose imprisonment would stir up loud protests abroad. Under Stalin it would have been inconceivable that Solzhenitsyn or Sakharov would be permitted to slander the socialist Fatherland, and yet remain at large; indeed neither would have been able to voice his protest or to put it in writing. Now, though submitting them to various chicaneries, the Brezhnev regime was at a loss how to silence its world-famous critics. The diehard Stalinists must have exploded in rage when the authorities finally decided to expel Solzhenitsyn from the USSR, thus giving him even a wider opportunity to denounce the evil system that had gripped his country.

Following his arrival in the West, Harvard's governing board was eager to have Solzhenitsyn honor its 1974 Commencement. The great writer curtly refused. If his answer was somewhat less than gracious (as I remember it, he simply scribbled on a piece of paper "I cannot come,") then his decision was reasonable. He had to find his footing in this new world and disliked being paraded about as an instant celebrity.

That year the university did confer an honorary doctorate on another famous Russian, Mstislav Rostropovich. He, too, had been expelled from the Soviet Union, and for sheltering Solzhenitsyn in his villa, among other sins. My wife and I enjoyed the privilege of escorting the famous cellist on that occasion.

A few years later, Solzhenitsyn did accept an invitation to the Harvard Commencement. Tradition dictates that one of those receiving honorary degrees address the university on the afternoon of graduation. It is no secret that his speech on that occasion disappointed, indeed alienated, a large part of this country's intellectual community. Some may have hoped the Russian author would join the "we are also guilty" chorus of the Western left, in that America's dereliction from principle, i.e., the Vietnam War, to some extent paralleled if not excused Soviet imperialism. But if Solzhenitsyn criticized the United States, it was precisely for its insufficient resolve in dealing with Communism, and insufficient firmness in maintaining the traditional, conservative values of the West. From now on the writer became for much of the liberal establishment a reactionary whose praiseworthy struggle against Communist oppression was not matched by an understanding and attachment to the democratic principles of the twentieth century.

I have always felt that both criticisms of the great writer were unreasonable. He is an extremely courageous man and a talented author, who has rendered tremendous service to the cause of freedom, both by his personal example and by his writings. No sociological or political tract could have matched the force and impact of his First Circle or Gulag Archipelago in showing the moral depravity of Soviet Communism. Once in the West, he, like many refugees and exiles, found it insufficiently alert to the danger of Communism, and itself flawed in its moral values. Proud of his national heritage, Solzhenitsyn could not but resent the condescending view that his nation has never been able nor would be able in the future to develop free institutions. Alas, post-Communist Russia must have saddened him much more than all the imperfections of the West: it has, at least for the moment, assumed some of the least attractive characteristics of capitalism without developing political and economic stability. And he, who once spoke for his nation's conscience, is now for the majority of his countrymen but a venerable relic of the past, his voice no longer attuned to their concerns and problems.

Solzhenitsyn's expulsion in 1974 was at least a partial victory for dissent. A thoroughly tyrannical regime would have confined him to a prison camp or eliminated him in an "accident." Had the rulers been more devious and intelligent, they would have let him stay in the country and write to his heart's content. They could have always kept his books from being widely circulated, and would have been credited with a certain broadmindedness. As it was, the dull-witted men in the Kremlin bestowed on the writer the encomium of quasi-martyrdom and made his voice resonate even louder in the Soviet Union and abroad.

Another sign of increasing political clumsiness on the part of the aging men of the Kremlin was their sponsorship of the Conference on Security and Cooperation in Europe. On its face, the conference was to provide a charter for European peace, and a solemn pledge by the thirty-four continental states as well as the US and Canada to abide by enlightened standards of international conduct and to observe in their domestic affairs rules consistent with human rights.

The original Soviet motivation for the conference was the desire to obtain a formal recognition of the post-World War II settlement and of the frontiers established "provisionally" in 1945 at the Potsdam meeting of the Big Three. But those frontiers, the division of Germany, Poland's Western frontier, etc. had already been affirmed by the series of agreements concluded by West Germany with Poland and the USSR between 1969-1972, and in the wake of the Nixon-Brezhnev meeting in 1972. Now in August 1975 the conference in Finland uniting the heads of the governments of those states, and which concluded with the Helsinki Final Act, brought the USSR little concrete advantage besides once more reaffirming that the participating parties consider inviolable each other's frontiers as well as other frontiers in Europe.

On the other hand, the Final Act listed also a number of rules the signatories bound themselves to observe in their internal policies. These included not hindering citizens seeking to be reunited with their families abroad, and allowing members of religious and professional organizations in any of the states to maintain contact and hold meetings with their fellow-believers and professionals in other states. And the introduction stated grandiloquently: "The participating states will respect human rights and fundamental freedoms, including freedom of thought, conscience, and religion They will promote and encourage the effective exercise of civil, political, economic, social, and cultural rights...[which] derive from the inherent dignity of the human person."

It is safe to say that none of the signatories, who included Brezhnev and President Ford, believed that the Soviet Union and other Communist states could or would abide by those admirable principles. After all, similar provisions were enshrined in the Soviet constitution, and there is no record of anyone publicly complaining to Stalin that Soviet practices concerning, say freedom of speech, fell somewhat short of the requirements of the law. Nor is it likely that Brezhnev in signing the Final Act thought that it would cause him and his colleagues any trouble. Who would be naive enough to urge that the Communist regime would observe all those provisions! The Soviets used to like to boast that their record in fulfilling their international obligations was "second to none." It certainly was, but not in the sense implied by the Kremlin.

But it was now more than twenty years since Stalin's death and quite a while since Khrushchev had opened the Pandora's box, which could not be tightly shut again. The dissenters now had a legal handle to denounce the abuse of human rights by the government. Committees to monitor the observance of the Helsinki declaration sprang up in the Soviet Union, and the Kremlin's chicanery could not eradicate them any more than it could the general phenomenon of dissent.

Subsequent international meetings on security and cooperation in Europe now resounded to the Western powers' complaints that the Soviet government was violating its commitments under the Helsinki Accords. The problem of human rights in the Soviet state thus became internationalized. The Kremlin could no longer speak with the same conviction about the impermissibility of foreign interference in domestic affairs of the Soviet Union. Of course it would defend itself with its usual vituperative power: how about racial persecution in the United States, Britain's repression in Northern Ireland, etc. But now it did so with just a hint of embarrassment. "Qui s'excuse s'accuse," as the French say. And so the autocratic system that had survived so many near catastrophes would eventually succumb because of its leaders' inner doubts and attempts at reform.

Yet as I studied Soviet-American relations at the time, in the mid-seventies, I failed to identify this mellowing of the Kremlin as a symptom of the decline of the Soviet regime. It was acquiring new client states in Africa, backing North Vietnam's takeover of the South, spurring on the Arab states' uncompromising stand toward Israel; in other words acting as scavenger in the world's trouble spots. Washington's policies seemed ineffective by comparison.

Little remained of the spirit of détente which, by the Presidential election of 1976, had become almost a dirty word in American politics.

21

Back to the Past with Revolutionary Fervor

Side trip into Revolutionary Russian history...the pathos and the drama.

From personal and public concerns I sought distraction by study-ing and writing on a subject that had until then been outside my pro-fessional interest. Russia of the last four decades of the 19th century particularly fascinated the contemporary West. To long-standing amaze-ment at the exotic features of the Empire, such as the anachronism of its absolutist monarchy and the absence of parliamentary institutions, was added sheer wonder at the persistence and intensity of the revolution-ary movement in the land of the Tsars, the movement which more than anywhere else in Europe came to engage in conspiracy and terrorism. The Russian revolutionary in exile in the West found his way to the pages of authors as diverse as Joseph Conrad and Arthur Conan Doyle. In Russia itself the radical-revolutionary mystique became the creed of the educated and professional class. Turgenev and Dostoyevsky were only the most prominent writers among the many in that golden age of Russian fiction who strove to portray the strange world of the men and women of "The Sixties," or the "New Men" as they became known to their sympathizers. (Nowhere else in Europe were women as numerous and active in the revolutionary ranks.)

One was struck by other similarities with our own tempestuous sixties and seventies. The rebels embraced the cause of ethnic groups in the Empire that suffered from discrimination, notably of Poles and Jews, and scorned the Victorian sexual mores, their very ap-pearance defiant of the conventional social code, men with long hair, women with cropped heads.

Those "activists" were hardly impressive in numbers, a minority within the intelligentsia, which was itself a small segment of the population. Their most important political movement, the Populists, found virtually no support among the peasant masses on whose behalf they allegedly strove and whose political consciousness they tried to awaken through agitation.

Frustrated by this lack of response, the Populists were driven increasingly to schemes of violence. The masses would have to be aroused by dramatic acts, such as the assassination of the Tsar, if he kept refusing to grant the country a constitution. Other branches of the movement scorned Western constitutionalism, and urged a semi-anarchic society based on the peasant communes.

Tsar Alexander II had pursued the course of moderate liberalism. He freed the serfs, instituted reforms of the judiciary, and established the rudiments of local self-government. He would willingly sign a constitution for the whole country, he declared, if he was not convinced that the Empire would then fall to pieces, a prophecy that brings to mind the fateful end result of Gorbachev's efforts to bring free institutions to his country.

In 1879 one faction of the Populist movement adopted the name of The People's Will and devoted itself to terrorism designed to compel the Tsar to summon a constituent assembly. For two years the conspirators, their core group never more than maybe forty people, managed to shake the foundations of the mighty empire by a campaign of assassinations of government officials. On March 1, 1881, they finally cornered their main prey. After escaping unscathed in six previous attempts on his life, Alexander II was mortally wounded by a bomb as he was returning to the Winter Palace.

The shock at the murder of the emperor broke the spell that the revolutionary mystique had cast over society. Even the liberal intelligentsia condemned it. There followed a period of reaction under Alexander III, who curtailed his father's reforms and abandoned a plan for a parliamentary body (with limited power) The revolutionary virus, however, remained within the tissue of society and would erupt with violence after another generation.

This brief review can hardly render justice to the pathos, romance, and drama of revolutionary Russia of those days. The genuine idealism of some of the rebels puts in stark contrast the sheer criminality, the lust for violence, of others. It is to one of the latter variety that we owe one of the world's great novels: Dostoyevsky's *The Possessed* is based on the lurid story of Sergei Nechayev's conspiratorial group. Interwoven with the conspirators' struggle is the regime's effort to cope with it through intermittent repression and reform, again a tale full of modern motifs, the revolutionaries infiltrating the ranks of the bureaucracy, the imperial police resorting to the use of agents provocateurs. In brief, the Russian scene of those times seems unbelievable, at once so relevant and similar to our own times, and yet crowded with people and events so exotic. As I wrote in my foreword *to In the Name of the People*, "It is little wonder that some of the most memorable works of Russian literature are based on true incidents in the struggle of a handful of men and women against the most powerful autocracy of the 19th century."

But it was not only the colorful scene or analogies with our own times that fascinated me and drew me to write the book. For all the thorough studies of the subject, there was still an air of mystery attending some of the crucial episodes of the revolutionary saga. Was a Doctor Kobilin, connected with the court circles, involved in the first attempt to assassinate Alexander II? What was the truth in the stories about several high officials being privy to the plots and rendering them secret assistance? Or the social and political puzzles, e.g., how could a woman who shot the St. Petersburg chief of police point-blank and in the presence of several witnesses be found not guilty by a jury of twelve loyal subjects of the Tsar, and how could a high official declare the occasion to have been "the happiest day of my life?"

If I contributed, at least partly, to resolving such mysteries and enigmas, it was probably because of my enduring addiction to the detective story!

22

The Communist World

China's stunning transformation in the 1970s...Death of ideology...Tottering oligarchs....Poland spells trouble!

A stream of Chinese visitors to America soon followed the Nixon-Kissinger breakthrough in US relations with China in 1972. First came officials of the Communist regime, then scholars, both carefully selected for ideological reliability, in far greater numbers than the Soviet visitors during the period of détente.

Quite a number of them turned up at Harvard. They showed little interest in visiting the famed Department of Far Eastern Studies but were eager to see our Soviet specialists. In meeting them I had sometimes to pinch myself: were those people from the same country whose rulers for more than two decades had viciously denounced the United States and upbraided their Russian fellow- Communists for being "soft" on capitalism? Now their language about the Soviet comrades was more abusive than that of the most fervent anti-Communist on this side of the Atlantic. The Kremlin leaders were to them "the new Russian Tsars," and surely the Americans were not going to be naive enough to believe that the "new Tsars" were serious about détente.

Some symptoms of the old doctrinal rigidity still persisted, and at times they took an absurd form. One of my visitors from the mainland left me a book about the Chinese Party Congress. In it there was a photograph of seven senior leaders of the regime. But they were not identified in the usual way: X in the center, so-and- so on his left and right. No, they were all on the left from number 1 to number 7. God forbid that any leader should be found "on the right" even for the sake of identification! It reminded me of the idiocies of the Cultural Revolution, when the youthful Red Guards demanded that traffic lights must be changed, so that red became a signal to go. But apart from such occasional absurdities, the new Communist China was obviously on the verge of launching a new Great Leap Forward, this time from the egalitarian and ruinous type of Communism to semi-capitalism, which would turn its leaders into real "capitalist roaders," one of their now-obsolete propaganda phrases, and from the most uncompromising enemies of the West into virtual allies of the US. The Chinese officials and professors I met struck me as sensible and well-informed men. How could the folly of one man have suppressed for so long the inherent pragmatism and common sense of the Chinese elite?

The man, Mao Zedong, the "Great Helmsman," died in 1976. As I read the Soviet press, it was obvious that the Kremlin was overjoyed at the demise of its most intransigent enemy. Usually the passing of a foreign Communist leader was marked by long and laudatory articles in Moscow's press. This time it was a six-line communiqué on a back page of *Pravda* that told its readers about the death of the master of the world's largest nation. But following the event there was a great deal of speculation about its consequences: could Mainland China preserve its unity, or would it become a scene of violent struggle between rival Communist factions? Would there not be an attempt by one such faction to restore good relations with the "Elder Brother," as the Party in happier times referred to the USSR?

All such speculation turned out to be wishful thinking. A brief turmoil within the Party ended with the defeat of the "Gang of Four," proponents of a radical course headed by Mao's widow and three other veterans of the Cultural Revolution, and the emergence of Deng as the supreme leader, a proponent of a pragmatic course in the economy and foreign policy. No contending faction, it seemed, sought a return to closer relations with the Soviet Union. Anti-Soviet, or rather anti-Russian feelings were by now deeply ingrained in the Chinese Communists. More important, playing the "American card" was obviously of much greater advantage to Beijing. Very soon the Republic of China (i.e. Taiwan) was with the silent complicity of the US ejected from the UN. Détente with America opened the prospects of Western and Japanese investments on the mainland, which, along with the common-sense restructuring of the Chinese economy, not only lifted it from the doldrums of Mao's times, but led to rapid GNP growth and higher living standards for at least some segments of the vast population.

The scene in the late 1970s and the next decade reminded me of my first year at Harvard in 1945, when I noted a large number of Chinese students from what was still a pre-Communist China. But there was a marked difference from their bearing then and now: thirty years before, they had seemed uninhibited in their speech, quite a number of them critical of Chiang Kai-shek's Nationalist government. Now their next-generation counterparts avoided political discussions. One of them would often be a kind of "commissar" watching over the behavior of the others. Still, they seemed more relaxed than the visitors from the USSR with whom I came in contact. In my lectures at the time I drew the students' attention to the differing attitude of the two Communist regimes. Moscow did not trust its young people; there were only about two hundred Soviet students in all American universities, most of them above college age, their families not allowed to join them. But from Communist China there were about two to three thousand students, watched, to be sure, but not nearly as constrained as their Soviet counterparts. The later drama in Tienanmen Square made it clear that China's young were also quite susceptible to the lure of the freedoms of the "decadent West." No, in this epoch the energy of democracy will not again be stopped by geographic and cultural boundaries.

I was more to the point in another conclusion drawn from the lesson of China's miraculous transformation: it made nonsense of all the ideological bans and pretensions of Marxism-Leninism. Private ownership of land, the profit motive, and privately run businesses returned to the nation where only a few years before even the peasants' individual households were being abolished and replaced by communal living. And even more drastic was the about-face on foreign policy: from an uncompromising hostility toward the US and support for the "wars of national liberation," to warm and cooperative relations with the US.

What then is left of the ideological core of Marxism-Leninism? Nothing, except continuous insistence on "the leading role of the Communist Party," i.e., on the Party bosses' monopoly of power. Having long complained about "bourgeois degeneration" of the Soviet state, Beijing's leaders have quite surpassed it in stripping their Communism of any ideological meaning.

To my mind the implications of China's transformation went far beyond affecting just the People's Republic. They spelled out the bankruptcy of both the Old and the New Left in the West.

The old Communists, those who blindly followed Moscow, were shaken in both their faith and allegiance by Khrushchev's revelations about Stalinism and his view of the Hungarian revolution, and by Brezhnev decreeing the invasion of Czechoslovakia in 1968. For a while, the New Left had looked approvingly at Mao's allegedly egalitarian and populist Communism. But now the Chinese, criticizing the Soviet Union, were reintroducing capitalism, and their new "helmsman" Deng would soon be entertained at the White House (1979). He would also send his troops into Vietnam, and the world would witness actual warfare between two Communist countries, a fine example of "proletarian internationalism!" As I've said, I couldn't foresee the dramatic events of the late 1980s, but could not help wondering how this death of ideology would affect the stability of the Soviet regime. Its citizens no longer lived in a society hermetically sealed from the outside world, as in Stalin's time. Modern technology, travel abroad, activities of the dissenters, clandestine circulation of books like Solzhenitsyn's Gulag dispelled the last illusions of at least the educated class, that Communism was the wave of the future and that their sufferings and deprivations would still be eventually rewarded by the building of a classless and flourishing society. The long years of acquiescence in the autocratic regime, the absence of any visible alternative, taught the lesson that it would be foolhardy to expect a spontaneous explosion to overthrow the system that had survived so many crises and had so many instruments of repression at its command! But something had to give. I did not then foresee that this something would be the self-confidence of the rulers: that among those fifteen or twenty bosses who constituted the Kremlin's inner circle there would be one who would initiate actions that would break up the Soviet Union and destroy Communism. The system would collapse not through any popular revolt, but through an implosion. And once that process reached the critical stage it was because of the ideological bankruptcy of Communism that the system could find no defenders and went down without a struggle.

Yet this was all to come in the future. In the middle and late 1970s, it was easy to believe that it was the capitalist system which was in trouble. The energy crisis provoked by OPEC seemed to arrest the miraculous growth rate of the Western economies. Echoes of Vietnam and Watergate still reverberated, and US prestige was at its lowest since World War II. It was easy for the Kremlin to obscure its own troubles by reading a lesson to America. In his speech before his Party's Congress in 1976, Brezhnev dwelt lovingly on the "intensification of the ideological and political crisis of capitalist society." In an unmistakable reference to Watergate and the troubles of his sometime partner in détente, he stated that corruption "has affected all the institutions of the capitalist system . . . Spiritually and culturally it continues to decline while crime and delinquency are becoming more rampant." All in all, "There is no future for capitalist society.")

There was enough truth in some of those allegations to distract the observers from the indications, then hard to see, that it was Communism that might not have much of a future. Among them was the General Secretary's harsh language about Chinese Communism, whose basic aim according to him was "To provoke a world war, and to exploit it for their own purpose." This horrendous accusation was paradoxically combined with a plea to Beijing to cease its evil ways and to resume its previous fraternal cooperation with the USSR, an admission of how helpless the Kremlin felt in the face of the Chinese challenge.

The realization of that ideological bankruptcy began to dawn on Communist parties throughout the world. Already Khrushchev's partial unmasking of Stalin sent a shock through the movement. Soviet harshness in Hungary in 1956 and then in Czechoslovakia in 1968 led to something unimaginable under Stalin: criticisms of the Soviet policies by West European Communists. To be sure, the Kremlin had long given up on the possibility of their Italian or French comrades coming to power. Those parties might fuss over the Soviet intervention in Czechoslovakia, Brezhnev told Dubek and his associates, after they had been dragged to a conference in Moscow, but so what?

Yet in fact the Kremlin could not afford to be completely indifferent to what the Western comrades were saying and doing. The 1970s witnessed the phenomenon of Euro-Communism, the Communist parties of Italy, France, and Spain trying to distance themselves from Moscow. The Spanish party actually announced that it was not opposed to Spain's adherence to NATO. The French Communists, though irritated by Moscow's flirtation with De Gaulle and his successors, found it difficult to shake off their long-standing servility to the USSR.

I visited Italy during those years and had an opportunity then, and later in this country, to meet with some of the leading leftist

ıls and Communists. Almost without an exception they
: as cultivated and humane individuals, without that com-
ᴜᴀ.. ss in political discussion so characteristic of their French
and American counterparts. It seemed inconceivable that those people
would want to impose an authoritarian system on their beautiful country or that they had for so long been in spiritual bondage to Moscow.
Yet even they were reluctant to sever their ties to the "Fatherland of
Socialism." After the fall and dissolution of the Soviet Union, the
Kremlin's archives revealed what had been suspected for a long time,
that Moscow had been subsidizing the Italian and other foreign parties.

But what had propelled those humane people to embrace the cruel
cult which had produced the Great Terror in Russia in the 1930s,
and the Great Folly of the Cultural Revolution in Mao's China? The
usual explanation for the spread of Communism in the West dwells
on the effects of the Great Depression and the rise of Fascism. But
while this answer may be persuasive respecting the mental state of
the ordinary French or Italian worker, it can hardly explain the attraction of Communism, with its cardinal element of faith in the Soviet Union, to a French, Italian, or American intellectual. They could
not have been unaware of what was going on in the USSR under
Stalin, and of the enslavement of the arts and sciences to the dictatorship whether there, China, or in other Communist states! The real
or imaginary inequities of capitalism could indeed lead to some intellectuals rejecting it, but was the total submission to a tyrannical
creed the sole possible response to social injustice? One suspects
that most of those scientists, artists, writers and the like who adopted
the Communist creed did so not out of misguided ideals, but precisely because Communism did demand unquestioning obedience
and faith in the Party and the leader. The most telling evidence that it
was a kind of intellectual masochism rather than idealism that mis-
led those people, appears in the decreasing popularity of Communism in the West after Stalin's death. A "normal" police state ruled
by a committee of elderly bureaucrats didn't have the same appeal
as a phantasmagoric terror-driven society headed by an infallible
leader.

A similar phenomenon could be observed in the pre-perestroika
Soviet Union. Brutal and murderous as Stalin's rule had been, it still
evoked loyalty and enthusiasm among the indoctrinated masses,
especially among the young. By contrast, Brezhnev could command

but little fear and certainly no enthusiasm, except perhaps in the ranks of the bureaucracy, now no longer exposed to terror or to sudden whims and changes of the boss's mood. For the first time in the history of the Soviet Union, the officials enjoyed something like job security. Except in cases of scandalous incompetence or senility they could count on their jobs and perquisites continuing until death. I pointed out before what geriatric cases Brezhnev's colleagues were, and during his last years Brezhnev himself was hardly equal to the rigors of his office, being afflicted by a variety of ailments and on the verge of senility. Within the inner circle the Secretary General enjoyed little respect; there was much disparaging talk of his passion for collecting all possible decorations and gifts, and there was a scent of corruption surrounding his personal friends. To be sure, contemporary China was ruled by even older oligarchs; but that practice was in keeping with tradition, and Beijing's oldsters, certainly Deng, appeared full of vigor. The decrepitude of the Soviet rulers could not be concealed from the Soviet people or the outside world: in newsreels Brezhnev could be seen being hauled in and out of planes by his security guards. Party leaders listening to his speeches were obviously watching him closely lest he stray from the text or keep repeating the same passage. People laughed seeing Brezhnev kissing on the mouth (rather than on both cheeks as Slavic custom prescribes) his pals and vassals like Hungary's Kadar or Bulgaria's Zhivkov, whom he would gather each summer in his estate on the Black Sea.

For all of its impressive military might and vast resources, the Soviet empire entered its stagnation phase during the Brezhnev era. The economy no longer grew at the rapid rate of the 1950s and 1960s, the growth of GNP having slowed down to one to two percent per year. Technologically, the Soviet economy was falling farther and farther behind the West, how much so we were to learn only after the break-up of the Soviet system. What would be confirmed then, when relevant statistics were no longer withheld or distorted, was the perennially lamentable state of Soviet agriculture, decline in the quality of health care, and a plethora of other socioeconomic problems and weaknesses. What must especially have worried the Kremlin was the low birthrate in the mostly Slavic part of the vast country compared with the high birthrate in the mostly Turkic part. Ethnic Russians would soon decline to less than fifty percent of the population of the empire, which had to be of concern to the rulers, whose claim to power and legitimacy was now grounded much more on Russian nationalism than on Marxism-Leninism.

Problems thus mounted for the Kremlin. When a few years later the entire system began to totter, I recalled a Polish official who visited me in the 1970s. A Communist party member for reasons of career rather than of conviction, he felt confident enough to let his fellow Pole know how he detested Communism. After bending my ears for some two hours with tales of the villainy of his and Soviet Union's governments, and of the Western powers' ineptitude in dealing with them, he announced: "Thank God the Russians live under Communism." I knew what he meant but feigned astonishment. "Well," he said, "if they had a decent system they could have long ago ruled the world." Quite a few visitors from my native country expressed similar sentiments, but no one else in such a succinct and quaint fashion.

Not surprisingly, Poland continued to prove the main trouble spot in the Soviets' East European empire. To the people's dislike of Communism was joined the age-long dislike of foreign domination. Nowhere else in the area was the Communist party viewed not so much as a political organization but as a foreign imposed garrison. Antigovernment riots erupted regularly. The riots of 1956 led to the replacement of the previous leadership of the Party by a group headed by Wladyslaw Gomulka. Because of his imprisonment under Stalin, he enjoyed national popularity and the reputation of being able to stand up to Moscow. Alas, those hopes were soon disappointed; personally honest but a man of narrow horizons, Gomulka soon revealed himself as that rare kind of Polish Communist, a genuine believer in Marxism-Leninism, and as such a fervent follower of "proletarian internationalism"— meaning following Moscow's line in foreign and domestic policies. Polish troops along with those of other Warsaw Pact countries participated in occupying Czechoslovakia in 1968, and in putting an end to the "Prague Spring." In 1970 another series of riots and strikes led to Gomulka's removal.

For a while Gomulka's successors were beneficiaries of the rising standard of living in the country. This was mainly due to increased exports to the West, and loans from the same source. Then the energy crisis, following the Middle East War in 1973, sharply cut Western Europe's imports and much of Poland's now reduced hard currency earnings had to go to servicing foreign debts. With the bubble of prosperity burst and under inflationary pressures, the government

resorted to raising prices on food and other necessities; this in turn
led to renewed workers' riots and strikes. The government revoked
the price increases, and the riots subsided. But this experience of the
workers' action that forced the regime to retreat was not lost on the
population and would embolden the workers to much more massive
and effective action in 1980.

What impressed me most about the Polish events of 1976 was
that we were witnessing a new type of protest against Communism.
After the partitions of the 18th Century destroyed Poland's independence, the violated nation arose several times against its ravishers,
most notably against Russia in 1830 and 1863. Neither revolt had
the slightest chance of succeeding against the enormous power of
the empire of the Tsars. Yet the tradition claimed, as I was duly taught
in school, that both uprisings were justified and morally necessary.
Now under Communism, Poland was in effect as much under alien
occupation as it had been during the Partitions (1795-1918). Yet the
reaction of the nation was quite different from what the old romantic, or today we would say existentialist, tradition would urge: it would
no longer resort to armed struggle just for the sake of the struggle. In
the modern age there was a new and better way to fight for independence, and this was industrial action by the working class. This
weapon was tried in 1970, and again in 1976. Perfected in 1980,
this mode of rebellion would shake the foundations of Communism,
and not only in Poland, and would contribute to its crash a few years
later. The nation found a new and more practical way to freedom.

The other, and in its immediate significance, much more important, event of 1976, the election of Jimmy Carter to the Presidency,
filled me with some misgivings. I have always considered myself a
Democrat, and most of the time I had voted accordingly. The new
President never had been exposed to foreign policy problems, and
at that time those problems were much more urgent than any domestic issues. The election meant that Henry Kissinger would no
longer steer our foreign policy, precisely at the point where his tal-
ents and experience were needed to restore the world's and its own
citizens' confidence in the United States after Vietnam and Watergate.
Kissinger had been at the tiller of our foreign relations craft even
before he became Secretary of State. Now its direction would be
shared and often disputed by the new incumbent of the office, Cyrus
Vance, and the new national security adviser, Zbigniew Brzezinski:
the former a cautious lawyer-diplomat type, the latter a former col-

league of mine at Harvard, an able student of East European affairs but prone to be imprudent in speech. People of such differing backgrounds and temperament, both ambitious, might have well complemented each other if the President had been more decisive and in command of the facts. Unfortunately, Mr. Carter, for all his admirable qualities, was ill-suited to face the complex realities of this sinful world. Like some of his predecessors he placed exaggerated importance on personal relations with the Soviet leaders, and on convincing them that far from supporting the cause of reaction throughout the world the United States stood for progress and social justice. When Kennedy spent some time at the Summit in Vienna in 1961, it was in a similar spirit that he tried to read something of the same lesson to Khrushchev. The US was not against revolutionary changes wherever social and economic conditions required them; it only insisted that they be carried out in a democratic way. Such protestations usually succeeded in persuading the Soviet leaders of the Americans' naiveté. They neither believed that Washington's policies were inspired by democratic virtue, nor cared if they weren't.

After President Carter's inauguration, speculation in the press worldwide about whether and how the Soviets would test him illustrated how greatly the calamities of the past decade had damaged US prestige. The Kremlin was unstinting in showing its displeasure with the new administration. Carter's outspokenness about human rights violations in the USSR provoked its ire. Andrei Sakharov addressed a public letter to the President asking him to persevere in his humanitarian efforts, and Mr. Carter acknowledged the letter publicly and answered it. Even more irritating to Moscow was the invitation and visit to the White House of Vladimir Bukovsky, a dissident recently expelled from the USSR, and in Pravda's words, a "convicted criminal."

Along with many others, I have been baffled by the problem of the proper degree of influence humanitarian ideals ought to have on our foreign policy. Had the true character of Stalin's regime been known to our statesmen and public during the second World War, would we have refused to help the USSR in its struggle against Hitler and thus risked the eventual outcome of the war? Should we now risk our alliance with Saudi Arabia, pivotal to our position in the Middle East, by publicly denouncing the authoritarian nature of its politics and the condition of women under its fundamentalist Muslim laws and customs? Or, more practical in today's world: how far should this government go in denouncing violations of human rights in Communist China, now on its way to becoming a superpower? One could go on almost indefinitely asking similar questions, most of this planet's governments not adhering, alas, to what we consider democratic virtue.

My early approach to this vexing problem was close to what I understood to be Henry Kissinger's position on the issue: the US government's main concern has to be the security of this country and its allies. We must not jeopardize that essential interest by putting an ally or a powerful rival "on the spot" by a public brawl about its domestic practices. If we want to alleviate the lot of the unjustly oppressed in those countries, this can be done best by "quiet diplomacy," without arousing a chorus of public and mutual recriminations.

People critical of that position have accused Kissinger of cynicism and of advocating pure power politics, demeaning the role of the US as a country supportive of human rights and democracy. But could this country demand in effect, that the Soviet Union change its political system before we negotiate with it about arms regulations, trade, etc.? The Roman maxim "Let justice be done even if the world may perish" expresses a noble sentiment, but now that we have nuclear missiles, we must not try to put it to any actual test.

Nonetheless I modified my attitude after the Helsinki Accords of 1975. Through them Moscow of its own volition agreed to observe certain constraints on its domestic policy. But—whenever he visited say, Paris, a Soviet potentate would make it a practice to arrange a visit with the head of the French Communist Party. Why then should the President of the United States not see a member of Mr. Brezhnev's opposition? This was a point that Washington should have made but never did.

Where Mr. Carter and his advisers blundered was in their belief that they could reprimand and mollify the Soviets at the same time. Right after the Sakharov and Bukovsky episodes, Secretary Vance was dispatched to Moscow with proposals for SALT II. The proposals were virtually the same as those to which the USSR had tentatively agreed at the Ford-Brezhnev Summit in Vladivostok more than two years before. Such over-eagerness gave the Kremlin a welcome opportunity to teach the new Administration a lesson. Brazenly denying that they had agreed to some of the proposals before, the Soviets refused to negotiate, and rather insultingly made it clear that

Vance had no further business in Moscow. In his statement, foreign minister Gromyko showed that this rude behavior was not unconnected from the Americans' solicitude for the dissenters: "We do not need any teachers (from abroad) when it comes to internal affairs of our country."

The Carter administration was not the first one to discover that propitiatory gestures toward the Kremlin were not reciprocated unless the USSR had its own reasons. The President upon entering into office talked about reducing the defense budget and withdrawing part of the US troops from South Korea. For me, and more importantly for Brezhnev & Co., such declarations by the new Washington team indicated its lack of self-assurance. Why is it that practically every new administration going back to the war years had to learn anew the lesson that the Soviet leaders did not care how liberal their American counterparts were, and more often than not interpreted such protestation as a sign of weakness? Had Mahatma Gandhi rather than Cyrus Vance been in charge of America's foreign relations, the Soviets would still not have believed Washington's assurances. As it was, the Carter administration's initial misstep put it at a disadvantage in the negotiations to reach a new agreement on nuclear arms control, SALT II, and undermined even further the already frail framework of détente.

I have always been reluctant to become one of the numerous "experts" engaged in unsolicited advice about this country's conduct of its foreign policy. It always seemed to me that the task of scholarship is different from that of policy-making, and that the former often becomes flawed if the scholar tries to assume the garb of policy maker, his work designed not so much to provide an objective assessment of the given problem situation but rather to catch the attention of the powers in Washington. In the post-World War II period one could not write about the Soviet Union and its foreign policy with the same detachment possible, say, in writing about ancient Greek tragedies. One could not out of an excessive concern for one's scholarly identity, abstain from supplementing an analysis of Soviet policies with an evaluation of American responses to them. When the job of special assistant to the President was first created, I believe under FDR, it was said that its holders should be "on tap rather than on top." Well, few of my colleagues circulating in the corridors of power in Washington limit their ambition to being just on tap.

My own contribution to the public dialogue on American policy toward the USSR consisted of three books that were published from the early 1970s. The first and most ambitiously conceived was the already mentioned Expansion and Coexistence, which covered the entire history of the Soviet Union's foreign policy from the beginning until 1973. Though it was widely used in university classes, I did not think that it could be influential in affecting the policy of this country. Both its size, about 800 pages, and my approach to the subject were not likely to attract many general readers. I didn't indulge in the then popular game of solemnly prophesying, "what the Russians will do next." I said in the conclusion that the Soviet leaders clearly faced a choice. They could opt for the dangerous and essentially futile course of attempting further imperial expansion, or they might, "mindful of the realities of the nuclear age, choose the goal of supra-ideological world order without which no state, no matter how powerful, can find security and true greatness." Now more than twenty years later, it is clear that Gorbachev and Yeltsin, in different ways and at cross-purposes, were attracted to the second course.

At the time, however, those two were in the wings and virtually unknown outside the USSR. One had to assume that for the immediate future the US would have to deal with leaders of Brezhnev's type, unable and unwilling to depart from the beaten path of seeking expansion of the Soviet power whenever it seemed safe to do so. And they were not likely to seek internal changes, though the changing society and economy would impinge more and more upon the authoritarian system.

My book *The Rivals*, a survey of Soviet-American relations from 1945-1971, dealt with the lessons of the past twenty-five years and what they portended for the immediate future. In reading it today I readily concede that at the time my crystal ball was somewhat clouded: "We should not expect that the regime we will deal with in Russia for many years to come will be other than an authoritarian one." Nor, I wrote, should we wish for a drastic change there. "Or that I would hope for their own sake as well as that of the world that the Soviet people should try to alter drastically the system under which they live. Requirements of peace, I should say more concretely, of preserving the world from a nuclear holocaust, which a tottering authoritarian regime might unleash, take precedence over those of democracy."

The reader can judge whether 17 counts as "many years." I shall specify later why I think 1988 is the real watershed, the year when the Soviet system ceased to be authoritarian. And who in 1971 could have believed that if the USSR went down, it would do so with barely a whimper? I believed, and I still do, that neither Khrushchev nor Brezhnev would have recoiled from a nuclear war, had they thought it was the only way to save the Soviet Union from disintegrating.

I was still not clairvoyant in my *Dangerous Relations*, which appeared in 1982. Then I wrote, "No one should expect Brezhnev or any conceivable successor of his to declare in effect, "Comrades, I am happy to say that the imperialist danger has disappeared. We can now devote all our efforts to the cultivation of our socialist garden." Six years later Gorbachev would prove me wrong. But I was more fortunate in my other opinion that a drastic reversal in the character of the Soviets' internal and external policies would threaten the existence of the USSR: "Applying the brakes so precipitately to the whole process and rhetoric of expansion would throw into turmoil not only the Soviet bloc but the USSR itself." By August 1991, Gorbachev must have come to that same conclusion.

Dangerous Relations was the closest I came to offering unsolicited commentary and critique of US policies toward the Soviet Union. It seemed to me that the first task of the American policy makers was to restore consistency and self-assurance to Washington's management of relations with Moscow, something sadly lacking since Watergate and Vietnam. The problem could not be handled by following simplistic formulas like "Russians respect only strength," or conversely by the Carter administration's intermittent and often pathetic attempts to convince the Russians that we were not the capitalist monsters the Kremlin allegedly believed us to be. The conviction that the Russians respected only military power came from anecdotes such as Stalin's alleged response to FDR in Yalta when the latter urged him to establish diplomatic relations with the Vatican: "How many divisions does the Pope have?" Even if this anecdote was not apocryphal, Stalin was too intelligent to minimize the importance of moral and ideological factors in politics. How many divisions did Lenin have when he returned to Russia in 1917 and within six months overthrew the government of the country? The internal cohesion of its adversary, its leaders' grasp of the world situation, were qualities, which in the eyes of the Kremlin were of great importance. To quote myself again:

"Military strength is a necessary ingredient of the prevention of war, but it is only Western unity and statesmanship that can provide conditions for allaying the East-West conflict and removing the main obstacles to real peace." Perhaps this sounds like a platitude, but at the time there were considerable strains within the Western alliance, and soon it would be put to new tests by Soviet diplomacy. And I could not agree with Mr. Carter's evident belief that having and proclaiming one's good intentions was all that there was to statesmanship.

Occasionally the Administration varied that course with what could be described as naive Machiavellianism. Brezhnev's visit to Washington, much desired by Carter, and the final formulation of SALT II, was supposed to take place about the middle of January 1979. But Mr. Carter thought it appropriate to announce that just after Brezhnev's visit, he expected to host China's supreme leader Deng and to conclude with him a treaty establishing formal diplomatic relations between the US and the People's Republic. National Security advisor Brzezinski urged this particular timing on the President despite the opposition of the Secretary of State. It was hoped that this dramatic display of the China card would make the Soviet Union eager to appease Washington on some still disputed details of SALT II. But as Mr. Vance justly feared, the Soviets refused to fall in with the scheme that would make Brezhnev appear to be hastening to Washington to mollify the US before the appearance of the Chinese statesman. The irate Secretary General canceled the visit, and addressed a personal message to the President. Trying to put a good face on an awkward situation Carter declared that Brezhnev's letter took a very positive view of the new ties between America and China. The Soviets then took the unprecedented step of revealing the actual content of the communication between the two Heads of State. The gist was quite opposite to Carter's interpretation, and contained the insulting warning that the USSR would watch closely the future course of American-Chinese relations and would draw appropriate conclusions. "Don't get too friendly or we might do something," was the unsubtle implication of the Brezhnev message. Conclusion of SALT II was indefinitely postponed, and Brezhnev would never again step on American soil. Somewhat more delicately than their boss, Soviet spokesmen on foreign relations warned that too strenuous US wooing of China would doom détente. Mr. Carter might well have asked, What détente?

In retrospect, I feel it not unfair to consider Carter's presidency as the lowest point in the management of our foreign relations since World War II. One cannot begrudge his administration one great success: its role in facilitating the understanding between Egypt and Israel; more precisely, in helping to bring together Anwar Sadat and Menachem Begin. There Mr. Carter displayed his great talent as a conciliator, in a situation when what was needed was to throw America's support to two parties willing to come to terms but inhibited by party enmity. He had less success in impressing America's actual and potential opponents with this country's power and determination not to allow encroachments upon its interests. Personally, he was the most likeable occupant of the White House since Harry Truman, but he lacked the decisiveness and, indeed, occasional ruthlessness which the role requires.

23

Novel Uncertainties

Late 70s, early 80s: US failures in foreign policy...clashes in the "fraternal"... Socialist Countries...The Afghan adventure

How far away must the late 1970s seem from today's perspective! The events that occurred then appear to belong to another century. The most startling changes have taken place in world politics. Then, the central fact in world politics was the enormous power and menace of the Soviet Union. The Western world was in retreat. The United States, barely recovering from the humiliation of Vietnam, had just suffered another blow to its prestige. With the obvious complicity of Iran's government, a fanatical Moslem fundamentalist mob seized the American embassy in Teheran, and took its personnel hostage. Washington stood by, apparently powerless to rescue its citizens.

Equally symptomatic of the West's inability to protect the rule of law in international relations was its feeble reaction to Soviet aggression in Afghanistan. The Carter administration indeed did suspend its action on SALT II following Moscow's coup in Kabul, but the nuclear arms control agreement, and with it the whole concept of détente, had obviously been virtually buried by the vagaries of American politics. What had to agitate the American policy makers was the recurrent question: when will the Soviets strike next? Surely the Afghanistan venture could be a prelude to a move against Pakistan, America's ally and, like Afghanistan, torn by ethnic tensions and hence a potential prey for the Kremlin's intrigues.

Adding to such fresh worries was a concern going back to the end of World War II and the appearance of nuclear weapons, the ever-present fear of a nuclear holocaust. In this country and in Western Europe this fear was currently intensified by what appeared to be the Soviet Union's quantitative superiority over the US. Some analysts and public figures argued no one could maintain that America's nuclear umbrella still protected Western Europe from the Red Army.

By the 1990s such fears and apocalyptic visions began to fade. To be sure, by now we have recovered from that rather excessive feeling of relief brought on by the crash of the Soviet Union and, in fact, of world Communism. No, we have not arrived at "the end of history" and the definitive triumph of democracy. Our smugness has been tempered by the realization that there are still well over a billion people living under regimes that call themselves Communist. Though perhaps the ghost of Lenin would not certify them as such, they possess calculable power and the ability to make mischief. And they are not the only ones that create trouble for us and unhappiness for their own people.

Yet fear afflicts the world much less today. The Cold War is over. The invasion of Afghanistan turned out not to be a prelude to the Soviets' triumphant march to the Indian Ocean and the Persian Gulf. On the contrary it might well have been the proverbial straw that broke the red camel's back. Russia is moving toward some sort of democracy, as are the former Communist nations of Eastern Europe. And neither friends nor potential foes would now characterize the United States as, to quote Nixon, a "pitiful, helpless giant." At the time there were few reasons to expect such a fortunate turn of events. What seemed to be ahead was at best a continuous indecisive duel between the West and the Soviet camp, at the worst, the possibility of the conflict escalating into a nuclear confrontation.

One favorable development on the chessboard of international politics was Communist China's now irrevocable estrangement from the Soviet Union. Against Moscow's expectations, this estrangement not only endured but deepened following Mao Zedong's death in 1976. And it was not only because of China that one felt that the Communist world was coming under increasing strains. It is true that very few Communist parties ranged themselves alongside Beijing and against Moscow. But the bonds between Moscow and the main parties in Western Europe were becoming frayed, the Italian Communists openly critical of the Soviet Union's foreign and internal policies, the Spanish Party endorsing their country's participation in the Atlantic Alliance. And where, as in Eastern Europe, Communism had been imposed from outside, one could sense increasing restiveness among the wide masses of the population.

One event seemingly detached from the sphere of politics would turn out to be an early harbinger of the forthcoming crash of the Soviet empire: the Polish workers' revolt of 1980. I remember hearing the news in a rather unlikely context. It was a fall afternoon in 1978. I was entertaining a Polish visitor, the editor of a Catholic journal in Krakow. To what little there was of the Catholic press in Poland, the regime allowed a modicum of editorial freedom, and my guest was an unrelenting critic of the Communist government. Apart from subservience to Moscow, its current leaders were guilty of gross economic mismanagement. The situation was close to a boiling point. Like all sensible observers, he certainly didn't want a violent confrontation between the people and the regime. That in all likelihood would bring Soviet intervention, as in 1968 in Czechoslovakia and 1956 in Hungary. And as with Hungary, that might end in a blood bath.

My guest excused himself; he had to chat with some local journalists. I profited from the interruption to drop in on a colleague who was following an important event on the radio: the Red Sox and the Yankees were engaged in a single game play-off to decide the American League pennant. As so often in its karmic history, the Boston team, after having forged ahead was tied. They were trounced in the last inning. But an announcement during the broadcast took my mind off baseball. I had a surprise for my visitor when he returned: the Cardinal Archbishop of Krakow had just been elected Pope!

His first reaction was "We've lost our bishop." But soon he laughed at himself for the parochialism of his remark. We had a long discussion about the significance of the election. Its stupendous importance in ecclesiastical history was obvious; this was to be the first non-Italian Pope since 1523. But what were likely to be its consequences for Poland?

Politically, the election of the Polish Pope was undoubtedly of great importance. This is not to say that without it you would not have had the Solidarity explosion of 1980. But the election strengthened the morale of anti-Communist forces in a cruelly tried nation. Also it must have increased the initial reluctance of both the Polish regime and the Kremlin to crack down on the rebellious workers' movement, which defied the Communist government. Despite the Pope's lack of divisions, he was to be a formidable opponent.

Stalin's real feelings about Catholicism were reflected by the Communists' cautious tactics in dealing with the Church after they seized power in Eastern Europe following the end of World War II. At first they avoided a frontal assault on the Church. It was only after they eliminated other political parties in 1948 that the Soviet-controlled government began a systematic campaign against the only social force and institution that still remained outside their control. In Poland, with 95 percent of the population the most Catholic of the Soviet satellites, the regime's first goal was to weaken, then sever entirely the Church's ties with Rome. Isolated, with its spiritual function called into question, the Church would become as submissive to the state as was the Russian Orthodox Church in the Soviet Union. Arrests and trials of priests were in full swing when the Kremlin despot died. With his death and the lessening of repression, the overt anti-Church campaign was put on hold. And in Poland after 1956, when the local Communists won a measure of independence from Moscow, the state and the Church arrived at a sort of non-violent if troubled coexistence. Yet the regime could not, in the long run, acquiesce in a situation where one sphere of national life remained outside its grip, and the Church stood both as a symbol and a custodian of national aspiration.

The election of the Polish Pope was bound to strengthen the morale of the anti-Communist forces; most directly in Poland but also in other Eastern European states. And how long before this strengthened spiritual power of the Catholic Church would lead to political troubles for Communism?

Some years before the historic event, I was amused to read a speech a Communist minister delivered to a meeting of Catholic clergymen. Perhaps it was alcohol that had loosened the dignitary's tongue, but what he said certainly had a kind of perverse logic. They should thank their lucky stars for living under Communism, he argued. There in the West, under those alleged bourgeois freedoms, the Catholic Church is under siege. Here in Poland you do not see or hear rebellious priests and nuns; no one preaches "liberation theology." It was a disarming acknowledgment of how life under Communism made the nonbeliever and even people who would ordinarily be anti-clerical rally around the one institution that rejected its theology and practice. Our speaker has undoubtedly found some satisfaction in post-Communist Poland, where indeed the Catholic Church's position on issues like birth control and abortion has stirred up criticism of its role in society. Quite apart from its other features, life under Communism has a curious make-believe characteristic: its ultimate element, lack of individual freedom, tends to make other problems appear distant and relatively unimportant. And it would take some time after the fall of the Soviet Union to make the former subjects of Communism realize that freedom brings its own uncertainties and dilemmas.

As I review my writings of the late 1970s and early 1980s, I find that I was rather timid when assessing the chances for fundamental changes in the Soviet Union's foreign and domestic policies. Writing about the possible successors to the sclerotic oligarchs of the Poliburo I allowed that "there may be a new Khrushchev among them, willing and daring to wake up the ossified state and party bureaucracy." But at the same time I warned, "No one would expect Brezhnev or any conceivable successor of his to declare: Comrades, I am happy to say that the imperialist danger has disappeared. We can devote all of our attention to the cultivation of our socialist garden." Austrian generals repeatedly trounced by Napoleon pleaded in their defense that the upstart Corsican adventurer violated all the accepted rules of civilized warfare: he would conduct his campaigns even in winter and march his troops at a feverish pace rather than in the leisurely fashion prescribed by the leading 18th century authorities on the art of war. And so I can plead that Gorbachev violated the accepted rules of Communist politics. But I'll write more about this when considering perestroika.

Today, and quite rightly, Jimmy. Carter is considered the very model of an ex-President. His humanitarian work at home, his efforts on behalf of international conciliation, and advancement of democratic institutions abroad have elicited universal and deserved praise. It may seem rather tactless to dwell on his less than brilliant stewardship of this country's foreign policy when President. And indeed most of the critical issues of that policy seem from today's perspective to have taken place not just a couple of decades, but centuries ago. Can many Americans recall how concerned Washington was in 1978-1979 about the Soviet-dominated government of South Yemen, which Cuban troops assisted? Yet here was a situation parallel to one that in 1990-1991 would lead to the Gulf War, where a hostile regime sat across the vital oil shipment route to the West, and directly threatened the security of Saudi Arabia. Then at the same time the installation of a puppet Communist government in

Afghanistan was again an implied threat to a friend of the US, Pakistan. What happened in Iran was the biggest blow of all: Iran, this country's principal ally in the area and hailed by Mr. Carter as an "island of stability" in the Middle East, fell in 1979 to a fanatical Moslem fundamentalist movement. Khomeini's regime was indeed far from being pro-Soviet, but was sufficiently anti-American to be welcomed by the Kremlin.

It would be unfair to blame all those blows to Western interests and influence on specific errors of the Carter administration. But one had to admit that the United States was suffering defeats on an important front of the Cold War.

And in the case of Iran, one could not absolve Washington from contributing to the crisis through its irresolute policies. To quote from *Dangerous Relations*, "Washington had to be seen as incapable both of disciplining its allies and of helping them in their hour of need. As long as the man [the Shah] appeared to prosper, the US government despite all its misgivings proved unable to curb his autocratic behavior or to resist his requests for vast quantities of the most sophisticated American weapons." When the unfortunate monarch's position became quite shaky but the Iranian army still held the balance of power, an emissary of the Carter Administration advised the generals not to resist Khomeini's takeover. And in a vain effort to appease the new masters, Carter refused the critically ill man asylum in the US.

Writing in 1980-1981, I could not say that the United States was holding its own against the Soviet Union over the struggle for influence in the Third World. But I did not consider my primary task to be that of evaluating American foreign policy, still less of offering unsolicited advice on how it ought to be conducted. I studied and tried to analyze Soviet policies. There were plenty of books written around the themes "How to stop the Soviets," meaning "What I would do if I were Secretary of State or the National Security Advisor," and indeed some of their authors hinted more or less subtly that they could be available for the jobs. Mine was a more modest endeavor: to seek what were the motives, methods, and goals of Soviet foreign policy, and how effective were the Soviets in their pursuit. My writings on foreign policy would thus have qualified me to be an advisor to the Politburo rather than to American policy makers. However, I was never offered the job!

About the Kremlin's goals, I have long believed that beginning with the middle 1920s, world revolution receded further and further from the Soviets' minds. Khrushchev was the last leader for whom the ideological canons of Marxism-Leninism had real importance, and that is probably why on several occasions the USSR under his leadership came close to a dangerous confrontation with the West. With the Brezhnev period, the erosion of the ideology as the guide to actual policies was almost complete. This doesn't mean that if given a polygraph test the Politburo members would have been found entirely cynical, caring only about their jobs and perquisites. By constantly parroting the state ideological formulas about the "class enemy," the malevolence of the "imperialists," and "proletarian internationalism," they probably convinced themselves that they were following in Lenin's footsteps and that what was good for them individually and collectively was good for the Soviet people and Communism. In my classes I would often be asked what the Soviet Union really wanted. I would remind my students what Samuel Gompers once said in answer to the question "What does American labor want?": "More." And so did Brezhnev & Co: more client states in the Third World, more and bigger weapons, and more defeats for the West on the checkerboard of international politics. Nothing remained of the early militant idealism and the apocalyptic vision of socialism clashing victoriously with world capitalism.

Indeed, how could anyone take seriously the mumbo jumbo about "proletarian internationalism" when the fact was that beginning with the 1960s the two Communist giants considered the threat from each other greater than that posed by the main imperialist power, the United States. Some of the diehard Marxists in the West had allowed themselves to believe that if the Soviet Union had indeed departed from the straight and narrow path of ideology, then in Communist China genuine Marxism-Leninism was still alive and well. Now such purists had to swallow hard when, even before the departure of the Great Helmsman, Nixon was greeted in Beijing as an honored guest. And after Mao's death Deng Xiaoping, who emerged as his successor, took his country resolutely on a path toward virtual capitalism. After having long vilified the Soviets for their "revisionism" in social and economic policies the Chinese Communists abolished collective farms and other egalitarian and dogmatic features of their economy. Though having censured Moscow for its alleged collusion with Washington, they were themselves in the late 1970s fashioning a united anti-Soviet front with the United States.

Eager to exploit the "China card" the Carter Administration found itself in an almost comical dilemma over how to play it. The rapprochement with China was intended to push the USSR toward a more amenable position on nuclear arms control and other issues in contention between the two superpowers. And indeed, arrangements were made for Brezhnev to come to Washington in the middle of January 1979, presumably to sign SALT II. But following such intimations, a group of Carter's more adventurous advisors, headed by the Assistant Secretary for National Security Brzezinski, persuaded the President to invite Deng to visit the United States at the end of January. They obviously hoped that a dramatic display of the China card would make the Soviets willing to agree to additional concessions in the treaty. Their arguments prevailed over those of the Secretary of State, Cyrus Vance, who justly feared a violent Soviet reaction. And indeed, Brezhnev would have been put in the humiliating position of appearing to rush to Washington to mollify the US lest the Americans get too thick with China!

The irate Soviet leader canceled the visit with a withering message to the President. To try to fix things, Mr. Carter then stated that Brezhnev's letter took a very positive view of the United States' romance with China. Piqued, the Kremlin released the text of what had been a private message from one head of State to another. The actual message was far from conferring Soviet blessings on Sino-American rapprochement, and made the Carter statement seem, to put it mildly, contrived. The letter then went on to state the obvious but in terms both insulting and menacing. "The Soviet Union will most closely follow what the development of American-Chinese relations will be in practice and will draw appropriate conclusions for Soviet policy."

The Cold War was very largely a war of nerves where the Soviet Union enjoyed a psychological advantage. How could a citizen of the democracies be sure that the Soviets did not really mean it when the Kremlin grimly threatened that this or that step in America's policies would be followed by "the gravest consequences?" Awareness of the terrible potential of nuclear weapons made such threats disturbing even when it was clear that the Kremlin was bluffing. But could one be sure? An analyst of Soviet policies laboring in academic settings would dismiss such threats and demonstrate their emptiness. Could the President of the United States afford even a slight risk that an action of his might unleash universal devastation?

The problem was compounded by the Soviet leaders' apparent belief that their country could afford a major nuclear conflict and yet emerge victorious. We knew that the sober and calculating men in the Kremlin did not believe it, but again could we be absolutely sure? It was only in 1978 that Brezhnev in a speech in Tula provided an inkling that perhaps he and his colleagues might acknowledge what was common sense, that there could be no victor in a nuclear conflict between the two superpowers.

One had to take more seriously their concerns about US-China rapprochement. During the Korean War, Moscow had pushed the People's Republic into an armed confrontation with the United States. Might not Beijing try to return the favor by pushing America into a war with the Soviet Union?

And in actual fact, the world soon witnessed a series of armed clashes between what in the Communist phraseology were "fraternal socialist countries." In the waning days of 1978 Vietnam launched an invasion of Cambodia. Its Khmer Rouge government was speedily overthrown, and Moscow immediately recognized the pro-Vietnamese regime. Beijing had sponsored the Khmer Rouge regime and movement, and therefore its fall constituted a challenge to China. The West was in a difficult position. The end of the Cambodian regime represented an extension of Soviet imperialism. Yet the Khmer Rouge during its short reign had earned the unenviable distinction of having been the cruelest of all dictatorships, right or left. Its weird ideology led to such a regimentation of a traditionally peaceable nation as to make Stalin's collectivization of the 1930s look like a moderate reform. It featured wholesale expulsion of the urban population to the countryside, accompanied by massacres that eventually liquidated a quarter of the people.

For once one could not quarrel with Moscow's characterization of its adversaries, for the Khmer Rouge rulers were clearly engaged in a genocide directed against their own people. Believers in "proletarian internationalism," whether in the USSR or the West, must have had a hard time during the American visit of China's leader. Indeed Deng's anti-Soviet rhetoric was so extreme that it aroused concern among his hosts. The Carter administration hoped to use the "China card" to induce Moscow to be more amenable on a variety of issues, while Deng openly insisted that Carter's optimism about the Soviet Union's ultimate intentions was unfounded and that there was really no point in negotiating with the Russians. In his private talks with

American officials, the mercurial Chinese leader intimated that very soon his country would teach a lesson to its former protégé and ally in Hanoi, and indirectly also to friends of the "new Kremlin Tsars," as the Chinese press now dubbed the Soviets.

The "lesson" misfired. The Chinese troops that invaded Vietnam on February 17 encountered stiff resistance and were unable to advance beyond the border area. They faced an enemy better equipped, organized, and better led than the People's Liberation Army, which still followed the tactics and logistics it had employed in Korea almost thirty years before. The first serious military conflict between two Communist states lasted sixteen days. Chinese losses were heavy; by Beijing's own count they included twenty thousand killed.

Yet perhaps the "lesson" did convey a somber warning to the Soviets. While the fighting was going on, the Kremlin indulged in its threatening rhetoric along the familiar line "the gravest possible consequences would follow" unless the Chinese broke off the action and left Vietnam. But Hanoi and other Asian regimes had to wonder what if anything Moscow would have done had the invasion been a success and China had kept trouncing Vietnam's army. After the fighting did stop the Kremlin was quick to claim the credit: Beijing had to withdraw not only because of the steadfastness of the Vietnamese, but also because of "military readiness on the part of the Soviet Union." Perhaps all three Communist regimes absorbed an important lesson.

It is indeed an open question what the United States could have done had the Chinese continued their invasion of Vietnam, and the Soviets responded by military steps against Beijing. But it was obviously not in the US interest to have the Sino-Soviet conflict pushed that far. No one could be less devious than the President and his Secretary of State. But even had Carter and Vance been more cynical, no sensible statesman could wish in this day and age for an armed conflict between two nuclear powers. Publicly the Soviets were insinuating that the US covertly cheered on the Chinese invaders, but in the Kremlin they knew better. By playing the China card, Washington hoped to bring Moscow to the negotiating table on SALT II, and to make it realize the futility of further conquests in the Third World. A real war between the two Communist powers would have had incalculable consequences for the United States and the entire world. Yes, modern politics and modem weapons rendered Machiavellian schemes in international politics obsolete, and the safeguarding of peace remained the only rational course for both superpowers. But it would be only with Gorbachev that the Soviet leadership would fully subscribe to that simple truth.

In the meantime the Kremlin acknowledged that the lowering of tension between the US and the USSR was clearly in its interest. The general outlines of SALT II were ready by the spring of 1979 and awaited a Summit meeting, which was now to take place in Vienna, replacing Brezhnev's canceled January visit to America.

There are two incidents, that I especially remember from that meeting. One is a picture of the Soviet leader being carried from his aircraft by two security aides. Indeed as we know from other sources, Brezhnev had been ailing for some time and was able to work just part-time at his job. But the inherent conservatism of the Kremlin made his colleagues reject his intermittent pleas that he be allowed to resign his onerous post.

Mr. Carter had long been telling his intimates that the last-minute obstacles to SALT II would be overcome if he could only "get his hands" on Brezhnev. Now came his chance. The dust cover on my Dangerous Relations carries the photograph of the President pulling the somewhat startled General Secretary into a close embrace. "God will not forgive us if we fail," said Brezhnev on the occasion. Such references, though in Russian no more than a turn of phrase, always intrigued Americans; were not Communists supposed to be atheists? Perhaps fearful that the devout Carter might misinterpret the phrase and bring God into the discussion of human rights, Gromyko tried to laugh off and explain away his boss's remark.

The technical provisions of the treaty, never ratified, were soon rendered irrelevant. One hotly discussed issue, however, deserves attention. The Soviet "Backfire" bomber, the American side insisted, should be counted as a strategic weapon carrier since with slight modifications it could reach the United States. The difficulty was solved by Brezhnev handing Carter a written declaration that the plane did not have intercontinental range and that the USSR would refrain from modifying it for strategic missions. At least for me, there remained a perplexing question in the event of a nuclear conflict: would the Soviet command remember Brezhnev's pledge and refrain from the use of the bomber, which could easily reach the western United States on a round trip from a Siberian base? I recalled learning as a graduate student the quaint notion of international law forbidding bombing of any enemy territory unless the attacker gave a twenty-four hour notice specifying the intended target!

Unlike those at the Moscow summit of 1972 that brought SALT I, the Soviet negotiators at Vienna firmly refused to discuss any issues beyond nuclear arms control. In his formal speech Brezhnev rebutted the slander that "the struggle of people for independence and social progress" was due to "Moscow's intrigues and plots." Therefore why blame the Soviet Union for "the objective course of history," i.e. what the Soviet military or their Cuban surrogates were doing in Angola, Ethiopia, etc.?

Nothing then in 1979 indicated that the Kremlin rulers would forsake the course, which I epitomized in the title of my earlier book *Expansion and Coexistence* and the hope of a world revolution was no longer a part of things. Rather the search for clients such as Angola or Ethiopia was intended to demonstrate the viability and dynamism of the Soviet system, which on other counts, such as living standards or citizens' rights, could not withstand comparison with the West. Dissent in the USSR was no longer a negligible force, even if far from a mass movement. Soviet society could no longer be sealed off from the outside world, as had been the case in Stalin's time. But Soviet patriotism, the legitimate pride of the mass of the people in their country's power and its growing influence all over the globe, was expected to counteract any longing for the West's liberties and material well-being. "Look how we push around the American and other capitalists all over the world," the regime was in effect saying to its people, hopeful that it proved a sufficient compensation for their deprivations as citizens and consumers. And as I thought at the time, "Soviet patriotism" i.e., Russian nationalism in ideological packaging, was quite effective in stemming any major manifestation of discontent with the regime.

How long could this last? Reform in Russia has almost always come from above, rather than in response to a popular uprising or pressure. Revolutionary movements often succeeded in defeating not the autocratic state but the forces for reform. What was it at decisive moments that frustrated or flawed the impulses toward liberation of Russia's revolutionaries and reformers?

I pursued that question in *Russia's Failed Revolutions*, published in 1981. It traced revolutionary and reform movements from the Decembrists, the army officers who rose against Tsarist autocracy in 1825, to the Soviet era dissidents who peacefully strove to combat

Communist dictatorship. What distinguished the latter from their predecessors was precisely the peaceful character of their struggle for human rights,and deliberate rejection of anything like a call to armed struggle or terrorism. What the revolutionaries between 1825 and 1917 only too often fought for was not freedom under the law, but a different yet still repressive kind of society intolerant of competing political creeds and movements. The party to which Lenin belonged was called until 1918, the Russian Socialist Democratic Workers Party, (but even before 1917 there were indications that once power was his, the "Democratic" part of the name would soon become irrelevant.)

The fact that the dissidents abjured the original sin of the Russian revolutionary tradition left the question of how their dreams of a freer society were to be realized. It was natural for a scientist like Sakharov to believe that the logic of events in the world at large, as well as in the Soviet Union, must bring down the oppressive system. For Solzhenitsyn it was the moral enormity as well as sheer absurdity of Communism that had to lead to its eventual doom. The prescience of both men was to be amply justified by the events of 1988-1992. But writing at the beginning of the decade, an analyst of Soviet politics had to wonder: when and how? To me, as undoubtedly to the men in the Kremlin, the power base of their system appeared almost impregnable. For the great majority of the people Soviet patriotism, that is, the belief that by Communism alone, however bad, their country became a superpower, seemed to ensure their loyalty to the regime. I concluded my book rather lamely "...it is the worldwide reputation of freedom which will largely determine its future in Russia." At the time I thought my answer was rather evasive; in a few years I would be able to flatter myself that even if unwittingly, I was not altogether wrong with only the most guarded commentary on the probability of Russians longing for freedom.

Winston Churchill recalled how as a young aspiring politician he visited a veteran liberal statesman and asked him what important events were likely to take place in international affairs. "My dear Winston," replied the sage with a complacency born of the most stable years of the Victorian era, "nothing ever happens." And almost immediately, records Churchill, big things began to happen: repeated crises, and the Great War itself. And so contemplating the world at the end of the 1970s, one assumed that the Soviet Union and the Cold War would continue into the foreseeable future; that nothing could happen to alter that picture.

And then in 1979, big things began to happen. In November, a Teheran mob, with the approval of the regime, seized the American Embassy. At the end of December, Soviet armed forces descended on Afghanistan, one detachment seizing Kabul and murdering the country's Communist dictator and his entourage.

The seizure of the embassy and its personnel would have been considered under normal circumstances an act of war. But the Cold War was not a normal time. The Soviet press, while allowing that the incident clashed with diplomatic conventions, declared that the US had clearly provoked the Iranians, and what Washington was doing now was blackmail of a sovereign state. And needless to say, should the Americans resort to the use of force, rather than giving into Iran's quite reasonable demands (such as turning over to Teheran the former Shah), it would lead to "the gravest possible consequences." In fact, four days after the seizure, Secretary Vance pronounced what by then had become America's liturgical formula when dealing with hostile usurpations: "It is a time not for rhetoric but for quiet, careful diplomacy." Well, during the next fifteen months such diplomacy would prove unavailing, while the nation kept anxious vigil over the fortunes of the hostages. There would be an ill-conceived rescue attempt that led to Secretary Vance's resignation. There is no doubt that the humiliating outrage contributed to President Carter's defeat in the 1980 elections. And that humiliation in turn would lead Washington to adopt a much firmer line toward the USSR. Khomeini's regime would also prove a great disappointment to the Kremlin. To the fanatical clerics who ruled Iran, Communism was almost as evil as "The Great Satan," the United States. And Iran was to extend help to the anti-Communist forces in Afghanistan. This is an edifying tale; don't gloat over your adversary's misfortune because it may come back to haunt you.

The invasion of Afghanistan came as a result of a series of mistakes by the Soviet leadership, mistakes which are still astounding when one recalls the Kremlin's prudence during the Brezhnev-Kosygin era. In the first place, there was no reason for Moscow to extend its protective mantle over the Communist regime, which came to power in Afghanistan following a military coup in April 1978. The previous government of Prince Mohammed Daud was a deferential client of the Soviet Union. The Afghan Communist Party was now divided into two warring factions, both bent into forcing radical socialist reforms upon the most conservative and backward society in Asia. The new Communist regime promised even then to be a source of trouble rather than of any tangible gains to the USSR. From the beginning, their rulers kept asking for the Soviets' armed help in their struggle against the great majority of their countrymen. In September the internal struggle within the ruling clique exploded, with the leader Number One and his entourage murdered by Number Two, Hafizullah Amin. At first acquiescing in the coup, the Kremlin soon developed suspicions (totally unfounded) about Amin seeking contacts with the Chinese. Between December 25 and December 27, Soviet airborne troops descended upon the capital, with motorized units crossing the Soviet Afghan border. Amin, whom Brezhnev only three months before had cordially congratulated on his assumption of power, was killed, along with his family. The Soviets installed a new puppet in his place. The dead leader was now officially characterized as an "agent of the imperialist circles of the US and of Beijing's leaders."

From the beginning, I viewed the Soviet intervention as a gross error and as evidence of a serious deterioration in the Kremlin's political skill. The charges against Amin were of course ludicrous, and even had they been true, hardly justified such a foolhardy action. Would the U.S. and/or China have sent troops to help Amin police Afghanistan? Now it was up to the Soviet military to subjugate the country, where the terrain was most unsuitable for motorized warfare, and where every adult male knew how to use guns. Confronted with a challenge to his authority by Tito, Stalin though infuriated still did not resort to force. And now his successors, for no valid reason, stepped into the morass of fighting guerrillas in a mountainous country, whose inhabitants were too uncivilized to admit that they did not have a chance against a superpower. Something was wrong at the Soviet Olympus. The collective brain of the system, the Politburo, appeared to have lost its previous expertise in managing foreign policy.

It was only after the fall of the Soviet state and the opening of the hitherto secret Party archives that we learned that indeed the Politburo of the day was operating by fits and starts. Its principal members Brezhnev and Kosygin, being aged and ill, were incapable of keeping up with the business at hand. Decisions on foreign policy thus fell to the inner group composed of Gromyko, Defense Minister Dmitri Ustinov, and the KGB chief Yuri Andropov. We know that the military leaders had at first opposed the Afghan venture. As it was, the number of Soviet troops in Afghanistan never surpassed 120,000. The unfortunate country became "Russia's Vietnam," the pro-Communist forces even with Soviet help never succeeding in overcoming the insurgents and in gaining control of the country-side. The land was devastated, millions of Afghans becoming refu-gees in Pakistan and Iran. The number of Soviet soldiers killed in the ten-year struggle was twelve thousand, one fourth of the losses incurred by the US in Vietnam. But the Soviet army and security troops had suffered much higher casualties in the three years fol-lowing World War II, fighting anti-Soviet bands in the Ukraine and the Baltic republics, and no one protested. Why then did the Afghan war become so widely unpopular in Soviet society? Principally be-cause the Soviet soldier could no longer be told, as he had been in 1945-1948, that in fighting the Ukrainian and Lithuanian partisans he was defending the socialist fatherland against alleged fascists. He was now in a ruthless struggle in a foreign land, and against people who fought for their country's independence—Russian society had greatly changed from the Stalin times.

The Afghan adventure buried what remained of détente. Presi-dent Carter called Brezhnev on the "hot line" only to be told that the "limited contingent" of Soviet troops entered the country at the invi-tation of the Kabul government, a statement rather hard to reconcile with the fact that the alleged host was killed by the alleged guests. When asked in a television interview what he thought of Brezhnev's statement, the shaken President answered that the General Secretary lied and that he'd now changed his opinion about the Soviet leader. The Administration requested the Senate to postpone its consider-ation of SALT II treaty. The United States also announced that it would not participate in the Olympic Games scheduled to be held in Moscow in 1980. And there were other US punitive measures bear-ing on the economic relations with the USSR. No other post-World War II President had come into office as intent on achieving a new relationship with the Soviet Union as Mr. Carter. None other was as confident that we could effect a significant change. And now the President had to confess failure. And as we know from materials that became available after the fall of the Soviet Union, Brezhnev did strive to better relations with the US. But by the late 1970s, he was largely a figurehead rather than the principal decision-maker in the

Kremlin. If we are to believe the reminiscences of one of his advisors, on one occasion the ailing leader turned to his Politburo colleagues and asked, "How did we get into that Afghanistan mess?"

Even in 1979-1980, I felt that the era of militant Communism was definitely over. From being implacable enemies of capitalism and of the USSR, the Chinese Communists turned into virtual allies of this country, and domestically, to use their colorful language, "Capitalist roaders," jettisoning all the nonsensical ideological baggage from the "Great Leap Forward" and the "Cultural Revolution." The Soviets had long since given up the dream of world revolution. They were still bent upon expansion, but signs were multiplying that the leaders realized its senselessness. I wrote in 1982 that "When Soviet expansion is analyzed. . . it brings with it costs and dangers not commensurate with real gains. Abroad, Communism in power is no longer a dependable servant of or even an asset to the Soviet Union. It may become a threat, as in the case of China, or a heavy burden as in Poland."

My impression that for all the breakdown of détente over Afghanistan, the Soviets might soon see a rapprochement with the West, was strengthened by reading Moscow's press coverage of the American elections of 1980. It has been assumed that the attitude of the Soviet press was very hostile to Reagan, and basically it would have been so in view of his identification with the right wing of the Republican Party. But then on the contrary, strange as it may seem, Reagan appears to have been the Soviet favorite in the Presidential race. To be sure, when it comes to foreign politics the Kremlin has seldom chosen to offend a prospective winner. And Mr. Carter had certainly gotten on the Soviet leaders' nerves with his sermons about human rights. After Mr. Carter's defeat in 1980, Moscow's verdict about him was unsparing. "Everything he did was out of place. He would suddenly bolt from one position to another and engage in sabre rattling." On Reagan, the Pravda writer was rather hopeful: "In Ronald Reagan's entourage are found such experienced public figures as former treasury secretary William Simon, economists Alan Greenspan and Milton Friedman, and former secretary of state Henry Kissinger." The Soviet journalist was not well informed: Henry Kissinger was not in the good graces of Reagan's wing of the Republican Party. But unwittingly, the writer was prophetic about that high priest of extreme laissez-faire capitalist philosophy Milton Friedman; his ideas would indeed influence the Reagan Administration. And what is really amazing: in twelve years Friedman would replace Marx and Lenin as the guiding light for most Soviet economists.

Thus in this most curious world, I was not surprised that the most conservative US President since Hoover achieved what had eluded FDR and his successors: a completely different relationship with Moscow and the end of the Cold War.

24

Poland: A Determined and
Non-Violent Resistance

"Communism fitted Poland like a saddle on a cow"...Now comes a real proletarian revolution...A Polish extravaganza...Jaruzelski hedges his bets...But in the long run it's what happened in the USSR that mattered.

Poland and Polish affairs were never far from my thoughts. To use the academic jargon, I didn't "specialize" in Polish politics and history, my main occupation in the 1970s and 1980s being Soviet politics and foreign policy. But there was a steady stream of visitors from my native country who passed through my home and office. I kept in touch through correspondence with various members of the Polish diaspora spread out after World War II throughout the world, and after 1956 it was also possible to maintain contact with what Communists called People's Poland. My brother Stan's contacts with the old country were more extensive; being a mathematician, he could communicate with and occasionally visit his scientific colleagues without arousing suspicions that inevitably attached to someone who studied and wrote about Communism.

Observing from afar and through personal contacts, one could still sense the growing tension between the people and the rulers. During the war Stalin, trying to reassure his allies that he had no designs on the Soviet Union's neighbor, unwittingly told the truth: "Communism would fit Poland like a saddle on a cow," he observed to Harry Hopkins. After more than thirty years the Polish Communists and their Kremlin bosses had still not succeeded in completing that incongruous task. Poland remained subdued but untamed. At times rebellious feelings erupted even within its Communist Party. In 1956, after hearing Khrushchev expose Stalin's crimes, Warsaw's boss Boleslav Bierut, quite likely anticipating an explosion within his country, committed suicide in Moscow. This fact was never acknowledged, the official cause of death was given as a heart attack. I discovered an incidental reference to it in an obscure Russian pamphlet of the post-Soviet period. And indeed, what would soon take place in Hungary almost happened in Poland. Seeking to appease the aroused nation, the Party turned to one Communist who because of having been disgraced and imprisoned in Stalin's time enjoyed a measure of popular support, Wladyslaw Gomulka, who was hastily installed as the head of the regime. At the news, Soviet troops in Poland were put on alert and Khrushchev himself hurried to Warsaw to bully the insubordinate Polish comrades. Once off of his plane and seeing Gomulka among the reception committee, the impetuous Nikita started to shake his fist at the gathered crowd. It took hours of negotiations to persuade the Soviet "guests" to acquiesce in the election of the man once described by the Moscow press as an "agent of the Zionists and Wall Street."

Gomulka's first two years were the only period when Polish Communism, largely because of the personality of its leader, enjoyed a degree of popularity. But this era of good feeling between the rulers and the ruled could not extend much beyond 1958. A patriot by his own lights, and a man of undoubted personal integrity, Gomulka soon revealed himself as a narrow-minded dogmatist. After initial liberalization the regime stiffened its controls over all areas of social activity. In 1968, Gomulka was one of the most insistent voices among the East European Communist leaders asking for an end to the liberal course of the Czechoslovak government. Polish detachments participated in the invasion of their fellow Slavic country. In 1970 the government raised food prices, the announcement being timed—benevolently—just before Christmas! There followed mass strikes and turbulence, especially in the shipyards on the Baltic seaboard. Gomulka having long outlived his popularity was now pushed aside, the new Communist boss again promising far-reaching reforms and rescinding the price rises.

For me it was now clear that a new explosion in Poland could perhaps be delayed, but barring a miracle was eventually inevitable. No matter who headed the Communist regime it would not be able to give the people what they wanted. For a few years, an improved economic situation helped contain the people's hostility toward their rulers, but by the middle 1970s the mirage of economic progress had faded: the energy crisis in the West adversely affected Polish exports. At the same time, the Western bankers became wary of granting loans to Warsaw, the loans which had made possible the bogus prosperity of 1970-1974. I'd always marveled at the Western bankers' eagerness to lend money to the governments of the Communist states. I once quoted to one of them a French proverb that freely translated runs: "He who gives to the poor gives to God, he who subsidizes a government gives one a good reason to laugh." Didn't they realize that come another crisis in Hungary or Poland they'd never see their money again? But surely, objected my interlocutor, the Soviet Union would assume the debts of the "fraternal socialist" states if they go bankrupt! Bankers can be the most naïve of people.

In 1976 the downturn in the economic situation led the government to try to adopt austerity measures Again price increases on food; and again the workers' violent reactions: strikes and attacks in some cities on the Communist Party headquarters. The government rescinded the austerity measures, but dealt harshly with the rioters. The punitive measures led a number of intellectuals and professional people to organize what became known as the KOR—the acronym standing in Polish for the Committee for the Defense of the Workers. As KOR proposed to act within the law, the government, though with ill grace, tolerated its existence. The stage was set for the subsequent drama of 1980, one additional though imponderable factor being the election of the Polish Pope in 1978.

It was said of the Bourbons when they returned to the French throne after the Revolution and the Napoleonic interlude that they neither learned from history nor forgot their absolutist ways. The same could be said of the Polish Communists. They showed themselves both ignorant and oblivious of the quite recent past. On July 1, 1980, the mindless oligarchy announced higher prices for meat and other products.

For reasons that to me were unfathomable, the Warsaw regime was regarded at the time not only by the bankers but also some political leaders in the West in a rather favorable light. Its head Edward Gierek, a run-of-the-mill Communist bureaucrat, was thought to be quite influential with the Kremlin and as such a probable intermediary between East and West. The announcement about the prices led to an immediate explosion of strikes and labor unrest which rather amazingly had not been anticipated by Gierek, who only a few days before delivered this upbeat prediction: "Knowing our nation, confident of its creative forces, we look with confidence to the future." And when the Polish working class began to demonstrate its "creative force," the complacent Communist Boss was in Strasbourg to receive the Medal of the International Institute for Human Rights.

In contrast to their rulers, the Polish workers had learned lessons from the past. The experience of 1970-1976 taught the strikers that they must not leave their workshops and indulge in demonstrations that afterwards turned into riots. There would be disciplined coordinated sit-down strikes. And as against the alleged leaders of the working masses—the Communist potentates—the striking workers found a genuine proletarian leader, Lech Walesa, an electrician in the Gdansk shipyard. The strikes turned into a mighty movement, first along the Baltic seaboard and then in the interior of the country.

Yes, it soon became a real proletarian revolution, probably the only one of this century. Neither of the two Russian revolutions of 1917 can be described as "proletarian:" the one of February was a consequence of food riots and a mutiny by a part of St. Petersburg's garrison; the "Great October" a military coup by the Bolsheviks. In the course of the year the movement, which adopted the name "Solidarity," swept almost every factory and workshop. The Polish working class rose against its oppressors, the Communist bureaucrats. But what would have surprised and shocked Karl Marx and Lenin even more was that in some struck shipyards the Catholic clergy began daily celebrations of the Mass, the workers lining up to receive Communion. In addition to divine help the strikers sought help from the intelligentsia and political dissidents, and several members of KOR enlisted as consultants to the strike committees.

In their dilemma the Communist bosses tried the traditional gambits: promises of economic concessions, reshuffling the Party command (its boss Gierek was fired on September 5 with hints that he might have to face criminal charges), the not so veiled warnings that if the foolishness was not brought to an end, Poland's great neighbor might react the way it had in 1956 in Hungary and in 1968 in Czechoslovakia. This time nothing worked. The government had to negotiate with the workers and offer concrete concessions rather than, as in 1970, just honeyed words and vague promises.

The basic agreement went far beyond the economic issues. Solidarity was recognized as a genuine workers' union and unlike the old "official" labor unions, given full freedom of activity. In the political field, the regime pledged to abide by the constitution, allow freedom of expression, and release political prisoners. Radio and television were to carry religious services.

In return, the workers agreed that the Communist Party should continue to play the leading role in the state and that Poland should remain an ally of the Soviet Union. This was a recognition of the ineluctable reality of the country's political and geographic situation, and of both sides' realization that there was a third party watching over the negotiators' shoulders.

My feelings about the Polish revolution were somewhat confused. As a student of politics I could not see how the government could abide by the agreement. It would take a super-miracle for Communism and even a modest version of political freedom to co-exist. We have seen before and after 1980 all kinds of Communist regimes. Against all the canons of Marxism-Leninism we have had a Communist state running a capitalist economy, as in China. Some regimes, such as pre-1989 Rumania, and into the present day North Korea, have strongly resembled hereditary monarchies. But a Communist state which allows freedoms of speech and the press and independent labor unions is something we have never seen, nor are likely ever to see. Would the Kremlin ever allow the perpetuation of such, from its point of view, a monstrosity?

Knowing my countrymen, I also felt that it was almost as unrealistic to expect them to tolerate for long partial freedom or as the agreement stipulated "the leading role of the Communist party." Sooner rather than later they would demand an end to the rule of those bureaucrats and parasites detested by an overwhelming majority of the nation.

Yet at the same time I could not but share in the irrational hope that the long-suffering nation would be allowed a respite from the horrors and the indignities that they had undergone for forty years. Perhaps it was possible—all sorts of improbable things had happened and were happening in the Communist world.

And so it was that for the next fifteen months I watched the Polish scene with both enthusiasm and apprehension. There was now a veritable stream of Polish visitors passing through my house and office. One of the most welcome was a brilliant journalist, Teresa Toranska. She had won acclaim as the author of *Oni* (They), a collection of perceptive portraits based on personal interviews with the oligarchy of the Stalinist era pensioned off after 1956. Teresa interviewed me for the Warsaw newspapers, basking now in their new

282 Understanding the Cold War

and precious freedom. I expressed to her my concerns: it was important not to aggravate the situation through any verbal attacks or demonstrations against the Soviet Union. At the same time both she and I knew that even the utmost restraint by Solidarity was unlikely to make the Kremlin acquiesce in the situation; the Soviet press spoke continuously about the "counterrevolutionary" activities in Poland abetted by the Western capitalists. Understandably, the greatest alarm was felt by the Communist bosses in other East European countries, and it was no secret that they were begging the Kremlin to put an end to the scandalous scene before it had repercussions in their own countries. Alarm was felt even among those Communist bosses who had distanced themselves from the Kremlin. The notion of genuinely free labor unions was incompatible with the basic foundation of any Communist system. Delighted as they usually were whenever the Russians experienced troubles in their empire, the Chinese expressed their disapproval of the anti-Party motif in the Polish revolution.

In the meantime, the Polish extravaganza was going on. With the regime now revealed as shaky, there was considerable exodus from the Polish Communist ranks. Membership in Solidarity would reach nine million, the movement having transcended its industrial workers' origin. In fact some members of the Party were joining Solidarity, which at one point seemed to be on the point of capturing the mainstay of the regime. In some ways the situation presaged what would happen in Eastern Europe and the USSR in 1988-1991: the ruling Communist parties becoming demoralized and disintegrating, the regimes seemingly incapable of arresting the trend, increasingly viewed as impotent by their societies.

But the final hour had not yet struck for Polish Communism. As we now know, but could have guessed at the time, the Soviets' contingency plans for dealing with the crisis were being formulated from the very beginning. Military intervention was considered as the last resort. Poland was much bigger than the previous beneficiaries of the Soviet Union's "fraternal help;" and the popular mood strongly anti-Russian. Unlike in Czechoslovakia, in 1968 there was a high probability of armed resistance to an invasion. It would take a considerable military force to subdue and garrison—for how long?—the country of thirty-five million people.

The much-preferred solution had to be an internal subjugation of the revolution. But how and by whom? In my talks with Solidarity and other anti-Communist activists, I received a strong impression that almost all of them discounted the possibility of the discredited and decrepit regime daring to attempt to subdue Solidarity. And frankly I myself did not see at first how it could be done. But the Communists had not as yet run out of tricks.

And so we watched with hope and fear this strange phenomenon of the Communist regime being gradually stripped of its powers, while the Soviet colossus seethed with rage, its rulers warning their partisans in Poland to put their house in order, or else... As Brezhnev put it in a speech, "In fraternal Poland, enemies of socialism helped by foreign forces have been instigating anarchy, thus hoping to turn the course of events in a counterrevolutionary direction...but the Polish Communists and working class can fully rely on their friends and allies...We shall not abandon fraternal Poland in its plight...Communists have never faltered before the enemy, and they have always prevailed." Ominous words, but how unconsciously funny when the speaker expresses his great solicitude for the Polish working class; almost all of it now enlisted in Solidarity.

Months were passing and still no Soviet tanks. As I had anticipated, Solidarity was growing ever more assertive and imprudent. In September 1981 its congress issued a declaration which must have raised the blood pressure of the aged men of the Kremlin. Addressed to the workers of Eastern Europe, including those of the "nations of the Soviet Union," the declaration called upon them to emulate their Polish comrades' example and "enter the difficult path of struggle for free unions." It was a virtual rephrasing of the appeal of the Communist Manifesto, as if saying "Workers unite, you have nothing to lose but the chains of Communism." Three months later Solidarity in fact repudiated its August 1980 pledge to respect the authority of the Communist Party, and called for a referendum to decide whether the country should exchange its present system for a fully democratic one. Most imprudent, such declarations were opposed by Walesa and the more realistic leaders. But, had Solidarity stuck scrupulously to its original agreement with the government, it still could not have been tolerated by Moscow.

By this time I had gotten rid of my initial illusion that the Warsaw regime was too inept and timid to attempt a crackdown on its unruly people. Developments of the past few months suggested increasing preparations for a military coup. In February General Wojciech Jaruzelski became Prime Minister. In October, he added leadership of the Party to his other offices. Military personnel were being inserted into the strategic positions in the state machinery. Civilian Communists having proved incompetent, it was the ones in uniform who were taking over.

And so on the night of December 13, 1981, this bedraggled and supposedly helpless regime staged a military coup. It was ruthless and technically almost perfect in a startling contrast to the amateurish one attempted by the Soviet opponents of reform in August 1991. Leading members of Solidarity who had unsuspectingly assembled for a meeting in Gdańsk (formerly Danzig) were scooped up, their organization dissolved. The press, except for government publications, was temporarily banned. Telephones and other means of communication went under strict controls. Jaruzelski in a nationwide address announced martial law and the formation of the Military Council for National Salvation, which assumed the plentitude of powers. It was an eloquent speech justifying the actions as necessary for the nation's salvation, Communism and socialism not being mentioned. Strikes were banned, thousands of Solidarity activists dragged to prisons.

But what of the general strike threatened by Solidarity if ever such emergency measures were to be used? What of the Polish army, which, as had confidently been predicted, would turn against its superiors if they tried to use it against their countrymen? The simultaneous arrest of thousands of activists left Solidarity leaderless. The regular army units were not used in the coup; its execution was carried out by special security forces. But all during the martial law period the regime was careful not to push the repressive measures too far: there were no executions (unlike in Hungary in 1956), and the political prisoners by and large were treated humanely.

One can picture the shock and fury of my Polish friends. They all agreed that if and when Polish Communism collapsed, something very unpleasant awaited the main architect of the coup. Well, when the regime did crumble eight years later and Solidarity triumphed, Jaruzelski, instead of swinging from the gallows, was asked to continue as president and for a year to preside over the transition to democracy! But then the good general turned out to be an exceptionally clever politician, easily the most cunning among the latter-day Communist potentates in Eastern Europe, the Soviet Union not excluded. He wrapped himself in the mantle of patriotism. After Brezhnev's death he obviously sensed that great changes were forthcoming in the Communist world, and he began to hedge his bets. Martial law was terminated, many of the Solidarity leaders were freed; and the regime turned a blind eye to much of the "subversive" activity in the country. Living in honorable retirement in post-Communist Poland, Jaruzelski wrote his memoirs. Reading them, I decided that the general would have also made an excellent defense lawyer. He almost convinced me that indeed it was sheer patriotism rather than the Kremlin's orders that prompted his coup. Had a man with his endowments, rather than Gorbachev, been in command in Russia at the critical period, we might still have the Soviet Union, and all the troubles associated with it.

For the moment my Polish friends could only curse Jaruzelski, his accomplices, and their Soviet bosses. And for all of the Warsaw government's concern that the coup should not be followed by atrocities, there were occasional cases of the security forces dealing brutally with the dissidents. Moscow of course was greatly relieved by "fraternal Poland" being again under the Communist version of law and order, even though the Kremlin could not be too pleased by the potentially dangerous precedent of military men rather than Party hacks now in charge.

Some of my visitors had immediate and prosaic concerns. They could not return to Poland and to almost certain imprisonment under martial law. For the most part they were enterprising and likable men and women and soon secured jobs in journalism, teaching, etc.

At the time, perhaps one could draw some consoling conclusion from what looked like another installment of Poland's tragic struggle against the facts of history and geography. More convincingly than ever before, it gave the lie to the myth that Communism represented the interests of the working class. And then for how long would the Soviet Union be able to stand armed guard over 100 million people in Eastern Europe? Soviet imperialism was becoming expensive: just as after the past invasions of Hungary and Czechoslovakia, to prevent the situation from heating up the Kremlin was obliged to follow pacification of Poland with considerable economic help. I did not as yet dare to believe that the Soviet Union would, in the foreseeable future, be constrained to give full freedom to its vassals in Europe. But wouldn't the Russians in their own interest find it reasonable to allow "Finlandization:" i.e., allow them internal freedom, on the condition that their foreign and defense policies be in accord with Moscow's? I propounded that solution in my writings, and when in

Russia I tried it on my Soviet acquaintances who I knew to be liberal-minded, and some of them agreed that indeed "Findlandization" of Eastern Europe would make sense from the Soviet point of view. But others would not buy it. Their rulers, they held, were not in the habit of giving up anything unless they had to. Once they started on the path of concessions the whole system would crumble—in eight years the skeptics would prove to have been right on both counts. When Gorbachev was ready to offer a new deal to the Poles, et al., he discovered that it was much too late: the Soviet Union's vassals did not want their Communist masters to become more liberal, they wanted the Communists to get out.

The lesson of Poland 1980-81 was thus not entirely discouraging. But it was more clear than ever that Eastern Europe's vassalage could not be terminated through some satellite's internal development, but only by an upheaval within the USSR itself.

25

Stan

Ebullient, full of life; he was—simply—the most charismatic, fascinating person in the world

Throughout much of the year 1984 professorial and political concerns could not be uppermost in my mind: In May, my brother Stan died very suddenly, just one day after returning from a European trip. As happens very often it took some time before I began to realize how much I missed his presence, and even longer, and this still continues, when I reflected at length on his remarkable life. He was far from fitting the stereotype of an unworldly scientist: clumsy in practical matters and in the usual business of life. On the contrary, Stan was very sociable, interested in politics, a connoisseur of classical and French literatures. At the same time he was, at least to me, the quintessential mathematician, often commenting on the mathematical aspects of quite commonplace phenomena, finding unceasing fascination in that most exalted and demanding of sciences. With it went a certain condescension toward the less rigorous disciplines. I think it was from him I heard the description of economics and political science as "conversational sciences."

Mathematicians as a rule exhaust their innovative and inventive potential very early, some would say by the time they are thirty. Stan was certainly an exception, his interest and scientific productivity continued undiminished till the end. Shortly before he died, he was telling me excitedly about the new possibilities of applying higher mathematics to tackle problems in biology.

Though in an English-speaking environment from his early twenties, my brother remained very much a European, and though cosmopolitan, his tastes and habits were grounded in his Polish youth. He was never as happy as when he could finally travel to the coun-

287

try of his birth and there renew his ties with those—alas few after the German occupation—friends and professional colleagues of the early days. As a young student in Lwów of the 1930s, he used to commune with fellow mathematicians in a café, the cafe Szkocka, or "Scottish Café." The scientists ranging from what he would call undergraduate to aged professors had their own table where they would spend hours intermittently gossiping and posing mathematical hypotheses and tentative solutions, which they wrote down in a special book kept on the premises. During the German occupation the *"Scottish Book,"* so named after the café, was hidden so that it would not share the fate of many of its contributors, murdered by the Germans bent upon eradicating the Polish intellectual class. After the war the "Scottish book" reemerged, and Stan was overjoyed to turn what had been loose-leaf notebooks into a printed book which has since been highly prized by the international mathematical community; a memorial to the vanished Lwów school of mathematicians, as well as to the continuing and robust Polish scientific culture.

My brother's wartime stint in Los Alamos has been duly noted in the vast literature dealing with the Manhattan Project. Ironically, it was mainly after his death that his name became associated with a controversy about the scientific discoveries that had led to the development of those dreadful weapons. Some authors were to claim that it was Stan's contribution that was fundamental to proving the feasibility of the construction of the H-bomb, rather than that of Edward Teller, long-known as the "father" of the bomb. As a layman, I am hardly competent to judge the merits of the case, nor do I recall my brother ever alluding to the subject. In his case it was not, I am sure, the lack of normal vanity, nor any compunctions about being instrumental in developing the dread weapon. He was simply more interested in what were to me very esoteric scientific problems in pure mathematics. He would have been thrilled by the recently announced solution of the celebrated "Fermat's Last Theorem" that had beguiled mathematicians for three hundred years. Heaven, where everything is known, must be a very exasperating place for mathematicians: no problems to solve!

26

Travels Abroad

1980s: Paris...Germany...Japan...Reagan & Star Wars

A student of the Soviet Union was expected to travel a great deal, attending domestic and international conferences on the then most pressing issue of the day. I partook probably less than many of my colleagues in that academic jet set. Not that I did not enjoy travel and meeting my foreign colleagues and former students. But my experience has been that most such conferences, while socially pleasant, and occasionally intellectually stimulating, are seldom very productive in furthering our knowledge of the knotty problems of history and politics. Unlike those in the exact sciences, such advances in the social sciences come usually from the work of individual scholars rather than that of collectives and conferences. Can one imagine a great work of literature being the product of a team? To be sure some worthwhile works, especially, in social history, have been co-authored. But in general, innovative ideas, and challenging analyses and hypotheses are more likely to emerge from a scholar's study, than a conference of paper-givers.

For all my admonitions, I am far from recommending that scholars should be confined to their cell-like studies and libraries rather than sent chasing after the foundation grants that would transport them to some charming locality in France or Italy, there to discuss problems like "Russia's Balance of Payments" or "Franco-Soviet Relations in the 1920." Scholars should occasionally be freed of the drudgery of tracking down what is known as "the sources" and agonizing about their correct interpretations, and enjoy some of the perquisites of the more affluent professions. And though I may now be weakening my stand against collaborative scholarship, personal contacts and exchange of ideas at scholarly gatherings do add zest to one's labors.

Whatever the advantages of travel, it tends to interrupt the rhythm of one's written work. I have always envied those of my colleagues who somehow are able to keep writing in hotel rooms and in airport lounges. For a historian it is well nigh impossible to dispense with voluminous notes, and prompt access to a library. Oh, to be a mathematician! I recall one of them, an old friend, Hassler Whitney. I once ran into him sitting on a bench at Union Station in Washington. His expression betrayed deep concentration. "Hassler, what are you doing?" "I am working," he said simply. And indeed a mathematician does not need notes or a laptop computer to run a gamut of those theorems and hypotheses, obscure to a layman but to him stimulating, even exciting. Often just a torn page from a notebook and a pencil will do.

As for me I have not been able to do any serious writing except in my study, not far from the splendid resources of Harvard's library. I could not work very effectively in any other place, even at home. At one time I was offered an office in the library itself, but I had to refuse. For someone like me to be in the immediate proximity of all those rich collections of books on every subject under the sun was simply too distracting. Even on my way to pick up some volume on Russian 19th century history I would spot a seductive title in an entirely different field, snatch the book from the shelf, and stand reading it for an hour or so, at the end of which time my mind was no longer engrossed by the problem on which I had been working. And so in writing under a tight schedule, I would often try to avoid the seductions of Widener .library, and ask my friends or research assistant to fetch the books I needed.

But, I did make a number of trips abroad in the early eighties which left me with the conviction that the dangers and anxieties of the Cold War were no longer felt in the rest of the world as acutely as they still were in this country. Years had passed and the horrors so frequently evoked twenty or thirty years before had not materialized: the Red Army had not poured into Western Europe, its Communist parties no longer threatened to take over governments of their countries, and the horrendous possibilities of nuclear war no longer preyed on the minds of the Europeans. It was a very human reaction: what had not happened for so long was unlikely to happen in the future. Back in the 1950s, on one of my visits to France, I discovered that the manager of the Paris hotel in which I was staying was learning Russian not because of a passion for the language of Tolstoy and Pushkin, but for some very practical reasons. "Perhaps I might have to use it in a year or two," he said with a Gallic shrug. But now such pessimistic, (and passive) attitudes had disappeared. You no longer had Stalin's Russia with its ominous posture, its armies seemingly poised to race to the English Channel. If political leaders were still nervous about the Soviets mounting new nuclear missiles, the average Italian or Frenchman was but little concerned. Even the local Communists no longer stood in awe of their Moscow comrades. While still pro-Soviet, they were no longer slavishly so. Italian Communists roused the wrath of the Kremlin by criticizing its foreign and domestic policies. Their Spanish comrades supported Spain's membership in NATO. Incomparably more powerful than in Stalin's time, the USSR no longer provoked either so much fear, or such blind loyalty either, as in the past. Besides it was really up to the Americans to handle the Soviet colossus, and since they were unduly agitated about the problem it was only right that they spend a much greater share of their GNP on defense than did their European allies.

Such nonchalance was not shared by the governments of the European powers. They were acutely aware of Moscow's continuing effort to split Western Europe from the United States. The Soviets' latest gambit in that direction was the propaganda campaign to prevent NATO from installing medium-and intermediate range nuclear missiles to offset similar weapons developed by the Warsaw Pact countries.

The Soviets' gambit in the chess game that constituted the essence of the Cold War was transparent. The Kremlin was saying in effect to Western Europe: "Our medium-range and intermediate-range missiles are trained on you. Do you really think that if, God forbid, we ever have to use our tactical nuclear weapons on you the US would dare to attack the Soviet Union with its strategic weapons and thus risk our strategic response which would kill 100 million Americans?" The moral was clear: Western Europe ought to cut its military links with the US and defer to the Kremlin. To counter that move, NATO proposed to install its own tactical weapons in Europe, 108 Pershing II ballistic and 464 ground-based Cruise missiles. Thus the threat of the Soviet tactical weapons would be checked by the European weapons, and Western Europe would not have to depend entirely on America's long-range missiles to deter the USSR from aggression.

There was an air of unreality about the game. Both sides pretended that a limited nuclear war was possible while they knew better: a Soviet SS20 takes out Amsterdam, NATO retaliates by a Pershing II devastating Kiev, and so on, without reducing both sides to radioactive rubble. But for NATO to refuse to play the game would have left the Soviets with a powerful psychological advantage, its tactical weapons suspended like the sword of Damocles over the West.

And so the somber chess game went on. It took a great deal of pressure to persuade West German public opinion to agree to accept the dread weapons on its territory. At the same time, both sides began negotiations over whether nuclear agreements previously limited to the strategic arsenals of the US and USSR could now be extended to tactical weapons. In a few years the whole question of those weapons, and of the possibility of a "limited" nuclear war, would be rendered irrelevant by the miraculous changes in the Soviet Union. But in 1982-85, the preposterous tournament continued.

Yet for all such weighty issues being discussed in the cabinets, parliaments, and also in the direct negotiations between the two camps, the majority of the people I observed in my travels did not appear greatly concerned. And perhaps this was fortunate. Had the full implications and dreadful possibilities of the curse of nuclear weapons continually agitated our minds, we might have witnessed mass hysteria similar to that which gripped 14th-century Europe after the onset of the Great Plague. Probably prematurely, we had become inured to the danger. Such previous irrational reactions as McCarthyism on the one hand, and the "better Red than dead" attitude on the other, had by the 1980s passed from the scene. And to be fair, one must admit that the Soviet leaders had finally relented somewhat in their game of intimidating the West by feigning equanimity at the prospect of nuclear war. Brezhnev's avowal in 1978, that such a war would be a universal catastrophe, was a landmark in this respect. But it would take Gorbachev, to his everlasting credit, to put an end to this dangerous game of "chicken" played so long by the Kremlin.

The Japanese, as I found on my trips to the Far East, were if anything even more complacent about "the Soviet danger" than the West Europeans. To me that attitude was rather disturbing. As I've mentioned before, I have never been an alarmist or believed that the men in the Kremlin were any less frightened of a nuclear holocaust than our men in Washington. Everything in the behavior of the Soviet leaders from Stalin to Brezhnev supported Winston Churchill's dictum that the Soviets did not seek war, but were greedy for the fruits of war. Yet might not that greed accidentally lead to war? Over and above such dangers, the real Soviet threat lay in Moscow acting as the scavenger in the world's trouble spots, and its apparent belief that international stability was not in its interest, that crises such as the Middle Eastern one should go right on festering, as long as it didn't thrust the two superpowers into an armed confrontation. Add to it the imperialist element in the leaders' mentality—like their 18th-century predecessor they believed that "what stops growing begins to rot." They did not understand that rot had already started to invade their domestic system even as they tried to add Afghanistan, Ethiopia, etc., to their vassals and clients.

The Soviet problem was thus not something that could be put aside and out of the democratic leaders' minds, even at a relatively quiescent period of the Cold War such as the early eighties. Much as the rulers of the Soviet Union, now elderly bureaucrats, probably would have preferred a quiet life, to enjoy their power and its perquisites, their political inheritance and the character of their rule constrained them to continue as troublemakers. Real peace, rather than a peaceful but strained coexistence with the democratic world, would not be tolerated by the Kremlin oligarchs. Wasn't it Churchill, whose sharp observations so often come to mind, who had said that they were as afraid of the West's friendship as of its hostility? And so, perhaps instinctively, they were. And indeed what happened under Gorbachev showed that such fears were not unfounded.

Thus, while the man in the street in Western Europe viewed America's preoccupation with the Soviet-Communist problem as an irrational obsession, the US had to continue countering the Soviets' moves. If the USSR found it easy to subdue Afghanistan, would it not be tempted to start another expansionist adventure in the region, say in Pakistan? One could hardly characterize the anti-Communist forces in Afghanistan as being devotees of democracy; for the most part they were bigoted Moslem fundamentalists. Yet Washington very rightly felt it had to help them. And it was largely because of the American military supplies, especially the famous Stingers, small, shoulder-fired anti-aircraft rockets, that the Afghan rebels were able to keep at bay the Soviets and their local puppets.

Such imperatives of America's policy found little understanding among the European politicians and scholars whom I encountered in my travels. Relative unconcern about Russia was even more evident in Japan. In fact I was amazed that even apart from politics there seemed to be but little interest in Soviet studies. Japan within forty years had fought two wars with Russia (perhaps more if one includes the undeclared frontier war of 1938-1939). There were still contentious territorial issues between the two countries. Yet except for one research institute in Hokkaido, this exceedingly prosperous land of 120 million had no center devoted to the policies, culture, and history of Japan's overseas neighbor. They have excellent scholars in the field, but these more often than not found employment at American universities rather than Japanese. There was and is also a core of experts on Soviet politics in Tokyo's foreign ministry, but again most of them were trained abroad; many in fact are my former students at Harvard.

That lack of interest in the country that has played such a crucial role in Japan's history, and will undoubtedly have an important impact on her future fortunes, reflects the changed political and social physiognomy of the former Empire of the Rising Sun. From the militaristically dominated society it was prior to 1945, it turned into one that has emphatically repudiated militarism and imperialism. When in modern history has a major nation accepted military occupation by a single foreign power so complacently? At the end of World War II, Stalin fully expected that the US, far from disarming Germany and Japan, would try to restore their military powers to use them as "catspaws" against the Soviet Union. Well, when it came to Japan, the US occupation authorities not only thoroughly disarmed the country, but bent all its efforts to demilitarize it in spirit. All of society's resources and efforts went into resuscitating and developing its economy. From a military power, Japan turned into an industrial colossus. Here again we witnessed something unprecedented in modern history: a capitalist state, the US, sparing no effort to rebuild the economies of its former enemies so that Germany and especially Japan, would become America's chief rivals in the world's markets. How does this square with the Marxist and especially Soviet view of capitalism and "U.S. imperialism"?

Walking in the beautiful Bavarian countryside on one of my trips, I found it hard to believe that its inhabitants, so hospitable and helpful to a stranger, had been the mainstay of Nazism in pre-1939 Germany. Traveling in Japan, I wondered how people so civilized had not long before found themselves under the spell of such a brutal militarism. The new cult of industrialization and technology never effaced the country's great cultural traditions.

On my first trip to Japan I was for the most part in the capable and kindly hands of my good friend and translator of my books, the gracious Hakushin Suzuki. I had barely emerged from my 17-hour flight from New York when he decreed that I had to go to Kyoto. And indeed very few of the world's cities I've known can rival the charm of this glorious city, the Florence of the Orient, as it is known. Kyoto's charm, as perhaps no other city in the world, epitomizes so well the artistic and a esthetic culture of a great nation.

Suzuki insisted that I must experience the ancient tea ritual as performed by Tokyo's most renowned master of the art. Preliminaries of the ceremony required the initiate to crawl through a succession of rooms, finally arriving at the master's studio. Here, sitting cross-legged on the floor, we were served green tea and bean cakes. My host then introduced me to his pupils, apprentices in the art. Were those young men going to devote their lives to the art, forsaking chances of lucrative jobs in banking and industry? But then I don't understand sumo wrestling either. And so amidst the throbbing business life of one of the world's largest and most modern cities one encounters enclaves of the entrancing past.

In Japan even more than in Western Europe, one could sense that the Cold War was very distant from the average person's everyday concerns. And the same—paradoxically—was true of the Soviet Union in those pre-perestroika days. There it was not only the preoccupation with the material and career exigencies of life that accounted for this indifference. The average Soviet citizen felt, and quite logically, that it was not within his power whether individually or collectively to affect the course of events in the world. Those fellows in the Kremlin had all the power, so unless one was a devout Communist or a fervent dissenter (neither category quantitatively significant), one felt that it was up to them to worry about issues like NATO and the Warsaw Pact organizations, their relative strengths in nuclear and conventional weapons, etc.

Soviet propaganda had in the past been quite successful in conjuring up the alleged dangers of American imperialism and German "revanchism," but was no longer convincing to the mass of Soviet citizens. The USSR was no longer virtually sealed off from the rest of the world as in Stalin's times. Increasing numbers of Soviet people had now traveled abroad and listened to Western radio broadcasts. Most of all, years had passed and none of those villainous capitalist plots against the Fatherland of socialism had materialized—one had to take all those horror stories emanating from the Kremlin with a grain of salt. The ordinary Soviet no longer felt seriously threatened by the capitalists. If anything, it was Communist China that aroused his deepest apprehensions. I recall a Party official saying to me that the United States and Russia were the only two major states that throughout their history have never been at war with each other. "Why should they now quarrel when the greatest threat to peace is obviously posed by Mao's China?"

I replied that I fully agreed with him. Nor did I believe that his government was any less apprehensive about the prospect of nuclear war than was Washington. Still, I pointed out, the Kremlin was relentless in stirring up trouble in many quarters of the world, and continuing to paint the US and its foreign policy as threatening the security of the Soviet Union. My interlocutor retorted that by 1975, Washington was virtually an ally of Beijing; didn't the Americans realize that the Chinese leaders' real goal was to steer our two countries into a catastrophic clash? Well, inconclusive as such discussions were bound to be, it was a relief to hear a Soviet official discuss Soviet-American relations dispassionately, rather than to parrot the official line about American imperialism, the dark demons of "Wall Street and the Zionists," as would have been the case a few years before.

It was not until 1984 that upon meeting Gorbachev for the first time Mrs. Thatcher, then Prime Minister of Britain, was to announce that one could "do business with the Russians." But as I discovered by the late 1970s one could have a sensible discussion with a Soviet dignitary. Russian discussion of public affairs whether foreign or domestic had long centered around two themes: "who is guilty" (title of a sentimental novel by Alexander Herzen) and "what is to be done" (the title of a celebrated but very bad novel by Nicholas Chernyshevsky, subsequently appropriated by Lenin for his political tract in 1902). It was an encouraging development that one could discuss Soviet-West relations no longer from the angle of who was guilty for the Cold War ("No, it was you who started it...And how about Vietnam?"), but what could be done to straighten out the mess.

That encouraging development was still confined to private conversation. Publicly, Washington and Moscow were still raging at each other. Our military supplies helped make Afghanistan a kind of Soviet Union's Vietnam. The Soviets reciprocated by furnishing arms to the rebels in Nicaragua and El Salvador. Was the change in the leadership of the two superpowers going to affect the picture?

By 1981 it was clear that Brezhnev was the leader of the Soviet Union in name only, and could not remain even the nominal leader for much longer. And America now had its most conservative president since. well, 1932. Even so, reading between the lines of the Soviet comments on the presidential election of 1980, one could see that the Kremlin preferred Reagan to his predecessor. Judging by my conversations with some Moscow journalists, they looked back on Nixon's administration as "the good old days," and still remained firmly convinced that Nixon's fall could not have been brought about by something so trivial and natural as spying on his political enemies. Obviously it was the enemies of Soviet-American rapprochement that engineered his downfall!

To be sure, Reagan's first pronouncements and policies could not have enraptured the Kremlin. He was clearly taking a tough line toward Moscow; preparing to increase the defense budget substantially. And then came his celebrated characterization of the Fatherland of Socialism as "the Evil Empire," and his strong line on the medium-range missiles for NATO.

But for all such demonstratively anti-Soviet statements and measures, the Reagan administration observed from the beginning considerable restraint on two issues of special importance to Moscow. Despite SALT II not having been ratified the US in fact continued to observe its provisions. And while Washington-Beijing relations remained friendly, the new US policy makers were careful not to appear too close to their Chinese counterparts. And very early in its first term the Reagan administration lifted the grain embargo on shipments to the USSR imposed by Carter after the invasion of Afghanistan.

I felt in 1981 that the new Administration might have been missing a bet by not opening a dialogue with Moscow. The Kremlin seemed to be quite agreeable to such a dialogue. Brezhnev, in his swan song — the speech to the Communist Party Congress in February-March 1981 — intimated that the Kremlin was now ready for comprehensive discussions with the US that would go beyond the nuclear arms control issues, and include subjects like Afghanistan. The latter was proving a much tougher nut to crack than the Soviets had thought before launching their ill-thought-out venture. The Soviet economy was clearly slowing down. The prospect of Euro-missiles, those medium-range nuclear rockets, and, the Cruise missiles that NATO proposed to install, clearly worried the Kremlin. Carter had irritated the Russians but did not particularly scare them. But they still did not know what to make of a conservative in the White House.

At the same time, there were good reasons why the new President and his advisors were reluctant to resort to premature "summitry." In the past, America's leaders often showed themselves too eager to initiate negotiation, too prone to illusions that personal contacts with the Soviet bosses could work wonders in the relations of the two superpowers. Kennedy rushed to a Summit in Vienna right after the Bay of Pigs fiasco; only to be bullied by Khrushchev, creating an impression of weakness that probably encouraged Khrushchev to embark upon the Cuban missile venture. Carter hastened to send his Secretary of State to Moscow without any prior agreement on the agenda to be discussed; it was meant as a demonstration of goodwill on his part. The Soviets reacted insultingly to Mr. Vance's proposals, virtually inviting him to leave Moscow. And so it was perhaps wise to keep the Kremlin guessing as to the intentions of the new Washington team.

In retrospect, one cannot fault Mr. Reagan's and his advisors' instincts as to how to deal with the Soviets. Of course like all successful statesmen they also happened to be lucky: it was during Reagan's presidency that the USSR began to experience the travails of perestroika, and by the end of his second term the whole Soviet system was ready to implode. I will return to the question of whether and to what extent US policies contributed. Here let me just register my opinion that it is a great oversimplification to assert that the US policies contributed decisively to the break-up of the Soviet Union, or that it was Mr. Reagan personally who "won the Cold War." Washington's role in the great drama reminds one of what a Gilbert & Sullivan ditty says about the House of Lords during the Napoleonic wars: "The House of Peers did nothing in particular and did it very well." The US official reaction to what began as an attempted reform of Communism and what ended as its self-emasculation were exactly right: Washington neither exulted nor unduly let down its guard at any stage of the crisis.

To be sure, those who insist that the US contribution to the ending of the Cold War wasn't limited to just avoiding false steps while the Soviet system was committing suicide, stress one initiative of Mr. Reagan's that probably hastened the process. In March 1983 the President formulated his Strategic Defense Initiative, which became celebrated as "Star Wars". The doctrine proposed a new strategy for deterring nuclear attacks upon the United States. Ever since the USSR had achieved a high level of nuclear and missile power, the guiding principle of deterrence had been MAD—the notion of Mutual Assured Destruction in the case of a full-fledged nuclear war. Any potential attack on the territory of the United States was, at least in theory, deterred by the threat of massive retaliation by this country. Now the US proposed to seek ways to develop a defensive deterrent, some means of preventing enemy missiles and bombs from reaching targets on its territory. The President did not minimize the enormous complexity and difficulty of the task. It would take years, or perhaps decades, before the appropriate technologies could be developed.

It has been held axiomatic ever since the invention of ballistic missiles which can traverse vast distances in a matter of minutes, that there could be no absolute defense against a nuclear attack, no reliable guarantee that some substantial number of hostile warheads would not reach and devastate their targets. Antiballistic defense could be perhaps partially effective in protecting single cities or missile sites, but it ran against common sense to think it could prevent unimaginable destruction from an attack carried out by a power with the nuclear arsenal of the US or the Soviet Union. And what Mr. Reagan proposed had still to appear as an unachievable dream: the erection of an impenetrable antinuclear dome over an entire country!

It is unlikely that the President's scientific advisors really believed that completely effective defense against a nuclear attack could ever be achieved. But the Star Wars gambit was good politics; it fitted that very American optimistic outlook of which Mr. Reagan was a veritable personification: there is nothing impossible for American know-how.

It is equally unlikely that the Politburo's scientific experts could have advised their bosses that complete immunity from a nuclear attack was in the realm of possibility. But the reaction was undoubtedly: "How can you be sure? Those damned Americans and their technological miracles!"

And so within days of Reagan's announcement, Yuri Andropov, Brezhnev's successor, raised the alarm. In an interview with Pravda the new General Secretary stigmatized the American initiative as an ill-concealed attempt to blackmail the Soviet Union, to make it vulnerable to a preemptive nuclear strike. "To have the means to destroy with antimissiles the strategic forces of another country, i.e., to deprive it of the possibility of retaliation. (would enable the US) to render the USSR defenseless in the face of a US nuclear threat." Andropov did not mention that Mr. Reagan promised that once the Star Wars technology was developed the US was ready to share it with Moscow. (Of course one did not have to be a Politburo member to be skeptical on that count.) And why did the US need Star Wars, asked Andropov, unless it intended to blackmail the Soviet Union? He rejected indignantly Reagan's alleged hints that under the current conditions "the United States was weaker than the USSR" and hence needed Star Wars to protect it from a preemptive strike. No, the strategic forces of the two superpowers are perfectly balanced, hence neither is in a position to carry out such a strike without leading to its own destruction, he contended.

It is interesting that Andropov was at great pains to stress that the Soviet Union was not stronger than the US insofar as its nuclear weapons capabilities were concerned. Twenty years before, Khrushchev had the gall to boast and bluster the reverse: that the USSR was better armed. In Washington no notice was taken of that assertion by the Soviet boss, which happened to be true. How could you believe what the Russians were saying? But to me the Soviet boss's protestations were significant. The Kremlin was losing its self-assurance, giving up its long-standing belief that it could always bluff the West.

But back to the question of Mr. Reagan's contribution to the winning of the Cold War. The president was not Machiavellian in enunciating SDI; he probably believed that it was indeed feasible. But even though it was a fantasy he did stumble upon a very effective psychological weapon against the Soviets; the Star Wars idea would have a chastening effect on their policies, and undoubtedly influenced Gorbachev's decision to seek a real detente with the West. Most of the Western experts, whether on defensive or offensive weaponry, scoffed at Reagan's initiative; it was utterly impractical; to try to get anywhere with it would not only be fruitless but ruinously expensive; it scared the Russians but in a wrong way by making

them more intractable and dangerous. But though not the most sophisticated of this century's presidents, Mr. Reagan was certainly,
and not only on account of his Star Wars, the luckiest.

If by America's victory in the Cold War we mean the fall of the
Soviet Union and the collapse of Communism, were those momentous events seriously affected by the new U.S. defense doctrine?
Some analysts and commentators would indeed have claimed so,
after 1991. According to their scenario the Republican
administration's greatly expanded defense budget forced the USSR
to try to match the US effort. But eventually Gorbachev decided that
the already ailing Soviet economy could not sustain the drain on its
resources that would be required to keep up with the US. Hence the
frantic and chaotic steps to heal the economy and the subsequent
realization that the cure would require a basic restructuring—
perestroika—of the Soviet political system. But the hasty and ill-
conceived reforms only weakened the system and eventually led to
its collapse.

But the factors that led Gorbachev to embark on perestroika, and
its subsequent failure, were not directly connected with their resolve
to set the relations with the West on a new basis. Let us give the
credit where it is due: the Reagan administration deserves it for facilitating Gorbachev's "new thinking," as he called it, on foreign
policy. For the failed reforms that broke up the Soviet Union the
responsibility lies squarely with the Soviet leader and his advisors.

When Gorbachev took over the reins of power in 1985 Mr. Reagan,
like everyone else on this side of the ocean, did not have an inkling
that in four years the Soviet state would be in the midst of a grave
crisis and in two more years it would cease to exist. It is difficult to
banish certain myths from history, especially those that flatter our
national pride. And so we shall undoubtedly continue to hear tales
of how America's cunning diplomacy and our democratic virtues
finally prevailed and brought down the "Evil Empire." But it wasn't
so. Let me briefly outline what actually did happen.

Back to 1984. The great and contentious issue between East and
West was the question of the Euro-missiles, NATO's installation of
medium-range rockets and Cruise missiles, necessary, the West argued, to offset similar weapons held by the Warsaw Pact countries.
Attempts at compromise, e.g. reducing the number of medium-range
missiles on both sides, had just broken down in the face of the Soviets' intransigence. Moscow learned to live with the fact that US war-

heads could land on the Soviet territory after a thirty-minute flight. But it viewed as intolerable that by placing the rockets in Europe they could reach Moscow in six or so minutes. Could both sides agree to eliminate entirely their medium range missiles? At that time it seemed an impossible dream; and the Soviets' obduracy (they walked out of the Geneva negotiations) also threatened any hopes of revising SALT II, and, gave rise to a new and dangerous East-West crisis.

It was fairly obvious that the Kremlin's stubborn stance was connected with this being an election year in the US. Why not wait out the election results? Mr. Reagan's toughness on the arms issue perhaps reflected political needs of the moment. Alternatively, should the unexpected happen and Senator Mondale emerge as the victor, the Democrats would need time to set their house and policies in order, and might prove more amenable to the Kremlin's position on some points.

Some time before the election I was asked by Robert McFarland, the President's security advisor, to prepare a confidential paper on the prospects of the Soviets returning to the negotiating table. I had no hesitation in stating that the Kremlin would definitely resume the negotiations. But they were bound to create more fuss and trouble in the case of a Democratic victory. For all their rhetoric to the contrary, the Soviet leaders did not really believe that NATO's medium-range missiles would pose a new danger to the USSR. After all, Britain and France had already had nuclear missiles capable of reaching their country in a matter of minutes. The same was true of missiles on American submarines. The Kremlin was simply probing: should NATO be bluffed into giving up or drastically modifying its ploy, America's European allies would have more reasons to question its commitment to their defense. By and large the Administration was following the right policy vis-à-vis the Soviets: it scared them a bit, but without throwing the Kremlin into a panic.

There is of course no way of proving that I was right. Very soon after the election Foreign Minister Gromyko announced that the USSR would resume the arms control talks. Perhaps he would have been equally accommodating with Mr. Mondale in the White House, but I don't think so. The new year was to see the main lines of US foreign policies firmly set, unaffected by the usual tumult and confusion attending a change in administration. Contrariwise, 1985 was to see a very fundamental change at the top of the Soviet system. The aged oligarchs who first made their mark under Stalin were now vacating the political scene. We in the West still couldn't be sure what it would portend for the system. But one could sense that something was not right with a political establishment headed by a succession of invalids: first Andropov, already in precarious health when elected General Secretary in 1982, and hospitalized during the latter part of his brief tenure; then Constantine Chernenko appointed in 1984, though his Politburo colleagues had to know that he was terminally ill.

27

Gorbachev and the Beginning of the End

Meeting Medvedev: man of courage... A "normal police state"....
The amiable Mr Gorbachev

1985: A historic year worthy to set alongside such other momentous dates as 1789 and 1917. I suppose that most people would be puzzled by this association. Surely, unlike the beginning of the French Revolution, or the focal period of the Russian one, 1985 did not initiate social convulsions and cataclysmic wars claiming millions of victims. Yet 1985 marked the start of a process, truly meriting the label revolution, that within a short time toppled a powerful empire and deeply crippled a world-wide movement that had sought to inherit the earth.

Our custom is to believe that great men make great moments in history. But here there was another departure from accepted convention. The year's claim to historic importance comes from Mikhail Gorbachev's election in March as General Secretary of the Central Committee of the Communist Party of the Soviet Union. At the time, the largely expected ascendancy of a run-of-the mill bureaucrat was hardly a world-shaking event. And even from today's perspective, the last General Secretary hardly appears to have been a towering figure. Surely no one would see another Robespierre, not to mention Napoleon or Lenin, in the amiable gentleman. Yet starting with his taking office and for six years thereafter, Mikhail Gorbachev was the leading actor in the drama which ended with the utter collapse of what Lenin and Stalin had built. To be sure, he certainly never consciously endeavored to bring about the collapse of the Soviet-Communist world. But he started the process, which was soon to get out of control. Had the Kremlin oligarchy on that day in March 1985 entrusted the leadership to someone else, a man without his reforming zeal, or conversely, to one who knew how to keep reforms from undermining his own and the Party's power, we might still have the Soviet Union as a going concern.

At the time I did feel that in the long run there were bound to be fundamental changes in the Soviet system. But to expect it to vanish within six years! So I still think it was the personality of one man, that peculiar mixture of Gorbachev's virtues and flaws, that played a crucial role in the timing of the Soviet Union's demise. The historian's usual incantation, "In the long run it was inevitable," may be right, but without Gorbachev the run might have been very, very long!

As I said, Gorbachev's rise to the top was hardly a surprise. Tradition had dictated that the likeliest candidates for the job were those members of the oligarchy who were both full members of the Politburo and secretaries of the Central Committee. When Constantine Chernenko departed the world in March 1985 only two Party worthies possessed those qualifications: Gorbachev and Gregory Romanov. Awaiting Chernenko's quite predictable end (even the official pictures could not conceal his condition), I thought at first that Romanov was a likelier choice. At sixty-one he was closer in age to his septuagenarian colleagues, and he had been made secretary quite recently, in clear anticipation of the eventual promotion. But soon there were insistent rumors that it was Gorbachev who presided over the Party councils during the ailing Chernenko's frequent absences. The Politburo oldsters must have had mixed feelings about handing over the leadership to Gorbachev, at fifty-three, a mere youth by their standards. In nominating him before the Central Committee, the foreign minister Gromyko, himself seventy-six, appeared to grope for justification: "Mikhail Gorbachev knows how to find solutions that fit the general policy of the Party." What a bad prophesy!

True until then nothing indicated that Mikhail Sergeievich was likely to depart from "the general policy of the Party." His recorded speeches with their standard references to the American imperialists and their dark designs had conformed to the officalese: As the man in charge of Soviet agriculture he had shown himself as unimaginative as his elderly colleagues. But there were some things in his record that seemed to justify Gromyko's hint at uneasiness. Quite unusually for a Soviet potentate, he had once chosen to spend his vacation in the West, traveling with his wife through the French countryside. Later on during perestroika I would joke with my colleagues that while in France, Gorbachev had been kidnapped by the CIA and a look-alike mole substituted in his place. By then some diehard Stalinists would have probably been ready to believe that I wasn't joking. He had made a good impression on his official visits to Britain and Canada. Mrs. Thatcher decided one could do business with him.

My own qualified optimism about the new leader centered first on his age and second, on his approach to foreign relations. He had not begun his career under Stalin, and was likely to see that the formulas and practices of the past would not serve the Soviet Union in the new age. What was the point of maintaining a high level of tension between the USSR and the United States? With the Sino-Soviet split a fact of international life, Moscow would never regain its absolute domination of the world Communist movement; and world revolution was no longer even a dream. The arms race was placing an increasingly heavy burden on the faltering Soviet economy. Unless one lessened the intensity of the conflict between the East and West a misstep on either side might bring the world to the brink of a nuclear war. And so a new and this time more solid détente could well be in the offing.

It was more difficult to project probable changes on the domestic front. Gorbachev should have been impressed by the economic progress of China, its Communist leaders having abandoned the economic shibboleths of Marxism-Leninism. But would he, like them, be venturesome enough to restore household farming by abolishing the collective farms, that veritable curse on Soviet agriculture? Socially as well as economically it would be a Herculean task, and even if he wanted to, it is unlikely that his extremely conservative and unenterprising Politburo colleagues would approve. Octogenarian though he was, Deng was showing himself mentally much more youthful than the Kremlin crew.

Would Gorbachev tamper with the authoritarian structure of the Soviet system? Nothing as yet indicated that he was a "closet liberal," but again there was his relative youth. Unlike his predecessors and colleagues he was quite removed from the mentality that characterized Stalin's officialdom with its almost pathological fear of nonconformity, whether in politics, the arts or anywhere else. For people of his generation, the Soviet system was so firmly established, the notion that a bit more freedom, or openness, would shake its foundations must have appeared preposterous.

I sought parallels in pre-Revolutionary Russian history. After Nicholas I's demise in 1855, Alexander II realized that Russia could no longer be ruled in his father's tyrannical ways. The new emperor believed firmly in autocracy, but also in his government coming closer to the people. So it was then that the term glasnost first came into use. It did not stand for completely free political discussion, nor for freedom from censorship, and certainly not for democracy. But the government could now be much more open with its society. It would let the people know how and why political decisions were reached. And it would tolerate a modest amount of criticism of its policies by journals and public bodies. But the Soviet ruling elite had been much more conspiratorial in its operations than the most absolutist of the Tsars. Some fifteen people in the Politburo could and did make in absolute secrecy decisions affecting every Soviet citizen's life, with no tolerance for any dissent or criticism. So why not lift that curtain of secrecy, and give the people some sense, even if largely illusory, of sharing in determining their own destinies? Surely after some seventy years the Soviet government was established firmly enough to afford public discussion of some of its policies. And such a modest version of glasnost would enhance the General Secretary's popularity at home, be welcomed by the main Communist parties in Europe, and take some of the sting out of Western criticism of the Soviet system.

Arguments like these persuaded me to foresee that Gorbachev might well embark upon glasnost, and make use of that term as part of his program. Like him I thought that application of the concept could be contained within limits safe for the regime and would not threaten the Soviet state and Communism. We were both wrong!

And so it was in the expectation of some albeit modest changes in the new regime that in the fall of 1985 I set out for the Soviet Union. Nothing during my stay really affected my views. None of my Soviet acquaintances, some of whom I had known for years, expected as yet any fundamental departures from the set pattern of Soviet domestic politics. Those who were pro-regime spoke of Gorbachev with approval, but hardly enthusiastically. He had given as yet no clear indication of initiating major reforms. Supporting his popularity was the contrast between him and his predecessors. For the first time in ten years the country had a leader who was not visibly ailing and who could really lead. There was a widespread feeling that Brezhnev in his last years was really a figurehead and did not or could not deal with ever-growing corruption. And whatever their political views, the Russians I talked to could not conceal a sense of humiliation that twice in a row their rulers had selected for the top post a man virtually on his deathbed. The movement that once confidently claimed to represent the future of mankind had unwittingly advertised itself as old and ailing.

Moving around in Moscow and Leningrad, I found there was no point trying to chat with the proverbial man in the street, for the cab driver or shop clerk I encountered would not discuss politics with someone like me who spoke Russian with an accent. But when talking, say, with academics, I noticed that they were much less inhibited in discussing ticklish subjects than they would have been a few years before. And even those on the periphery of the Establishment, newspapermen, members of government institutes and the like, did not bristle at criticisms of Soviet ways. That great pall of fear that hung over the entire society in Stalin's time had largely disappeared. One had still to be circumspect in talking with a foreigner but no longer terrified that a wrong turn in conversation might cost a job if not worse. A former student of mine who had worked for the CIA but never inside the USSR decided upon retiring from the agency that he would like to see the country on which he had worked for so long. He had applied for a Soviet visa, not making a secret of his former profession. A few years before, such a request would have been preposterous, and the trip if permitted quite a foolhardy venture. But in the early 1980s, he had no trouble in being allowed into the Soviet Union, and encountered no unpleasantness while there.

But I shouldn't exaggerate the extent of liberalization in Russia on the eve of perestroika or during its early phase. I was still followed when on an occasional excursion outside Leningrad or Moscow, and I have no doubt that my activities in the two cities were monitored. Also, and perhaps paradoxically, somebody like myself who was known to be a student of Soviet affairs did not arouse as much suspicion from the authorities as a casual tourist who might actually be a spy! When I flew from Moscow to Paris I sat next to a minister in the Algerian government, which was then quite friendly to the Soviet Union. He was seething with anger, he told me, over having been spied upon during his entire stay.

Conversations with my official hosts, representatives of two foreign affairs institutes, did not lead to confrontations, as so often had been the case in the past To be sure when the conversation turned to current issues such as Star Wars, the dialogue at times would take a sharper turn, but even then without reaching incivility.

I was both embarrassed and amused when during a discussion with a group of Moscow University professors I was asked whether I thought the Soviet Union as of then was a totalitarian or an authoritarian state. I could hardly launch into a methodological disquisition on the meaning of the two terms, and I knew I would sadden my listeners by classifying the USSR as the former. And so perhaps not quite candidly I opted for "authoritarian." My answer clearly pleased my audience. For many who had lived under Stalinism it was evidently flattering to hear from a foreigner that their country had now progressed so far as to be a "normal" police state!

Those who would publicly criticize the regime were of course unavailable; they were either in exile abroad or under lock and key. Roy Medvedev was the very rare exception. Few people in the West besides students of Soviet affairs would now recall this courageous man. Yet along with Solzhenitsyn he was the earliest and most influential harbinger of glasnost. Circulating clandestinely, his writings showed the Soviet reader a stark and horrifying picture of Stalinism, at a time when even after Khrushchev's revelations the official picture of the despot was of a great leader who on certain occasions abused his powers. Solzhenitsyn and Medvedev proceeded from two quite different points of view. For Solzhenitsyn, Stalinism was a natural consequence of the Communist system. For Medvedev it was an aberration. In his main work, titled in English translation *Let History Judge*, Medvedev wrote, "...only a resolute and honest Communist self-criticism...will cut the ground from under bourgeois propagandists who have long used these perversions in their fight against socialism." To the last he remained a convinced Communist, even though thrown out of the Party, who believed that by revealing the full truth about the past, he might help restore the Soviet system to its humane and constructive principles. The clear implication was that by not telling the full truth about Stalin and his misdeeds, Khrushchev, and even more so his successors, was hindering the healing of Communism and putting at risk its survival. And from the same book, "...it is the Communists who should be the strictest judges of their own history. Otherwise it will be impossible to restore the unity, moral purity, and strength of this great movement."

By the same token foreign scholars, no matter how well informed, were simply incapable of understanding the tragedy of the Soviet people, or evaluating objectively their past or present. Despite such reservations, I did find in his subsequent works occasional references to and citations from my works. Conversely, while working on the biography of *Stalin*, I profited greatly from *Let History Judge*. It was a product of years of painstaking labor. Not even Solzhenitsyn in his *Gulag* succeeded in gathering so much material about the bloodstained years of Stalin's tyranny. Medvedev collected a mass of reminiscences from the survivors of Soviet jails and penal camps. He researched literally hundreds of life stories of the victims of the savage terror. It is true, however, that even Medvedev's work was incomplete and, in a way, one-sided, for he concentrated on the purges within the Party, government and military elites in the period 1937-1941, with little attention to other strata of society or to the appalling story of forced labor and camp conditions between 1929 and 1933, with their millions of peasant victims. But given the conditions under which the author had to work and the data to which he had access, it still stands today as an imposing work, undimmed by the profusion of information brought to light in the 1990s by the opening of hitherto secret files. Here was one man working alone, undoubtedly aware that any day his research might be cut short by arrest. Under Gorbachev the regime finally appointed an official commission to investigate Stalin's crimes, and its findings would prove trifling compared to those that this brave individual had produced some twenty years before.

We met for dinner at the home of a mutual acquaintance. For all his fulminations against bourgeois writers on the Soviet Union, he was polite and gracious in our conversation. Yes, he had my *Stalin* translated into Russian for his personal use, but would neither compliment nor upbraid me for my work. We talked about the current situation. No, he did not expect great changes from the Gorbachev regime. There might possibly be a new NEP under which the government would as in 1922-1928 allow some private initiative in the economy. (During that time, though Stalin was already taking charge, political repression was relatively restrained compared with the previous and later periods. There was no point in engaging Medvedev in a debate about his beliefs in the recuperative powers of the Soviet system. The apartment was almost certainly bugged. A car with two agents inside it was parked in front of our building. Medvedev told me he was quite accustomed to such solicitude for his safety on the part of the police. Why was he allowed to be still at large, free to talk with the "bourgeois falsifiers" of Soviet history? As far as I could figure out, because by now it would have been embarrassing for the Kremlin to crack down on a man who was a professed Leninist, who did not seek to organize any political grouping or movement, and who just wrote. To diehard Stalinists this must have seemed inexcusable weakness. For them the Medvedevs represented a much greater threat to the regime than the open enemies of everything Soviet, like Solzhenitsyn. As it would turn out, they were right.

His prognosis was not cheering. A very perceptive observer of the political scene could see no fundamental changes in the future. But for me, an outsider, the situation appeared less bleak. I considered the two of us, one a man who in the official view had discredited the Soviet past; and a Western scholar allowed to meet and talk but under discreet police surveillance. In the past the KGB would have frowned at such meetings, or exploited them as provocation: obviously the Russian was transmitting state secrets to a Western agent. Now the more civilized attitude of the authorities suggested that perhaps something was changing in this land.

Spying was still very much in fashion. Around the time of my 1985 Moscow visit some US Marine guards at our embassy were arrested on charges of consorting with female KGB operatives. The whole affair was blown out of proportion. The guards were young marines and lacking the depth of experience to handle a tour of duty in the fatherland of modern espionage. On the Soviet side, the whole affair smacked of the KGB trying to justify its swollen personnel roster. What secrets could those guards have communicated to their KGB friends? Washington presumably had more sense than to circulate really important political and military data through the Moscow embassy, where even the "safe" room could not have been really safe, given the technological ingenuity of the KGB. In any case, subverting the Marine guards must have been superfluous.

At the time, many of the embassy's employees were Soviet nationals. Who knows, that middle-aged hefty female cheerfully dispensing hamburgers and scrambled eggs in the building's cafeteria may well have been a KGB colonel. The ethos of espionage had permeated the entire Soviet society in Stalin's time, when every citizen was supposed to be a volunteer collaborator of the secret police, and when a teenager became a national hero for denouncing his father as "an enemy of the people." By the 1980s, the secret police were less dreaded but still everywhere. At times my Soviet contacts would drop a hint that this amiable professor X or editor Y whom I had just seen was moonlighting at a rather confidential sort of job!

But it was not an internal plot or a foreign intrigue that would bring down Communism. By 1991 there was the greatest of all possible paradoxes: that it was the President of the United States who would try to help Gorbachev to preserve the unity of the USSR, while it was the KGB that mounted an inept plot against its own government. All that saturation of an entire society with spies and informers hastened rather than prevented the sudden collapse of the Communist state.

As of September 1985 I felt that if any major changes were forthcoming they would likely come from the top. The material situation of the average Soviet citizen was slowly improving. His daily life, with one exception, was freer from the regime's intrusion than before. The glaring exception was Gorbachev's ill-conceived campaign against alcoholism. Like the American "noble experiment" of Prohibition, the campaign was motivated by both idealistic and very practical reasons: addiction was taking a heavy toll on the health of the citizens and that of the economy. But the means employed soon turned out to be counterproductive. The government didn't resort to outright prohibition; that would have produced a revolution. It introduced a complicated scheme that made buying alcohol difficult through reducing vodka production and introducing rationing. Predictably the thirsty masses turned to making the precious substance on their own with whatever materials were available. Sales of tubes of toothpaste, toilet waters, and of other conceivable ingredients rose drastically. The government lost revenue, while the cause of sobriety did not gain.

Where one did discern signs of restlessness was among the intelligentsia. They certainly were not the base of demands for instant democracy or anything resembling revolutionary sentiments. Rather I sensed, even in conversations with some Party members, a feeling of embarrassment that their country was not ruled in a more civilized way, embarrassment that one had to feel awkward in the presence of a Westerner who was certainly not anti-Russian but knew and had written on Soviet history. By the same token I encountered many fewer Soviet intellectuals who were ready to spout official Soviet propaganda, and to be aggressive defenders of Communism. The Moscow stage was currently featuring a couple of historical plays by Mikhail Shatrov. They featured a theme missing in Soviet

literature since Khrushchev's fall in 1964: Stalin's betrayal and per-
version of Lenin's principles, and they played to sold-out audiences.
I was already hearing references to the period between Khrushchev
and now as one of stagnation, or Zastoy, the term which soon would
be featured in Gorbachev's official oratory. But then the spectacle of
the new leader's belittling or even clearly condemning the preceding reign had not lately been so unusual. According to his unsenti-
mental colleagues Khrushchev had been dismissed for his "hare-
brained" schemes. And during his short term at the top Andropov
took as one of his main tasks the fight against government corruption, swollen under Brezhnev. In this continuum of change, I took
leave of my Soviet hosts, who except for a few tense moments had
treated me with true Slavic hospitality, with a feeling that some
changes indeed were coming, but still not convinced that time was
running out on the Fatherland of Socialism.

The first portents of more dramatic change came in US-USSR
relations. The president of the United States and the new Soviet leader
were to hold a Summit meeting in Geneva. In the past, positive results of such summitry had proved to be short-lived or illusory, at
most a lessening of the tension, soon followed by another conflict.

Witness for example Mr. Carter embracing Brezhnev in Vienna in
June 1979 and then being obliged in December to call him a liar
after the Soviet invasion of Afghanistan. But this time the prospects
appeared much more promising. The Soviets had not succeeded in
dividing the US and the Europeans over the Euro-missiles. They
obviously had a stake in reducing military expenditures and stop-
ping the US from embarking on the Star Wars project. Gorbachev
would not try to bully Reagan as Khrushchev had Kennedy in Vienna
in 1962. Vietnam and Watergate no longer burdened America's
policymakers. Probably for the first time the President of the United
States would be going into a meeting with the Soviet General Secretary without any illusions and not on the defensive.

Prior to the meeting, Mr. Reagan had invited me, along with several students of Soviet affairs, to a session in Washington. Unaccus-
tomed as I was to the corridors of power I booked my flight from
Boston for a mere two hours before I was supposed to attend a working lunch in the White House. A very bad idea: anything—bad
weather, a flight delay—could make me miss the occasion. On my
future expeditions this experience taught me to take the plane the
night before the meetings. And indeed my unwitting nonchalance

about setting out to meet the great of this world made me almost miss the occasion. My plane started on time but after taxiing out to the runway turned back with engine trouble. I called a White House aide and explained my plight. He in turn, very flatteringly for my vanity, proceeded to scold the airline agent for not being able to provide transportation for an important person to an important meeting with the President. Surprisingly enough, the ailing aircraft quickly recovered, and I landed at National Airport some ten minutes before my appointment.

But this was not the end of my troubles. Destiny seemed to be against my helping to formulate policies that would tame the Evil Empire. I was met at the aircraft by a White House car, and also by the news that a storm had flooded the main route to Washington. The driver sped through red lights and one-way streets in a reasonable imitation of a Hollywood car chase. Though traumatized I also experienced a heady feeling of self-importance. Then the predictable police car caught up and stopped us. The driver expostulated: "Officer, this man is in a hurry to meet with the President." "I don't care if he is going to meet the Pope," was the cop's rejoinder as he got out his notebook. Here on an inspiration, I opened the window on my side and said, "Officer, I *have* met the Pope." It was not exactly a lie; I had met John Paul II when he visited Boston while still a Cardinal. In any case the policeman threw up his hands, and we sped off, arriving at the White House just a few minutes late. No other of my visits there was so dramatic.

I remember rather little of the actual discussion over White House chicken salad, wine, and iced tea. Each of the visiting experts delivered a little speech on what could be expected from the Soviets. The President listened attentively but said very little. The Secretary of State asked some questions. But most of the National Security Council members present looked rather bored. They must have attended many sessions like this one, and read countless memoranda on the impending Summit meeting. My own presentation summarized what I've written here: we should not expect the Summit to bring a magic transformation in US-Soviet relations. But there were good reasons to believe that this time the Russians were eager to meet us at least half-way. Gorbachev needed positive results to bolster his position at home. The Kremlin was in a chastened mood after its failure to split NATO, and likely to be reasonable about the medium-range nuclear missiles. The Soviets might be open to discussing Afghanistan. This time, for a change, we were dealing with them from a position of strength, and the precept "never fear to negotiate" was appropriate to the moment.

I was too measured in my optimism. The Geneva meeting did transform the atmosphere of relations between East and West, and tangible results would soon follow. The next summit, held in Iceland in October, 1986, brought momentarily, as befitted its location, new frigidity to the Cold War. But in fact the circumstances that had led to the meeting demonstrated how badly Gorbachev wanted to put relations with the West on a new basis.

A Soviet diplomat had been arrested in the US for spying. In its time-honored way, Moscow retaliated by imprisoning, on fabricated charges, Nicholas Daniloff, an American journalist in Moscow. Nick, my colleague in the Russian Research Center at Harvard, was needless to say innocent of any wrongdoing. But this game of tit-for-tat which some years before would have been quite normal, and would have been quickly concluded with the expulsion of both individuals from the respective countries, created a great deal of commotion here, coming as it did after all that cordiality in Geneva. To cover up its blunder (Daniloff had been sent home in a blaze of publicity), the USSR unexpectedly proposed a new Summit in Reykjavik. Hastily convened, it obviously could not lead to any concrete agreements. Gorbachev, probably because he could not think of anything else at the moment, proposed the phasing out of all nuclear weapons in the hands of the USSR and the US, if the latter abstained from developing SDI (Star Wars). Overwhelmed, and most likely confused by the scope of the proposal, Mr. Reagan felt constrained to reject it. Now, it is unlikely that Gorbachev meant his offer seriously. It would have been irresponsible and potentially catastrophic for world peace if the two superpowers gave up all their nuclear deterrents, while other states including Israel, South Africa, India, Pakistan, Iraq, North Korea, etc., retained those weapons and/or the capacity to develop them.

Gorbachev couldn't have meant it. Or could he? Whatever the national arguments against his proposal, they may have been momentarily overlooked under the emotional impact of the catastrophe that befell the Soviet Union the preceding spring. On April 26 there had been a meltdown and an explosion at the antiquated Soviet nuclear plant at Chernobyl. Even today we don't know the extent of the explosion at the badly managed plant and the consequences in lives lost and environmental damage, but they were certainly disastrous. A Soviet journalist gave me one estimate that would have much of Byelorussia's soil and rivers polluted for generations, and thousands of its population condemned to suffer the long-range after-effects of radiation.

The catastrophe could not be concealed. Radiation levels in even quite distant European locations increased sharply. After trying to minimize the deadly incident, Gorbachev eighteen days later felt obliged to address the subject in a nationwide broadcast. Some of his oratory reflected old habits. He claimed, falsely, that the US government had taken even longer to inform the world about a near-catastrophe at an American nuclear plant. In fact Three Mile Island was a potential disaster, but Chernobyl an actual one. He could not let the occasion pass without accusing, again falsely, "the ruling circles of the US" of gloating over the disaster.

For all such insinuations, the General Secretary struck if not a new note, then one now endowed with special and unprecedented emphasis. "We understand it as yet another tolling of the bell, another grave warning that the nuclear era calls for new political thinking, for new policies...a stop to the heinous arms race, in order to improve radically the climate of world politics." Gorbachev well understood that the effects of Chernobyl were a pinprick compared to what even a "limited" nuclear war would produce. It was one thing to talk of the nuclear danger in abstract, and another against the background of the exploded nuclear reactor spewing out radioactivity over large areas of the Ukraine and Byelorussia. And so after all, it may have been strong emotion that prompted Gorbachev to make his incautious proposal at Reykjavik. It would seem impossible that in a Soviet leader emotion could prevail over cold calculation. But then all sorts of "impossible" things were to happen in the Soviet Union in the next five years.

Failure of the Reykjavik summit did not long sour the American-Soviet dialogue. The fresh face of Soviet diplomacy was well expressed by the new Minister of Foreign Affairs, Eduard Shevarnadze. A mercurial Georgian, close to Gorbachev, he provided a striking contrast to his predecessor Andrei Gromyko, whose dour appearance and sarcastic manner had seemed to epitomize the spirit of the Cold War during his almost thirty years in office. Contacts with Soviet officials became much easier, and freer from the strain one had usually felt on such occasions prior to the Gorbachev era. It was a venerable tradition in Russian politics long before the Bolshevik Revolution: a signal from the top, and all the officials, newspapermen, etc., would sing the new song. Those stone-faced bureaucrats were now smiling at you, those journalists previously vilifying everything American now praised Soviet-American friendship and extolled the "new thinking" of Moscow's foreign policy. I had to pinch myself during such encounters: could these be the same men who a year or two before had spewed out venom about the West.

I got to know quite well some of those converts to real coexistence. I would often run into Gennadi Gerasimov, the new official spokesman for the Soviet Foreign Ministry. Some time in 1987 he asked me what his government could do to solidify the breakthrough in East-West relations. For a beginning, I said, it would help if the Soviets announced the date for a pullout from Afghanistan. Also, why not recognize the realities of Eastern Europe and let its nations be free to choose their rulers, rather than carry the burden of keeping those Communist regimes in power? Poland, Hungary, etc., would still defer to the USSR in their foreign policies. This was in line with what I had been writing for some time about the "Finlandization" of Eastern Europe; huge were the advantages that would accrue to the USSR if it no longer had to stand armed guard over 100 million people who detested their Moscow-imposed Communist puppets.

Gennadi was shocked; at the time my suggestions seemed to him impossibly far-fetched. Moscow News featured our debate, Gerasimov using it as an example of how even those Americans who were familiar with the Soviet Union tended to be utterly unrealistic in their expectations.

I was proved wrong but not in the sense Gerasimov meant. In two years Soviet troops would actually be out of Afghanistan. And events also outran my "Finlandization" idea. By 1989 Communist ministers all over Eastern Europe were hurriedly packing their belongings and vacating their offices. And the Soviet Union lost control not only over domestic but also over foreign policies of the liberated nations.

In my writings I think I betray the fact that I'd never been able to make up my mind about the knotty question of whether the Soviet Union, or its rulers, could really afford friendly relations with the West. That siege mentality which the Kremlin had impressed on its subjects was always rationalized by the ever-present danger coming from the "imperialists," and the incessant intrigue directed by Wall

Street against the Soviet people, and the threat to world peace coming from the West German "revanchists," etc., etc. And now with the
world at peace how could one justify the repression of the Soviet
citizen and his deprivation of decent consumer goods? Would
Gorbachev's colleagues, some of them undoubtedly nostalgic for
the days of Stalin when they began their careers, allow him to say in
effect, "Moment, stay, thou art fair?" And didn't the man himself
realize how vulnerable the Soviet system was to peace and harmony
in international relations? In 1985, I tended to become more san-
guine on the subject. After all there was the example of China. Its
leaders were now quite friendly with the West and seemed not to
fear that such friendliness was undermining their power. In three
years, though, demonstrations and repression at Tienanmen Square
would show the government's abiding sensitivity. And so I told
myself that it was silly to be pessimistic when things were on the
mend, when the Great Fear which could be another name for the
Cold War was now receding and common sense was asserting itself
in international relations.

Curiously, my thinking about the incongruity of a new era of peace
with the Soviet system found its parallel in some Soviet writers' observations expressing similar doubts about the ability of the US to
handle the end of the Cold War. "How would America be able to live
in a world in which it has no enemies?" impishly wrote Georgi
Arbatov, head of Moscow's US Institute, and for years his country's
leading "Americanologist." I had occasionally crossed swords with
Arbatov, for years a participant in practically every conference on
Soviet-American relations, a man with many American acquaintances. I knew he was too intelligent a man to believe that the US would
greatly miss a hostile Soviet Union. But some less sophisticated Soviet commentators took the question seriously. Marxism-Leninism
teaches that capitalism must develop periodic, ever-increasing de-
pressions. How were they then to explain that the United States has
escaped such predicaments since the end of World War II? Simple:
its rulers invented the phantom of the "Soviet danger," and spent
billions on the military. Without the alleged Soviet threat, the ruling
capitalists would not be able to keep bolstering the economy through
those policies, and mass unemployment would soon grip the West.
In fact our Marxist-Leninist sages would have done better to worry
about their own society. It was Marxism-Leninism that was in deep
trouble.

It wasn't the capitalist economy but the field of "Sovietology" in the West that would be stricken by the disappearance of the Soviet Union, and with it the "Soviet danger." Prior to WWII, to most Americans Russia was a little-known exotic land. The war and then the Cold War enormously enhanced public interest in things Russian. But what aroused that interest was only partly the recognition of the historic and cultural importance of the land of Pushkin, Tolstoy, and Tchaikovsky; mainly it was the public's apprehension of what the new superpower's policies portended for the world.

And then of course, in 1991-1992 the Soviet Union collapsed into 15 separate states. The main successor state, Russia, bankrupt and supplicant for Western help, no longer loomed as a threat, although it must not be forgotten that those long-range nuclear missiles are still there. Public interest in things Russian declined. Just as the Department of Defense was now shutting down army and naval bases, so colleagues and universities were curtailing their offerings in the Soviet-Russian field. The media turned to other subjects.

But back in 1986 the Sovietology studies industry was thriving, in part because of the attractiveness of change as the Cold War evolved into something calling for constant revision. It's not that prior to the Gorbachev-Reagan romance, the public had been panicky about the possibility of an actual clash between the two superpowers. Such fears had largely subsided since the 1950s and 1960s. Still, with all the trouble spots in the world, Berlin, the Near East, Africa, could one be sure that the Washington-Moscow tension over them would not escalate into a fatal confrontation? And now, amazingly, the Geneva summit opened a period of five years when Soviet-American relations would grow ever friendlier, confounding all the fears of the past forty years.

Thus it was natural that America's interest in Russia would reach its peak during those five years. That amiable Mr. Gorbachev was promoting not only a new look in Soviet foreign policy, but also domestic reforms. Was it possible that he was steering the Soviet Union toward democracy? Was it conceivable that he might succeed? Gradually this man won the sympathy of the American public as no other Soviet leader had done before. He was certainly moving with the times, also in his personal life. How many Americans had heard of Mrs. Khrushchev or Mrs. Brezhnev? They usually stayed home while their husbands stalked the world scene. But not Gorbachev; the brave new world of perestroika was also affecting the hitherto strictly masculine style of Soviet politics. The old and the new were vividly and incongruously illustrated in those traditional pictures of the General Secretary, home from his travels, being greeted by other members of the Politburo. Here was this row of dour old men all in fedora hats, looking like FBI agents of the 1930s; and in their midst a high-fashion woman standing next to her husband. No, the other potentates would not have dreamed of bringing their wives for the occasion! Yes, said Raisa Gorbachev to a TV reporter, he discussed political issues with her.

Gorbachev's acquisition of an affectionate nickname further underlined his status as an American celebrity. Prior to "Gorby" the only Soviet figure so honored was Joseph Stalin, the "Uncle Joe' of those distant pre-Cold War days.

The Gorby era stimulated the popularity of Soviet studies in America and increased the demand for Sovietologists. Scholarly traffic between the two countries greatly increased, and conferences between Soviet and American notables and scholars proliferated. Where once such gatherings labored in a strained atmosphere, they now took on the character of veritable love feasts.

Unlike some previous periods of rapprochement with the USSR, this one provoked almost no skepticism in the media or from politicians. No one could question Mr. Reagan's conservative credentials or think that Moscow could dupe the man who coined the term "The Evil Empire." One of my fellow participants in some of those White House sessions was Ms. Suzanne Massie, an authority on Russian cultural history, author of some delightful books on the subject. It was she, I believe, who suggested to the President a Russian proverb which feely translated into English comes out, "Trust your partner but be sure to check the facts." The President did act in that spirit. And rather surprisingly for someone with no experience with foreign cultures, he knew how to set exactly the right tone in his dealings with the Soviets, and personally with Gorbachev. Russians have always been sensitive to any suggestion that they were not being treated as equals, and conversely quick to spot a foreign statesman's lack of self-assurance. No one could fault Mr. Reagan on either count.

And so "summitry" flourished, with meetings in Washington in December 1987, Moscow in June 1988, and New York in December. The President's trip to Russia in 1988 had to rival Nixon's visit to China in 1972 as a candidate for the most spectacular event in recent diplomatic history. The most conservative American President of the era made a state visit to what was still the self-proclaimed Fatherland of Socialism. And on the occasion he had the opportunity to address the Soviet people on national TV and give a talk to an audience of university students. Did he still think of Russia as "The Evil Empire?" No, things have changed, replied the President. His speeches were seeded with appropriate Soviet proverbs, and even an occasional quote from Pushkin and Pasternak, a gracious tribute to the cultural heritage of his hosts. The President's advisors and speech writers had risen to the occasion. The two leaders took an "informal" stroll through Red Square chatting with and answering questions from the Muscovites. What bourgeois leader ever had a reception like that in Moscow!

The spectacle could not have pleased the spirit of the mummy enshrined in the Red Square mausoleum. Pointing to the edifice, Gorbachev assured his guest that this, meaning the Leninist foundations of the Soviet State, was one thing not subject to perestroika. "This is one sphere in our nation's life which does not require a change." Events proved him wrong. In a few years almost everything that Lenin and his monument stood for would be gone from the land of his birth. Equally pathetic in retrospect appear Pravda's biting comments on Reagan's meeting with a group of dissidents, characterized by the journal as "active enemies of socialism and perestroika." Yet even here the Soviet organ struck a new note: as Russian society becomes more democratic, it wrote, those gentlemen calling themselves dissidents will become irrelevant and of no interest to the Americans. This amounted to an admission by the Soviet press that the Soviet Union needed more democracy.

The June 1988 meeting represented the high point of the Gorbachev-Reagan relations. By the time of the next summit, in December of the same year, it would already be clear that the Soviet leader's position was unstable and perestroika was in trouble.

Like many others I beheld this love-feast between the President and the General Secretary first with incredulity, then with a growing conviction that we were indeed witnessing a momentous turn in history. We were witnessing what might have been called a revolution of common sense: both superpowers acknowledging the obvious fact that there was no intrinsic reason for their menacing grimaces at each other. It was clear that neither threatened the vital interests of the other

Yet at some point in the late 1980s I developed doubts on the latter count. I recalled an offhand remark, I believe of Winston Churchill's that the Soviets were more afraid of friendship with the West than of outright hostility. During the Cold War the United States had to be continually fearful of what the USSR might do. For its own part, Moscow, despite its incessant protestations to the contrary, was well aware that the West had no aggressive intentions toward the Soviet Union. But no diehard Communist could approve of friendship with the West, if this friendship meant that Western ideas, political, cultural, and social, would seep into the Soviet Union and thus undermine the bases of their authoritarian society. According to the Kremlin's traditional code of behavior, Marxism-Leninism could not tolerate coexistence with non-objective art, permissive sexual mores, rock and roll, and other indulgences of decadent bourgeois culture. One could not enforce political conformity without also maintaining social standards.

One day in 1988 I happened to look at a Moscow magazine and was startled by one of the articles in the otherwise sedate publication. It described, with photos, the competition for "Miss or Mrs. Bosom of Moscow." The magazine's reporter asked one of the contestants' husbands if he was embarrassed by his wife appearing in public half naked. Not a bit, replied the man; it was quite an appropriate manifestation of the country's advance toward democracy. It was another trumpet blast toward tumbling the walls of the totalitarian Jericho.

But as of 1986-1987 it was still hard to believe that Gorbachev and his team would allow the attrition of the Communist code of behavior to go that far. The General Secretary's goals and policies seemed quite sensible and practical to the bulk of the ruling class, a meaningful détente with the United States plus moderate liberalization domestically. No one at home or abroad quite understood what was meant by perestroika. To be sure some of his elderly colleagues in the Politburo must have sensed danger, but then Gorbachev through his still masterful political skills succeeded in removing the most obstreperous ones. He had obviously learned from the outcome of Khrushchev's attempt to shake up the Communist establishment. By proclaiming glasnost, or making political decision-making up to a point subject to public scrutiny, Gorbachev appeared as champion of the people's rights. It would not have been easy for his Politburo colleagues to deal with him as they had dealt with Khrushchev.

For all his books and appearances on the international lecture circuit, the Gorbachev of the 1990s has still not told us what he really meant to achieve with his slogan perestroika. Probably by now he can't; how could he reproduce his state of mind in 1986-1987 when he held what was an office still much more powerful than that of the President of the United States? Yet we can take for granted that he did not intend to dismantle the Soviet Union or the Communist system. My own feeling was that he came closest to defining his goal when he talked of the Soviet Union becoming a "state under the law." This language evoked the 19th -century political concept of the Rechtstaat, an arrangement not necessarily a democracy, nor even a state where every citizen knows his rights and enjoys protection from arbitrary actions by the authorities. Great Britain was such a state for at least a century and a half (1660-1832) before the reform of the House of Commons made it a democracy in the modern sense.

But could a Communist state ever become a "state under the law?" Supportive as in those days we all were of Gorbachev and his perestroika, I never doubted that the answer to the question was no. The very essence of the Communist system implied that its rulers' powers could not be restricted by laws. Would a citizen of the USSR be allowed to denounce Communism, organize a rival political party, or openly condemn the government's policies? If so, the USSR would cease to be a Communist state. Today's Communist China has abandoned most of the tenets of Marxism-Leninism, and economically has virtually embraced capitalism. But it is certainly not a state "under the law": for no higher establishment of laws constrains the arbitrary power of the ruling Communist elite. It is the unrestrained power of the Party's high command which has been the main distinguishing characteristic of the Communist state.

But how could Gorbachev, a man of undoubted intelligence, and an experienced Party apparatchik, have missed a point so obvious to so many analysts of the Soviet scene? I have believed the answer lies in the contrasting mindset of different generations. His predecessors reached their political maturity and began their careers under Stalin. They all absorbed their terrible master's principle that the Soviet system could not dispense with repression, and that the one thing it could not afford was the people being entirely free of the fear of their rulers. But Gorbachev had grown up in a society, which, compared with Stalin's, was but mildly repressive and yet except for a handful of dissidents seemingly content with Communist rule. And so to introduce the rule of law struck him as both safe and desirable. The emphasis on legality, far from destroying the Soviet system, would only make it stronger and more popular. Thirty years had passed since Stalin's time; and the Soviet state stood more powerful than ever, its people solidly united behind the Party. How ridiculous of his conservative colleagues to think that the system could not afford an infusion of legality.

As subsequent events were to demonstrate, Gorbachev was even more fatuously optimistic concerning the problem of nationalities within the USSR. Practically to the moment of its break-up he could not see that the Soviet Union was a Russian empire, and as such resented by many of its non-Russian citizens. Again, for a lifelong Communist official it would have been difficult to perceive how divisive the nationalities question would become once the Soviet people were given a voice in determining their destiny. The ruling Communist oligarchy did include non-Russians: it was Stalin, a Georgian, who established the pattern of Russian domination over the other ethnic groups. Thus Gorbachev saw nothing unnatural or troublesome in the fact that the Russians were, as the official statements would often proclaim, "the leading nationality of the Soviet Union." It did not enter his mind that given the chance some nations, notably the Baltic ones, would opt for full independence, and that the others would at least demand that what had previously been the dead letter of the phony constitution: full equality and autonomy of the constituent fifteen republics of the Union. Nor did it enter his mind that, say, the Lithuanians could prefer to have their own tiny state rather than to stay within the mighty Soviet Union; or that the Ukrainians might decide to break their three-hundred-year association with Russia. Such fantastic ideas could be entertained only by small groups of fanatics within those nationalities; for the vast majority of the non-Russian inhabitants of the Soviet empire the words of the Soviet Union's national anthem expressed an immutable fact of political life: "An unbreakable Union of free republics was forged forever by Great Rus." I used to tease my students by asking them to spot three factual errors in that single verse. On paper, the Union was not unbreakable since the constitution "guaranteed" the right of the constituent republics to secede; the republics were certainly not free; "Rus," usually applied to medieval Muscovy and had nothing to do with the formation of the empire, which Russia conquered from the 17th century on.

Much as I appreciated the explosive potential of the nationalities question, I could not foresee until 1987-1988 that within a few years the giant state would become partitioned into fifteen independent entities, or that even smaller ethnic groups like the Chechens would seek to secede from Mother Russia. My reason for believing in the durability of the Soviet Union was different from Gorbachev's. He assumed that the Ukrainians, Uzbekis, Lithuanians, etc., were well content to live in "fraternal union" with the Russians. For my part I had no such illusions. But I thought the enormous power of the state plus the support of the Russian element in the population was strong enough to quash any aspirations toward independent statehood by any other component of the USSR. It was Russian nationalism, that was the main psychological prop of the regime. It was not by appealing to Marxism-Leninism but by evoking Russian patriotism that Stalin succeeded in saving the Soviet Union in the fall of 1941 when the German invader was close to Moscow. Surely "the leading nation of the Soviet Union" would defend that Union in the face of any challenge.

Well, I was quite mistaken. The moment came in 1990-1992, the empire tottered and then fell, while the bulk of the Russian population didn't rally to the defense of what first the Tsars and then Stalin had built over three centuries. Russian patriotism had been a powerful weapon when invoked against the foreign invader. But when the task was defense of the authoritarian structure, patriotism was not there. Pride in the imperial role and power of one's nation may at times soothe political and social grievances. Though living in an essentially oligarchic and plutocratic society, 19th century British workers, for example, were not insensitive to the Rome-like glory of the British Empire. But the mass of the Russian people was unlikely to experience such nationalistic stirrings. With awesome impartiality, Stalin's terror had struck "the leading nationality of the Soviet Union" just as hard as it did the other ethnic groups. One could eulogize the Communist empire as the patrimony of the Russian people, but evaluated unsentimentally, it was really the property of top officials of the Party and the government.

How paradoxical was the Russian-Soviet connection in those last years manifested interestingly in the appointment of Constantine Chernenko as General Secretary in 1984. Since the aged oligarch's name sounded Ukrainian, the official announcement reviewing his curriculum vitae stated flatly, "He is Russian." It was correctly assumed that the man elevated to the most powerful position in the state was virtually unknown to his fellow citizens. There must be no misunderstanding about his nationality. This man who had spent his entire career in the Party apparatus and whom a handful of Kremlin potentates now promoted behind closed doors, was more remote from the mass of the Soviet people, Russians, or non-Russians, than any 19th century Tsar.

I do not question the enormous latent power of Russian nationalism, and that some time in the future it might again assume imperialist aspirations. In fact we already see such aspirations in the reborn Communist Party, which came close to winning the presidential elections in 1996 and in Vladimir Zhirinovsky's preposterously named Liberal Democratic Party. The shadow of Stalin, this time in its ultra-Russian nationalist emanation, hovered over the Russian political scene. But during the breakup of the Soviet empire the nationalist emotion was muted. And not only among the Russians. People of all the ethnic groups were awakening from a catatonic supine state long imposed by the political system, and it was getting rid of that system that was mainly on their mind.

But the collapse of the Soviet Union and Communism, surely one of the most astounding developments in world history, requires a more detailed account. In the falsely seductive period of perestroika during the late 1980s, Communism was to receive a human face. Without abandoning the achievements of socialism, the Soviet Union was to become a state under the law, possibly with a dash of democracy. The whole world smiled upon Gorbachev. And indeed how many men in history have matched what he attempted to achieve, evidently successfully: the transformation of a despotism into a humane law-abiding society. And that without a revolution or violence. As yet his political maneuvers could not be faulted. Systematically and without much fuss he eliminated the diehard Stalinists from the Party and state posts. Glasnost kept the demoted and disgruntled oligarchs from mounting a coup like the one which had brought down Khrushchev. Were they to try such a gambit against Gorbachev they would risk a popular revolt.

At the end of 1986 occurred an act symbolic of the reconciliation of the regime with the dissenting intelligentsia. Its most prominent figure, the physicist Andrei Sakharov, had for some years dwelt in humiliating exile in Nizhny Novgorod. One day he received an unexpected amenity, a private telephone. And then the General Secretary himself called and invited him to return as a free man to his home and laboratory in Moscow.

Some years before, I had met Sakharov's wife Yelena Bonner when she was in the US for medical treatment. At the time she was very eloquent in describing the indignities that she and her husband had suffered in their exile in what was then Gorky (the city that after the Soviet Union's fall reclaimed its ancient name of Nizhny Novgorod) An energetic, forthright woman, she undoubtedly contributed to turning her husband, who, until their marriage, was best known as a dedicated scientist, into an advocate of human rights and a dignified opponent of the Soviet regime. Moderate in his views and with no discernible ideological bias, the distinguished physicist was closer in his views to the Western liberal community than Solzhenitsyn. Yet like his fellow fighter for freedom, Sakharov was very Russian in his appearance and demeanor.

A man like Sakharov could not be expected to endorse perestroika, and if Gorbachev had hoped to secure his support for his half-hearted revolution, he was in for a great disappointment. Typical of the progressive intelligentsia, what Sakharov would argue for was, if not an instant democracy, then the dismantling of the main features of the Soviet system. Gorbachev's vision of a future in which there was to be room both for the monopoly of political power in the Communist Party, and for the state under the law; both for the expanded rights of the Union republics and for centralized control by Moscow, was certainly not Sakharov's vision nor that of like-minded reformers. The saying, "Those who make revolution by halves dig their own graves" would certainly fit the career of the unfortunate last General Secretary of the Central Committee of the Communist Part of the USSR.

The inherent contradictions of perestroika were first clearly discernible in Gorbachev's speech on the 70th anniversary of the October Revolution. On one hand it was a severe and uncompromising condemnation of Stalinism: "Through mass repression and lawlessness Stalin and his entourage had sinned before the Party and the nation." And yet, "From the viewpoint of historical truth it is indisputable that Stalin contributed to the struggle for socialism and its defense in the ideological struggle." Stalin, continued Gorbachev, contributed significantly to the Soviet victory in the War. His imposition of forced collectivization "created the social base of modernization and for guiding it along the path of cultured development."

At the time Gorbachev's speech could be taken as a clever maneuver designed to appease and disarm the suspicions of diehard Communists: to paraphrase Winston Churchill's declaration in 1942 about the British Empire: he, Gorbachev, was not going to preside over the dissolution of the Soviet Empire. But the truth was that there were two Gorbachevs: one an unsparing critic of the system, seeing its history as rooted in crime, falsehood, and brutal abuse of power by its rulers; and the other a defender of Communism eager to preserve it as a higher and more progressive form of society. And indeed for the remainder of his ill-fated reign the two Gorbachevs would continuously and incongruously struggle with each other. But at the time, November 1987, it was clear that it was the critic Gorbachev to whom the majority of the politically conscious intelligentsia were listening. Those people were no longer ready to accept any extenuating facts about the Stalin era. They repudiated the notion of Stalin's great contribution to the victory in World War II. While the General Secretary was extolling the social and economic virtues of collectivization, articles and books were already appearing with the truth: a brutal and ill-conceived feat of social engineering that cost millions of human lives and was still crippling the Soviet Union's agriculture and general economy. In sum, how hollow and unwittingly ironic must have sounded Gorbachev's praise of Stalin for having contributed "to the struggle for socialism and its defense in the ideological struggle." And even to the unsophisticated general public, it must have appeared incomprehensible and perverse that a man officially branded as a mass murderer could have been at the same time a wise social and economic reformer and a great military leader.

And what picture of Soviet history did their highest leader present to the Soviet people? Thirty years of unremitting tyranny under Stalin, plus twenty years of political and economic stagnation under Brezhnev and his short-lived successors. As yet only the brief period of Lenin's leadership was exempt from blame, and the ten years of Khrushchev's tenure remained as a kind of gray area. But history could not absolve even them. Lenin after all elevated Stalin to the position that enabled him to build his dictatorship. Khrushchev had been one of Stalin's closest collaborators. What other nation in modern history has endured so much for so long! And if that was the balance sheet of the seventy years of the existence of Communism, what did it say about the system itself and its guiding ideology? In

his October Revolution anniversary speech, Mikhail Gorbachev
sounded a dissonant chord, incongruously out of tune with the music of time.

28

To the Bialowiezha Forest

(Belavezhskaya Puscha)

The 19ᵗʰ Party Conference...Gorbachev's dilemmas...Yeltsin: the coup of 1991.....The end of the USSR

The British Empire, a wit once said, was created in a fit of absence of mind: a clever saying but hardly accurate. Generations of statesmen, soldiers, and capitalists had striven for centuries to expand Britain's rule over distant lands and seas. But how much more fitting it is to describe the fall of the Soviet empire as having occurred in a fit of absence of mind. None of the main actors in the drama sought or wished for the collapse. Gorbachev, dreaming of combining Communist power with democracy, believed to the last that he was just liberalizing the structure built by Lenin and Stalin. To the extent he for his part had a conscious design, Boris Yeltsin worked to transform the Communist giant into a confederation of national republics.

Barely recovering from the shock of dissolution, those local Party bosses who proclaimed themselves national leaders of Ukraine, Kazakhstan, Lithuania, etc. were mostly interested in maximizing their personal power. Those who had been dissenters, who opposed the Communist dictatorship, had given hardly any thought to the future possibility of the USSR being transmuted into fifteen separate states. Even the non-Russians among the dissenters thought of independence as perhaps a distant goal, their immediate demand being real autonomy for their nations.

Among the people the dream of independence lingered mainly in the Baltic lands and in Western Ukraine, the more recent acquisitions of the Communist empire. It was only on the eve of the crash, in 1988-1990, that the dream seemed to be something that could be fought for and won. For three generations the enormous power of the state had lain heavily on Russians and non-Russians alike, making it virtually impossible to all but a handful of dissidents even to think of an alternative. And then the burden lightened. The regime began to unravel. Except in the Baltic area, the people even then did not stir in revolt. No one overthrew the regime; rather the very men who had been its custodians and rulers cast it aside like a set of outworn clothes.

I am not among those who believe in the notion of "inevitabilities," that "underlying social forces" turn the wheels of history unaffected by the presence of a charismatic individual, or the intervention of a crucial event, initiating the transition from the old to the new. Had Louis XVI not convened the Estates General in 1789, the absolutist monarchy might have continued; had the senile president Hindenburg not been bamboozled into appointing Hitler Chancellor in January 1933, the scourge of Nazism might have been contained and the Weimar Republic saved. Clearly the Soviet Union was bound to change once Mikhail Gorbachev started to talk about perestroika, and the doctrine of glasnost bared the criminal past of the Communist regime. But his attempt to give actual meaning to his restructuring was the crucial blow that helped bring down the edifice of Communism.

The occasion was the 19th Party Conference, which opened on June 28, 1988, and which under Gorbachev's prompting adopted far-reaching changes in the governance of the USSR that were soon fatal for the Soviet state. Already the atmosphere of the gathering should have given a warning to the would-be reformers. A cardinal element of the Soviet system was the infallibility of the leadership in place. Past leaders could be criticized in a form prescribed by the current leader, as for example Khrushchev had denounced Stalin for his crimes. But between 1925 and the current conference, no gathering of the Party notables had heard anything but extravagant praise of the leader and his closest comrades at arms. Criticisms, again in a form prescribed from above, were reserved for the inferior officials, or those the leader decided to disgrace. But now the epidemic of glasnost struck the Party itself. Could one imagine Khrushchev or Brezhnev, not to mention Stalin, pleading with the comrades, as did Gorbachev, "We have not gathered here to deceive each other. Why do some of you believe that the leadership will always trick you, and try to wrap you around its finger?"

But here was Boris Yeltsin, who had been fired the preceding year from his post as boss of the Moscow Party organization, removed from the Politburo, and assigned to a minor office to keep him quiet. To Gorbachev's marked discomfort he insisted on addressing the conference, and in his talk attacked the current Politburo, which included Gorbachev, for its undemocratic ways, and on indulging in a scandalous criticism of the Soviet system for failing in seventy years to solve the basic problem of "how to feed and clothe the nation."

Yeltsin was then speaking only for himself. But while he chastised the Party leadership, several other speakers expressed doubt about the quick pace of reforms, and feared that reforms themselves undermined the traditional—read authoritarian—character of the regime. "It is not by undermining our past that we should secure a better future," said a well-known conservative writer who aptly compared perestroika to a plane that took off without the pilot (Gorbachev) being sure there was a landing strip at his destination. Clearly dissipating was that aura of awe that had traditionally surrounded the General Secretary, even when, as during Brezhnev's last years, he was ailing and only a figurehead.

More serious than this breakdown in Communist discipline was the character of Gorbachev's political and constitutional reforms that the Conference unenthusiastically accepted. The government had duly proclaimed Stalin's 1936 constitution the most democratic in the world. In addition to a range of civil rights, every citizen was guaranteed gainful employment. The Union republics, unlike the states in the United States, were free to secede from the federation. The only trouble was that most of the constitutional provisions bore no relationship whatsoever to the actual political reality of Soviet life. How was there to be a real constitution, and real elections, when there was only one Party-designated candidate for each seat, with, equally traditionally, some 98 to 99% of eligible voters duly casting their votes for him? With Gorbachev's reforms the voter was to be given choice: there could be more than one candidate running for a seat and they could be nominated independently of the Party.

Was the USSR to become a pluralist political society? No, the Communist Party was to remain the only legitimate political body in the country. In this lay a fatal flaw, for Gorbachev was striving for an impossible simultaneous arrangement of democracy and monopoly of power for the Party. This was to be accomplished at several levels. The central feature was to be the new Parliament called the Congress of the People's Deputies, an assembly of 2,250 representatives, two-thirds elected by popular suffrage and one-third by social organizations, a description encompassing such diverse organizations as the Central Committee of the Communist Party (one hundred delegates) and the Academy of Sciences (twenty). The Congress would meet annually and select one-fifth of its membership to constitute the Supreme Soviet, a two-tiered legislature that would be expected to function as a Western-style legislature. The reasoning behind the cumbersome scheme was obvious. With more than one candidate running in each district, quite a few of those elected by popular suffrage might turn out to be independents critical of this or that aspect of the regime. But the overwhelming majority of the deputies sent by "social institutions" would dependably be Party line adherents, and hence Gorbachev loyalists. The overall design would thus produce a freely elected legislature with a firm majority that guaranteed one-party rule.

But in a revolutionary situation, such as was approaching in the Soviet Union, constitutional niceties count for little. The Bolsheviks had been in a minority in the Constituent Assembly that convened in 1918. They chased out the majority with impunity after one day. Now for the first time in seventy years there were to be some free elections, some voices denouncing the regime from the podium of the legislative assembly. It was bound to be contagious, if only because of its novelty. What matter that the critics would be in a minority? They could and would ask questions and pose demands which many voiceless Soviet citizens must have had on their minds. Why preserve the system that had sent to death or the Gulag millions of innocent people, and kept their standard of living below that of even other Communist countries, while keeping the privileged few in luxury?

In his quest to marry democracy to Party rule, Gorbachev devised another unfortunate proposal. The organs of local government, called Soviets, corresponded in their powerlessness and purely decorative character to the old All-Union legislature. In Kiev, for example, the secretary of the Kiev Party organization was the local boss, not the chairman of its city council. Gorbachev promised that now those local organs were to have real power. But, he added, the local Party secretary should also assume the chairmanship of the local Soviet. Here some delegates perceived obvious objections. If the local Soviet is to be a truly independent body how can you prescribe that it would elect as its chairman the Party boss, or even that the Party boss would have been elected to the local Soviet at all? All that Gorbachev could answer was that somehow the system would work. He would be proved wrong.

After reading the proceedings of the Conference I became convinced that perestroika and with it the Communist regime were doomed. One delegate asked Gorbachev a very sensible question: "How shall we be able, while preserving the Soviet form of society and the one-party system, to secure the democratic character of social life?" To me it became clear that neither perestroika nor Communism could survive this sort of fatuous experiment. Here was a man who for all his political skill and benevolent intentions had no sense of history. Fear and apathy had so far preserved Communism. But fear had been steadily eroding since Stalin's death. For what you could now say freely, you and your family would have been destroyed in Stalin's time, you yourself would have received a prison term under Khrushchev, and only lost your job under Brezhnev. Apathy was undoubtedly a powerful force in enabling the system to go on. The average Soviet citizen was at a complete loss over how and for what purpose the status quo could be changed. But now the government itself was pushing the people to become active citizens, to vote as they actually wished. The great majority would undoubtedly still vote for the official candidates, would still be fearful of a sudden change, lest their now-bearable existence be threatened by some unknown, like anarchy or a new Stalin. But there would be others, and their number would grow, who would find their national life intolerably undemanding. For them perestroika was already becoming a meaningless slogan. They were being told, and this time not by Solzhenitsyn or Sakharov but by Gorbachev and his people, that the record of Communism was execrable. After thirty years of Stalin's tyranny and criminality, there followed a gray era of unconsummated reforms under Khrushchev, followed by what Gorbachev characterized as "Zastoy," political and economic stagnation, with Brezhnev. Why preserve this system? There was still a sizable body of defenders of Communism, but most of them were not with Gorbachev. For them, he was a traducer of the glorious record of the Soviet people. It was Russian-Soviet nationalism rather than Marxism-Leninism that agitated the diehard defenders of the old system. They gloried in the memory of Stalin, and installed him in the pantheon of history alongside Peter the Great. A chemistry teacher, Nina Andreyeva, became a spokesman for that view in an article published in March 1988. She would not give up her principles, she wrote, to take up the currently fashionable exaltation of glasnost concentrating on denouncing Stalin. To be sure he could be cruel and unjust. But so had been Peter the Great, who had made Russia a modern state, while Stalin had industrialized the country and turned it into a superpower feared and respected all over the world. Communism and Russia's Soviet Union's greatness were inseparable.

Seemingly at the height of his popularity and power, in September 1988 Gorbachev fired most of the old-timers from the Central Committee; but Gorbachev was in fact losing what in American politics would be called grass-roots support. Perhaps the General Secretary could have retained a firmer grip on events had there been a dramatic improvement in the country's economic situation. One of the slogans and promises of perestroika had been "uskorenye," designating an accelerating economic progress. But as with the other slogans this one raised expectations without providing concrete achievements. While the leading Soviet economists became advocates of market economics almost overnight, forsaking the precepts of Marxism, the same was not true of the vast economic bureaucracy, confused and alarmed by the call to change their habits and methods of a lifetime. Of course, the would-be reformers themselves were not of one mind. There were exhilarating calls for the decentralization of the unwieldy economic machinery, for abandoning the traditional Soviet reckoning of economic success in terms of quantity in favor of quality, and for more attention to modern technology; but there was no agreement as to how those goals could be attained. The old taboos and articles of faith were slow in giving way to new ideas. Habituated to Leninism, Gorbachev could not agree to surrender such dubious achievements of Communism as collectivization and shift to family farming. Chinese Communists had no such inhibitions. Under Deng they had dissolved collective farms, and soon those once ultra-dogmatic Marxists turned their economy almost 180 degrees, embracing the fundamentals of capitalism. But Beijing refused emphatically to follow the economic with a political perestroika. They refused to tamper with the authoritarian structure of one-party rule.

In any case the mixed signals coming at the policy makers did not help them deliver the country's economy from stagnation. Declining GDP plus rising inflation were bound to follow the political and economic chaos, and would then afflict the USSR with the failure of perestroika. A half-hearted and confused attempt to combine the old command economy with one offering a degree of decentralization, privatization, and profit-driven enterprise brought what might be expected, a festering economic crisis. The fifteen components of the CIS have still not overcome the situation that they inherited from its eruption in the last years of Gorbachev's reign.

Thus at midsummer 1988 I could not see how Gorbachev could be saved, or the Communist system, perhaps even the unity of the Soviet state. It was impossible to contemplate with equanimity something as momentous as the crash of the Soviet empire. Would it be peaceful? Could the ruling elite accept its defeat or in an attempt to save its waning powers or might it provoke a civil war? An even more frightening possibility was that in a state of panic the rulers would once more call up the phantom of danger from the West to blame for all the political and economic malaise. The USSR was militarily still a superpower with a vast array of nuclear weapons.

But what different policies could have arrested the drift to disaster? Anatoli Sobchak, the reformist mayor of St. Petersburg, was probably right when he said that the task of reforming the old system was hopeless; it had to be completely abandoned. Alternatively, some unrealistic scenarios can be conjectured. Imagine that the man working with the consequences of perestroika was not a latter-day Kerensky but what might be called a "liberal Stalin," a man who could crush all opposition and forcibly install a semi-democracy. But clearly Gorbachev hardly fit the description. For quite a while he was able to outmaneuver his dull conservative opponents, elderly oligarchs who were simply too stunned by events to devise a timely counter strategy. But he lacked that essential prerequisite for leadership, the ability to secure loyal followers. Those close to him would note that he was brusque and irascible in personal relations; and incongruously both dictatorial and indecisive in laying down policies. Eventually he would be toppled by the very people in whom he had put his trust.

Typical of Gorbachev's flaws was the one great hope that sustained him when the realization of perestroika appeared completely blocked. This was the delusion that the West, or mostly the US, would offer vast economic help, a new Marshall Plan, for the faltering Soviet economy, and thereby save his reforms and his regime. This belief flowed from a completely unrealistic reading of the world situation, or of the willingness of the West to provide an enormous volume of aid. Nor was there a clear reason for it. The USSR had not been recently ravaged by a devastating war; it was a country of huge resources and potentialities. There was also something unseemly about the leader of a superpower traveling in supplication to the meetings of the main capitalist powers and begging for inclusion in their councils. Much of the lethargic state of the Soviet economy in the last decade proceeded not only from the general faults of Communism, but also from the specific lack of incentives, whether for the factory director or assembly-line worker and collective farmer, to improve performance quality. It was up to "them," eventually the bureaucrats in Moscow, to prescribe production quotas, and devise new techniques. If Gorbachev's hopes for substantial US aid could be realized, even "they" could relax. Why tamper with established procedures and antiquated technologies if the capitalist powers would pour in money and experts to arouse the economy from its sluggish torpor? Thus at the end of 1988 I had to conclude that short of a miracle nothing could save perestroika and with it its architect and the Soviet system. The blow came with the installation of new institutions and the elections to the Congress of People's Deputies in March 1989. Yes, Gorbachav did win his majority, and in a normal parliamentary system it would have been an impressive, overwhelming victory for the government. But for perestroika it was a calamitous setback. Several of the regime's notables lost their elections. And in the big cities, where electoral fraud would have been difficult, the Party slates also lost heavily. Thus the first secretary of the Leningrad Party failed to get elected, though running unopposed, for failing to secure the prescribed 50% of registered voters. Gorbachev's ingenious scheme of linkage between the Party organizations and corresponding local government organs was exposed as fatuous. How could a Soviet citizen, even if not truly anti-Communist, deny himself the pleasure of doing something unimaginable for sixty years: voting against the once local divinity, the Party boss?

The victories of the critics and future enemies of the regime overshadowed the defeats of the celebrated. The most spectacular win was that of Boris Yeltsin, who in a district co-terminous with Moscow received six million votes, crushing a Party hack put up against him. Despite considerable pressure on the Academy of Sciences not to elect Andrei Sakharov he was eventually voted in. And the eminent scientist was by now a determined enemy of that halfway democracy dreamed up by Gorbachev.

Equally ominous was the appearance on the scene of nationalist opposition in the non-Russian areas. In Lithuania proponents of far-reaching autonomy or independence won thirty-one of thirty-nine districts. Not so long ago the mere expression of such aspirations would have won the new People's Deputies not a trip to Moscow but to the camps in Siberia. How wise the Chinese Communists were. While introducing capitalism in their country, they prudently rejected anything resembling free elections!

But even so, China soon felt the demoralizing effects of events in the USSR, and other parts of what was called, but soon would cease to be, the "socialist camp." For some time now leaders of other communist countries had watched with increasing horror what was to them democratic bacchanalia in the USSR. In some states, such as the German Democratic Republic, the government banned the now "subversive" Soviet press. But of course such precautions were in vain. While the oligarchs trembled, their subjects' reactions to the news were probably not much different from what an English poet described as the feelings aroused abroad by the French Revolution: "bliss in that dawn it was to be alive, but to be young was very heaven." And to be sure it was mostly the youth in those vassal countries of the Soviet Union who would soon be demolishing the Berlin Wall and demonstrating against their frightened rulers, now no longer serene in the knowledge that if trouble came they could always rely on the restorative treads of Soviet tanks.

While losing ground at home and scandalizing the Communist world, Gorbachev was becoming ever more popular in the West. It was a situation rich in irony. Who could have predicted a few years before that the capitalist world would take an intense interest in the success of the former "evil empire," and that not only many American students of Russia, but even some politicians and businessmen would nourish Gorbachev's illusions by urging massive economic help for the USSR? At Harvard there developed what might be called a veritable lobby for perestroika. In its Kennedy School of Government, several professors, including Graham Allison, the school's dynamic dean, were developing several strategies for rescuing the Soviet economy from its doldrums. They received a constant stream of visitors from the USSR, and agitated for a variety of the Marshall

Plan for an entire range of Communist countries now beginning to shed the shackles of Marxist-Leninist dogmas.

This solicitude for the former Cold War enemy and the cult of perestroika was not peculiar to the United States. A stout conservative such as Mrs. Thatcher, who claimed the credit of first discovering that "one could do business with Gorbachev," now adopted a virtually maternal attitude toward the embattled Soviet leader. All over the West, statesmen, economists, and businessmen hastened forward with praise and advice for the Soviet reformers.

For some of us who had followed Soviet affairs for a long time this enthusiasm seemed both premature and potentially counterproductive. Some Western well wishers, who found ready followers in the East, were advising what came to be known as shock therapy, an overnight shift from a state-controlled and centralized economy to a free market one. I felt that in the case of the USSR at least, such a drastic step would indeed shock but not be therapeutic. I would tell my Soviet visitors that for all his sins Lenin did leave behind one maxim relevant to the present conditions, contained in the title of one of his articles: "better less but better."

My own Russian Research Center, which the Soviet establishment once viewed in all likelihood as a branch office of the CIA, now appeared to it in a much more favorable light. Few Soviet visitors to these shores whether official or not neglected to stop by the Center and participate in the seminars and discussions. The new atmosphere was reflected in the way the visitors treated my colleague, the exiled historian Sasha Nekrich. Previously rather shy about meeting him, they now greeted him warmly. And in the USSR his long-banned book about how Stalin was responsible for Soviet unpreparedness for war was now republished in a large printing. An official representative of the waning Soviet power could not however be overjoyed at meeting a former dissident. When in 1990 I introduced Nekrich to the visiting Soviet ambassador, he chose to be acerbic: "Shall I call you 'mister' or 'comrade?'" he asked pompously. Just Alexander Moiseyevich, answered Sasha imperturbably. In two years comrade as a form of address was to fall from favor in Russia.

Nekrich entertained an interesting array of personalities at the Center. There was Yuri Afanasyev, historian and rector of one of Moscow's universities, an enthusiastic and radical proponent of reforms, for whom Gorbachev was a temporizer, and in 1988 already a spent force. His views were shared by Gary Kasparov, the world's chess champion, and unusual in a practitioner of the craft, deeply and intelligently interested in politics. At the other end of the ideological spectrum was novelist Alexander Chakovski, a venerable pillar of the pre-perestroika establishment as the editor of the influential Literary Gazette. He did not enjoy a good reputation and was rumored to have denounced some fellow writers in Stalin's post-war purge of Jewish intelligentsia. Just to be safe, I arranged for some Harvard police officers to gather discreetly in the corridor behind the seminar room where Chakovski was giving his talk. But the speaker's notoriety evidently did not reach Boston, and there was no incident. Why invite such types? I felt that we were in the business of examining all aspects of Soviet reality, warts and all.

Andrei Sakharov, for so long the voice of conscience of Russian dissidents, was our honored guest shortly before his untimely death. In his appearance and manners, he did not fit the usual stereotype of the Russian intellectual. He had none of the typically expected talkativeness and expansive manner; indeed, his awkward movements and reserve were rather peasant-like. He was obviously deeply under the influence of Yelena Bonner, his wife, her treatment of him being at once affectionate and a bit authoritarian. Listening to his impassioned indictment of the old regime one again realized the still-continuing tragedy of the Russian intelligentsia. Brutally repressed before, it was now liberated but still out of touch with the political realities of the country. They were now disenchanted with Gorbachev. But if the old system was going to crash down, there was little to suggest that democratic socialism would follow it, as Sakharov and many others had hoped. In all likelihood it would be, as in fact it has become, the Russia of technocrats, bankers and political operators, with many of the unattractive traits of capitalism at its worst.

I had never imagined that one day I would be invited to write for the Soviet press. But in the new atmosphere much was now possible that a few years before had seemed fantastic. My books had been receiving scant notice in the USSR, if any at all. Now, in 1988 and 1990, *Izvestia* asked me to write some articles; it was one of the two major national newspapers. The other one, *Pravda*, with its direct tie to the Communist Party, was losing readers. *Izvestia*, until now identical to *Pravda* in format and ideological line, was beginning to differentiate itself. And so I wrote on Soviet-American relations, on

Stalin, and other subjects. I could and did write as I would for the American press, but sadly without any honorarium.

My journalistic debut in the "Evil Empire" brought me many letters in response, for *Izvestia*'s readership was still in the millions. One that sticks in my memory came from a young lady in Minsk. She had all the skills, she wrote, expected of a young Soviet woman: housekeeping, cooking, sewing and the like. Now she wanted to be married, but most of the young men she knew were not good prospects because they were all drunks! Could I find her a suitable American? Sadly the letter was quite serious, and it seemed amazing that she could not find a good man in Minsk, a city of over a million people. And the USSR already had a service for bringing young men and women together, a likely consequence of the waning of the Komsomol, the Communist Youth League, which once had millions of members. This was a puzzle. I could not very well advertise her virtues in the personals column of the *Harvard Alumni Bulletin*. I had at last to concede my inability to act as a matrimonial agent for someone three thousand miles away. I never heard again from my Irina, and I can only hope that she did find a man worthy of her. I note in passing that in 1945, Stalin forbade those Soviet women who during the war had married members of the British and American missions to leave the USSR, and the prohibition held until his death in 1953. And even after that, had a Soviet censor intercepted a letter such as my correspondent's from Minsk, she would have had, at least, to answer some very probing questions from the police. Yes, the USSR had certainly changed in those few years of Gorbachev's rule.

But in 1989 "change" was an inadequate term for what was happening in the Communist world. This was the year which witnessed the crumbling of the Soviet "external" empire, the Communist regimes in Eastern Europe, and the beginning of the dissolution of the "internal" empire, the Soviet Union itself. Both processes were triggered by perestroika or to be more precise, by its very concept as well as by its failure.

Here again some personal characteristics of Gorbachev contributed to the crash, if they did not indeed cause its implementation. Essentially of the post-Stalin generation, he did not understand, for one thing, that Eastern Europe had not been converted to Communism but conquered by the Soviet Union, and that once the threat of armed Soviet intervention was lifted, the Communist regimes there were doomed. His enthusiastic reception in Czechoslovakia in 1987, and in Poland during his visit there in 1988, appeared to bolster his belief that once those countries went through their own version of perestroika their peoples would be content to continue in the "socialist camp" with their fraternal Soviet people. But the reason he was cheered, apart from the Slavic tradition of hospitality, was that the welcoming crowds sensed that in view of what was going on in the USSR, they no longer had to be afraid of the Russian tanks and soldiers appearing on their streets. By the same token their rulers, alarmed, tried to put a liberal veneer on their regimes. But to no avail.

A similar delusion clouded Gorbachev's judgment about the nationality problem within the USSR. The constituent republics, and nationalities, were granted some rights, as against the fictitious ones contained in the Stalin constitution. Surely they now would be content to coexist happily with their Russian brothers. Perhaps more skillful policies could have avoided or delayed the disintegration of the Soviet Union. Moscow's rule was not resented as much in the Ukraine as it was, say, in Poland. But still, to the non-Russians, the USSR was a Russian empire. Had Gorbachev hastened to grant full autonomy to the Union republics the crash might have been avoided. If Eastern Europe could not have been held except by force, the Soviet Union could perhaps have been saved.

Gorbachev's awkwardness in dealing with the nationality issue was demonstrated when in 1986, he appointed an ethnic Russian to be the boss of Kazakhstan. This tactless step led to widespread riots by young Kazakhs. On the face of it the outburst appeared puzzling. The previous long-time first secretary of the republic's party, though an ethnic Kazakh, had long been an obedient servant of Moscow, respectful of the domination of his region by the Soviet Union's "leading nationality." But now one had to tread carefully on the nationality issue. Gorbachev's pronouncement on the subject could hardly be endorsed even by a most pro-Union Kazakh or Ukrainian. "History had decreed that a number of big and smaller nations became united around Russia...this process was assisted by the openness of the Russian nation, its readiness to work as equals with people of other nationalities..." This was a very romantic notion of the creation of the Russian and then the Soviet empire, founded chiefly on force and denial of self-determination to its subject nations. Perhaps the Soviet leader would have elicited a better response had he said to the non-Russians something like, "I know you have been oppressed by our rulers, but so have the people of Russia." Though by only a year or two, Gorbachev came too late to understand and act on the national aspirations of the non-Russians.

The watershed year for this matter proved again to be 1989. On August 23, the fiftieth anniversary of the Soviet-Nazi Pact that led to their subjugation by Stalin, over one million inhabitants of Lithuania, Latvia, and Estonia formed a human chain throughout the three small republics in an impressive demonstration for freedom. Sensing the drift of history, even the local Communist leaders were transformed overnight into nationalists and advocates of emancipation from the USSR.

Elsewhere the resentment at being ruled from Moscow had not yet taken the form of clear demands for independent statehood. And as the cloud of fear lifted from the Soviet scene, not only national assertiveness but also ethnic conflicts erupted into the open. Inhabitants of an Armenian enclave within the Azerbaijani Union Republic demanded to be freed of that association. It was a vivid illustration of the difficulties of managing upon any other basis an empire built and maintained through force. There were just one hundred eighty thousand people in the district of Nagorno-Karabakh. In pre-perestroika times, disorder in the tiny area would have been speedily quelled by the KGB and concealed from the mass of Soviet citizens and the world. Under Stalin any hint of revolt and most of the population might have found itself "relocated" to distant areas of central Asia. Now the Armenian-Azerbaijani conflict would fester through the final years of the USSR and beyond. But the use of force by the government could not now have passed unnoticed or unprotested. In the spring of 1989 the army intervened brutally against a nationalist demonstration in Tbilisi; twenty demonstrators were killed and many more injured. Moscow tried to shift responsibility to local officials, but many placed the blame on the regime leaders, especially those in charge in the Kremlin while Gorbachev was abroad.

The year 1848 had passed into history as the "springtime of nations," on account of the revolutions which then erupted against authoritarian governments all over central Europe. But perhaps that term could be better applied to 1989, which all over Eastern Europe witnessed different stages of collapse of the communist regimes and which ended appropriately in November with the demolition of the

Berlin Wall. The German Communist government collapsed within a month. Some years before, Ronald Reagan, standing nearby, called rather theatrically upon Gorbachev "to tear down this wall." Actually the hated barrier was pulled down by the people of Berlin, but in a wider sense it was perestroika which did away with it.

Perestroika likewise smashed the Communist system in Poland. In 1988 the labor union Solidarity, emboldened by what was happening to the East, emerged from its semi-clandestine existence and began a program of strikes against the regime. Rapidly losing confidence that the USSR would promptly stifle perestroika, the Polish government entered into negotiations. A bargain was struck early in 1988: Solidarity would be legalized and allowed to compete for one-third of the seats in the Diet, the lower house, the rest being reserved for the Communists and their allies. But for the weaker part of the legislature, the Senate, Solidarity would be allowed to run for all 100 seats. Here was a kind of Polish perestroika that would probably have pleased Gorbachev: an aged repast reheated and served with a garniture of democracy. But this time history had no use for compromises. To its own amazement Solidarity won all the seats it stood for in the Diet and 99 out of 100 Senate seats. Astounded by its triumph, Solidarity was still amenable to some sort of coalition rule with the Communists, most of whom believed the game already lost. Communists were now eager to shed power, but their opponents were hesitant to grasp it, and rather embarrassed by the extent of their victory. In the equally ironic resolution, Solidarity took over the government, and Gen. Jaruzelski, once the bête noire of democratically minded Poles, briefly remained figurehead president. And the whole momentous transformation to a Poland free for the first time in fifty years went off entirely peacefully.

The "Springtime of Eastern Europe" lengthened into fall and winter. Other Communist regimes tried last-minute rescue operations like changing their leaders, promising an end to the police state, and introducing political pluralism; but all in vain. For some time it had been clear that most of those puppet governments were vanishing, but not East Germany. Here, three hundred thousand Soviet soldiers stood guard. Surely whatever happened elsewhere in its domain the Kremlin would not let slip this great prize of the victory in World War II! And true to form, Gorbachev prophesied fallaciously here too. With the Wall breached, and the East German Unity Party dying, he seemed in his speech to his Central Committee on December

9, 1989, to challenge the West in the old style of Brezhnev or Khrushchev, "We must declare solemnly that we shall not let down the German Democratic Republic. It has been our ally and member of the Warsaw Pact. One must accept the realities of the post-World War II situation, the existence of two sovereign states." Set against the situation of the moment those words sounded pathetic. Even before its collapse the USSR had abdicated its role as a superpower. It did let down the German Democratic Republic. In a few months both it and the Warsaw Pact would be but historical memories. The winds of change were blowing Communism away all over the globe.

In May Gorbachev had gone to China. This was the first summit meeting between the two Communist colossi since 1959. Only a few years before, the meeting would have been seen as a momentous event riveting the attention of the world, arousing new hopes of Communists everywhere, and equally vivid apprehensions in the non-Communist world. But now the meeting aroused neither fears nor hopes. It was just a diplomatic event and as such turned out to be an embarrassment both to the hosts and the visitors.

The contagion of perestroika did not spare Communist China. Much as they had abandoned the economic side of Marxism-Leninism, China's rulers, headed by the eighty-four year old Deng, clung to their authoritarian pattern of rule. And that in turn led to student unrest and mass demonstrations against the regime, centering in Beijing. For the Chinese partisans of the Democracy Movement, the Soviet reformer's visit was an opportunity not to be missed. They intensified their protest, and the vast area of the Tiananmen Square was occupied by a vast throng of demonstrators. What could come out of the meeting of two leaders, one with his power evaporating, the other facing an incipient revolution? For the moment neither side had anything to fear or expect from the other.

Within three weeks of the visit the Chinese leaders proceeded to suppress the Democracy Movement. Troops and tanks were used to clear Tiananmen Square, the massacre claiming hundreds of lives and precipitating widespread arrests.

I was on a trip to Japan and, I hoped, China when the tragedy erupted. I landed at Tokyo airport just as the media were announcing the massacre. Shortly afterwards I received telephone calls from my contacts in Beijing and Shanghai warning me against continuing; at best I would be forced to spend my entire visit in a hotel. The atmosphere was certainly not conducive to interviews and seminars. I decided to stay in Japan.

The collapse of Communism was thus not limited to the Soviet Union and its former vassal states; it was worldwide. I recalled telling my students that virtually dead as Marxism-Leninism was in the USSR, it obviously had greater staying power in China. The USSR skimped on sending its young to study abroad, and those allowed to go usually could not take their families with them. But Beijing obviously trusted its students. By the eighties there were thousands of them in the United States and elsewhere in the West. But now there was a virtual uprising of a significant part of China's youth, and their protests and grievances were echoed by their countrymen attending Western universities and research institutes. The Communist oligarchy in China, their leaders being tougher than Gorbachev, would maintain themselves in power. But by almost every other standard, you could hardly apply the label "Communist" to mainland China.

That ideological vacuum was now prevalent more than ever in the Soviet Union. Like Khrushchev before him Gorbachev had begun his campaign under the slogan "back to Lenin." But glasnost, which was destroying the remnants of Stalin's myth, had not spared Lenin. It was his autocratic ways, his legitimizing of mass terror, which were now seen as having set the stage for his terrible successor. What precisely could be the end product of perestroika? And what was the point of having a Communist Party at all? As of the end of 1989 an article still in the Soviet Constitution, now suffering continual and meaningless amendment, proclaimed "the Communist Party armed with Marxism-Leninism determines the general perspectives of the development of society, directs the great constructive effort of the Soviet people and imparts a planned systematic...character to their struggle for the victory of Communism."

In view of the actual situation that pompous declaration now sounded not only anachronistic but also ridiculous. Pressure was being exerted on Gorbachev to remove this Article 6 from the constitution. But rather than quickly agree and be done with this embarrassment from the past, he fought the proposal with language as fatuous as that of Article 6 itself: "The Central Committee will resolutely fight any attempts to denigrate the importance of the Party and to undercut its authority among the masses...[the proposal] is an attempt to demoralize the Communists..." As everyone knew, membership in the Party had for long been little more than a status symbol, and now it was ceasing to be that; more and more people were leaving the once 19-million-strong "Party of Lenin and Stalin." On February 27, 1990, despite its leader's pleadings, the Congress of People's Deputies removed the offending article from the constitution.

The Soviet Union during late perestroika was like a rudderless ship, carried along by a current of events defying all attempts of its helmsman to put it into a safe haven. Gorbachev's constitutional improvisations were failing to arrest the growing political chaos. Hoping to offset his rapidly evaporating authority, Mikhail Sergeievich prevailed upon the Congress of the People's Deputies to elect him president, a new office and title in the Russian political nomenclature. As such he was invested with an impressive-sounding array of powers. And some in the West were indeed impressed. A noted American political scientist was impelled to write in 1990 that Gorbachev was now more powerful than Stalin at the height of his rule. But no one in the USSR would have agreed with such a statement.

To be sure some who had hailed perestroika and admired its author were now accusing him of having dictatorial ambitions. In a public speech the embattled leader complained rather pathetically, "If Gorbachev is a man who lusts after absolute power then why did he give it up when he had it? I did have it; the General Secretary in those days was a dictator with powers unparalleled in the world." He was exaggerating, for one did not automatically become a Stalin upon being elected general secretary. What such deluded critics overlooked, however, was that if after 1989 Gorbachev had tried, not indeed to become dictator but to assert his authority, he did so because of the realization that the country was on the verge of chaos. On the right he was blamed for undermining the awesome edifice of the Communist bloc; on the left his critics, mainly from the intelligentsia, blamed him for not having brought about instant democracy.

How brave had appeared the new world of perestroika when first proclaimed, and how gray had become its reality by 1990! And for the average Soviet citizen the most perceptible effect of the new order was the perceptible lowering of his living standard. This reality stood in ironic contrast to those exhilarating slogans of but two of three years before. There was "acceleration," that is, of economic growth; there was liquidation of the old "command administrative" system of managing industry and agriculture in order to free the creative and innovative forces of producers. And indeed, freed from obsolete Marxist-Leninist dogmas, the Soviet economy would overcome its stagnation and for a time begin to match the rate of growth of the West.

But in the economy as in politics the task of overcoming seventy years of sins and errors was proving to be beyond the powers of the faltering leadership. It was easy to agree on what was wrong: the old ideological shibboleths had crippled society's vital forces. There was no such agreement upon the cure. Some of Gorbachev's advisors pleaded for the government to take a direct plunge into a free market economy, applying deregulation of prices, plus aggressive privatization of industry and agriculture. Others advised a more gradual transition, warning of the hardships and dangers likely to follow too drastic a change of course. Foreign advisors were almost unanimous in urging the former course; it was perhaps easy from the perspective of Cambridge, Massachusetts, or some other Western fount of economic wisdom to underestimate the hardship and political dangers inevitable with the adoption of shock therapy.

Confronted by a variety of often clashing prescriptions for curing the ailing economy, the government pursued a zigzag course of privatizing an industry here, and there subjugating it to a new set of regulations and bureaucratic interference. Soon the entire economic scene reflected the muddle. Some of the inherent flaws of socialism persisted alongside the characteristic phenomena of capitalism in crisis, growing unemployment and severe inflationary pressures. By 1990 the average Soviet citizen would look almost nostalgically at what Gorbachev had denounced as the stagnation of the Brezhnev times. Back then one enjoyed guaranteed social security. Now I would read almost daily indignant letters to the Soviet press the gist of which was the complaint that the alleged blessings of free enterprise had not materialized, and that under the old system a family could make ends meet but now could hardly pay the rent or afford the basic necessities. Strikes by the workers, who had often not been paid for months or whose wages had become derisory through inflation, became frequent. Perestroika lay in shambles.

The last two years of Gorbachev's tenure in office were dominated by his struggle to preserve the Union. The Soviet constitution still retained from Stalin's times the amazing provision: "Each Union republic shall retain its right to secede from the USSR." In 1936 it was intended to be yet another demonstration of Soviet superiority to the bourgeois states in democratic virtue. Until recently no one in his right mind could have imagined that this Article 72 could have any practical application. But in 1989, this meaningless adornment of Soviet politics turned into a very clear and present danger for the regime.

Beginning in 1989 most of the fifteen Union republics were impelled to declare themselves sovereign states. Some of the autonomous republics, and even smaller units, then followed their example. The hitherto entirely fictitious federalist mosaic of the USSR was exploding into reality. In any revolutionary or transition situation the use of political terminology is bound to become blurred. "Sovereignty" in plain English is synonymous with "independence." In the USSR during its last two years of its existence the intended meaning of the term comprised both independence and an assertion of far reaching autonomy. The Lithuanian parliament, for example, asserted sovereignty in May 1989, then proceeded in March 1990 to proclaim the country independent. The process of the decomposition of the USSR was in full swing.

The world watched in wonderment the agony of this once mighty empire. The United States now recalled that it had never recognized Stalin's takeover of the three small Baltic States. Washington was put in a strange and paradoxical position. It felt bound to warn Moscow against trying to coerce Lithuania. At the same time it was constrained to support the attempt to preserve the territorial outline of the Soviet Union, the rationale being that Gorbachev's fall might lead to a civil war, and perhaps in the long run, to a revival of Stalinism. The situation had other ironies. In January 1991 the foreign minister of Czechoslovakia summoned the Soviet ambassador to warn him gravely against his government's attempts to stifle Lithuania's independence. Shades of 1968!

For those with historical memories, Gorbachev in his latter phase must have evoked memories of Kerensky, who had been a well-intentioned reformer unable to cope with the forces he himself had helped to unleash. In terms of political influence Gorbachev was by 1990 increasingly challenged by Boris Yeltsin. Indeed, against the proponents of the "deeper" causes of great historical transformation, it is possible to assert that the fall of the Soviet Union was greatly hastened by the personal rivalry and enmity of the two men. As head of the Russian Republic Yeltsin soon assumed leadership of the struggle of the Union republics against the central role of Moscow. At first he did not seek the dissolution of the Union. But already in 1990 compliance with his demands would have made real federalism meaningless. For Yeltsin the laws of the constituent republics should have taken precedence over those of the Union. Hardly less destructive to the continued existence of the USSR was Yeltsin's insistence that it was up to the government of the Russian republic to decide how much of the general taxation should be turned over to the central organs.

What motivated Yeltsin to advocate and carry out policies clearly destructive of the system and the regime which he had served for most of his adult life? No doubt personal rancor against the man who had humiliated him and sought to bar him from politics played a part. Then there was the trauma of breaking with Communism, the faith, which had been his for so long, and which had so clearly been revealed as but a sham. In 1990 he formally left the Communist Party. In any case if Gorbachev had weakened the foundations of Communist autocracy, then it was Yeltsin who gave the edifice a decisive push, which brought down the Soviet Union.

With fascination I watched Gorbachev's preservation efforts. Again, as so often in the Soviet drama since 1985, the events did not follow the usual scenario of the decline and fall of empires. Except for the Baltic States and Western Ukraine there was no visible popular pressure for dissolving the Union. But by the same token one hardly could speak of any widespread sentiment for its preservation. The apparent passivity was especially striking among the hitherto dominant ethnic group. At first glance the Russians' indifference to the preservation of the empire their own ancestors had built over three hundred years had to appear astounding. True, the actual architects of the imperial colossus had originally been the Tsarist bureaucrats and generals, and then their Soviet successors. But still one would have expected some resistance, based on national pride, to shrinking what had always been Russia to the approximate size of mid-seventeenth century Muscovy, with a population but half that of the USSR. And in surrendering those conquests of the past, citizens of the Russian republic would have also to acquiesce in losing millions of their fellow nationals. Russians were the most numerous ethnic group in vast Kazakhstan, millions strong in Ukraine, and numerous in practically every other Union republic. In ceasing to be the heart and master of an empire Russia would lose vast economic resources. It was bound to lose its status as a superpower. Yet this great empire, for so long an object of wonder and fear to the rest of the world, would pass into history not only without a bang but with hardly a whimper.

Years of repression had anesthetized Soviet society to the point of losing its power to react to what the Communist masters had been doing. Glasnost had begun to reawaken it, making the people recognize the myths and evils of Communism. But even glasnost had entered society not as a result of a popular revolt or agitation, but as a doctrine that once authorized by the rulers was taken up by the intelligentsia. And so it is understandable that the prospect of breaking up the Union failed to arouse either popular enthusiasms or revulsion. The struggle over either reforming or liquidating the Soviet Union was being fought among rival groups of politicians.

Gorbachev and his now-dwindling group of followers sought to fight this battle through constitutional and legal improvisation. His proposals envisaged both cosmetic changes, such as renaming the USSR the Union of Sovereign Socialist Republics and proposing extensive new powers for the constituent units. Had those proposals been made two or three years before they might have at least delayed the final crash. Now with the regime's authority visibly crumbling they stood little chance of succeeding. Except for those in the Baltic most of the Union republics would not opt for full independence until the drama of August 1991. But afraid of being outbid and replaced by their local rivals, those long-time obedient servants of Moscow were now advancing claims that would have made nonsense of the federal system, demanding separate military establishments and independent foreign policies.

The Gulf War demonstrated the Soviet Union's rapid descent from the status of a superpower. Iraq had long been Moscow's client and recipient of its military help. Had it still been pre-Gorbachev USSR the United States might well have hesitated to wage war vigorously against Sadam Hussein and would have hardly been assisted by so many other states. As it was, the Soviets were reduced to passive observers of the military destruction of their ally; their half-hearted attempts to mediate the conflict and to help reach a compromise solution were virtually disregarded by Washington.

In a desperate attempt to preserve the Union Gorbachev resorted to a referendum, held on March 17, 1991, but six republics refused to participate. On the surface the result still seemed to bolster Gorbachev's stand, for nearly 70% of the voters agreed that the USSR should continue as a federal Union of "sovereign socialist states." But the result again demonstrated the futility of counting heads in a revolutionary situation. The real question was how many would be willing to fight for the preservation of the Union. The obvious answer was very few. I was reminded of the elections to the Constituent Assembly in 1918 after the fall of Kerensky's government. The Bolsheviks were able to gain only about one-fourth of the votes and seats of the Assembly. But Lenin's party was willing and able to fight for power. Its democratic opponents were not. In 1991 very few, whether Uzbeks or for that matter Russians, were inspired by the passion for separate statehood or had a clear comprehension what it would actually mean. Most were willing to wait upon events.

There was another ironic paradox during those last days of the Soviet Union. Only a few years before, the prospect of the "Evil Empire" breaking up would have seemed to an American an impossible dream that, if ever miraculously made real, would have been the consummation of the fondest hopes of this country's policy makers ever since 1945. But here was Washington rendering its moral support to Gorbachev's desperate effort to save as much as possible of the empire of Peter the Great and Stalin. On his trip to the USSR in July 1991 President Bush applied much effort to supporting its faltering leader. Addressing the Ukrainian legislature he implied very strongly that the US was not in favor of Ukrainian separatism. My Ukrainian friends in this country were disgusted by Bush's performance, which they dubbed the "Chicken Kiev speech."

Ever since the beginning of Gorbachev's reforms I had expected the conservatives within the Communist hierarchy to mount an effort to overthrow him. How much more modest were Khrushchev's reforms, which in no sense challenged the authoritarian foundations of the regime, or the power and privileges! Yet one day in October 1964 his colleagues on the Politburo dismissed him, and there was absolutely no popular reaction. Surely following that Party Conference of 1988 those diehard oligarchs must have realized what all those proposed changes meant for their own job security and for the future of Communist power. And yet there were no signs of an anti-Gorbachev conspiracy as one by one the bricks of the foundations of the Soviet autocracy were removed, and the whole edifice clearly became structurally unsound. Glasnost had demoralized and weakened the resolution of Gorbachev's opponents within the Party hierarchy. They lacked the courage to demand the return to old practices now associated in the people's minds first with mass murders under Stalin, and then with his successors' withholding the truth about the past. It is instructive to note that when the attempted coup did come, in August 1991, none of the Party officials previously dismissed by Gorbachev lent his hand to it. The inept conspirators were those second and third-rate bureaucrats with whom Gorbachev had chosen to surround himself. Those superannuated Party bosses merit the benefit of the doubt: perhaps it was some feeling of shame for their past which kept them from lending a hand to restoring the old order.

As in many other countries, August in the Soviet Union is vacation time. Having patched together what was to his satisfaction a ploy for a new federal state Gorbachev departed for his residence on the Black Sea. One must agree with the hapless conspirators on one thing: there was no earthly chance that the proposed new constitution could hold the country together. It was at once too vague and too specific, vague in delineating the authority of the center, but very specific in granting constituent units powers amounting to virtual independence.

If some measurement could be devised for political ineptitude then Gorbachev in his last months would have to be given high marks, along with those who schemed to overthrow him. The August 19th coup was mounted by a junta, which included the president's deputy, his ministers of defense, police, and the secret service. The initial supporters of the attempted putsch included all but one of the remaining members of the council of ministers as well as chiefs of his personal staff and of his personal security detail. Gorbachev certainly knew how to pick them!

The awkward name chosen by the plotters for the junta, The State Committee for the Emergency Situation, epitomized the amateurish character of the enterprise. Anyone with a sense of history would have called it A Committee for National Salvation or Unity. Gennadi Yanayev, the obscure Party hack whom Gorbachev had chosen shortly before as vice president, was the head of the Committee. The plotters neglected such elementary conspiratorial precautions as securing the cooperation of the key army and KGB units in arresting key public figures who might stand in their way, such as Yeltsin, and former foreign minister Shevardnadze.

A call from CBS News awakened me early in the morning of August 20th. Had I heard the news from Moscow? Gorbachev, allegedly sick, had been replaced by one Yanayev; some committee had been set up. All I could say was that if it was a coup it was at least two years late.

A few hours later the picture became clearer. It was an attempted coup. TV carried statements from the heads of Ukraine and Kazakhstan, who were clearly waiting to sense the direction of events. The wretched Emergency Committee issued a lengthy declaration that they were acting to save the Union. A few more hours, and I felt confident that the putsch would not succeed. Yeltsin in Moscow, and the mayor of St. Petersburg respectively mobilized crowds against the usurpers. Had they acted more resolutely the plotters might have temporarily succeeded, for popular resistance in the two capitals was not overwhelming. Like the Party bosses, the military leaders were hesitant. But ever since 1989 power had become too difficult to be scooped up in one sudden motion. There would have been fighting, but after a few days or weeks the conspiracy would have collapsed. As it was, the imbecility of the enterprise became immediately apparent: resolute revolutionaries would have proclaimed that Gorbachev had resigned or approved the coup. Instead they sent a delegation to plead with him. Appearing on TV their leaders showed themselves nervous and unsure of themselves, some of them clearly drunk. Who would follow leadership like that? The state and the movement which began with the real drama of October 1917 ended in fact with the tragicomedy of August 1991.

And with it also ended the Gorbachev reign. No one has noticed that the real and successful coup took place on Gorbachev's return to Moscow, after his brief detention in his summer residence. Without having the slightest legal authority for his actions, Boris Yeltsin vetoed the USSR president's list of replacements for the mutinous ministers, and imposed his own nominees. Publicly humiliating Gorbachev before a session of Russia's parliament, Yeltsin also took upon himself to order the dissolution of the Communist Party and the termination of its press facilities. Gorbachev meekly resigned as the General Secretary of the already abolished Party. All over the country crowds were dismantling the statues of Lenin and other greats of the Soviet era. One such dethronement recorded by television was especially evocative: Lenin had been pictured in his typical pose with an outstretched arm. Now as the statue was being lowered from its pedestal the father of the Revolution seemed for a moment to be pleading for his life's work to be spared before being ignominiously dropped to the ground.

A question that I have not seen posed was why Yeltsin was content just to humiliate Gorbachev rather than seeking to replace him as boss of the Soviet Union. If such a thought had entered his mind he must have promptly dismissed it. Reassured by the fiasco of the conspiracy, the Party bosses of Ukraine and Kazakhstan quickly shed their Communist identity and proclaimed themselves nationalist leaders of their countries. It must have appeared an almost hopeless task to create meaningful federalism in what was now but the ghost of the Soviet Union. Capable of occasional acts of bravery and self-assertion, Yeltsin, as his whole career demonstrated, lacked that fixity of purpose and passionate energy required of a great state and system builder. He was at that time content to remain the leader of Russia.

For a few months Gorbachev would continue trying to resuscitate the dying empire. A treaty of Union was signed by ten states that approved the political arrangements, chaotic as they were. The Congress of People's Deputies voted itself out of existence, a fitting end for an inept contrivance which rather than creating a new order only hastened the destruction of the old. Those proceedings bore little relation to reality.

The final end of the Soviet Union came as a singular anticlimax. There were no armed clashes, no mass demonstration for or against, no parliamentary votes or even debates. Certainly the dissolution of a business firm usually entails more formalities and discussion than did this abrupt burial of one of history's mightiest empires.

Some 35 miles north of the Poland-Belarus border town of Brest, an ancient forest spreads across a small area of both countries. It is the Belavezhskaya Puscha, (Bialowiezha Forest) or "Forest of the White Tower," named after a 13th century structure. Yeltsin and his counterparts from the Ukraine and Belarus met on the December 8th, 1991, in a government residence in Viskuli in the forest, and proclaimed absolute and unqualified independence for their countries, thereby putting an end to the USSR. The meeting was hastily arranged; the president of Kazakhstan was also supposed to attend but missed a crucial telephone call. The leaders' deliberations were assisted by considerable consumption of alcohol, which accounts perhaps for certain of their pronouncements. It could also be read as constituting some sort of league of the three Slavic countries, dubbed the Commonwealth of Independent States, admission to which would be open to other former Union republics, in fact to any other states. In a move that had an eloquence of its own, the first statesman Yeltsin telephoned to announce the fait accompli was President Bush.

The atmosphere of confusion that followed the announcement was well expressed in the next day's headlines in the Moscow press: "We are now living in a new country...Yes.. No...Maybe." A lingering speculation is that had Gorbachev reacted vigorously to what was clearly an illegal and unconstitutional act by the three presidents; perhaps the issue could have been put to a referendum. And to be fair, it was unlikely that any real force could have been mobilized in the defense of the Union.

In a few days the situation clarified. The other shoe had dropped; there was no USSR. The Commonwealth of Independent States was a phantom, still existing on paper to this day. There was a bitter dispute between Yeltsin and Gorbachev following the latter's resignation, but it dealt only with the perquisites the ex-president would enjoy. He ended up with a large dacha, an office building, and a limousine, though not the luxury model he fancied. An undignified ending to a great drama. But who can regret that a regime born and maintained amid so much bloodshed expired without the loss of a single life?

29

Russia Again

Improbable in appearance to the point of miraculous as late as 1987-1988, the collapse of the Colossus promised to free us from most of our worries and fears. Belief was widespread that we could now freely concentrate on our domestic politics, problems, and scandals. A former student of mine proclaimed enthusiastically that this was, indeed, the "end of history." Democracy had definitely triumphed. The US was the only remaining superpower, and who would dare to challenge it, or prevent the spread of American values all over the globe?

To me such enthusiasm was both premature and excessive, and today we can see quite clearly that the evaporation of the Soviet Union has not condensed into an era of peace and world stability. The likeliest most important threat to peace and democracy has gone, but many others remain.

It may also appear premature to pronounce a requiem on Communism. Isn't the largest nation in the world still under the rule of a party that continues to call itself Communist? Aren't similar regimes in power in Vietnam and North Korea? Former Communist parties with new titles featuring the magic word "democratic" remain influential in a number of countries including, surprisingly enough, some in Eastern Europe.

But these political facts should not obscure the central fact of the demise of Communism, in the sense this term was meaningful before the collapse of the Soviet Union, and more convincingly, before the burst of hostility between the Soviet and Chinese Communists. Communism derived its strength and worldwide appeal from its humanitarian and socialist phraseology, fraudulent as it was, in view of actual events in the Fatherland of Socialism. Today that appeal has been muted. After contending for two decades with the

359

Soviet Union for leadership of the "socialist camp," China has not sought to occupy the place left vacant by the former's collapse, or to indulge in any ideological crusade on a world scale. Rather than appeal to the world's proletarians, it seeks to enhance its own role and power within the international capitalist system. Each of the remaining Communist states has now become explicitly nationalist, forsaking any missionary zeal on behalf of Marxism-Leninism.

In the structure of the existing Communist regimes, what remains from the past is their authoritarian character and the central role of the state in their economies. The early egalitarianism had long since gone overboard. The label national socialist could arguably apply to the surviving Communist regimes, save that another and horrifying movement permanently preempted use of the term.

But what of the erstwhile "Fatherland of Socialism?" Could Russia regress into an authoritarian regime? Could its government lapse into what we here characterized as a national socialist or an outright fascist pattern?

The dizzying events of the last two decades make an outright prophecy far too hazardous. But some cautious speculation about the future of Russia remains in order. The outstanding fact about Russia's condition as of 1998 was its still far from stable political system. Its society still has not fully absorbed the shock of the disintegration of "Greater Russia," once the Soviet Union, and of the loss of superpower status. Though no longer ruled autocratically, Russia is still far from being a working democracy. Many, especially those associated with the Communist Establishment and their families, continue to view the dismantling of the USSR and the repudiation of Communism as acts of betrayal by Gorbachev, Yeltsin and their associates. A typical expression of this nostalgia for the past would indeed grant that there had been horrifying cases of repression and abuse of power under Communism, and yet claim that, all things considered, the country had grown steadily in military and industrial power; while now it has become a virtual satellite of the United States. A book I read recently, the memoirs of a man in his sixties, exalts Stalin and his times. Never mind that the author's father was executed and his mother imprisoned at the dictator's orders. The writer argues in time-honored fashion that Stalin's subordinates misinformed him. But back then, Russia was great and was feared by the capitalists. And now the country gathers in the fruits of the celebrated reforms; and the harvest is of general impoverishment while a few are making fabulous fortunes, and of corruption pervading the entire governmental machinery, and an alarming fall in the moral standards of the younger generation. One does not have to be a partisan of Communism to see much truth in this nostalgic Stalinist's complaint about the current Russian reality. And its most indisputable point is the failure of the new system to improve the lot of the average citizen. Quite to the contrary, GDP still lags far behind where it was during the last years of Communism. Workers in state enterprises are often not paid for months on end. The state not surprisingly finds it difficult to collect taxes. For the mass of people those much-advertised blessings of capitalism and the free market must still seem chimerical, while their negative features are all too apparent. For a nationalist, even if democratically inclined, Russia's dependence on loans and subsidies from the West cannot but lead to bitter reflections.

There is another and more hopeful part of the story. Glasnost has now fully triumphed, and freedom of speech and political pluralism, however marred by corruption, are taking hold. Prior to the collapse of Communism and the empire, few could have believed such momentous changes could take place without a civil war and attendant social convulsions. Yet amazingly, except for the unfortunate case of Chechnya, the transition has been peaceful. For all its shortcomings Yeltsin's regime deserves credit for not adopting a chauvinist posture; it has addressed by negotiations rather than by military threats issues such as the dispute with Ukraine over the Crimea or the rights of the Russian minority in Latvia.

The precarious condition of the post-1991 regime reflects largely the strength and weaknesses of the man who headed it. Boris Yeltsin, a former Communist Party boss, delivered the coup-de-grace to the USSR and Communism. He kept the country on a pro-Western pro-democracy course. But his leadership lacked firmness and consistency. The president's uncertain health and personality traits have prevented him from being steadily at the helm of the ship of state. Many Russian citizens would second a housewife's complaint in a letter to the editor toward the end of perestroika, "I don't care about democracy. All I know is that under Brezhnev I could make ends meet and I cannot now." Such feelings show up in the strength of the neo-Communists in parliamentary elections and in constant clashes between the President and the Duma, the lower and dominant house. Yeltsin's ministerial team, frequently changed, could not exert a firm grip on the country's economy and, its members mostly technocrats, has proved incapable of inspiring the nation's confidence. And so reminiscent of Moses, having freed his people from the slavery of Communism, Boris Yeltsin failed to bring them to the promised land of stable democracy and economic growth.

One would like to think that the winds of change that have swept through Russian society since Gorbachev's time have made impossible the return in totalitarianism. The bulk of the people while not convinced of the benefits of democracy would not acquiesce in a return to a one-party regime and loss of their recently acquired freedoms. The great danger for the future lies elsewhere. Even under Yeltsin Moscow has recently sought to emphasize its differences with the West on foreign policy issues such as Bosnia, and attitudes toward what Washington terms "rogue regimes" like Iraq. A future undemocratic leader might well decide to challenge the basic idea of cooperation with the West. He might also abandon the wise restraint Yeltsin showed in his dealings with the new states emergent from the old Soviet Union and seek a new imperial role for his country. We must not forget that because of its nuclear arsenal, Russia still remains a superpower.

It is clear first of all that America's predominant foreign concern must be to help Russia's continuing progress toward an orderly democracy, and its most important precondition, a stable economy.

The issue of economic help for what was then the USSR first arose in the West with Gorbachev's perestroika. At that time I strongly opposed any such help. No matter how extensive, it could not cure the basic ills of the Soviet economy. On the contrary, economic aid was likely to delay the Russians' resolve to deal realistically with their problems, to adopt needed reform and to reduce the swollen defense budget and other nonessential expenses. And indeed, the phantom of a new Marshall Plan of Western billions painlessly buying perestroika, proved greatly harmful to Gorbachev's reforms and to him personally. It blocked or delayed needed economic reforms, greatly contributing to rampant inflation and diminished industrial production. The sight of Gorbachev appearing at meetings of the Big Seven industrial nations practically begging for aid humiliated national pride and haunted him ever since. Voters gave him less than one percent of their ballots in the 1996 presidential elections.

But then harm has been done, and in the post-Soviet period substantial Western help is of crucial importance in enabling democracy and pro-Western orientation to succeed in the new Russia. The major responsibility for saving the young and fragile democracy must of course rest with the Russians, but for the economy, outside help through agencies such as the IMF and the World Bank could make the crucial difference.

From my perspective, the Russian scene presents an incongruous mixture of the new and the old. The Lenin Mausoleum still stands in the middle of Red Square. In one way it has now been degraded to a tourist attraction, but it is also a reminder that the burden of the Soviet past still weighs heavily on the country's present. In contrast, nothing appears as dead and irrelevant to Russia's present and future as Marxism-Leninism. That 19th century scholastic dogmatism and its inhumane 20th century version now find fewer adherents than in some countries of the West. Not even the neo-Communists propose to revive the old cult, and they cast their critique of the present situation in the nationalistic rather than in the old ideological idiom.

If the mass of the people have yet to embrace democratic values wholeheartedly, they do find strong support among Russia's intelligentsia. Just as in the pre-revolutionary period the thinking class was the conscience of the nation, since perestroika it has equally proved to be the main catalyst of the reassessment and rejection of the Soviet past. Academics, lawyers, and artists provided the bulk of those who pressed for reforms. From the intellectuals have come the writers who described Stalin's murderous career without the qualifications that Khrushchev and even Gorbachev employed to mollify their condemnation of the tyrant. The same intellectual milieu produced critics who breached the last sophistic defense line of Communism by exposing the myth of Leninism as the antithesis of Stalinism. Perhaps for the younger generation of Russians such tales from the past hold little interest for being irrelevant to their daily concerns. But just as the story of the Holocaust must never be allowed to be just a footnote in the histories of the twentieth century, so must the sufferings of the Russian people never be forgotten or trivialized, nor the transgressions of their government during the Soviet era.

Apart from the moral and political imperative to draw the proper lessons from the history of the Soviet period, the fact is that much of that history remains obscure. While many archives from the period have opened up, and documents hitherto secret may be studied, the Communist era presents special difficulties for the historian. The

Nazi leaders more often than not effectively boasted about their inhumanities; they made no secret of their determination to exterminate the Jews and of their achievements toward that end. Communist ideology, on the contrary, claims to represent the highest moral aspirations of mankind and the quest for social justice. The Kremlin therefore covered departures from such lofty aims by obfuscation, or more bluntly, by a tissue of lies. Furthermore, politics in Russia have by long tradition often been veiled in an air of mystification. The people simply were not supposed to know the true reasons behind their rulers' decisions or to grasp the often lamentable consequences to their country's conditions. Unquestionably, no mention could be made of the terrible famine of 1932-1933, during which the government exported huge quantities of foodstuffs. Today we can only speculate how many millions were let starve to death.

Complete veracity and candor are not characteristic of governments. Few, however, have tried to deceive their own people as much as that of Moscow. There was the story that following Stalin's death that a crowd of Soviet and Chinese officials were cropped out of a 1950 photo to leave only Stalin, Malenkov, and Mao together (see p.). And there was Khrushchev's gratuitous canard in his 1956 "secret" deconstruction speech, that Stalin strategized WWII on a schoolroom world globe.

Such uses of political spin seem in retrospect merely funny or pathetic. But how difficult the task of the historian when he has to deal with the really important incidents of Soviet history, which he finds covered with layer upon layer of deception and mystification. There was perhaps the supreme example of how hard it has been to ascertain who and what was behind Sergei Kirov's assassination. The same is true of the real reasons that prompted Khrushchev to send missiles to Cuba in 1962.

The other side to extracting the truth out of this veritable sea of misinformation is that a careless writer or one prone to sensationalism would tend to see all the acts and declarations of the Soviet government prior to the Gorbachev time as inspired by ulterior motives and reflecting the intent to deceive. The fact is that even at the height of terror there were some high officials and other prominent figures who died of natural causes! In 1952 the Soviet government proposed to the West a new arrangement to solve the German question. The Kremlin expressed its readiness to consider giving up East Germany, in exchange for which a unified Germany would forswear any military alliances. At the time such a proposal deserved to be explored by the West; certainly Washington and London were interested in lifting Communist rule from East Germany. But by then, and understandably so, the Western powers had no confidence that Moscow could ever negotiate in good faith. Washington brusquely rejected the proposal. Yet in retrospect this appears to have been one of those rare occasions when the Soviets were in earnest. The Korean War had heated up the East-West conflict, and the Kremlin had an obvious interest in lowering the level of tension and a willingness to pay for West Germany not entering NATO, something which was already under discussion and would take place three years later.

Soviet political history has long suffered clearly fictitious treatments. Many writers outside the Soviet Union, for example, insisted on bestowing on Stalin the non-existent Rosa Kaganovich as his third wife. Equally frequent have been the stories of Stalin having had a relationship with an agent of the Tsarist secret police prior to the Revolution. In some cases such tales, often emanating from Russian émigrés in the West, have been repeated in good faith by Western writers. A subject veiled in secrecy and deception will often attract unfounded gossip, which then develops into accepted fact. One has to be careful in accepting at face value the stories of fugitives from the USSR. Most of them have been scrupulously honest in relating their experiences and speaking only of things with which they've had firsthand acquaintance. But now and then writers have felt that their stories needed the dramatic energy of a sensational "revelation" which had no factual basis.

A historian's lot in this field is not an easy one. It is far more challenging than that of a scholar dealing with modern Western history, where there are ample reliable documents and accounts. True it is that myths and other traps attend the stories, say of the Third Republic in France, or of the New Deal in the US. But nowhere else, it is fair to say, has the course of politics, and of the life of society, been overlaid for some eighty years with so much secrecy and intentional deception.

The financial crisis that began in Asia and spread in time to Russia, led in the fall of 1998 to a dramatic bear market on the Moscow Stock Exchange and made our media switch their fleeting attention from President Clinton's personal troubles to Russia's most recent travails. Once again, I and my colleagues at the Center heard our phones ringing with queries from TV and radio stations and national and foreign journals asking what next in Russia? That American complacency that had accreted after the breakup of the Soviet Union was considerably shaken. Now everyone recalled that the humbled, impoverished nation still possessed thousands of nuclear weapons and missiles. Russia in chaos might pose a greater potential threat to this country and world stability than the old USSR under its cautious septuagenarian Communist masters.

It would be erroneous to give way to pessimism or to equally unfounded optimism concerning the future. Our "victory" in the Cold War was largely due to the peculiar qualities of American democracy, as well as to the prudence and courage of its leaders. But a large part of our good fortune must be ascribed to sheer luck. Immoral and covetous as the successive Soviet leaders had been, they lacked the recklessness of Hitler, for whom the vision of successive military triumphs banished all other considerations. It was an unusual piece of luck for the world that a man like Gorbachev rose to the top and exorcised the evil propensities of Communism. And so we must hope that out of the present condition of Russia there will emerge men, and even more important, one man who will keep the country on a course toward democracy and will not allow economic difficulties to divert it from the path. Having entertained doubts about the Yeltsin regime's plunge into what was supposed to be free market capitalism, I still do not think it desirable for the economy to revert to complete state control. But in the short run some central controls are inevitable if the country is to avoid a ruinous hyperinflation. And if any government is to succeed in the struggle for economic salvation, then it must adopt draconian measures to free the business community from the influence of the criminal element. It is an ironic commentary on Russia's faltering start in capitalism that it has been crime, until then largely a prerogative of the Soviet government, that has been most widely "privatized." By some Russian estimates, forty percent of the business enterprises have been compelled to pay tribute to the Mafia-like syndicates. And non-payment of taxes has been at least as widespread.

To repeat, the fall of the Soviet Union was one of the most dramatic and surprising events in all history. We in the United States were spoiled by the peacefulness of the development, and by how Russia slid overnight into the community of democratic states, moving from previous hostility to friendship and partnership with the

West. Thus we must not be surprised that the Russian people have traded previous troubles for new ones.

We are in for a long period of uncertainty and danger. And differently from during the Cold War, the challenge to the United States and other democracies is all the greater because the danger will be continually shifting in its nature and identity.

Part Four

Postlude

30

Other Thoughts and Memories

...The Office...the Red Sox...the Family...

The Office

(*Harvard Crimson*, Fall Registration Issue 1975)

"...Adam B. Ulam, the Russian Research Center's director and professor of Government, has an office in room 105, at the middle of a long corridor on the first floor of 1737 Cambridge Street. The room resembles the kind of scholar's study that would appear in a Victorian novel: papers are everywhere, ashtrays are full of the professor's pipe tobacco and cigarette butts, and books lie in every manner of arrangement—books with fifteen bookmarks, books face-down on their binding, and books lying fallow—most of them with the dull dark red covers of the University libraries.

There is a rumor around the Center that a couple of years ago, one of Ulam's research assistants found the documents and materials Ulam had used to write his first books, roughly 25 years before. At any rate, Ulam's den is heated like a greenhouse, with the windows closed and the director sweating it out in rolled-up sleeves and undone collar.

Ulam, a European, old-world scholar, was one of the Center's original members, finishing his Ph.D. dissertation on the British Labor Party in 1948, when the Center was founded with anthropologist and Freudian Clyde Kluckhohn as its first director. (Even then, Ulam says the Center was sensitive to charges that it was a Cold War front for US imperialism, thus Kluckhohn—an expert on the Navajo Indians—was apparently chosen in part because he seemed so utterly non-political.....Like most institutions, a favorite word describing many topics is used at the Center—"deplorable"—and when asked about the Center's present financial condition, the director focuses on his pipe and responds "it's deplorable."......The Center is in financial trouble and if something big is not quickly forthcoming, neither Ulam nor any of the other 100 or so scholars affiliated with the Center will have a spiritual or physical home next year....In July 1976, the Ford Foundation will cease to provide about 80 per cent of the Center's annual operating budget—and the Center, consequently, is going public this year, with industries doing Soviet business and other foundations as the main foci of a $1 million fundraising effort.

As in New York City and London, however, there are no visible signs of crisis at 1737 Cambridge Street—the phones still work, the paint isn't peeling, and the mid-morning coffee hour, at which Ulam is said to regale fellow members with recitations of Polish poetry, is still going strong...(Last year) State contracted with the Center for a set of studies and Washington seminars to be prepared by five of the Center's Scholars like Ulam...among them...This year, State has accepted a contract extension that will engage about five more scholars on issues like US Soviet trade. Soviet agriculture, and long-range economic thinking and guesses on Soviet succession (i.e "Kremlinology"—who's sitting next to Brezhnev at what state dinners, and so on)...This hasn't brought in all that much money—most of that is absorbed by costs—The Center's scholars seem hardly thrilled by the lure of government power. Ulam seems to speak for the Center's members when he says, "We don't want to study for the twentieth time the Soviet succession..."

Most members of the Center are neither Harvard faculty members nor post-doctoral researchers or fund-raisers, however; many more or less permanent members are drawn from the Boston area social science faculties, while visitors for one or two-year periods come from other universities—usually during a paid sabbatical since the Center's finances allow few stipends to visiting scholars, no matter how expert or promising. For their traveling, the visitors are rewarded (by) occupying cubicles right down the corridor from luminaries such as Abram Bergson and Marshal Goldman, experts on the Soviet economy, and ...Ulam, himself..."

The Red Sox

One grows stale in intellectual work, unless it is properly balanced by exercise and other forms of relaxation. I adhere to Lord

Chesterfield's advice: morning is for work (I seldom have been able to write at any other time), afternoon for games, evenings for "sociability" (even if we don't mean by it what he undoubtedly meant, port and wenching). My only active sport has been tennis, which I have played fervently, if alas, not very skillfully. When it comes to games in a passive sense, mine has been baseball, which, as for many foreign born, has been a path to partial acclimatization. For me living in Boston, it was tragically inevitable that I became seduced, then intermittently enraptured, betrayed, and let down by the Red Sox. No other team in baseball or in any other sport epitomizes as vividly the pathos of American life: seemingly unlimited possibilities, triumphant progress through much of the season, inexplicable recession in fortunes, followed by an equally incredible recovery and then a heart-rending failure, the loss of the pennant or the World Series by a single game. Such at least had been the picture during the years of my intense interest and suffering with the Sox from the middle forties to the end of the fifties.

Later on, I grew more philosophical. In the well-worn phrase I have tried to convince myself that "It's only a game." But as I write this chapter, there is a fresh ray of hope they are leading their division. Maybe this will be the year! But even so, my fifty years' experience cautions against such hopes. I hear again the apocalyptic warnings of the TV announcers on the first day of the pennant race, or in the seventh game on those rare occasions when the team made the World Series, "There is no tomorrow." And indeed the idiom of baseball is as studded with platitudes as that of current social sciences. "No one knows where Russia's process of modernization will take her" in some ways parallels that classic answer of a ballplayer to the question of how his team is doing, "We are taking it one game at a time."

A decade later, after repeated disenchantments, my interest in the game was sustained by that of my younger son. Very early Joseph became a veritable encyclopedia of baseball. Once we were on our way to Fenway Park in a taxi, with my golden-haired eight-year-old in his then high-pitched voice, discoursing learnedly on the sport. At one point the cab driver could not stand it anymore and interjected: "All right, wise guy, I bet you don't know who was the only player who ever pinch hit for Ted Williams!" Out piped the instant reply, "Carroll Hardy;" and we almost crashed as the man took his hands off the wheel and turned back to look at this Mozart of baseball lore. In fact the personality cult of Ted Williams was an important component of my addiction to the game. I did attend his last appearance at Fenway in September 1960, when to avoid an anti-climax after his home run in the seventh, Williams was replaced by Hardy. John Updike immortalized the entire scene in The New Yorker.

HR: "Adam belonged to a subset of a small and diminishing group—now, alas, nearly all gone—I'm thinking of the important refugee scholars... far too few of whom, it should be added, found homes at Harvard in the 1930s and 40s. Of course, Adam was largely educated in the United States, but in style and substance he was the brother of that older generation. He also belonged to the very special subset of that generation. I would describe them as the fellowship of Harvard Red Sox fans—sporting the heavy and distinctive accents of Central Europe. Their discussions always reminded me of the famous scene in the movie Casablanca..."

Henry Rosovsky, The Lewis P. and Linda L. Geyser University Professor Emeritus; former Dean of the Faculty of Arts and Sciences, at Harvard University.

The Family

My long bachelorhood came to an end. In January 1963, I married Mary Hamilton Burgwin, a charming Radcliffe-Harvard graduate. Within the next few years we demonstrated our faith in the future by having two delightful sons. Though some authorities would not agree, the joys of fatherhood, I was to discover, greatly surpassed even those of its literary equivalent.

Joseph Ulam: Some Family Memories

Lying in bed with him and Alexander on Sunday mornings before breakfast seemed to be one of the few times he'd actually relax...sitting at the breakfast table, in his bathrobe drinking Earl Grey tea...always the same two tea bags, allowed to steep for a long time...he loved to give directions. I remember that were I to make tea, he'd always tell me to let it steep for awhile...he was fascinated by differences in taste...always asking me what I liked, if I liked my tea as strong as his, etc. I think he was curious if there were some genetic reason for our tastes. He was obsessive/compulsive about things like unplugging the toaster, would ask me multiple times to make sure I remembered to do it...he had his habits, like putting margarine on one half of his muffin, butter on the other half...he liked to wait about ten minutes after a meal before he ate his ice cream...he loved chocolate mixed with some sort of sorbet...would always offer that it would be 'obscene on top of chocolate cake.' He was always grumpy during holidays, Christmases, etc., he'd get very thoughtful...seemed depressed... probably thinking about his family...loved to analyze Suzy (the dog) and figure out how many words she understood..

Joseph Ulam is Director of Annual Giving, Columbia University Development & Alumni Relations

31

Ending

MU: Adam wrote this book in the late 1990s. Although he became increasing disabled after a back operation in 1992, he continued to go to the office until November 1998.

MK: "...Unfortunately, another curtain fell in Adam's life nearly sixty years later, on Thanksgiving Day, 1998. That was the day he collapsed at around 2:00 a.m. and had to be brought to the hospital. David Powell, my brother David, my father, and I had been planning to get together with Adam and his son Joseph for dinner that day, but the Ulams didn't show up and we couldn't figure out what had happened. That evening we found out that Adam was in the hospital. From then on, he never made it back to the Davis Center. A curtain had fallen over his past life."

During the last year-and-a-half of his life, Adam was housebound part of the time and in the hospital the rest of the time. For quite awhile, he was hopeful of recovering, but this year he had begun to lose hope. Still, even as recently as a couple of months ago, just before he had a major operation at Brigham and Women's Hospital, he discussed with me a few things he still hoped to do. In descending order of likelihood, these were: returning to the Davis Center, something I had long been urging him to do, even if only in a wheelchair; second, making a brief visit back to Poland and western Ukraine (or what Adam jokingly called Ukrainian-occupied Poland), something he deeply regretted not having done; third playing tennis again, something that by this point he had largely realized he would never do again; and, fourth and least likely, seeing the Red Sox win the World Series. Adam readily conceded that "this, alas, is something none of us will ever live to see."

MU: After our divorce in 1991, I had moved to Charlottesville, VA, but when Adam first became ill in 1992, he asked me to come and help him and I began making monthly trips back to Cambridge to supervise his medical care. He had many operations...and much discomfort. .He was not used to being ill...In the last year, his walking grew progressively worse...and he went from a cane to a walker...He kept his resolve however, to get better...well enough to return to his office. Then at the end of January 2000, he was diagnosed with a fast-growing cancer...He asked me not to leave him again and I said I wouldn't.

Six weeks before he died, he started to weaken rapidly. When he didn't feel like anything else, he always would feel like working on the book...so that's what we did... He said he hoped he would live long enough to enjoy the book's publication...He was amused and pleased we were publishing it ourselves. He named the publishing company Leopolis Press and entitled his book Understanding the Cold War: A Historian's Personal Reflections.

One day he asked me if I was glad I married him...I said that I never would have married any one else.

I asked him several times during the last months why he had divorced me...His only reply was that "it had been a great mistake."

Another time, he turned his head to the wall and murmured to himself ... "Anger is such a waste..."

During the last weeks he kept repeating that he wanted to live for me and Alexander and Joseph.

JU: Next-to-last day

My mother made a quick trip to Charlottesville to see her doctor. My brother, Alexander arrived a day later, Saturday, to spell her and I took his place on Sunday for two days. On Monday, I took him outdoors in his wheelchair, and he seemed happy...deeply breathing in the fresh air...when he was in his bed, he was slightly uncomfortable; I kept having to go over and pull him up further on the bed...we watched "Law & Order," and he seemed to enjoy it, smiling at me several times at some of the jokes...In the afternoon, the doctor came in and gave him a rather pessimistic prognosis...he was very discouraged...the physical therapist came in and asked if he wanted therapy...he said 'no, but starting tomorrow, very intense therapy'. He was very sad. I put him in the wheelchair, and asked him to try to stand up...I brought the walker over to him, and he made several valiant efforts, straining with all his might to get to his feet...finally, with my help he stood for several moments...a brief flicker of hope seemed to flash across his face. We watched another episode of "Law and Order," and then I left to catch the bus...I never saw him alive again.

MU The last day

Adam called me and asked me to return immediately. He told me he loved me very much. I arrived back late Monday evening....He was agitated, irritable, impatiently switching the TV dial...He wanted to see the movie, "Laura", but couldn't get Channel 44.....I took the TV Guide down to the nurse's station...Mr. W. was there. He wrote out the channels that were available on the hospital TVs. He also told me that I could borrow the physical therapy department's video machine in the evenings, so I signed up for the next day, Tuesday evening.

I went back to Adam's room and he was asleep.

The next morning around 5:00, he called to me ...A little later he asked me to hold his hand.

Then about 9:00, after I came back from breakfast, he asked me if he was going to die...I said emphatically, no!

He continued to cough a lot... when he did I called the nurse who would come and siphon the ever-increasing phlegm from his lungs...

Around 11:00, he said quietly that he was dying. I sat on the bed and put my head down on his chest and looked up at him and wept. I said please don't leave me. He looked down at me with that intent look he had from time to time...when I first met him he looked at me the same way.... like an eagle.

His lunch came, but he scarcely touched it...The special nurse was there and we both urged him...He took a bite from his sandwich but would have no more...I tried to make him sip some Boost...He tried, but then refused.

The nurses came and put him in the wheelchair...

The lawyers came to take care of some financial matters.

Then he wanted to go back to bed and I sat on the bed and again laid my head on his chest...I asked him if he forgave me for all the stuff in the 70s...he rested his hand on my head.

....Sometime in the afternoon, I don't remember when....they replaced the oxygen tube with an oxygen mask.

The nurse practitioner came to the door and waved me out into the hall. In a low voice she said to call the boys. Uncomprehending... I did,..at the front desk...Then I went back to the room and wheeled in the video machine....I asked him if he would like me to get him a "goody" from the Faculty Club and a video...He looked at me and smiled an uncharacteristic smile of great sweetness...

...Later, after he had the oxygen mask, I asked him what he would like to see. I couldn't understand his answer through the oxygen mask, so I gave him paper and pencil and he wrote out the name of a Polish film, "With Fire and Sword" ... His coughing and choking increased; the special nurse and the nurse practitioner came in about 10 to 5....The nurse practitioner said to him that they were going to give him a little morphine to relax him...I asked him if he still wanted me to go...He nodded emphatically...and I went on my errands.

Five minutes later he closed his eyes and slipped away.

He died March 28, 2000.

"...I shall miss that dark integrity of his..."

Samuel H. Beer, Eaton Professor of the Science of
Government, Emeritus, Harvard University

32

Adam and His Friends

Abbott Gleason

A great deal of Adam's charm and fascination had to do with way he united qualities often appearing in the world as opposites. He was a man of towering intelligence, with a tremendous grasp—partly intuitive—of the workings of large intellectual architectures, of complex systems. At the same time, he was someone with an extraordinary memory, who understood the importance of the singular. To use a Sherlockian phrase (and Adam was a Sherlockian), he knew how important it was to find out why the dog didn't bark in the night.

Adam was a believer—the way few modern people are—in the importance of decorum. And yet there were few people who were so ready to jettison decorum, if the occasion was right. This was an aspect of his aristocratism. There must be rules, but civilization consists entails knowing when to break them. He was cautious about extolling democracy's virtues. Fulsome tributes made him uncomfortable. He believed in a certain amount of hierarchy, but manifested it in his behavior only on certain occasions, as he chose.

Adam admired the English upper class, but his admiration, though real, was ironical and he had a deeper feeling for Paris than London. His love for these two bastions of the West was intertwined with a kind of Polish baroque spirit that usually, but not always, remained beneath the surface.

Adam was a great individualist, who felt that Ted Williams—refusing to tip his cap after hitting a home run—was a kindred spirit. And yet, few individualists of that sort have inspired such communal warmth. Few such bold and apparently self-contained spirits have had so many friends. He inspired conviviality the way no one else I know could.

Adam was a profound realist, who set out to dominate the world by his intellect. At the same time, he was vulnerable to the world's brute physicality, to its refusal to submit to the spirit. His extraordinary mix of security and insecurity was surely abetted by his bereavement—and the resultant sense of the precariousness of things—that took place during World War II, and about which pages in this book speak so eloquently. This was a subject about which I never heard him speak personally but was clearly absolutely central to his identity. The resulting paradox contained within it a kind of pathos, which could draw loving friends closer to him, which could create between us a kind of undefined league of mutual protection.

Many people, having heard of Adam's death, commented—after expressing their personal grief—that it marked the end of an era. Perhaps this is because of the particular character of his culture and experience, and its richness. He sprang from the Jewish portion of the Polish middle class and knew the aristocracy too. Then there was the Russia that he spent his life studying. The mores of the upper class in France and Britain were a subject of interest to him and found some strong echo in his character and personality. And he spent his life at the center of the university world of the United States, at the apogee of its power and influence during the Cold War—as well as during what Adam regarded as its decline in recent years.

His life was a great adventure, although perhaps paradoxically much of it took place in his office. The United States at the turn of the millennium contains very few people of comparable diversity of experience. Today more than ever he seems larger than life.

But no such analytical recital can begin to explain Adam and why his friends will miss him so much. His talent for friendship was a product of his enormous strengths and his vulnerabilities in their mutuality.

But finally—like the ultimate virtues—it was inexplicable. No one can take his place in our lives.

Abbott Gleason is the Barnaby Conrad and Mary Critchfield Keeney Professor of History, Brown University

33

Review of Adam Ulam's Professional Career

Mark Kramer

"... Adam Ulam was one of the world's foremost authorities on Russia and the Soviet Union. He was a member of the Harvard faculty from 1947 until his retirement in 1992. Over the years, he trained thousands of undergraduate and graduate students who went on to leading posts in academia, government, business, and the media. He was affiliated with Harvard's Russian Research Center (renamed the Davis Center for Russian Studies in 1997) for more than fifty years. He twice served as the Center's director, from 1973 to 1976 and from 1980 to 1992. During his tenure, the Center became one of the leading institutions in the world for the study of the Soviet Union. It also was widely known for its convivial and collegial atmosphere. Ulam wrote eighteen books, many of which remain classics in the field. He started out in 1951 by publishing a book on *The Philosophical Foundations of English Socialism* and followed it up a year later with *Titoism and the Cominform*. After that, Ulam began writing about Russia and the Soviet Union, a focus he maintained for the rest of his life. Although the Soviet archives were still closed, he combined an intuitive genius with prodigious reading of open sources to produce works that have held up remarkably well amid fresh archival revelations since the collapse of the Soviet Union. His study: *The Bolsheviks*, published in 1965, is still regarded as one of the definitive treatments of the party led by Vladimir Lenin, which seized power in Russia in November 1917. The book is as much a study of Lenin as it is an analysis of the party itself. It was hailed by reviewers as "an intellectual biography of the highest sort," a "stunningly insightful look at this key period," and a "masterful study of the Communists' rise to power in Russia." One reviewer commented:

"We used to be told it was worth learning Italian to read Dante. Here is a new one: it is worth developing an interest in Lenin to read Adam Ulam." Ulam's 760-page biography of Joseph Stalin, *Stalin: The Man and His Era*, met similar acclaim when it was published in 1973. Reviewers described it as a "mammoth and altogether splendid volume," "an absorbing study of power won and terrifyingly applied," a "superb biography of Stalin," and a book that is "morally as well as historically definitive." The book was issued in two subsequent editions, in 1987 and 1989. In the final edition, Ulam included a new introduction that allowed him to take advantage of some of the disclosures that emerged in the Soviet Union during the "glasnost" period of the late 1980s. Ulam's magisterial survey of Soviet foreign policy, *Expansion and Coexistence*, first published in 1967, is often regarded as the most influential book on the subject ever to appear. Through several editions and reprintings, it was a standard text for courses on Soviet foreign policy and is still widely used. A reviewer described the last (1976) edition of the book as a "tour de force" and a "work of astonishing breadth and erudition." Ulam wrote a sequel to it, *Dangerous Relations*, in the early 1980s. The two books together covered Soviet foreign policy through almost the whole period before the rise of Mikhail Gorbachev. Ulam never published a book length study of Gorbachev's foreign policy, but he did cover the subject in his final book, *The Communists* (1992), and in a preface he wrote in 1994 for the translated memoirs of Valeri Boldin, a former top aide to Gorbachev. Ulam's scholarly work was notable not only for the depth of his insights, but also for the sparkling wit he displayed. A reviewer of Ulam's biography of Stalin described the author as "a sardonic connoisseur of human folly." ...Another reviewer expressed admiration for the book's fundamental "humanity—often sardonic but never unfeeling—of its witness to hell." Although the topics Ulam was analyzing were often grim and deadly, he was able to highlight the absurdities of Soviet life in a way that kept his books from being ponderous..."

Mark Kramer, Director, Cold War Studies Project, Harvard University

34

Notes on Lwów

Julian Bussgang;
family notes by JB&MU

Jewish Citizens of Lwów

The ethnic composition of the population of Lwow was quite mixed. Just before World War II, the population numbered 330,000. Approximately 50% were Poles, 30% Jews, and 15% Ukrainians. There were also many Armenians, Austrians, Hungarians and other ethnic groups. The city prided itself on its diversity and its cosmopolitan character. Ukrainians were a minority within the city, but a majority around it. Nationalistic feelings ran high among the Ukrainian farmers in the countryside. Jewish citizens of Lwów, often acted as the swing vote in the local elections and tended to side with the Poles on most issues rather than with the Ukrainians.

Jews had lived in Lwów since the thirteenth century. As far back as 1383, there was the first written reference to a "Jewish street" in the city. Jews were given special rights in Lwów by various Polish kings, well before they became accepted as full citizens in other cities of Poland.

Lwów had one of the first "Progressive" synagogues in Poland, established in 1844, reflecting the so-called Haskalah (Enlightenment) movement that began in Germany. In the United States this German Progressive Judaism evolved into Conservative and Reform Judaism, so prevalent today.

Between the two world wars, the Jews of Lwów were quite assimilated and well integrated into the community. Many of the city's businessmen and professionals were Jewish. Jews played a major role in the political life of the city and the region. During the years immediately before the war, the elected Deputy Mayor of Lwów, Wiktor Chajes, was Jewish, as were several elected members of the Polish Parliament (Sejm) and Senate. Most Jewish children attended public schools and generally spoke Polish rather than Yiddish at home. The trend was toward secularization and away from Orthodoxy. The Zionist movement was strong; some claim it originated in Lwów.

Religious life and social and educational services for Jews were under the direction of a Kahal (community council), which enjoyed a large degree of autonomy and was administered by elected activists. One of the three members of the leadership of the Lwów Kahal just before World War II was Michal Ulam, Adam Ulam's uncle. The harmonious relations enjoyed by the Jews of Lwów with their neighbors became strained when a wave of anti-Semitism began to sweep Poland in the 1930s. First, informal quotas in the departments of law and medicine were introduced at the University of Lwów. Then the Polish National Democratic Party (Endecja), fashioned after the Nazi movement in Germany, gained followers among university students. A formal doctrine known as *numerus clausus* was adopted at the universities, restricting the number of Jewish students allowed to study there. Eventually Jewish students were confined to special "ghetto" benches and often beaten by their Catholic colleagues. Clearly, such a situation was unacceptable to many Jews, and those who could afford it began sending their college age children to study abroad.

The Ulam Family of Lwow

Adam Bruno Ulam, born in Lwow on April 8, 1922, was the son of Dr. Jozef Ulam and his wife, Chana, maiden name Auerbach, born in Stryj. Adam's two siblings were much older: Stanislaw, born in 1909, and Stefania, born in 1912.

Adam's father, Jozef (born 1877), was the second of four prominent Ulam brothers. A doctor of law, he was a highly-respected lawyer in private practice. The Ulam family was well established in Lwów. Jakub Ulam (1876), the older brother of Jozef, was the owner of a bank. A younger brother, Michal (1879), was an architect and building contractor, and the youngest, Szymon (1883), a major lumber dealer. Abraham Berl, Adam's grandfather, had been a prominent building contractor in Lwow.

My family's relationship with the Ulams was quite close because my mother's oldest sister, Salomea Philipp (or Aunt Lusia, as we called her) was married to Jakub Ulam, Adam's uncle. Jakub, owner of the Ulam Bank (Dom Bankowy Ulam), was my father's banker. Keeping an eye out for a proper match for his sister-in-law, Jakub introduced my father, Joseph Bussgang, to Stefania Philipp, and they were later married. Jakub Ulam died shortly before I was born (in 1925), and I was named Julian Jakub Bussgang in his honor. The only son of Aunt Lusia and Jakub, Andrzej was born in 1906. He succeeded his father as the head of the Ulam bank. My aunt and her second husband, Izydor Goldberg, had no children from their marriage. I was the youngest nephew, and they treated me very specially. Andrzej and Adam's brother, Stanislaw, in addition to being cousins through their fathers, were good friends, being fairly close in age. Andrzej was, of course, my cousin as well, as our mothers were sisters. He had his own apartment in the same house as his mother and stepfather. Although I was quite a bit younger than Andrzej, our families were very close, and we saw Andrzej frequently.

My first recollection of meeting Adam was at age eleven when I entered Public High School No. 7 in Lwów. The school was named for the Polish freedom fighter Tadeusz Kosciuszko, who had led a Polish peasant revolution against the Russian Tsar. Young for my grade and not knowing anyone, I was told by my family to look for Adam, who was attending the same school. Adam, by then fourteen and two grades ahead of me, was very cordial to me during the two years we overlapped and sometimes became my protector. Our school was in a rather modest building without much of a yard. We spent intermissions crowded into the corridors outside of our classrooms or playing on the small street in front of the building. I remember distinctly that on a couple of occasions, when some bigger boys were harassing me, Adam, who was tall and strong, ran to my defense whirling his fists, and the other boys quickly disappeared. I was very grateful.

Even before meeting Adam, one of my closest friends throughout elementary school had been Julek (Juliusz) Ulam, Adam's younger cousin and the only son of the youngest of the four Ulam brothers, Szymon. My dimunitive name was also Julek, so we were known in school as "the two Juleks." I especially enjoyed visiting Julek's house in the evening to gaze at the stars through a telescope his father had mounted for Julek on their balcony.

Julek's father, Szymon Ulam, is described in the 1937 Jewish Almanach of Lwów as a leading lumber industrialist who served on the National Wood Industry Council, advising the Ministry of Commerce and Industry, and was chairman of the board of the Central Bank of Lwów. He was also active in charitable and cultural activities and was vice chairman of Dror, the major Jewish sports club in Lwów, where my mother was also active. Following the German invasion of eastern Poland in 1941, Szymon became a member of the Judenrat (Jewish governing council). In early 1943, along with other Judenrat members, he was sent to the Janowska Road concentration camp and later perished in Dachau. Julek's mother, who was Catholic, survived the war in Lwów, hiding Julek in the attic of their home. After the war, Julek and his mother went to France, where my wife, Fay, and I visited him in 1961. Unfortunately, Julek died only a few years later.

A fourth Ulam brother, Michal, was an architect, a building contractor, and a prominent lumber industrialist who served on various professional boards. He designed and constructed a series of significant buildings, including municipal and school buildings, as well as the yeast factory in Lesienice managed by my uncle, Izydor Goldberg. Michal Ulam was one of the leaders of the Jewish community of Lwów, a member of its governing body, the Kahal. Michal died in 1938, well before the war began. After the outbreak of the war, my father, mother, sister, and I escaped together with my aunt and uncle Goldberg, heading south, crossing the border to Romania on September 17, 1939. Andrzej also escaped through Romania and quickly made his way to the United States. Andrzej had a visa to attend the New York World's Fair and had no problem entering the U.S. The Goldbergs followed, arriving in New York on January 9, 1940 by way of Cuba. Both they and Andrzej settled in New York City. Sadly, Andrzej died of pneumonia less than two years later, before I arrived in the US.

I spent the war years first as a refugee in Palestine, where I finished high school, and then joined the Free Polish Army, a part of the British Eighth Army. Our army fought in Italy and led the final assault in the famous battle at Monte Cassino. After the war, I wanted to emigrate to the US, and my aunt in New York turned to Adam's older brother, Stan, to help me. Stan was then teaching at the University of Southern California and was able to arrange for me to be admitted to USC. When I went to the US Consulate in Genoa to apply for a visa, I was asked whether I wanted to stay in the US. When I unfortunately answered, "Yes, of course," I was immediately refused a student visa. My aunt and uncle sent me an affidavit to come to the USA, which made the application for an immigration visa possible, but because of the restrictive Polish quota, it would take me several more years to obtain the visa.

The Polish soldiers who did not wish to return to Poland were transferred from Italy to England. There I was able to enter an undergraduate program at the University of London. Adam was then at Harvard, and my aunt sent me his address. I wrote to Adam from London that I was interested in mathematics and engineering and that I would love to study at Harvard when I got to the US (of course, I not only had no money, but I had no idea of the cost of an American education). Adam wrote back that if I was interested in engineering, I should apply to MIT. I had never heard of MIT, and I was a little upset about being discouraged from applying to Harvard, but I followed his advice. I sent my paperwork to MIT and was admitted.

In March 1949 I arrived in New York, where my parents and sister had just settled following a brief stay in England..The United States was then in an economic recession, and I could not find a job. My parents barely supported themselves. A kind man in New York, hearing that I had been admitted to MIT, told me not to miss the opportunity and lent me some money. And so it was that in September 1949 I traveled to Cambridge, with very little money. Again Stan helped me. He wrote to Professor Victor Weisskopf of MIT, whom he knew from his Los Alamos days, asking that he help me find some means of support. Weisskopf was in the Physics Department, however, and since I wanted to study electrical engineering, Weisskopf asked Jerry Wiesner, then head of the Research Laboratory for Electronics, to assist me. Wiesner arranged for me to get a job as a part-time technician at the Research Laboratory for Electronics, and this helped pay my tuition. Wiesner became my master's thesis avisor. Later, long after I graduated, he served as President of MIT Soon after arriving at MIT, I contacted Adam, the only person I knew in Cambridge, who was then a tutor at Eliot House at Harvard. In those early days, Adam would sometimes treat me to dinner at one of the nice Harvard Square restaurants that I otherwise could not patronize. I always cherish how nice he was to me.

In the fall of 1951 Stan and his French-born wife, Françoise, came toCambridge, as Stan was spending the year as a visiting professor at Harvard. They invited me to their home several times, and that is how I finally got to know Stan, who had been my mathematical hero since childhood. In 1954, after five years in the US, I was able to become a citizen. I needed two witnesses, so I asked Adam, since he had known me longer than anyone else, and he gladly accepted. By the time I married Fay in 1960, I was already employed, and we first rented an apartment in Watertown and then moved to Lexington. We saw Adam now and then, at our home or at a restaurant, and later, we visited him and Molly in their house in Cambridge.

Julian Bussgang, retired engineer,
Lexington, MA

MU: Adam's maternal grandfather, Michael Auerbach, was a prominent industrialist from Vienna who dealt in steel under the Austro-Hungarian Empire. He represented factories in Galicia and Hungary. He raised his family in the beautiful town of Stryj, which is situated near the Carpathian Mountains, not far from Lwów. His daughter Anna (Hania), married Adam's father. Another daughter, Klara, bore four children, one of whom was Stasia, the wife of the painter Zygmund Menkes, both of whom are mentioned in the text. Adam described his mother as extremely beautiful, passionate and highstrung. She was sickly thoughout most of her married life..

Adam's paternal forebears were prominent citizens in Lwów. His great-grandfather emigrated from Venice sometime before the 20th Century. Adam knew only that he had been a stonemason. Adam described his own father as a small man with an austere demeanor who was rather distant in his relations with his younger son. This description is somewhat contradicted by Stasia Menkes, who described Jozef Ulam as a "quiet man of great warmth and kindness who loved to welcome people to his house." Perhaps Adam's memory was colored by the fact that during a good part of his childhood, his mother was ill with cancer. He told me that she took periodic trips to Vienna for cancer treatments. She never told him the purpose of these visits. Her last trip was in 1938. She never returned.

Adam described his sister, Stefania Francesca, as beautiful, but quiet.She adored him. After the mother's death, Stefania had a falling-out with her father over her marriage to a man "in trade." Although he came from a loving and close-knit family, Adam told me that his childhood was rather lonely. He was left pretty much to his own devices. Perhaps it was his mother's lengthy illness that took his parents' attention away from him.

It was just a year after his mother died, that Adam set forth with his brother on his voyage to this country, which was to take him from his family forever, and from Lwów, to which he never returned.

35

A Letter from John Kenneth Galbraith

Dear Molly,

...For close on half a century I have known and been delightfully informed by Adam Ulam—often during a daily encounter for lunch at the Faculty Club. He was the central spokesman on Soviet and Russian matters for all those years at Harvard. I did not always agree: I was always informed and enchanted. We have lost Adam, to our sorrow and regret, but we have this book which tells wonderfully of what we once found so alert and interesting.

I add my voice in gratitude that we still have this memory of one of the most distinguished and articulate members of the Harvard community, one we remember with both affection and gratitude.

Yours faithfully,

John Kenneth Galbraith
Paul M. Warburg Professor of Economics, Emeritus, Harvard University

Index

Polish for the Committee for the Defense of the Workers, 279
Polish National Democratic Party, 386
"Polish" Pope, importance of, 261-263, 279
Polish Socialist Party, 25
Powers, Gary, 149, 227
"Prague Spring", 203
Pravda, 275, 300, 341-342
Providence Journal , 48

R

Reagan, President Ronald
    election of, 275-276
    "Evil Empire" and, 321-322
    Moscow visit, 321-322
    Soviet democracy steps, 323
    USSR policies of, 297-298
Republic of China, economy of, 244
Reykjavik Summit, arms control discussions, 316-317
von Ribbentrop, Joachim, 44
Rockefeller, Nelson, 123-124
Rokossovsky, Konstantine, 68
Romanov, Gregory, 306
Roosevelt, President Franklin
    British support from, 60
    legislation blocking of, 21
    Lend-Lease programs, 65
    post-war Europe dividing, 79-80
    Stalin's feelings about, 191
    vs Willkie campaign, 58-60
    Yalta conference, 3, 79-80, 128
Roslyakov, Mikhail, 222
Rostropovich, Mstislav, 234
Rothfels, Hans, 68
Russell, Bertrand
    "better red than dead", 229
    vs USSR, 230
Russia
    "activists" non-support, 239-240
    archives opening up, 363-364
    Cold War victory of, 366

conspirator killings, 240
ethnic group embracing, 239
future of, 360-361
idealism vs criminality, 240-241
incongruity of, 363
intelligentsia support, 363
1998 financial crisis, 365-366
post-1991 regime, 361-362
reforms of, 270-271
Soviet political history and, 365
U.S. challenges with, 366-367
U.S. economic help, 362-363
West fascination and, 239
world financial crisis, 365-366
See also Soviet republics independence; Soviet Union
Russian Research Center, founding of, 115
Rydz-Smigly, Edward, 37

S

Sakharov, Andrei, 229, 233, 327, 339, 341
SALT I treaty, 225, 229, 230
SALT II treaty, 253
    Carter and, 269-270
    halting of, 259, 274-275
    proposals for, 253
Saturday Evening Post , 202-203
Schlesinger, Arthur, 138, 230
Scottish Café, 7-8
Sea Lion (operation), 55
Sergeievich, Mikhail, 306
Shevardnadze, Eduard, 317
Simon, William, 275
Sobchak, Anatoli, 337
Solidarity, birthplace of, 34
Souvarine, Boris, 189
Soviet republic's independence
    advise for reformers, 340
    Central Committee membership firing, 336
    China and, 339, 346-347